BEWARE THE SERPENT

"...And the woman said, The serpent beguiled me, and I did eat." (Genesis 3:13)

"But I fear, lest by any means, as the serpent beguiled Eve through his subtlity your minds should be corrupted from the simplicity that is in Christ." (2 Corinthians 11:3)

Satan is symbolized as a serpent in many scriptural references. In the Garden of Eden it was Satan who beguiled Eve which lead Adam and Eve to be cast out in the lone and dreary world. Today Satan has taught the many different religious leaders to be the deceivers of the world—preaching one God or another. In terms of the Christians, there are thousands of different religious sects who teach Christ's teachings in different ways and giving different meanings to the same passages of the Bible creating a great deal of confusion. When studied, most of these religions have some truth as represented in the Bible. This is Satan's plan! Having only a portion of the truth that confuses a sincere Christian. This confusion alone will keep one from investigating the truth and ultimately from entering into the kingdom of God.

In the picture, we see the snake's back because very seldom does Satan directly confront us. Satan's method of operation is to deceive. He works on us slowly and takes small steps in breaking us down. Before we know it, we dig ourselves into a big hole—a pit that seems impossible to climb out of. The snake represents the men who now beguile their followers into believing something that will keep them out of the kingdom of God. These religious leaders have forgotten or lost many of the important teachings like those of the temples, the Melchizedek Priesthood, the nature of man in God's image, the Sabbath day observance, the law of tithing and even baptism by immersion.

The snake also represents the fear that is instilled in people to not search for the fullness of truth. It represents the fear of giving up false teachings, the fear of losing the approval of men, the fear that the way is too hard. Fear is immobilizing. Hopefully, this book will help many overcome fear and lead them to obtain exaltation in the kingdom of God. The goal of this book is to help one recognize, in all this religious fervor, who is teaching the fullness of truth and who is only teaching a part of the truth. God and Jesus Christ really do want all Christians in the unity in faith. Hopefully this book will help you sort out the different truths being taught so that you too can become unified in faith.

COMMENTS

"As a new convert, when I asked a question I demanded that the answer be backed by the Bible. This book does a good job of scripture references and includes them in the text." Barbara Garcia, San Antonio, Texas

"Many years ago as an investigator being taught about Joseph Smith and the restored gospel, the main question I asked over and over again was, "Can you show me where it speaks of this in the Bible?" How I wish this book that Kendall Mann has written was available to me then. No other book so clearly uses the Bible to identify and substantiate all the core LDS principles and beliefs. It walks you right through in such a logical process. It's all in one book, a great missionary tool." Cheryl Linder, San Antonio, Texas.

"After going over the chapter on polygamy I guess I can't say anything about polygamy anymore!" J. Kenneth Mann, Grass Valley, California. Ken Mann, the author's father, who believes in God but does not believe in organized religion. This statement was made after going over the chapter on polygamy.

BEWARE THE SERPENT

WAS JOSEPH SMITH A PROPHET?
BIBLICAL ANSWERS TO HARD QUESTIONS.

BY
KENDALL L. MANN

Published by
Mann-Lee, LLC
San Antonio, Texas

Visit us at josephsmithandthebible.com

First printing in 2007.

ISBN 978-0-9787295-0-9

Published in the United States of America

Printed in India by Sai Printopack Pvt. l td.,
New Delhi-110 020
Exported by Shubhendu Trading House,
New Delhi-110 045, India.
Email: shubhendutrading@vsnl.net

BEWARE THE SERPENT

Dedicated to
All those children of God who with open hearts
and open minds sincerely seek to know the only true
God and Jesus Christ–
and once they find it–will defend it!

John 17:3 – And this is life eternal, that they might know the only true God, and Jesus Christ, whom thou hast sent.

Knowledge Leads To Glory.

"First generation members constitute more than half of the membership of the (LDS) Church"

(Paul B. Pieper, Quorum of the Seventy, Oct 2006 General Conference)

Answer your family's and friend's questions with only the Bible!

The LDS Biblical Support Chain insert cards are a scripture marking system designed to:

• Increase your ability to teach 92 of Joseph Smith's teachings from the Bible.
• Establish a Bible scripture chain that leads you from one supportive scripture to the next.
• Enable you to find quick answers to hard questions.
• Provide the topical references that you need—at your fingertips.

Visit us at
josephsmithandthebible.com

THE LDS BIBLICAL SUPPORT CHAIN   josephsmithandthebible.com

Saved By Works (Saved-Works)–2 Pet 3:15-17; James 1:22; 2:14-26; Gal 6:7,8; Rev 20:12,13; Matt 16:27. (Ch 10)
Scriptures-All Acceptable (Scripts Accept)–2 Tim 3:15-17. (Ch 7)

Temples–Baptisms for the Dead (Temple-Baptism)–1 Cor 15:29; 1 Kings 7:23-25; 2 Chron 4:2-4; Jer 52:17,20. (Ch 14)
Temples–Build (Temple-Build)– ... 5:3-5; Hab 2:20; Zech 1:16; Zech 6:12,13. (Ch 14)
Temples–Make Covenants (Te... ... 6:27. (Ch 14)
Temples–Garments (Temple-G... ... 9; Isa 52:1; Isa 61:10...
Ezek 42:14; Rev 16:15; M...
Temples–God Dwells (Tem...
Deut 31:15; 2 Chron 1:...
Temples–Latter Days (Te...
9:11,12; Acts 15:16,17...
Temples–Law of Worth...
22:6-11; **To Enter:** ...
97:15-17; **The Pen...**
Luke 19:45-46; Jo...
Temples–New Nam...
Temples–Ordinanc...
(Ch 14)
Temples–See G...

THE LDS BIBLICAL SUPPORT CHAIN

Apostasy–New Testament (Apos NT)–2 Thes 2:2,3,7; Acts 20:29-31; 1 Cor 11:18,19;
Gal 1:6,7; 2 Tim 3:1-7; 4:3,4; 1:15; 1 Tim 4:1; 2 Tim 2:16-18; Matt 24:5,24. (C
Apostasy–Old Testament (Apos OT)–Isa 24:5; 29:13; Amos 3:7; Isa 60:2; Amos 8:11. (C
Bible Contradictions (Bible Contras)–Acts 24:5; 29:13; 2 Tim 3:17; 1 Cor 5:9; Matt 27:5 & Acts
2:5-9 & Gal 6:7,8; John 10:30 & Gen 1:26,27; Gen 32:30. Acts 7:55,56; John 1:18 & Acts
Gen 32:30, Exo 24:9,11. (Ch 7)
Bible-Missing Scriptures (Missing Script)–Exo 24:4,7; Num 21:14; Josh 10:13; 2 Sam 1:1
37:15-17; Luke 4:17-20. (Ch 7)
Blacks & Priesthood (Blacks-PH)–Ezra 2:62; Rom 2:10; Eph 3:5,6; Isa 56:3-7. (Ch 18)
Book of Mormon Support (BofM Spt)–2 Cor 13:1; Isa 29:1-4; Psalms 85:11; Isa 29:
Book of Mormon-Add to Bible (BofM-Add to)–Rev 22:18; Deut 4:
Book of Mormon-Linage (BofM Linage)–Ezk 37:15-18; Deut
Deut 33:13-16;Isa 16:8. (Ch 8)
Calling/Election Made Sure (Election S...
130:3; 67:10. (Ch 5)
Church Organization ...
3:22,23

FORWARD

The four hundred year old battle between Christian religions has been about who is right and who is wrong? Who has the truth and who does not have the truth? Who is going to heaven and who is going to hell? This controversy has its roots from Jesus Christ Himself! He taught:

> *Matthew 7:13,14 – 13.* **Enter ye in at the strait gate:** *for wide is the gate, and broad is the way, that leadeth to destruction, and many there be which go in thereat:* 14. **Because strait is the gate, and narrow is the way, which leadeth unto life, and few there be that find it.**

> *Matthew 7:21-23 – 21.* **Not every one that saith unto me, Lord, Lord, shall enter into the kingdom of heaven;** *but he that doeth the will of my Father which is in heaven. 22. Many will say to me in that day, Lord, Lord, have we not prophesied in thy name? And in thy name have cast out devils? And in thy name done many wonderful works? 23.* **And then will I profess unto them, I never knew you: depart from me, ye that work iniquity.**

It is clear here that Christ was talking to His followers when He said that *"strait is the gate, and narrow is the way, which leadeth unto life, and few there be that find it"* and *"Not every one that saith unto me, Lord, Lord, shall enter into the kingdom of heaven."*

Christ who did not stop with these two statements. The parable of the ten virgins is also related to this topic of many Christians not making it into the kingdom of heaven—in this particular parable 50% of the Christians will not make it into the kingdom of heaven when Christ comes.

> *Matthew 25:1-13 – 1. Then shall the kingdom of heaven be likened unto ten virgins, which took their lamps, and went forth to meet the bridegroom. 2. And five of them were wise, and five were foolish. 3. They that were foolish took their lamps, and took no oil with them: 4. But the wise took oil in their vessels with their lamps. 5. While the bridegroom tarried, they all slumbered and slept. 6. And at midnight there was a cry made, Behold, the bridegroom cometh; go ye out to meet him. 7. Then all those virgins arose, and trimmed their lamps. 8. And the foolish said unto the wise, Give us of your oil; for our lamps are gone out. 9. But the wise answered, saying, Not so; lest there be not enough for us and you: but go ye rather to them that sell, and buy for yourselves. 10.* **And while they went to buy, the bridegroom came; and they that were ready went in with him to the marriage: and the door was shut. 11. Afterward came also the other virgins, saying, Lord, Lord, open to us. 12. But he answered and said, Verily I say unto you, I know you not.** *13. Watch therefore, for ye know neither the day nor the hour wherein the Son of man cometh.*

Question: Why would Jesus Christ deny His followers' entrance into the kingdom of heaven?

The answer to this question is because He wants all His followers to be a perfect man *"in the unity of faith, and of the knowledge of the Son of God."*

> *Ephesians 4:11-14 – 11. And he gave some, apostles; and some, prophets; and some, evangelists; and some, pastors and teachers; 12. For the perfecting of the saints, for the work of the ministry, for the edifying of the body of Christ: 13.* **Till we all come**

in the unity of the faith, and of the knowledge of the Son of God, unto a perfect man, unto the measure of the stature of the fullness of Christ: 14. That we henceforth be no more children, tossed to and fro, and carried about with every wind of doctrine, by the sleight of men, and cunning craftiness, whereby they lie in wait to deceive;

In this last passage Paul taught that Christ gave some apostles and prophets for the perfecting of the saints. Paul also in addition to the command to have *"unity of faith"* he warned us about men who *"lie in wait to deceive."* In Mark, Christ warned about false Christs and false prophets.

*Mark 13:21,22 – 21. **And then if any man shall say to you, Lo, here is Christ; or, lo, he is there; believe him not: 22. For false Christs and false prophets shall rise, and shall shew signs and wonders, to seduce, if it were possible, even the elect.***

Paul continued to expound on the teaching that Christians will be deceived and that those *"who preached any other gospel"* would be cursed.

*Galatians 1:6-9 – 6. **I marvel that ye are so soon removed from him that called you into the grace of Christ unto another gospel: 7. Which is not another; but there be some that trouble you, and would pervert the gospel the gospel of Christ. 8. But though we, or an angel from heaven, preach any other gospel unto you than that which we have preached unto you, let him be accursed. 9. As we said before, so say I now again, If any man preach any other gospel unto you than that ye have received, let him be accursed.***

Knowing now that the Christians who let themselves be deceived and the deceivers who lead these people astray will not make it into the kingdom of heaven it is our responsibility to find out who are the real deceivers. The Christian leaders who are leading the fight against Joseph Smith and the Mormons may be doing this with all sincerity of their hearts! After all Christ did warn against *"false prophets."*

How to Know Who Is the Deceiver. With all these warnings about false prophets and men waiting to deceive the very elect, Christ did provide a way to know who is a true prophet. Christ taught us how to know a true prophet in Matthew.

*Matthew 7:20 – **Wherefore by their fruits ye shall know them.***

One can know a true prophet by the fruits that he accomplishes. To help one understand what kinds of fruits of a prophet are good, a few examples of the works of the prophets in the Bible will be given. Noah saved mankind by building a boat for the great flood. Through Moses God established the Ten Commandments, the first tabernacle or portable temple, and led the Jews out of bondage. Through Abraham He established the 12 tribes of Israel. Through Isaiah God prophesied of Christ's coming, His crucifixion, resurrection and His second coming. Through Solomon He built the Solomon Temple. It appears that each prophet had his own mission to accomplish and each did it well. An important characteristic of each prophet was that they all talked with God. The apostle Paul also stated something similar as to how he taught the gospel of Jesus Christ.

*Galatians 1:10-12 – 10. For do I now persuade men, or God? **Or do I seek to please men? For if I yet pleased men, I should not be the servant of Christ. 11. But I certify you, brethren, that the gospel which was preached of me is not after man. 12. For I neither received it of man, neither was I taught it, but by the revelation of Jesus Christ.***

Paul taught that the gospel of Jesus Christ should be taught by revelation of God. Following the examples of the prophets mentioned above, in order to obtain the teachings for the church, a true prophet should be able to talk to God or Jesus Christ. This will be one of the first tests of a prophet…he should claim the opportunity to talk with God or Jesus Christ.

The Biblical Support Challenge. A second test of a true prophet will be the teachings that the prophet presents to his followers. This book will use only the Bible to thoroughly examine over 90 of Joseph Smith's teachings. If Joseph Smith actually talked with Jesus Christ, as he claimed, then the Bible will support his teachings. Christ commanded us to be perfect.

> *Matthew 5:48 – **Be ye therefore perfect, even as your Father which in heaven is perfect.***

In order to measure just how close the teachings of Joseph Smith and the other Christian churches are to perfection a Biblical Support Challenge is provided. This challenge will take each topic or teaching and provides the opportunity to mark whether there is biblical support for that particular topic or not. At the end, each religion can add up and calculate an actual percentage that reveals how close their leader or church is to what the Bible states.

This Biblical Support Challenge is meant to reveal the fruits of Joseph Smith and those of the leaders of the other churches who challenge the teachings of Joseph Smith. If properly and sincerely completed the Biblical Support Challenge will help reveal who is the true deceiver! It will reveal who is teaching the precepts of man and who is teaching the true doctrines of God.

I personally believe that a righteous sincere man who teaches part of the truth of God is a good man. Christ's followers will still receive some blessings. Christ backs these feelings in Matthew.

> *Matthew 10:41 – **He that receiveth a prophet in the name of a prophet shall receive a prophet's reward; and he that receiveth a righteous man in the name of a righteous man shall receive a righteous man's reward.***

This book will reveal, according to the Bible, the differences between a "prophet's reward" and a "righteous man's reward." It is up to each one of us to choose between the rewards of a prophet and the rewards of a righteous man.

One Jot or One Tittle. While using the Bible to examine the fruits of Joseph Smith and fruits of the men who claim he is a false prophet the following statement by Christ will be used.

> *Matthew 5:18 – For verily I say unto you, Till heaven and earth pass, **one jot or one tittle shall in no wise pass from the law, till all be fulfilled.***

It is the author's interpretation of this passage that *"**one jot or one tittle shall in no wise pass from the law, till all be fulfilled"*** means that all prophesies, principles, laws, and practices of the Old and New Testaments, whether great or small, given by the prophets will be fulfilled or realized. One of Joseph Smith's most quoted scriptures is about Elias coming to *"**restore all things."***

> *Matt 17:11 – And Jesus answered and said unto them, **Elias truly shall first come, and restore all things,***

Following the *"one jot and one tittle"* command from Christ this last scripture indicates that all the old prophet's statements about the future and the actual *"restoration of all things"* include all the same organization that Christ set up. The organization includes many of the practices and laws of the Old and New Testaments. It is the author's conclusion, that a church restored by Jesus Christ, would be fully supported, in some way, by the Bible. It is critical to understand that the LDS Church is not the "restoration of new things!" The teachings of Joseph Smith seem to be new and unusual to most of the Christian churches today. In actuality they are not new. If a particular teaching is supported by the Bible, then it is not a new teaching!

In understanding the *"one jot and one tittle"* statement in relation to the *"restore all things"* statement, the question that should be asked about the Mormon Church is not whether it is true or not. The question should be: Is the Mormon Church the restored church spoken of in Bible? If not, is there another church that may to be the restored church? If there is no restored church on the earth, then you should be waiting for the restoration of Christ's church to come to pass.

What Is Our Cross to Bear? When compared to the passages mentioned about the many Christians who will not make it into the kingdom of God, these small and insignificant teachings and prophecies may be the difference between which Christians make it into the kingdom of God. Referring back to the parable of the ten virgins. It is important to note that 50% of the Christians were denied entrance into the wedding or the kingdom of heaven. These 50% were denied entrance because of a little insignificant element—not having their lamps full of oil. This seems very trivial and most Christian churches tend to ignore this small requirement of being prepared. The question that must be asked about this parable is:

> **Question: What is the "oil" that will keep 50% of the Christians out of the kingdom of God?**

Like most Christian religions teach, each person has his/her own cross to bear. This "oil" could be different for the many different people trying to get into the kingdom of God. There will be several times that a small "jot or tittle" element of salvation that is quoted in the Bible will be raised to see if it might be your "oil." For example, Christ gave a parable about a king who gave a wedding. In this wedding there was a man who was not wearing the "wedding garment." The king had this man bound up and cast into outer darkness.

> *Matthew 22:11-14 – 11. And when the king came in to see the guests, **he saw there a man which had not on a wedding garment:** 12. And he saith unto him, **Friend,** how camest thou in hither not having a wedding garment? And he was speechless. 13. Then said the king to the servants, Bind him hand and foot, and take him away, **and cast him into outer darkness;** there shall be weeping and gnashing of teeth. 14. For many are called, but few are chosen.*

In this example Christ casts out a "friend" because he does not have on the "wedding garment." This is similar to the parable of the 10 virgins were 50% of the virgins are refused entrance into the wedding because their lamps were empty of oil. With the final statement in verse 14, "For many are called, but few are chosen" it is possible that in both these examples the wedding of the 10 virgins and this wedding of the king could mean the invitation of the practicing Christians into the kingdom of God.

> *Revelation 16:15 – Behold, I come as a thief. **Blessed is he that watcheth, and keepeth his garments,** lest he walk naked, and they see his shame.*

> **Question: Could these special *"wedding garments"* be the oil that will keep you from entering into the kingdom of God?**

Like this example there will be several more statements about single principles of the gospel that may be the oil that keeps many Christians out of the kingdom of God. It is important that all Christians know these small but very important principles! If you read this book you will know these principles!

Know the Only True God. One of the main charges against Joseph Smith and the Mormons is that we do not believe in the same Christian God of the Bible that other Christians believe in. It is also the intent of the Biblical Support Challenge to "shed some light" on this accusation. It is a commandment from God to know Him and Jesus Christ.

> *John 17:3 – **And this is life eternal, that they might know thee the only true God; and Jesus Christ,** whom thou hast sent.*

It is the intent and goal of this book to bring both Mormon and non-Mormon Christian closer to the teachings of God so that *"they might know the only true God; and Jesus Christ."* After completing the Biblical Support Challenge one will probably know who is closer to believing in the true God of the Bible. Each individual reader who sincerely wants to know God and Jesus Christ can only answer this for himself/herself.

The Bible. Knowing there are many different translations of the Bible available for study, the King James Version of the Bible is used here. The main reason for using this version is because it was translated before all the different Christian religions came into existence. Many of the current translations are interpreted according to the interests of the person or church doing the interpretation. Great are the variations between the different interpretations. The King James Version is a more neutral translation.

Unfortunately, the Bible is not the perfect "How to Manual" that explains the exact organization of the Church and how to operate the church, and instructions on what exactly the followers of the Bible should believe in. The New Testament is a compilation of letters that the original Apostles wrote to the different memberships in many different locations.

In many cases, the letters are written in a form that addressed that particular audience and their problems. The authors of each letter, without writing the detail of specific church organization and list of beliefs, commented on those specific problems. Knowing that the local audience already knew the doctrine that was being addressed, the Apostles would comment on the existing problems. This resulted in many passages being vague to current readers of the Bible. Which leaves the interpretation of many doctrines to the imagination of the different religious scholars involved, to include Joseph Smith.

With most biblical passages, there are two ways to interpret them. First, is what the passage states in plain English—"What it says is what it means." Second is the symbolism that some passages include. This symbolism is where most of the different interpretations come about between the different religious sects.

Therefore, in most cases, it is the intent of this author to use the passages basic statement – in other words, "what the passage basically states is what it basically means." There will be very little explaining of the symbolism that a passage may contain.

Knowing that one particular passage could be interpreted in several different ways according to the different scholars of the Bible, it is not the expectation of this book to define the different doctrines of Joseph Smith or any other sect. The intention of this book is to quote the particular teaching of Joseph Smith, show where he obtained that teaching, and compare it with some kind of support, whether it be simple or complicated, from the Bible. It is up to the person reading the book to decide if many of the scriptures could in fact support the case for the teachings of Joseph Smith. This is not meant to argue or contend with the different Christian religions, it is only to show you where, if any, there could be support for the teachings of Joseph Smith in the Bible. You the reader can draw your own conclusions on my interpretations of the different passages used.

General Information. In this book I have written out almost all of the passages quoted from the scriptures. I have done this primarily to make the book easier to read and study. I have read many religious books where a passage is mentioned but not quoted. I then have to look up the scripture and it takes a long time to read the books.

A second reason I have included the passages in this book is because in the different "anti-Mormon" books and pamphlets that I have read, many passages are mentioned, but never quoted. When I take the time to look them up, the passage is grossly misquoted or does not even state anything close to what the authors are interpreting.

Therefore, each passage quoted here is written for the ease of the reader and to insure that you know what I am talking about. Any mistake in transcribing the passages is due to human error only. There is no willful intent to change the passages for my own benefit of interpretation. All of the bolded parts of the passages are placed by me and are there for my own emphasis to help the reader zero in on what I am talking about at the time.

I have placed an open page at the end of most chapters for taking notes. Please use this space for writing down your questions, concerns, and thoughts on the different topics. Then after finishing the entire book, go back to those notes and review those particular topics. You can also visit the web site – josephsmithandthebible.com – for more information on how to present the teachings in this book. You will also be able to leave your comments and thoughts on this book.

I hope this book will enlighten you as to who are the deceivers out there in the Christian world and most of all I hope that this book will help bring you closer to *"knowing the only true God; and Jesus Christ."*

TABLE OF CONTENTS

PART I: THE CHURCH CHRIST ORGANIZED

CHAPTER 1

THE APOSTASY

The Apostasy Defined. The apostasy is defined as the "falling away" from the original church organization, doctrines, and teachings. While Christ was on the earth, He organized His church with apostles, prophets, and other offices. Christ established that church with power of the priesthood with accompanying ordinances. He also established rules and/or commandments for His disciples to live by. Then He called the general membership to go two-by-two out into the world to spread His gospel. This "falling away" is a full or partial departure from the organization and teachings that Christ and His apostles set up while they were on the earth.

The Roman Catholic Church, headquartered in the Vatican, claims to be the original church that Christ organized. Recognizing the priesthood that was present in the original church, and the necessity for a line of authority, the Catholic church has a record of all the leaders of the Catholic church, or "Popes," from the time of the first "Pope" or Peter. Since the days of the reformation, most of the existing Christian churches in Europe and North America are churches that disagreed with the Catholic Church and broke off making their own sect. In the eyes of the Catholic Church, these churches that include the Church of England, the Lutherans, the Protestants, the Methodists, the Presbyterians, the Baptists, and etc, are apostate groups from the Catholic Church.

Joseph Smith's Teachings of the Apostasy. One of the key elements of the Mormon Church and one of Joseph Smith's first teachings is the "great apostasy" from the original church of Jesus Christ. If there were no apostasy, then there would be no need for a restoration, thus leaving the Mormon Church unnecessary.

The Biblical Teachings of the Apostasy.

The Old Testament Prophecies of the Apostasy. One of the first prophecies of the apostasy was Isaiah's. He speaks specifically of the leaders and members of the church who have changed the ordinance and broke the everlasting covenant. The leaders of the Roman Catholic Church, somewhere between 300 A.D. to the 1500's, changed the ordinance that was established by the Lord. These many changes instituted by the Roman Catholic Church led to the Protestant Reformation in the 1500's.

> *Isaiah 24:5 – The earth also is defiled under the inhabitants thereof; **because they have transgressed the laws, changed the ordinance, broken the everlasting covenant.***

In another prophecy by Isaiah, the church members and leaders in the latter days are again revealed for their shallowness of sincerity towards God. God describes many members of the Christian faith here that "*draw near me with their mouth, and with their lips do honour me but have removed their heart far from me.*" Then Isaiah hits the church leadership very hard…"*their fear toward me is taught by the precept of men.*"

> *Isaiah 29:13 – Wherefore the Lord said, **Forasmuch as this people draw near me with their mouth, and with their lips do honour me, but have removed their heart far from me, and their fear toward me is taught by the precept of men:***

In this passage, the religious leaders are accused to be teaching the things of God by their own precepts or beliefs, not by the inspiration of God through His prophets as was done throughout the history of the Bible. The prophet Amos tells how God works through His leaders in the following passage.

> *Amos 3:7 –* **Surely the Lord God will do nothing, but he revealeth his secret unto his servants the prophets.**

Isaiah continued prophesying of the apostasy from Christ's original church in the following passage.

> *Isaiah 60:2 – For,* **behold, the darkness shall cover the earth,** *and gross darkness the people; but the Lord shall arise upon thee, and his glory shall be seen upon thee.*

In this past passage, Isaiah foretold of the "dark ages" where the world did not progress. The "dark ages" happened while being directed by the leaders of the Roman Catholic Church. It was and still is the official doctrine of the Roman Catholic Church that the "heavens are closed" and there is "no more direct revelation to prophets." This belief here is why the leader of the Roman Catholic Church is not called a prophet, but instead is called a Pope. It is my understanding that nowhere in the Bible is a position called the "Pope." Christ never in His teachings established the position of the Pope.

It is this official policy of " the heavens are closed" that fulfills Amos' prophecy of the "famine in the land" that was a famine of "hearing the words of the Lord."

> *Amos 8:11 – Behold,* **the days come,** *saith the Lord God,* **that I will send a famine in the land, not a famine of bread, nor a thirst for water, but of hearing the words of the Lord.**

The Apostle Paul's Teachings on the Apostasy. Paul was very aware of the upcoming apostasy from Christ's church. He preached to many of the different congregations about the apostasy and continually warned of it. One of his clearest messages was to the congregation in Thessalonia where he prophesied to them that the second coming of Christ cannot come until there was a "falling away" first.

> *2 Thessalonians 2:2,3 – 2. That ye be not soon shaken in mind, or be troubled, neither by spirit, nor by word, not by letter as from us,* **as that the day of Christ is at hand.** *3.* **Let no man deceive you by any means: for that day shall not come, except there come a falling away first,** *and that man of sin be revealed, the son of perdition;*

Paul warned the Thessalonians that the mystery of that iniquity of the "falling away" was already working before the death of the apostles.

> *2 Thessalonians 2:7 –* **For the mystery of iniquity doth already work:** *only he who now letteth will let, until he be taken out of the way.*

Paul also warned the saints that after he left grievous wolves would enter in among the membership not sparing them. And he warned them that from their own membership men will arise and speak perverse things that would draw away disciples. The apostasy again, working through the leaders of the church.

> *Acts 20:29-31 – 29. For I know this, that* **after my departing shall grievous wolves enter in among you, not sparing the flock. 30. Also of your own selves shall men arise, speaking perverse things, to draw away disciples after them.** *31. Therefore watch, and remember, that by the space of three years I ceased not to warn every one night and day with tears.*

Paul talked to the current membership in Corinth where he acknowledges that there are already divisions amongst the leaders and membership of the church.

> *1 Corinthians 11:18, 19 – 18. For first of all, when ye come together in the church,* **I hear that there be divisions among you;** *and I partly believe it. 19.* **For there must be also heresies among you,** *that they which are approved may be made manifest among you.*

Paul wrote Titus, who was in Crete, of the membership who professed that they knew God, but in works they denied Him, being abominable and disobedient.

> *Titus 1:15,16 – 15. Unto the pure all things are pure: but unto them that are defiled and unbelieving is nothing pure; but even their mind and conscience is defiled. 16.* **They profess that they know God; but in works they deny him, being abominable, and disobedient, and unto every good work reprobate.**

The last warning of the apostasy by Paul was to the saints in Galatia. Paul was surprised that they were so soon to pervert the ways of Christ, which was taught them by Paul and the other apostles. Paul even accused them of perverting the gospel of Christ.

> *Galatians 1:6,7 – 6.* **I marvel that ye are so soon removed from him that called you into the grace of Christ unto another gospel:** *7. Which is not another;* **but there be some that trouble you, and would pervert the gospel of Christ.**

Paul's Views to the Apostle Timothy on the Apostasy. In Timothy Paul actually prophesied of the apostasy on three different occasions. The first was talking about the apostasy from the original Church of Jesus Christ. Paul warns of perilous times that will come and that the leaders and members will have a form of godliness, but they actually deny the power of God. Paul describes them as people that are always learning, but they never are able to come to the knowledge of truth.

> *2 Timothy 3:1-7 – 1.* **This know also, that in the last days perilous times shall come.** *2. For men shall be lovers of their own selves, covetous, boasters, proud, blasphemers, disobedient to parents, unthankful, unholy, 3. Without natural affection, trucebreakers, false accusers, incontinent, fierce, despisers of those that are good, 4. Traitors, heady, highminded, lovers of pleasures more than lovers of God; 5.* **Having a form of godliness, but denying the power thereof;** *from such turn away. 6. For of this sort are they which creep into houses, and lead captive silly women laden with sins, led away with divers lusts, 7.* **Ever learning, and never able to come to the knowledge of the truth.**

In the few writings toTimothy that exists in the New Testament Paul prophesied a second time of the apostasy from the original church. He speaks of the church not enduring sound doctrine, the teachers are leading after their own lusts, and they turn away from truth and go for fables.

> *2 Timothy 4:3,4 – 3.* **For the time will come when they will not endure sound doctrine; but after their own lusts shall they heap to themselves teachers, having itching ears; 4. And they shall turn away their ears from the truth, and shall be turned unto fables.**

As was with the apostle Paul, Timothy was experiencing similar problems with the leaders and membership of the church. It was mentioned that the membership that was established in Asia had already turned him away.

> *2 Timothy 1:15 – This thou knowest, that* **all they which are in Asia be turned away from me;** *of who are Phygellus and Hermogenes.*

In Timothy Paul also found himself correcting some of the leaders of the saints. He described them as having *"swerved"* into teaching *"vain jangling,"* and desiring to be teachers of the law, but not understanding what they teach.

> *1 Timothy 1:6,7 – 6.* **From which some having swerved have turned aside unto vain jangling; 7. Desiring to be teachers of the law; understanding neither what they say, nor whereof they affirm.**

An example of what these particular leaders taught is that the resurrection was already past.

> *2 Timothy 2:16-18 – 16. But shun profane and vain babblings: for they will increase unto more ungodliness. 17. And their word will eat as doth a canker: of whom is Hymenaeus and Philetus; 18. Who concerning the truth have erred,* **saying that the resurrection is past already; and overthrow the faith of some.**

A very interesting perception of Paul reveals that not only did he know of and also prophesy of the apostasy, he also understood the restoration of the gospel in the latter times. Knowing that after the apostasy and the "dark ages," the fullness of the gospel would exist, he prophesizes that in those latter times some will also depart from the faith giving heed to the doctrines of devils.

> *1 Timothy 4:1 – Now the Spirit speaketh expressly, that* **in the latter times some shall depart from the faith, giving heed to seducing spirits, and doctrines of devils;**

Jesus Christ even had a few words to say about the apostasy.

> *Matthew 24:5 –* **For many shall come in my name, saying, I am Christ: and shall deceive many.**

> *Matthew 24:24 –* **For there shall arise false Christs, and false prophets,** *and shall shew great signs and wonders; insomuch that, if it were possible,* **they shall deceive the very elect.**

A Brief History of the Churches.

Having the teachings of Jesus Christ, the apostles, and some prophets on the falling away of the truths taught by Jesus Christ, a brief history of the original Church of Jesus Christ is now introduced. One may apply the actual history with what was written in the Bible.

The Evolution of Christ's Original Church.

In order to understand the current situation with the many different religious organizations a very brief history of the Christian religious movement will be reviewed. Much of the history and all of the diagrams included in this history are quoted out of the pamphlet "Christian Religions – A Comparative Chart Vol. II," by Rex Bennett.[1]

Under the direction of God the Father, Christ organized His church. Christ gave the twelve apostles the responsibility to spread the gospel to the whole world. The apostles accomplished this over the next forty to fifty years until they were martyred. Once the original apostles had all died there was a second generation of church leaders that led the churches. As did the original apostles, these church leaders wrote letters to the different congregations, they traveled and visited the different congregations, and also gave their lives as a testimony of Jesus Christ. Many of them were fed to the lions in the Roman arenas.

The writings of the second generation of church leaders are translated, published and available in many bookstores. One set of writings is "The Writings of the Apostolic Fathers." These writings also record some of the early teachings and expected behavior of the general membership.

In the period 307-337 A.D., the Roman Emperor Constantine I, having trouble hanging onto the Roman empire, decided to adopt the belief of the Christians as the state's organized church. Constantine himself was a sun worshiper. After this state adoption of Christianity, the Roman Emperors in Constantinople had complete power and control over the Christian religion for about 700 years. Although the falling away was a gradual process, this adoption of the Christian movement by the Roman empire could be, "officially," the actual time of the great apostasy from the original Church of Jesus Christ.

In about 1054 A.D. another apostasy occurred. This is when Rome and Constantinople split and created the Roman Catholic Church. Based out of Rome (the Vatican) in the west, and the Eastern Orthodox Catholic Church in the east, based out of Constantinople.

The early 1500's began yet another apostasy, what is called the Protestant Reformation. This is after Martin Luther began his questioning of the teachings of the Roman Catholic Church. The Roman Catholic Church viewed this as an apostasy from Christ's church and Martin Luther was subsequently excommunicated from the Roman Catholic Church. This incident led to the separation of the Church of England, the branching off of Calvinism, and other "radical sects" that wanted to teach what they thought was the correct teachings of Jesus Christ.

Diagram 1
The Evolution of the Original Church of Jesus Christ

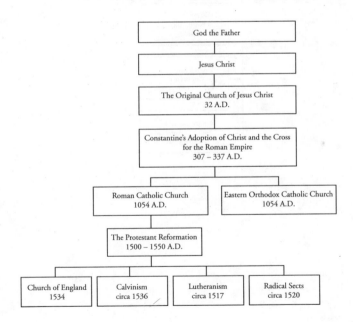

The Lutheran Church.

After Martin Luther's excommunication from the church he did not immediately establish the Lutheran church. There was a group of people who started an apostate church, which adopted Martin Luther's name for their church. This church eventually sponsored the American Lutheran Conference of 1878 and 1900. The religious movement eventually became the United Lutheran Church in America (1918).

Diagram 2
The Evolution of the Lutheran Church

The Church of England.

The political leadership in England, in short, wanted its own power over the people, so for political reasons, broke off from the Roman Catholic Church and named their movement **The Church of England.** The American branches of the Church of England became the Protestant Episcopal Church and the Methodist church. As the church progressed in America it branched into several different faiths of the Methodist Church that are listed in **Diagram 3.**

Diagram 3
Evolution of the Church of England

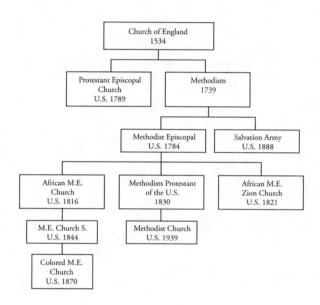

The Calvinist Movement.

The Calvinism movement (approximately 1536) introduced the Reformed Churches, the Presbyterian Church, the United Presbyterian Church, and the Evangelical Churches.

Diagram 4
Evolution of Calvinism

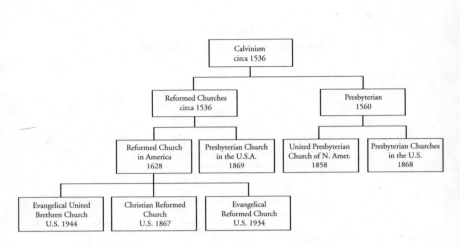

The Radical Sects.

The last major break from the Roman Catholic Church was the "Radical Sects" (approximately 1520). They began with the Anabaptists that sprung forth the Baptists, the Southern Baptist Convention, the northern Baptist Convention, the Free Will Baptists, the Churches of Christ, the Mennonites, the Church of the Brethren, the Disciples of Christ, the National Baptist Convention U.S.A., the Adventist movement (the Seventh Day Adventists), the Congregational (Brownists) churches, and the Unitarian churches.

It is history that the Baptist church actually apostatized from the Roman Catholic Church. The Baptist's official position is that the Roman Catholic Church had lost many of the original truths that Jesus Christ set up while on the earth.

Diagram 5
Evolution of the Radical Sects

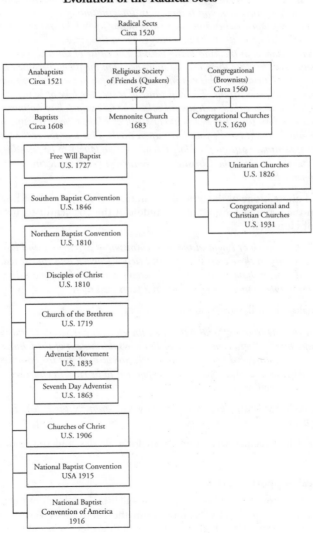

The Apostasy Recognized. In the book "The Great Apostasy"[2] written by James E. Talmage, a leader in the Mormon Church as well as a religious scholar wrote many of the historical and religious reasons for the apostasy from the original church of Jesus Christ. In his study he concluded that the Catholic Church was part of the apostasy from the original church. Talmage also portrayed the original men who broke off from the Catholic Church to start their own churches were actually sincere men who recognized that many of the original teachings and truths had been lost from the Catholic Church. Here are two of quotes from major reformers. The first is from John Wesley who lived from 1703 to 1791 A. D. and ranks as chief among the founders of Methodism. John Wesley comments on the apostasy of the Christian Church as evidenced by the early decline of spiritual power and the cessation of the gifts of the Spirit of God within the Church:

> *"It does not appear that these extraordinary gifts of the Holy Spirit (I Corinthians, chapter 12) were common in the Church for more than two or three centuries. We seldom hear of them after that fatal period when the Emperor Constantine called himself a Christian, and from a vain imagination of promoting the Christian cause thereby heaped riches and power and honor upon Christians in general, but in particular upon the Christian clergy. From this time they almost totally ceased, very few instances of the kind being found. The cause of this was not, as has been supposed, because there was no more occasion for them, because all the world had become Christians. This is a miserable mistake; not a twentieth part of it was then nominally Christians. The real cause of it was the love of many, almost all Christians so-called, was waxed cold. The Christians had no more of the spirit of Christ than the other heathens. The Son of Man, when He came to examine His Church, could hardly find faith upon earth. This was the real cause why the extraordinary gifts of the Holy Ghost were no longer to be found in the Christian church—because the Christians were turned heathens again, and only had a dead form left."* [3]

The second quote is one of the official declarations of the Church of England when it first broke from the Catholic Church in the middle of the 16th century. This quote is found in the Book of Homilies.

> *"The Church of England makes declaration of degeneracy and loss of divine authority in these words:"Laity and clergy, learned and unlearned, all ages, sects, and degrees, have been drowned in abominable idolatry most detested by God and damnable to man for eight hundred years and more."*

Talmage makes the following statement.

> *According to this official statement, therefore, the religious world had been utterly apostate for eight centuries prior to the establishment of the Church of England. The fact of a universal apostasy was widely proclaimed, for the homilies from which the foregoing citation is taken were "appointed to be read in churches" in lieu of sermons under specified conditions.*

Talmage concluded with *"The great apostasy was divinely predicted; its accomplishment is attested by both sacred and secular writ."*

These sacred and secular writs were from John Wesley and the leaders of the Church of England.

The Biblical Support Chart.

This Biblical Support Chart is the section that will list whether or not the teachings of Joseph Smith's will have some kind of support from the King James Version of the Bible. It is important to note that not all religious sects will interpret the listed passages the same way

Joseph Smith interpreted them. What is important is that in the passages listed, do they talk about what Joseph Smith taught? Or do they or could they support, in basic English, what Joseph Smith taught?

In the author's opinion, there is credible belief that the Bible comments on the potential of an apostasy in both the Old Testament and the New Testament.

THE BIBLICAL SUPPORT CHART	
Is the following topic supported in the Bible?	**Yes or No**
Does the Old Testament support Joseph Smith's teaching on the Apostasy? (Isaiah 24:5; 29:13, 60:2; Amos 8:11)	Yes
Does the New Testament support Joseph Smith's teaching on the Apostasy? (2 Thes 2:2,3,7; Acts 20:29-31; 1 Cor 11:18,19; Titus 1:15,16; Gal 1:6,7; 1 Tim 4:1; 2 Tim 3:1-7; 4:3,4; 2 Tim 1:15; 2:16-18; Acts 20:29-31; Matt 24:5,24)	Yes

Author's Note: I would like to comment on my admiration of two people in particular who question the necessity of organized religion. The first is my father, J. Kenneth Mann. My father recognized at an early age that he did not need organized religion to guide him through life. My father taught me that organized religion was for the weak minded and they existed to control the people.

My father was not an atheist, he has always believed in God who created this earth and everything on it. He just did not believe or could not follow the teachings of the organized religions. It is very understandable to me after studying the "apostasy" that my father did not buy into organized religion's confusion that was prophesied in the Bible. I admire him for recognizing the fallibility of the teachings of most religious leaders and not wanting to follow these churches.

The second person that I admire is Scott R. Stahlecker, who is a personal "best" friend. Scott is a trained minister who, like my father and many other people in the world, has recognized the weaknesses of the teachings of organized religion. Scott has authored a book called *How to Escape Religion Guilt Free*[4]. In this book Scott questions the existing religious thought and does a tremendous effort to compare their teachings with the characteristics of God.

In both cases, their common sense outlook on life recognizes the spiritual confusion that exists in the organized religious world. It is my hope that they both read this book, which is a common sense look at the teachings of Joseph Smith and how these teachings compare to the Bible.

As this chapter related, there was an apostasy from the original Church that Jesus Christ set up. This is the reason for the many different and confusing Christian religions on the earth today. The founder of the Mormon religion, Joseph Smith claimed to have seen God the Father and His Son Jesus Christ. Joseph Smith claimed to able to converse with Jesus Christ face to face and claimed to be able to ask Him questions.

After reading this past evolution of the Christian churches many readers may wonder where the LDS Church falls into the over-all evolution chart. Joseph Smith, who could be known as a major reformer, is the only founder that has claimed direct contact with Jesus Christ. Or in other words, Joseph Smith is the only reformer that Jesus Christ Himself has appeared to and personally directed the organization of the Church of Jesus Christ of Latter Day Saints. With this knowledge, the only two churches with divine authority and guidance from Jesus Christ in setting up the Church of Jesus Christ was the original church and the second church set up through the prophet Joseph Smith—The Church of Jesus Christ of Latter Day Saints.

Diagram 6
Where the Church of Jesus Christ of Latter Day Saints Fits

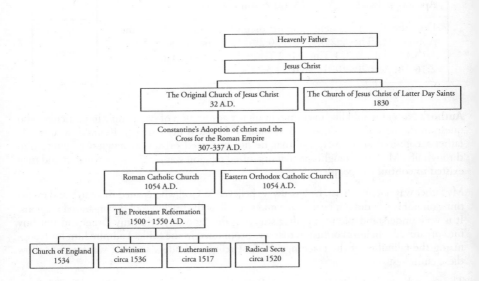

Even though all the major reformers mentioned in this chapter were apostates from the Catholic Church, these men were all sincere followers of Christ that recognized the "apostasy" from the original Church of Jesus Christ. They were doing what they thought was best for their followers who agreed with them.

In the next chapter, **The Restoration,** a detailed look at Joseph Smith's claim to restoring the original Church of Jesus Christ back on earth will be researched using only the Bible to either support or dispel this claim. If this claim of a restoration is supported—oh!…the many questions that could be answered!

NOTES

NOTES

CHAPTER 2

THE RESTORATION

The Restoration Defined. The restoration of the fullness of the gospel of Jesus Christ is just that…Christ, himself, bringing back all the precious elements of his original church. This includes the priesthood, teachings, ordinances, temples, covenants, mysteries, organization, and etc.. In Christ's own words he stated:

> *Matthew 5:17, 18 – 17. Think not that I am come to destroy the law, or the prophets: I am not come to destroy, but to fulfill. 18. For verily I say unto you, Till heaven and earth pass, **one jot or one tittle shall in no wise pass from the law, till all be fulfilled.***

As Christ said, not "one jot or one tittle" will be forgotten or passed over from the law. Christ was talking about fulfilling all that the prophets have foretold in the scriptures, both Old and New Testaments. This includes the prophecies of the prophets, apostles, and Christ himself about the apostasy. It also includes what the prophets teach about The Restoration, which shall be presented hereafter.

The Restoration. The doctrine or theory of the restoration of the fullness of The Church of Jesus Christ in the latter times creates a dilemma for all the Christian churches. This doctrine leaves these churches to 1) accept the restoration of the fullness of the gospel of Jesus Christ and leave the current church with which they are affiliated or 2) reject this doctrine of the restoration and continue on with partial truth. In the case of the different church leaders, they become what Christ himself warned against—***Deceivers of the word.***

Currently, many members of the different churches have heard of the restoration of the gospel according to Joseph Smith and have accepted it. Resulting in the LDS church being the fastest growing church in America where these converts are taking advantage of the fullness of Christ's blessings and ordinances.

Unfortunately, most of the leaders of the different churches have rejected the restoration or have failed to fully investigate the restoration. They charge Joseph Smith with being a false prophet, teaching false teachings, thus falling into Christ's category of being a "deceiver." The main charges being that Joseph Smith does not believe in the Bible and that the Bible does not support his teachings. It is the purpose of this book to outline most of the Biblical support, or lack thereof, for what Joseph Smith has taught.

Many churches do not believe in the restoration and those who do acknowledge those prophecies, do not believe they will happen until Christ comes in his glory at the second coming. They quote the following passage for their support.

> *Acts 3:19-21 – 19. Repent ye therefore, and be converted, that your sins may be blotted out, **when the times of refreshing shall come from the presence of the Lord; 20. And he shall send Jesus Christ, which before was preached unto you: 21. Whom the heaven must receive until the times of restitution of all things, which God hath spoken by the mouth of all his holy prophets since the world began.***

In a way these church leaders are correct that the "*refreshing*" will come with Christ, but what these leaders count on is the fact that Christ can only come when He comes in all His glory at the end of the world. What the leaders reject or ignore is the fact that Christ does have the power and ability to come and visit the earth before He comes in all His glory.

Isaiah taught that the Lord will "*set his hand again the second time*" to recover the remnant of his people.

> *Isaiah 11:11,12 – 11. **And it shall come to pass in that day, that the Lord shall set his hand again the second time to recover the remnant of his people,** which shall be left, from Assyria, and from Egypt, and from Pathros, and from Cush, and from Elam, and from Shinar, and from Hamath, and from the islands of the sea, 12. **And he shall set up an ensign for the nations,** and shall assemble the outcasts of Israel, and gather together the dispersed of Judah from the four corners of the earth.*

Jeremiah taught that in the last days the Lord would make a new covenant with the house of Israel and the house of Judah.

> *Jeremiah 31:31 – Behold, **the days come, saith the Lord, that I will make a new covenant with the house of Israel, and with the house of Judah:** 32. Not according to the covenant that I made with their fathers in the day that I took them by the hand to bring them out of the land of Egypt; which my covenant they brake, although I was an husband unto them, saith the Lord: 33. But this shall be the covenant that I will make with the house of Israel; After those days, saith the Lord, I will put my law in their inward parts, and write it in their hearts; and will be their God, and they shall be my people.*

Daniel taught that the God of heaven will "*set up a kingdom, which shall never be destroyed*" and that "*it shall stand for ever.*"

> *Dan 2:44 – **And in the days of these kings shall the God of heaven set up a kingdom, which shall never be destroyed;** and the kingdom shall not be left to other people, but it shall break in pieces and consume all these kingdoms, **and it shall stand for ever.***

In responding to the church leaders who believe the restoration will not happen until Christ comes in all His glory, these last three prophets have demonstrated that the Lord can and will in fact do this restoration Himself.

Christ's Teachings of the Restoration. A very important happening in Christ's ministry was the transfiguration of Jesus, where, with the glory of God the Father, Moses and Elias appeared to Jesus while in the presence of Peter, James, and John.

> *Matthew 17:1-8 – 1. And after six days Jesus taketh Peter, James, and John his brother, and bringeth them up into an high mountain apart, 2. **And was transfigured before them: and his face did shine as the sun, and his raiment was white as the light.** 3. **And, behold, there appeared unto them Moses and Elias talking with him.** 4. Then answered Peter, and said unto Jesus, Lord, it is good for us to be here: if thou wilt, let us make here three tabernacles; one for thee, and one for Moses, and one for Elias. 5. **While he yet spake, behold, a bright cloud overshadowed them: and behold a voice out of the cloud, which said, This is my beloved Son, in whom I am well pleased; hear ye him.** 6. And when the disciples heard it, they fell on their face, and were sore afraid. 7. And Jesus came and touched them, and said, Arise, and be not afraid. 8. And when they had lifted up their eyes, and they saw no man, save Jesus only.*

As they were coming down from the mountain, the apostles asked Jesus about Elias and why the scribes say that Elias must come first. Jesus answered them with verse 11.

> *Matt 17:11 – And Jesus answered and said unto them, **Elias truly shall first come, and restore all things.***

Here Christ tells them that Elias "*shall first come and restore all things.*" Recognizing that Christ has already come and organized His church, Christ then tells the apostles "*that Elias had already come and the people knew him not.*" They were thinking of Elias being John the Baptist, who was rejected and killed.

> *Matthew 17:12,13. 12. But I say unto you,* **That Elias is come already, and they knew him not,** *but have done unto him whatsoever they listed. Likewise shall also the Son of man suffer of them. 13. Then the disciples understood that he spake unto them of John the Baptist.*

Although Elias had already come, he was to come again and "**restore all things.**"

The Apostle's Teachings of the Restoration. After Christ taught the apostles about the "restoration," the apostles had a few words about this subject. Paul commented that there would come the "*times of refreshing from the presence of the Lord*" and the "*times of restitution of all things.*"

> *Acts 3:19-23 – 19. Repent ye therefore, and be converted, that your sins may be blotted out,* **when the times of refreshing shall come from the presence of the Lord; 20. And he shall send Jesus Christ, which before was preached unto you; 21. Whom the heaven must receive until the times of restitution of all things, which God hath spoken by the mouth of all his holy prophets since the world began.**

The apostle Paul also stated to the Ephesians "*that in the dispensation of the fullness of times all things would be gathered together in Christ.*"

> *Eph 1:10 –* **That in the dispensation of the fullness of times he might gather together in one all things in Christ,** *both which are in heaven, and which are on earth; even in him:*

Paul also wrote about the Jews (branches) being broken off until the fullness of the Gentiles.

> *Romans 11:25 – For I would not, brethren, that ye should be ignorant of this mystery, lest ye should be wise in your own conceits; that blindness in part is happened to Israel,* **until the fullness of the Gentiles be come in.**

Question: When is the "fullness of the Gentiles?"

Question: Is not the "fullness of the Gentiles" going on now with the tremendous amount of Christians, most of which are gentiles?

John also taught about the restoration. In his Book of Revelations he actually saw the angel who came down and initiated the restoration.

> *Rev 14:6 –* **And I saw another angel fly in the midst of heaven, having the everlasting gospel to preach unto them that dwell on the earth, and to every nation, and kindred, and tongue, and people.**

If there were no apostasy and the Catholic church indeed still had the power of God, then there would need no "*restitution of all things,*" or "*times of refreshing,*" or an angel "*having the everlasting gospel to preach unto them that dwell on the earth.*"

God Will Raise Up a Prophet. Now that it is established by some of the Old Testament prophets, the New Testament apostles, and Christ Himself that there was to be a "restoration of all things,"

Question: How is God going to do this restoration?

In the same passage that Paul spoke in Acts 3:17-21, where he spoke of the "*times of refreshing will come from the Lord,*" Paul continued to tell how this would be done. It was through a prophet that the Lord would "*raise up.*"

> *Acts 3:22 – For Moses truly said unto the fathers,* **A prophet shall the Lord your God raise up unto you of your brethren, like unto me;** *him shall ye hear in all things whatsoever he shall say unto you.*

Knowing that God will do nothing except reveal His secrets through prophets:

> *Amos 3:7 –* **Surely the Lord God will do nothing, but he revealeth his secret unto his servants the prophets.**

It is very important that everybody listen to that prophet, because if they don't, Paul stated that "every soul, which will not hear that prophet, shall be destroyed from among the people."

> *Acts 3:23 – And it shall come to pass,* **that every soul, which will not hear that prophet, shall be destroyed from among the people.**

Not only did Paul speak of this prophet that would be raised up, but Moses also spoke of him in Deuteronomy.

> *Deuteronomy 18:15 –* **The Lord thy God will raise up unto thee a Prophet from the midst of thee, of thy brethren, like unto me; unto him ye shall hearken;**
>
> *Deuteronomy 18:18 –* **I will raise them up a Prophet from among their brethren, like unto thee, and will put my words in his mouth; and he shall speak unto them all that I shall command him,** *19. And it shall come to pass, that whosoever will not hearken unto my words which he shall speak in my name, I will require it of him.*

Question: Who is this prophet that is supposed to be raised up by the Lord to restore all things?

This prophet that is supposed to be raised up is commonly accepted as Jesus Christ Himself. But, Paul is speaking after the time of Jesus Christ's death and resurrection. Jesus Christ was already raised up. Paul was now specifically speaking of the "*times of refreshing.*"

Question: Could Paul be speaking of another prophet that will be raised up in the "times of refreshing?"

For the members of The Church of Jesus Christ of Latter Day Saints, there is another prophet and his name was to be Joseph. This is found in 2 Nephi of the *Book of Mormon.*

> *2 Nephi 3:11-15 – 11.* **But a seer will I raise up out of the fruit of thy loins; and unto him will I give power to bring forth my word unto the seed of thy loins—and not to the bringing forth my word only, saith the Lord, but to the convincing them of my word, which shall have already gone forth among them.** *12. Wherefore, the fruit of thy loins shall write; and the fruit of the loins of Judah shall write; and that which shall be written by the fruit of thy loins,* **and also that which shall be written by the fruit of the loins of Judah, shall grow together, unto the confounding of false doctrines and laying down of contentions, and establishing peace among the fruit of thy loins, and bringing them to the knowledge of their fathers in the latter days, and also to the knowledge of my covenants, saith the Lord.** *13. And out of weakness he shall be made strong, in that day when my work shall commence among all my people, unto the restoring thee, O house of Israel, saith the Lord. 14. And thus prophesied Joseph, saying; Behold, that seer will the Lord bless; and they that seek to*

> destroy him shall be confounded; for this promise, which I have obtained of the
> Lord, of the fruit of my lions, shall be fulfilled, Behold, I am sure of the fulfilling of
> this promise; 15. **And his name shall be called after me; and it shall be after
> the name of his father.** And he shall be like unto me; for the thing, which the
> Lord shall bring forth by his hand, by the power of the Lord shall bring my people
> unto salvation.

To the non-Mormons and "anti-Mormons" this is what this book is set out to clear up. We
will be looking at the "*fruits*" of Joseph Smith's labors. As the *Book of Mormon* passage states,
this book will help to bring together the writings of "*the fruit of the loins*" of Joseph and the
writings of "*the fruit of the loins of Judah* **unto the confounding of false doctrines and laying
down of contentions.**"

Other Precious Principles To Be Restored. When Christ stated that "*one jot or one tittle
shall in no wise pass from the law, till all be fulfilled,*" he meant that all prophesies stated by
the prophets and apostles would be fulfilled.

> Matthew 5:17, 18 – 17. Think not that I am come to destroy the law, or the
> prophets: I am not come to destroy, but to fulfill. 18. For verily I say unto you, Till
> heaven and earth pass, **one jot or one tittle shall in no wise pass from the law,
> till all be fulfilled.**

The House of the Lord. There are several important things that need to be added to the
restoration of all things in the latter days. The first is the temples or "Houses of the Lord."
The temples were something sacred to the Lord and when His sheep were righteous, they
always had a temple to perform certain ordinances and covenants. These temples were
prophesied that they would be restored in the last days. The first prophecy was Isaiah.

> Isaiah 2:2-3 – 2. **And it shall come to pass in the last days, that the mountain
> of the LORD's house shall be established in the top of the mountains, and
> shall be exalted above the hills; and all nations shall flow unto it.** 3. And
> many people shall go and say, Come ye, and let us go up to the mountain of the
> LORD, to the house of the God of Jacob; and he will teach us of his ways, and we
> will walk in his paths; **for out of Zion shall go forth the law,** and the word of the
> LORD from Jerusalem.

Another Old Testament prophet, Micah, also foretold about the same temple in almost an
identical statement.

> Micah 4:1-2 – 1. **But in the last days it shall come to pass, that the mountain
> of the house of the LORD shall be established in the top of the mountains,
> and shall be exalted above the hills; and people shall flow unto it.** 3. And
> many nations shall come, and say, Come, and let us go up to the mountain of the
> LORD, to the house of the God of Jacob; and he will teach us of his ways, and we
> will walk in his paths; **for the law shall go forth of Zion,** and the word of the
> LORD from Jerusalem.

In addition to Isaiah and Micah, Ezekiel also prophesied of a "sanctuary" or God's "tabernacle" being set up by the Lord.

> Ezekiel 37:26 – 26. Moreover **I will make a covenant of peace with them; it
> shall be an everlasting covenant with them;** and I will place them, and
> multiply them, **and will set my sanctuary in the midst of them for evermore.**
> 27. **My tabernacle also shall be with them: yea, I will be their God, and they
> shall be my people.** 28. And the heathen shall know that I the Lord do sanctify
> Israel, when my sanctuary shall be in the midst of them for evermore.

Isaiah, Ezekiel, and Micah were very clear that in the last days the house of the Lord will be established. One reason this House of the Lord was to be set up in the last days was to provide a place for the Lord to "*suddenly come*" and visit. Malachi foretold of the Lord's sudden visit.

> *Malachi 3:1 – BEHOLD, I will send my messenger, and he shall prepare the way before me; and the Lord, whom ye seek,* **shall suddenly come to his temple, even the messenger of the covenant,** *whom ye delight in; behold, he shall come, saith the Lord of hosts.*

In order for Malachi's prophecy to come to pass there has to be at least one modern day temple built and open. It was from the beginning of Joseph Smith's ministry that he was commanded to build a temple. The first temple was in Kirtland, Ohio. After moving from there, they built another temple in Nauvoo, Illinois. After moving from Illinois to the Salt Lake Valley, Brigham Young had them almost immediately build the temples in Salt Lake City, Ogden, and Manti, Utah. There are currently over 126 temples built worldwide.

Question: How could the Lord fulfill these prophecies without having a temple built in the latter days?

More important and critical information on the temples can be found in **Chapter 14 – The Temples.**

Other Signs of the Restoration. Malachi also prophesied of Elijah the prophet coming before the great and dreadful day of the Lord to turn the heart of the fathers to the children and the heart of the children to the fathers.

> *Malachi 4:5,6 – Behold,* **I will send you Elijah the prophet before the coming of the great and dreadful day of the Lord: 6. And he shall turn the heart of the fathers to the children, and the heart of the children to their fathers,** *lest I come and smite the earth with a curse.*

Isaiah spoke of a "*marvelous work and a wonder*" being done amongst the people while many people worship God with their lips but their hearts are far from them! This period would be during the last days after the apostasy.

> *Isaiah 29:13-16 – 13. Wherefore the Lord said, Forasmuch as this people draw near me with their mouth, and with their lips do honour me, but have removed their heart far from me, and their fear toward me is taught by the precept of men; 14. Therefore, behold,* **I will proceed to do a marvelous work among this people, even a marvelous work and a wonder;** *for the wisdom of their wise men shall perish, and the understanding of their prudent men shall be hid. 15. Woe unto them that seek deep to hide their counsel from the Lord, and their works are in the dark, and they say, Who seeth us? And who knoweth us? 16. Surely your turning of things upside down shall be esteemed as the potter's clay: for shall the work say of him that made it, He made me not? Or shall the thing framed say of him that framed it, He had no understanding?*

The Old Testament prophet Joel also spoke of a period when the Lord would "*pour out my spirit upon all flesh.*"

> *Joel 2:28 – And it shall come to pass afterward,* **that I will pour out my spirit upon all flesh;** *and your sons and our daughters shall prophesy, your old men shall dream dreams, your young men shall see visions:*

In Matthew, it was stated that this gospel of the kingdom would be preached to the entire world and then the end would come.

> *Matthew 24:14 – And* **this gospel of the kingdom shall be preached in all the**

world for a witness unto all nations; and then shall the end come.

How the Restoration Occurred. It is the claim of the Church of Jesus Christ of Latter Day Saints, that God the Father and Jesus Christ restored the fullness of Christ's church and gospel back onto the earth through a prophet that Christ *"raised up."* This young man was Joseph Smith, Jr.. This is Joseph Smith's own story of some of his experiences.[5]

> *I was born in the year of our Lord one thousand eight hundred and five, on the twenty-third day of December, in the town of Sharon, Windsor County, State of Vermont…My father, Joseph Smith, Senior, left the State of Vermont, and moved to Palmyra, Ontario (now Wayne) county, in the State of New York, when I was in my tenth year, or thereabouts. In about four years after my father's arrival in Palmyra, he moved with his family into Manchester in the same county of Ontario—*

> *Some time in the second year after our removal to Manchester, there was in the place where we lived an unusual excitement on the subject of religion. It commenced with the Methodists, but soon became general among all the sects in that region of country. Indeed, the whole district of country seemed affected by it, and great multitudes united themselves to the different religious parties, which created no small stir and division amongst the people, some crying, "Lo, here!" and others, "Lo there!" Some were contending for the Methodist faith, some for the Presbyterian, and some for the Baptist.*

> *I was at this time in my fifteenth year. My father's family was proselyted to the Presbyterian faith, and four of them joined that church. During this time of great excitement my mind was called up to serious reflection and great uneasiness; but though my feelings were deep and often poignant still I kept myself aloof from all these parties, though I attended their several meetings as often as occasion would permit. In process of time my mind became somewhat partial to the Methodist sect, and I felt some desire to be untied with them; but so great were the confusion and strife among the different denominations, that it was impossible for a person young as I was, and so unacquainted with men and things, to come to any certain conclusion who was right and who was wrong.*

> *In the midst of this war of words and tumult of opinions, I often said to myself: What is to be done? Who of all these parties are right; or, are they all wrong together? If any of them be right, which is it, and how shall I know it?*

> *While I was laboring under extreme difficulties caused by the contests of these parties of religionists, I was one day reading the Epistle of James, first chapter and fifth verse, which reads:* **If any of you lack wisdom, let him ask of God, that giveth to all men liberally, and upbraideth not; and it shall be given him.**

> *Never did any passage of scripture come with more power to the heart of man than this did at the time to mine. It seemed to enter with great force into every felling of my heart. I reflected on it again and again, knowing that if any person needed wisdom from God, I did; for how to act I did not know, and unless I could get more wisdom than I then had, I would never know; for the teachers of religion of the different sects understood the same passages of scripture so differently as to destroy all confidence in settling the question by an appeal to the Bible.*

> *At length I came to the conclusion that I must either remain in darkness and confusion, or else I must do as James directs, that is, ask of God. I at length came to the determination to "ask of God," concluding that if he gave wisdom to them that lacked wisdom, and would give liberally, and not upbraid, I might venture.*

> *So, in accordance with this, my determination to ask of God, I retired to the woods*

to make the attempt. It was on the morning of a beautiful, clear day, early in the spring of eighteen hundred and twenty. It was the first time in my life that I had made such an attempt, for amidst all my anxieties I had never as yet made the attempt to pray vocally.

After I had retired to the place where I had previously designed to go, having looked around me, and finding myself alone, I kneeled down and began to offer up the desires of my heart to God. I had scarcely done so, when immediately I was seized upon by some power which entirely overcame me, and had such an astonishing influence over me as to bind my tongue so that I could not speak. Thick darkness gathered around me, and it seemed to me for a time as if I were doomed to sudden destruction.

But, exerting all my powers to call upon God to deliver me out of the power of this enemy which had seized upon me, and at the very moment when I was ready to sink into despair and abandon myself to destruction—not to an imaginary ruin, but to the power of some actual being from the unseen world, who had such marvelous power as I had never felt in any being—just at this moment of great alarm, I saw a pillar of light exactly over my head, above the brightness of the sun, which descended gradually until it fell upon me.

*It no sooner appeared than I found myself delivered from the enemy which held me bound. When the light rested upon me I saw two Personages, whose brightness and glory defy all description, standing above me in the air. One of them spake unto me, calling me by name and said, pointing to the other—**This is My Beloved Son. Hear Him!***

I was answered that I must join none of them, for they were all wrong; and the Personage who addressed me said that all their creeds were an abomination in his sight; that those professors were all corrupt; that, "they draw near to me with their lips, but their hearts are far from me, they teach for doctrines the commandments of men, having a form of godliness, but they deny the power thereof."

He again forbade me to join with any of them; and many other things did he say unto me, which I cannot write at this time. When I came to myself again, I found myself lying on my back, looking up into heaven. When the light had departed, I had no strength; but soon recovering in some degree, I went home.

Question: Does not this experience of Joseph Smith sound similar to the experience of Peter, James, and John that the apostle Matthew wrote?

*Matthew 17:1-8 – 1. And after six days Jesus taketh Peter, James, and John his brother, and bringeth them up into an high mountain apart, 2. **And was transfigured before them: and his face did shine as the sun, and his raiment was white as the light. 3. And, behold, there appeared unto them Moses and Elias talking with him.** 4. Then answered Peter, and said unto Jesus, Lord, it is good for us to be here: if thou wilt, let us make here three tabernacles; one for thee, and one for Moses, and one for Elias. 5. **While he yet spake, behold, a bright cloud overshadowed them: and behold a voice out of the cloud, which said, This is my beloved Son, in whom I am well pleased; hear ye him.***

Question: Could a fourteen-year-old boy have made up a story such as this?

Many religious leaders have questioned why the Lord would choose a young boy and not a religious leader of the time to be the prophet of the restoration. To answer this, we will look at how Jesus Christ set up His original church. When He called the twelve apostles, Christ did not choose any of the Jewish leaders to be one of those apostles. Jesus Christ's reasoning for this was, in His own words:

> *Matthew 9:17 – **Neither do men put new wine into old bottles:** else the bottles break, and the wine runneth out, and the bottles perish: but they put new wine into new bottles, and both are preserved.*

> *Mark 2:22 – **And no man putteth new wine into old bottles:** else the new wine doth burst the bottles, and the wine is spilled, and the bottles will be marred: but new wine must be put into new bottles.*

> *Luke 5:37 – **And no man putteth new wine into old bottles;** else the new wine will burst the bottles, and be spilled, and the bottles shall perish.*

These last three scriptures were of the account where some Pharisees were dining with Christ and they were asking Christ questions. One account had the disciples of asking why the apostles did not fast, like the Pharisees. These questions were about organizing Christ's church. In the same manner that Christ organized His church in His day, Christ repeated the same act—He chose a person that was not greatly affiliated with or trained by the current churches of the time. The important fact to consider is that Christ did choose a certain person to be His mouthpiece here on earth—a prophet.

> *Amos 3:7 – **Surely the Lord God will do nothing, but he revealeth his secret unto his servants the prophets.***

According to the LDS church, the restoration of the gospel of Jesus Christ continued over the next twenty-four years. As the restoration took place Christ and His angels revealed a few secrets here and there as Joseph Smith and the saints were prepared to receive them. Many of these "secrets" and their details will be discussed in the following chapters.

The Biblical Support Chart. It is in the author's opinion, that there could be credible belief that the Bible commented on the potential of the restoration in both the Old Testament and the New Testament. There is also potential support for the way Joseph Smith claimed that the restoration took place, that is, through a prophet by celestial beings appearing to him.

THE BIBLICAL SUPPORT CHART	
Is the following topic supported in the Bible?	**Yes or No**
Does the Old Testament Comment on the possibility of a "Restoration of all things?" (Isaiah 11:11,12; Jer 31:31; Dan 2:44)	Yes
Does the New Testament Comment on the "Restoration of all things?" (Acts 3:19-23; Matt 17:11; Eph 1:10; Romans 11:25; Revelations 14:6)	Yes
Does the Bible support the visitations of angels and/or ancient prophets appearing on the earth? (Matt 17:1-8)	Yes

Author's Note: Now that the apostasy and the restoration of the original Church of Jesus Christ has been substantiated in the Bible, it will be interesting to look at the actual organization of that church. Assuming the original Church of Jesus Christ was lost and then restored, a good look at the "jot and tittle" from the Bible will be looked at to see just how that Church was organized and operated. It will give the non-Mormons and the "anti-Mormons" a good opportunity to compare the organization of their own churches with that of the original church. The next **Chapter 3 – The Organization of the Original Church of Jesus Christ,** will give some great detail on this matter.

NOTES

CHAPTER 3

THE CHURCH AS ONE

Be One. In organizing the Church of Jesus Christ of Latter-day Saints with apostles, prophets, the priesthood, and revelation from the Lord, Joseph Smith established a very strong, central leadership core that followed the same leadership pattern as the original Church of Jesus Christ. Joseph Smith then required strict obedience to the laws and doctrines of the leadership—the prophet and apostles of the church. Joseph Smith apparently learned very well from the Bible. He understood that the Lord wanted no confusion within the church.

> *1 Cor 14:33 – **For God is not the author of confusion, but of peace, as in all churches of the saints.***

Joseph Smith also taught that there was just one organization of the church. The apostle Paul also taught the Ephesians that there is "*One Lord, one faith, one baptism.*" That the members are to "*keep the unity of the Spirit in the bond of peace.*"

> *Ephesians 4:3,4 – Endeavouring to **keep the unity of the Spirit in the bond of peace.** 4. **There is one body, and one Spirit**, even as ye are called in one hope of your calling: 5. **One Lord, one faith, one baptism,***

Paul was also very clear when he taught the Corinthians. He told them that "*they all speak the same thing,*" that "*there should be not divisions among you,*" and that they "*should be perfectly joined together in the same mind and in the same judgment.*"

> *1 Corinthians 1:10, 11 – Now I beseech you, brethren, by the name of our Lord Jesus Christ, **that ye all speak the same thing, and that there be no divisions among you; but that ye be perfectly joined together in the same mind and in the same judgment.** 11. For it hath been declared unto me of you, my brethren, by them which are of the house of Chloe, that there are contentions among you.*

Paul continued teaching that "*by one Spirit we are all baptized into one body.*"

> *1 Corinthians 12:13 – **For by one Spirit are we all baptized into one body,** whether we be Jews or Gentiles, whether we be bond or free; and have been all made to drink into one Spirit.*

Not only are we all baptized but also we must not have any contentions or "*schism*" in the church.

> *1 Corinthians 12:25 – **That there should be no schism in the body;** but that the members should have the same care one for another.*

Again, Paul taught the Philippians the same "unity" principle.

> *Philippians 2:2 – Fulfill ye my joy, **that ye be likeminded, having the same love, being of one accord, of one mind.***

> *Philippians 3:16-19 – 16. Nevertheless, whereto we have already attained, **let us walk by the same rule, let us mind the same thing.** 17. Brethren, be followers together of me, and mark them which walk so as ye have us for an ensample. 18. (For many walk, of whom I have told you often, and now tell you even weeping, that they are the enemies of the cross of Christ: 19. Whose end is destruction, whose God is their belly, and whose glory is in their shame, who mind earthly things).*

The apostle Timothy was also teaching the **"unity"** principle when he wrote about the people in Macedonia not teaching the proper doctrine. Timothy told of people who wanted to be "teachers of the law," but in reality, they did not understand the law at all.

> *1 Timothy 1:3, 7-10 – 3. As I besought thee to abide still at Ephesus, when I went into Macedonia,* ***that thou mightest charge some that they teach no other doctrine,*** *7. Desiring to be teachers of the law; understanding neither what they say, nor whereof they affirm. 8.* ***But we know that the law is good, if a man use it lawfully;*** *9. Knowing this, that the law is not made for a righteous man, but for the lawless and disobedient, for the ungodly and for sinners, for unholy and profane, for murderers of fathers and murderers of mothers, for manslayers, 10. For whoremongers, for them that defile themselves with mankind, for menstealers, for liars for perjured persons, and if there be any other thing that is contrary to sound doctrine;*

It is again reaffirmed that the members should not be teaching false doctrines or listening to false doctrines.

> *Hebrews 13:9 – Be not carried about with divers and strange doctrines.*

The Consequences of Not Following the Apostles and Prophets. It is with great importance that the apostles taught that the original organization of the church with apostles and prophets was to be used until "*we all come in the unity of the faith, and of the knowledge of the Son of God,*" that "*we henceforth be no more children, tossed to and fro, and carried about with every wind of doctrine, by the sleight of men, and cunning craftiness, whereby they lie in wait to deceive.*"

> *Ephesians 4:11-14 – 11.* ***And he gave some, apostles; and some, prophets; and some, evangelists; and some, pastors and teachers; 12. For the perfecting of the saints,*** *for the work of the ministry, for the edifying of the body of Christ: 13.* ***Till we all come in the unity of the faith, and of the knowledge of the Son of God, unto a perfect man, unto the measure of the stature of the fullness of Christ: 14. That we henceforth be no more children, tossed to and fro, and carried about with every wind of doctrine, by the sleight of men, and cunning craftiness, whereby they lie in wait to deceive;***

It is in the same conversation of Paul's when he spoke that there should be "*one body*" and "*that there should be no schism in the body*" that he also described the body with apostles and prophets:

> *1 Corinthians 12:27,28 – 27. Now ye are the body of Christ, and members in particular. 28.* ***And God hath set some in the church, first apostles, secondarily prophets,*** *thirdly teachers, after that miracles, then gifts of healings, helps, governments, diversities of tongues.*

Joseph Smith taught, that the consequences of not following the apostles and prophets, is to be cast out. Joseph Smith said that when Christ spoke the following verses, He was speaking of the many people who believed in Him, but would not make it because they never really "knew" Christ.

> *Matthew 7:21-23 – 21.* ***Not every one that saith unto me, Lord, Lord, shall enter into the kingdom of heaven;*** *but he that doeth the will of my Father which is in heaven. 22.* ***Many will say to me in that day, Lord, Lord, have we not prophesied in thy name? And in thy name have cast out devils? And in thy name done many wonderful works? 23. And then will I profess unto them, I never knew you: depart from me, ye that work iniquity.***

Christ also taught that:

> *Matthew 7:13,14 – 13.* ***Enter ye in at the strait gate: for wide is the gate, and***

broad is the way, that leadeth to destruction, and many there be which go in
thereat: 14. Because strait is the gate, and narrow is the way, which leadeth
unto life, and few there be that find it.

Jesus Christ did not only teach this teaching that "only a few of the Christians will make it
to the kingdom of God" once. He also taught the same principle in the parable of the
ten virgins.

> *Matthew 25:1 – 1. Then shall the kingdom of heaven be likened unto ten virgins,*
> *which took their lamps, and went forth to meet the bridegroom.*

Joseph Smith taught that these 10 virgins are all believers in Christ.

> *Matthew 25:2-4 – 2. And five of them were wise, and five were foolish. 3. They*
> *that were foolish took their lamps, and took no oil with them: 4. But the wise took*
> *oil in their vessels with their lamps.*

Christ designated five as wise and five who were foolish. Joseph Smith taught that the
foolish were ones who did not follow the true doctrine of Christ—or did not follow the words
of the apostles and prophets.

> *Matthew 25:5, 6 – 5. While the bridegroom tarried, they all slumbered and slept. 6.*
> *And at midnight there was a cry made, Behold, the bridegroom cometh; go ye out to*
> *meet him.*

Many religions believe that when the bridegroom comes is the actual second coming of
Jesus Christ.

> *Matthew 25:7-9 – 7. Then all those virgins arose, and trimmed their lamps. 8.*
> *And the foolish said unto the wise, Give us of your oil; for our lamps are gone out. 9.*
> *But the wise answered, saying, Not so; lest there be not enough for us and you: but*
> *go ye rather to them that sell, and buy for yourselves.*

At the second coming the virgins who were not prepared, needed to go back and get
prepared. Those virgins (or members) who were prepared went into the wedding.

> *Matthew 25:10 – 10. And while they went to buy, the bridegroom came; and they*
> *that were ready went in with him to the marriage: and the door was shut.*

Those who were not prepared, or did not listen to the words of the prophets, were shut out
and not recognized by Christ.

> *Matthew 25:11-13 – 11. **Afterward came also the other virgins, saying Lord,***
> ***Lord, open to us. 12. But he answered and said, Verily I say unto you, I***
> ***know you not.** 13. Watch therefore, for ye know neither the day nor the hour*
> *wherein the Son of man cometh.*

I remind you that all these people turned away by Christ, were Christians, who actually
believed in Jesus Christ! Christ continues to warn us of false Christs and false prophets.

> *Mark 13:21,22 – 21. **And then if any man shall say to you, Lo, here is Christ;***
> ***or, lo, he is there; believe him not: 22. For false Christs and false prophets***
> ***shall rise, and shall shew signs and wonders, to seduce, if it were possible,***
> ***even the elect.***

Paul continued to expound on the teaching that Christians will be deceived and that those
"who preached any other gospel" will be cursed.

> *Galatians 1:6-9 – 6. I marvel that ye are so soon removed from him that called you*
> *into the grace of Christ unto another gospel: 7. Which is not another; **but there be***

some that trouble you, and would pervert the gospel the gospel of Christ. 8. But though we, or an angel from heaven, preach any other gospel unto you than that which we have preached unto you, let him be accursed. 9. As we said before, so say I now again, If any man preach any other gospel unto you than that ye have received, let him be accursed.

How to know a True Prophet? Joseph Smith taught that this message means that there will be many Christians who profess Jesus Christ as their savior and follow many of the teachings and commandments of Christ, but will not make it to the kingdom of heaven. After Christ spoke the last statement, He spoke of false prophets.

*Matthew 7:15 – **Beware of false prophets, which come to you in sheep's clothing, but inwardly they are ravening wolves.***

Christ taught how to know who the true prophets are:

*Matthew 7:16 – **Ye shall know them by their fruits.** Do men gather grapes of thorns, or figs of thistles?*

*Matthew 7:20 – **Wherefore by their fruits ye shall know them.***

Being in the position of Joseph Smith, when he was fourteen years old and trying to find the true church to attend, there were many churches to choose from. It is very similar today. There are many different churches available and they are all teaching "*all manner of doctrine.*"

The important doctrine of Christ that is still in effect is:

*Matthew 7:21-23 – 21. **Not every one that saith unto me, Lord, Lord, shall enter into the kingdom of heaven;** but he that doeth the will of my Father which is in heaven. 22. **Many will say to me in that day, Lord, Lord, have we not prophesied in thy name? And in thy name have cast out devils? And in thy name done many wonderful works? 23. And then will I profess unto them, I never knew you: depart from me, ye that work iniquity.***

Question: How does one find out which church is true, or which church should one join?

One potential answer is to find out which prophet, or which leader of the many different religious sects is a true prophet. This book is to investigate the truthfulness, or the "*fruits*" of the claimed prophet Joseph Smith. It is still proposed that if Joseph Smith were a prophet of God then all of his teachings would be supported in the Bible.

The Biblical Support Chart. Continuing with the case of the organization of the Church of Jesus Christ of Latter-day Saints (LDS church) i.e. with prophets, apostles, revelation, and now to include being well organized and unified in all its teachings, doctrines, and practices. The important factor is to identify how well the LDS Church is living up to the original teachings and organization of the Prophet Joseph Smith.

Currently, the LDS Church is still organized with a prophet heading the church with twelve apostles that assist in leading the church. The LDS Church is so organized that every congregation (or ward) in the United States receives the same manuals for teaching their Sunday School and Priesthood classes. Each class should be teaching the same doctrine as every other class throughout the United States. In foreign countries the individual congregation also has the same organization and lessons. Each in its own specific language.

When a person or leader gets off tangent from the directed doctrines of the prophet, or when a leader starts teaching false doctrines, that leader is called to repentance. If that leader repents and gets in line, fine. If he does not stop teaching the false doctrines, then he is excommunicated. With this strictness of organization the LDS Church is still the fastest growing church in America.

THE BIBLICAL SUPPORT CHART	
Is the following topic supported in the Bible?	**Yes or No**
Does the Bible support the Joseph Smith's teaching of being one organization? (1 Cor 14:33; Eph 4:3,4; 1 Cor 1:10,11; 1 Cor 12:13,25; Phil 2:2; 3:16-19; 1 Tim 1:3,7-10; Heb 13:9)	Yes
Does the Bible support the strictness of Joseph Smith's teaching of having one doctrine? (Heb 13:9; Eph 4:11-14; Matt 7:13,14; 21-23; 25:1-13)	Yes

Question: How does the LDS Church hold up in the Biblical Support Chart for unity of faith and organization?

NOTES

CHAPTER 4

THE ORGANIZATION OF THE ORIGINAL CHURCH OF JESUS CHRIST

Joseph Smith claims to have organized the Church of Jesus Christ of Latter Day Saints much in the same way as the church was organized in the New Testament. This includes the naming of the church, the addressing the membership as saints, the formal organization with apostles and prophets. Joseph Smith continued the organization with revelation being prevalent in the church along with the priesthood, the need for the power of the priesthood, and a strong unity with emphasis on obedience of its members. Each one of these elements of the Mormon church will be targets for biblical support.

The Naming of the Mormon Church. Joseph Smith is theoretically not the person who named the Mormon church as The Church of Jesus Christ of Latter Day Saints. The official naming is found in the compilation of revelations given to Joseph Smith from the Lord, called the Doctrine and Covenants (D&C). The D&C is organized by sections and verses. Each section has a header that explains the circumstances and date of the claimed revelation. It is in the D&C section 115, verses 1-4 (or D&C 115:1-4).

> *D&C 115:1-4 – 1. Verily thus saith the Lord unto you, my servant Joseph Smith, Jun., and also my servant Sidney Rigdon, and also my servant Hyrum Smith, and your counselors who are and shall be appointed hereafter; 2. And also unto you, my servant Edward Partridge, and his counselors; 3. And also unto my faithful servants who are of the high council of my church in Zion, for thus it shall be called, **and unto all the elders and people of my Church of Jesus Christ of Latter-day Saints,** scattered abroad in all the world; 4. **For thus shall my church be called in the last days, even The Church of Jesus Christ of Latter-day Saints.***

Joseph Smith taught that since the restored church is that of Jesus Christ, then it is appropriate to name it The Church of Jesus Christ. It has been commented that if the church were named after another person, whether it be John the Baptist, Martin Luther, and etc., then the church would be officially that particular person's church, and not the church of Jesus Christ.

Joseph Smith continued teaching that Jesus Christ distinguished His original church from the restored church by adding the "of the Latter-day Saints." Which brings up the next important element of Joseph Smith's restored church, which is the naming of the general membership.

The Saints. It was common in the 19th Century and is still prevalent today that a "saint," especially in the eyes of the Catholic Church, was a superior person who is "canonized," and becomes a figure to be idolized or greatly admired. It is not a position for the masses of membership.

Joseph Smith taught that each member of the general membership of the Mormon Church was to be called a saint. Having changed a major doctrine of the Catholic Church, then there must be some comments from the Bible on this particular doctrine.

The Old Testament Use of Saints. The following passages are some of the references of saints in the Old Testament. These passages are examples of where symbolism may be used in the interpretation of the use of "saint." Wanting to remain basic in what the verse is saying and away from the symbolism, all you, the reader, have to do is substitute the word "member" for the word "saint," and see if it fits. The first passage is in Deuteronomy.

> *Deuteronomy 33:2,3 – 2. And he said, The Lord came from Sinai, and rose up from Seer unto them; he shined forth from mount Paran, **and he came with ten thousands of saints:** from his right hand went a fiery law for them. 3. **Yea, he loved the people; all his saints are in thy hand: and they sat down at thy feet; every one shall receive of thy words.***

The next few uses of "saints" are in Psalms. Using the word "member" is a bit clearer here.

> *Psalms 50:5 – **Gather my saints together unto me; those that have made a covenant with me by sacrifice.***

> *Psalms 89:7 – **God is greatly to be feared in the assembly of the saints,** and to be had in reverence of all them that are about him.*

> *Psalms 97:10 – Ye that love the Lord, hate evil: **he preserveth the souls of his saints; he delivereth them out of the hand of the wicked.***

One of the last uses of "saint" in the Old Testament is in Zechariah.

> *Zechariah 14:5 – And ye shall flee to the valley of the mountains; for the valley of the mountains shall reach unto Azal: yea, ye shall flee, like as ye fled from before the earthquake in the days of Uzziah king of Judah: and the Lord my God shall come, **and all the saints with thee.***

Using the simplest of basic terms in the Old Testament, one could conclude that "saints" are not just a few very great men who where "canonized" for the great works that they did. They could very well be the general membership of the church at that time.

The New Testament Use of Saints. The New Testament use of "*saint*" is more explicit. When the different apostles were writing their letters to the general membership they sometimes addressed the membership as "saints." The following passages denote this usage of the term "saint" in their introductory of their letters.

> *Romans 1:7 – **To all that be in Rome, beloved of God, called to be saints:** Grace to you and peace from God our Father, and the Lord Jesus Christ.*

> *1 Corinthians 1:2 – **Unto the church of God which is at Corinth, to them that are sanctified in Christ Jesus, called to be saints,** with all that in every place call upon the name of Jesus Christ our Lord, both theirs and ours;*

> *2 Corinthians 1:1 – Paul, an apostle of Jesus Christ by the will of God, and Timothy our brother, unto the church of God which is at Corinth, **with all the saints which are in all Achaia:***

> *Eph 1:1 – Paul, an apostle of Jesus Christ by the will of God, **to the saints which are at Ephesus,** and to the faithful in Christ Jesus:*

> *Philippians 1:1 – Paul and Timotheus, the servants of Jesus Christ, **to all the saints in Christ Jesus which are at Philippi,** with the bishops and deacons:*

> *Colossians 1:2 – **To the saints and faithful brethren in Christ which are at Colosse:** Grace be unto you, and peace, from God our Father and the Lord Jesus Christ.*

The term "saint" was not just used in the introduction of the letters. There are many instances where the apostles talked about "going down to the saints" and "ministering unto the saints." These are some of those uses when reading about the "saints" one can substitute the word with "member(s)" and there will be a total congruence with the meaning.

> *Acts 9:13 – Then Ananias answered, Lord, I have heard by many of this man, **how***

much evil he hath done to thy saints at Jerusalem:

*Acts 9:32 – And it came to pass, as Peter passed throughout all quarters, **he came down also to the saints which dwelt at Lydda.***

*Romans 15:25 – **But now I go unto Jerusalem to minister unto the saints.***

*Eph 2:19 – **Now therefore ye are no more strangers and foreigners, but fellowcitizens with the saints,** and of the household of God.*

*Eph 4:11,12 – 11. And he gave some, apostles; and some, prophets; and some, evangelists; and some, pastors and teachers; 12. **For the perfecting of the saints,** for the work of the ministry, for the edifying of the body of Christ:*

*Hebrews 6:10 – For God is not unrighteous to forget your work and labour of love, which ye have shewed toward his name, **in that ye have ministered to the saints,** and do minister.*

Another use of the term "saint" was when Paul brought Tabitha back from the dead. After he did this, he presented her to the "saints."

*Acts 9:40,41 – 40. But Peter put them all forth, and kneeled down, and prayed; and turning him to the body said, Tabitha, arise. And she opened her eyes: and when she saw Peter, she sat up. 41. And he gave her his hand, and lifted her up, **and when he had called the saints and widows,** presented her alive.*

Having read the preceding passages about the use of "saint" each of you will have to judge yourself whether or not the term "saint" could be an outstanding "canonized" person as the Catholic Church defines them, or if a "saint" could be just the general membership of the church.

The Organization of the Church. Joseph Smith organized the Mormon Church in the following manner. The head or president of the church is regarded as a Prophet. The prophet then has twelve apostles who are there to help direct the church. There are other members of the church leadership which are priests, elders, teachers, deacons, bishops, and etc. Most of these positions are within the priesthood which will be defined later.

The most important element of the organization of the church is the leadership role of the apostles and prophets. This is what Joseph Smith believes the Bible has to say about this. First, the prophet Amos declared that the "*Lord God will do nothing but he revealeth his secret unto his servants the prophets.*"

*Amos 3:7 – **Surely the Lord God will do nothing but he revealeth his secret unto his servants the prophets.***

Using a prophet as a way to communicate His will to His people is certainly the way the Lord operated during the entire Old Testament and after His death and resurrection in the New Testament. Paul explained the organization of the church in several different passages of the Bible.

*Ephesians 2:19-22 – 19. Now therefore ye are no more strangers and foreigners, but fellowcitizens with the saints, and of the household of God; 20. **And are built upon the foundation of the apostles and prophets, Jesus Christ himself being the chief corner stone;** 21. In whom all the building fitly framed together groweth unto an holy temple in the Lord: 22. In whom ye also are builded together for an habitation of God through the Spirit.*

Paul continues with:

> *1 Corinthians 12:27, 28 – 27. Now ye are the body of Christ, and members in particular. 28. **And God hath set some in the church, first apostles, secondarily prophets, thirdly teachers,** after that miracles, then gifts of healings, helps, governments, diversities of tongues.*

Paul continues explaining the organization of the church and gives specific parameters for this organization.

> *Ephesians 4:11-14 – 11. **And he gave some, apostles; and some, prophets; and some, evangelists; and some, pastors and teachers; 12. For the perfecting of the saints,** for the work of the ministry, for the edifying of the body of Christ: 13. **Till we all come in the unity of the faith, and of the knowledge of the Son of God, unto a perfect man, unto the measure of the stature of the fullness of Christ: 14. That we henceforth be no more children, tossed to and fro, and carried about with every wind of doctrine, by the sleight of men, and cunning craftiness, whereby they lie in wait to deceive;***

Paul explained that this organization with apostles and prophets was to exist for:

1. *"the perfecting of the saints"*

2. *"until we all come in the unity of the faith, and of the knowledge of the Son of God"*

3. *"that we no more be children tossed to and fro, and carried about with every wind of doctrine, by the sleight of men, and cunning craftiness, whereby they lie in wait to deceive"*

Referring to the first two chapters on the possibility of the apostasy from the original church and its restoration, then the restored church would still be under these three rules. A few questions one must ask itself.

Question: With the numerous different Christian churches in America alone, have the Christians "come in the unity of the faith, and of the knowledge of the Son of God?

Question: Are the members of these numerous different Christian churches being "tossed to and fro, and carried about with every wind of doctrine, by the sleight of men, and cunning craftiness, whereby they lie in wait to deceive?"

Question: If Christ were to restore His church in its fullness, would He have prophets and apostles?

The Continued Need for Apostles. When Joseph Smith set up the LDS church with apostles he also established a manner for them to be replaced when they transgressed or died. Most Christian churches today do not have apostles within their organizations. These leaders claim that the need for apostles was done away with the dying off of the original apostles.

Joseph Smith's teachings were to the contrary and if Joseph Smith was indeed a prophet, then the Bible should support this fact. Joseph Smith pointed out that in the book Acts, the remaining apostles, after Judas killed himself, got together and selected a new apostle to replace Judas.

> *Acts 1:21-26 – 21. Wherefore of these men which have companied with us all the time that the Lord Jesus went in and out among us. 22. Beginning from the baptism of John, unto that same day that he was taken up from us, **must one be ordained to be a witness with us of his resurrection. 23.** And they appointed two, Joseph called Barsabas, who was surnamed Justus, and Matthias. 24. And they prayed, and said, **Thou Lord, which knowest the hearts of all men, shew whether of these two thou hast chosen, 25. That he may take part of this ministry and***

apostleship, from which Judas by transgression fell that he might go to his own place. 26. And they gave forth their lots; and the lot fell upon Matthias; and he was numbered with the eleven apostles.

Revelation. The next important element that Joseph Smith taught was the importance of revelation that played in the restoring of Christ's church. Joseph Smith never claimed to have organized anything on his own judgment. Joseph Smith always recognized the divinity from Jesus Christ from whom he received directions to organize the church in the original manner, to teach the doctrines of the church, and to reveal the mysteries of the church.

Much like the prophets of the Bible who would receive a revelation from the Lord and then write it down. These writings are now compiled in the Holy Scriptures called the Bible. In Joseph Smith's case, he wrote down each revelation that he received and then published these revelations in a book called The Doctrine and Covenants.

The important element of these revelations recorded in The Doctrine and Covenants is the "revelation" itself. Most of the Christian churches today do not claim any form of official revelation from their leadership. This includes the Catholic Church, which should be founded on the foundation of apostles and prophets.

Here is what the Bible has to say about revelation and its part in the church. The first passage is when Christ was talking to Peter.

> *Matthew 16:13-18 – 13. When Jesus came into the coasts of Caesarea Philippi, he asked his disciples, saying, Whom do men say that I the Son of man am? 14. And they said, Some say that thou art John the Baptist: some, Elias; and others, Jeremias, or one of the prophets. 15. He saith unto them, But whom say ye that I am? 16. And Simon Peter answered and said, Thou art the Christ, the Son of the living God. 17. And Jesus answered and said unto him, Blessed art thou, Simon Bar-jona: **for flesh and blood hath not revealed it unto thee, but my Father which is in heaven.** 18. And I say also unto thee, That thou are Peter, and **upon this rock I will build my church;** and the gates of hell shall not prevail against it.*

Joseph Smith teaches that "*this rock*" that Christ will build His church on is "revelation." Joseph Smith teaches that it was not "*flesh and blood*" that revealed to Peter who Christ was, but it was Christ's "*Father which is in heaven*" who revealed that knowledge which was a "revelation" to Peter. Then Christ goes immediately into "*upon this rock*" which is receiving knowledge directly from our Father in heaven, or revelation, is what He will build His church.

Joseph Smith teaches that "revelation" is again back on the earth and that the "*heavens,*" where God dwells, are again open. Paul taught the Galatians that he learned his knowledge of God from revelation.

> *Galatians 1:6-12 – I marvel that ye are so soon removed from him that called you into the grace of Christ unto another gospel: 7. Which is not another; but there be some that trouble you, and would pervert the gospel of Christ. 8. But though we, or an angel from heaven, preach any other gospel unto you than that which we have preached unto you, let him be accursed. 9. As we said before, so say I now again, If any man preach any other gospel unto you than that ye have received, let him be accursed. 10. For do I now persuade men, or God? Or do I seek to please men? **For if I yet pleased men, I should not be the servant of Christ.** 11. But I certify you, brethren, that **the gospel which was preached of me is not after man. 12. For I neither received it of man, neither was I taught it, but by the revelation of Jesus Christ.***

> *Galatians 2:2 – **And I went up by revelation,** and communicated unto them that gospel which I preach among the Gentiles, but privately to **them** which were of repu-*

tation, lest by any means I should run, or had run, in vain.

*1 Corinthians 13:2 – **And though I have the gift of prophecy,** and understand all mysteries, and all knowledge; and though I have all faith, so that I could remove mountains, and have not charity, I am nothing..*

Two important passages that Joseph Smith and the Mormons always like to emphasize are about prophets and revelation.

*Amos 3:7 – **Surely the Lord God will do nothing but he revealeth his secret unto his servants the prophets.***

*Proverbs 29:18 – **Where there is no vision, the people perish:** but he that keepeth the law, happy is he.*

Maybe this passage from Proverbs has to do with the following passage.

*Acts 3:22,23 – For Moses truly said unto the fathers, **A prophet shall the Lord your God raise up unto you of your brethren, like unto me;** him shall ye hear in all things whatsoever he shall say unto you. 23. And it shall come to pass, **that every soul, which will not hear that prophet, shall be destroyed from among the people.***

The Biblical Support Chart. In the case of the organization of the Church of Jesus Christ of Latter-day Saints (LDS church) i.e. with prophets, apostles, revelation, and down to the naming of their membership as saints, one must consider that Joseph Smith was fourteen years old when he claimed to have received his first revelation from God and Jesus Christ. Being educated in neither formal schooling nor any clerical training, Joseph Smith organized the LDS church in a manner closely related to the original church that Jesus Christ set up. The Bible, as related to the organization of the LDS church, does give support to the way Joseph Smith set it up.

THE BIBLICAL SUPPORT CHART

Is the following topic supported in the Bible?	Yes or No
Does the Bible support naming the general membership of the LDS church, saints? (Deut 33:2,3; Psalms 50:5, 89:7;97:10; Rom 1:7; 1 Cor 1:2; 2 Cor 1:1; Eph 1:1; Phil 1:1; Col 1:2)	Yes
Does the Bible support the organization of the church with prophets and apostles? (Amos 3:7; Eph 2:19-22; 1 Cor 12:27,28; Eph 4:11-14; Acts 3:22,23)	Yes
Does the Bible support the continued need for having 12 apostles? (Acts 1:21-26)	Yes
Does the Bible support that the fullness of the Church of Jesus Christ should be based on revelation? (Matt 16:13-18; Gal 1:6-12; 2:2; 1 Cor 13:2; Prov 29:18)	Yes

NOTES

CHAPTER 5

THE PRIESTHOOD

In organizing the Church of Jesus Christ of Latter-day Saints, Joseph Smith claims that he received the priesthood of God through the administration of celestial beings. This priesthood of God was divided into two different priesthoods called the Melchizedek Priesthood and the Aaronic Priesthood. The first visit was by John the Baptist who, as a celestial being, gave to Joseph Smith and Oliver Cowdery the Aaronic Priesthood. Joseph Smith called this the "Lesser Priesthood." This is Joseph Smith's account:

> **Joseph Smith History** *1:68-72 – 68. We still continued the work of translation, when, in the ensuing month (May, 1829), we on a certain day went into the woods to pray and inquire of the Lord respecting "baptism for the remission of sins, that we found mentioned in the translation of the plates. While we were thus employed, praying and calling upon the Lord, a messenger from heaven descended in a cloud of light, and having laid his hands upon us, he ordained us, saying:*
>
> *69. Upon you my fellow servants, in the name of Messiah, I confer the Priesthood of Aaron, which holds the keys of the ministering of angels, and of the gospel of repentance, and of baptism by immersion for the remission of sins; and this shall never be taken again from the earth until the sons of Levi do offer again an offering unto the Lord in righteousness.*
>
> *70. He said this Aaronic Priesthood had not the power of laying on hands for the gift of the Holy Ghost, but that this should be conferred on us hereafter; and he commanded us to go and be baptized, and gave us directions that I should baptize Oliver Cowdery, and that afterwards he should baptize me.*
>
> *71. Accordingly we went and were baptized. I baptized him first, and afterwards he baptized me—after which I laid my hands upon his head and ordained him to the Aaronic Priesthood, and afterwards he laid his hands on me and ordained me to the same Priesthood—for so we were commanded.*
>
> *72. The messenger who visited us on this occasion and conferred this Priesthood upon us, said that his name was John, the same that is called John the Baptist in the New Testament, and that he acted under the direction of Peter, James and John, who held the keys of the Priesthood of Melchizedek, which Priesthood, he said, would in due time be conferred on us, and that I should be called the first Elder of the Church, and he (Oliver Cowdery) the second. It was on the fifteenth day of May, 1829, that we were ordained under the hand of this messenger, and baptized.*

According to the Mormon Church history, the Melchizedek Priesthood was later given to Joseph Smith by Peter, James, and John, the original apostles of Jesus Christ. This is recorded in the Doctrine and Covenants.

> *D&C 27:12,13 – 12. And also with Peter, and James, and John, whom I have sent unto you, by whom I have ordained you and confirmed you to be apostles, and special witnesses of my name, and bear the keys of your ministry and of the same things which I revealed unto them; 13. Unto whom I have committed the keys of my kingdom, and a dispensation of the gospel for the last times; and for the fullness of times, in the which I will gather together in one all things, both which are in heaven, and which are on earth;*

In order to substantiate the division between the two priesthoods, the Aaronic and the Melchizedek, the presence in the Bible must be made of both priesthoods and that there was one priesthood that was higher than the other priesthood.

The Aaronic Priesthood. The Priesthood of Aaron or the Lesser Priesthood was mentioned in the following passages.

> *Numbers 3:3,8-10 – 3. **These are the names of the sons of Aaron, the priests which were anointed, whom he consecrated to minister in the priest's office.***
>
> *8. And they shall keep all the instruments of the tabernacle of the congregation, and the charge of the children of Israel, to do the service of the tabernacle. 9. And thou shalt give the Levites unto Aaron and to his sons: they re wholly given unto him out of the children of Israel. 10. **And thou shalt appoint Aaron and his sons, and they shall wait on their priest's office:** and the stranger that cometh nigh shall be put to death.*
>
> *Numbers 18:1,7,8 – 1. And the Lord said unto Aaron, Thou and thy sons and thy father's house with thee shall bear the iniquity of the sanctuary: **and thou and thy sons with thee shall bear the iniquity of your priesthood. 7. Therefore thou and thy sons with thee shall keep your priest's office for every thing of the altar,** and within the vail; and ye shall serve: I have given your priest's office unto you as a service of gift: and the stranger that cometh nigh shall be put to death. 8. And the Lord spake unto Aaron, Behold, I also have given thee the charge of mine heave offerings of all the hallowed things of the children of Israel; unto thee have I given them by reason of the anointing, and to thy sons, by an ordinance for ever.*
>
> *Joshua 18:7 – But the Levites have Jno part among you; **for the priesthood of the Lord is their inheritance:** and Gad, and Reuben, and half the tribe of Manasseh, have received their inheritance beyond Jordan on the east, which Moses the servant of the Lord gave them.*

The Melchizedek Priesthood. The Melchizedek or Greater Priesthood is mentioned in the following passages. Melchizedek was a king in Salem (or Jerusalem) and a priest.

> *Genesis 14:18 – **And Melchizedek king of Salem brought forth bread and wine: and he was the priest of the most high God.***

As taught by Joseph Smith, the writings in Psalms and the apostle Paul also confirm that an office of the priesthood was named after Melchizedek.

> *Psalms 110:4 – The Lord hath sworn, and will not repent, **Thou art a priest for ever after the order of Melchizedek.***
>
> *Hebrews 5:6 – As he saith also in another place, **Thou art a priest for ever after the order of Melchizedek.***
>
> *Hebrews 5:10 – **Called of God an high priest after the order of Melchizedek.***

The Greater and the Lesser Priesthood. Now, apparently after there being biblical support for the two priesthoods, the Aaronic and the Melchizedek, there must also be a reference to one being the lesser priesthood and the other being a higher priesthood. Joseph Smith organized the priesthood offices into the following categories with their major assigned duties.

- The Aaronic Priesthood (or the Lesser Priesthood, or the Levitical Priesthood).
  - Deacons – Passes the sacrament.
  - Teachers – Prepares the sacrament, visits families.
  - Priests – Blesses the sacrament, baptizes.
- The Melchizedek Priesthood (or the Greater Priesthood).

Elders – Baptizes, confirms the Holy Ghost, heals the sick.
Seventies – Same as Elders and responsible for missionary work.

- High Priests – Same as all others plus the administering to all the members, all of the ordinances of the temple and leading the congregations.

One of the first indications in the division of the two priesthoods is found in 2nd Kings.

> *2 Kings 23:4 –* **And the king commanded Hilkiah the high priest, and the priests of the second order,** *and the keepers of the door, to bring forth out the temple of the Lord all the vessels that were made for Baal, and for the grove, and for all the host of heaven: and he burned them without Jerusalem in the fields of Kidron, and carried the ashes of them unto Beth-el.*

The apostle Paul elaborates on the two priesthoods in his letter to the Hebrews. Paul explains how great was the man Melchizedek. Demonstrating how great this man was, Abraham paid his tenth part of all his increases to Melchizedek.

> *Hebrews 7:1,2,4 – 1.* **For this Melchizedek, king of Salem, priest of the most high God,** *who met Abraham returning from the slaughter of the kings, and blessed him; 2.* **To whom also Abraham gave a tenth part of all;** *first being by interpretation King of righteousness, and after that also King of Salem, which is, King of peace;*
>
> *4.* **Now consider how great this man was, unto whom even the patriarch Abraham gave the tenth of the spoils.**

Paul continues to tell of the differences of the two priesthoods.

> *Hebrews 7:11,12 – 11. If therefore perfection were by the Levitical priesthood, (for under it the people received the law),* **what further need was there that another priest should rise after the order of Melchizedek, and not be called after the order of Aaron? 12. For the priesthood being changed, there is made of necessity a change also of the law.**

Noting that there was a change in the law for the two priesthoods, Paul told of the priesthood that Jesus Christ received, and the office.

> *Hebrews 5:5,6 – 5.* **So also Christ glorified not himself to be made an high priest;** *but he that said unto him, Thou art my Son, to day have I begotten thee. 6. As he saith also in another place,* **Thou art a priest for ever after the order of Melchizedek.**

Paul continued telling about Christ and His mission and then repeated the same office that Christ received.

> *Hebrews 5:8-10 – 8. Though he were a Son, yet learned he obedience by the things which he suffered; 9. And being made perfect, he became the author of eternal salvation unto all them that obey him; 10.* **Called of God an high priest after the order of Melchizedek.**

The Power and Authority of the Priesthood. Joseph Smith claimed that the proper priesthood is the only power in which one could return to the kingdom of God. Any other semblance or claim to the priesthood of God would not be accepted in the eyes of God. Joseph Smith taught that with the apostasy from the original church God withdrew His priesthood from the earth until it was given back to Joseph Smith by Peter, James, and John. Joseph Smith teaches that the Bible supports this doctrine.

The first passage is one that is well known among most religions. It is the one about baptism and the gift of the Holy Ghost being a requirement to enter into God's kingdom.

> *John 3:5-7 – 5. Jesus answered, Verily, verily, I say unto thee, **Except a man be born of water and of the Spirit, he cannot enter into the kingdom of God.** 6. That which is born of the flesh is flesh; and that which is born of the Spirit is spirit. 7. Marvel not that I said unto thee, **Ye must be born again.***

Many religions dispute the interpretation of this statement and many religions do not even emphasize the ordinance of baptism as necessary. Some of these religions accept the previous baptisms of other churches. Joseph Smith brings to light a passage in Acts that demonstrates the need for the correct baptism. This is when the apostles re-baptized some people who thought they were already baptized.

> *Acts 19:1-6 – 1. And it came to pass, that, while Apollos was at Corinth, Paul having passed through the upper coasts came to Ephesus: and finding certain disciples, 2. He said unto them, **Have ye received the Holy Ghost since ye believed?** And they said unto him, **We have not so much as heard whether there be any Holy Ghost.** 3. And he said unto them, Unto what then were ye baptized? And they said, Unto John's baptism. 4. Then said Paul, **John verily baptized with the baptism of repentance, saying unto the people, that they should believe on him which should come after him, that is, on Christ Jesus. 5. When they heard this, they were baptized in the name of the Lord Jesus. 6. And when Paul had laid his hands upon them, the Holy Ghost came on them; and they spake with tongues, and prophesied.***

Question: If the proper authority were not necessary for baptism, why would Paul re-baptize these people, who, having faith in Jesus Christ, did get baptized?

Paul answers this question himself in his letter to the Ephesians.

> *Ephesians 4:3-5 – 3. Endeavouring to keep the unity of the Spirit in the bond of peace. 4. There is one body, and one Spirit, even as ye are called in one hope of your calling: 5. **One Lord, one faith, one baptism,***

Question: *"One Lord, one faith, one baptism"*—can it be much clearer than what Joseph Smith taught?

Priesthood Power. Joseph Smith taught that this authority is "the power" of God to do Christ's work here on earth. The following are examples from the Bible that demonstrate the power and authority of the priesthood. While on earth even Jesus Christ at one time did not have *"the power."* He stated himself that *"All power is given unto me in heaven and in earth."* This *"power"* was given to Jesus Christ.

> *Matthew 28:18 – And Jesus came and spake unto them, saying, **All power is given unto me in heaven and in earth.***

If Christ needed to be given the power to do His Father's will, then it is logical that man also must be given this power to do God's will. It is reinforced by Paul's teachings that *"the kingdom of God is not in word, but in power."*

> *1 Corinthians 4:20 – **For the kingdom of God is not in word, but in power.***

A few examples of Christ giving *"the power"* to His apostles and other priesthood holders are:

> *Matthew 10:1 – And when he had called unto him his twelve disciples, **he gave them power against unclean spirits, to cast them out, and to heal all manner of sickness and all manner of disease.***

*Luke 10:19 – Behold, **I give unto you power to tread on serpents and scorpions,** and over all the power of the enemy: and nothing shall by any means hurt you.*

Christ gave the disciples the power to overcome unclean spirits, tread on serpents, and heal the sick. Joseph Smith taught that this power was in the greater or Melchizedek Priesthood. Stephen, full of this *"faith and power,"* was able to do great wonders and miracles.

*Acts 6:8 – **And Stephen, full of faith and power, did great wonders and miracles among the people.***

The Sadducees, leaders of one sect of the Jewish religion recognized the need for the power of God to act in His name. Having received the offices of High Priests and Priests since ancient times, they asked Peter and John by what *"power"* were they acting under.

*Acts 4:7 – And when they had set them in the midst, they asked, **By what power, or by what name, have ye done this?***

Another important lesson on receiving the proper *"power"* was the example of Simon, who seeing the apostles gave the gift of the Holy Ghost to the newly baptized members, offered money to obtain this power.

*Acts 8:18-22 – 18. And when Simon saw that through laying on of the apostles' hands the Holy Ghost was given, **he offered them money,** 19. Saying, **Give me also this power, that on whomsoever I lay hands, he may receive the Holy Ghost.** 20. But Peter said unto him, Thy money perish with thee, because thou hast thought that the gift of God may be purchased with money. 21. Thou hast neither part nor lot in this matter: for thy heart is not right in the sight of God. 22. Repent therefore of this thy wickedness, and pray God, if perhaps the thought of thine heart may be forgiven thee.*

As is written here, the apostles greatly chastised Simon for thinking he could buy his way into the priesthood. They quickly called Simon to repentance. It is the teachings of Joseph Smith that nobody can choose to be in the leadership of the Mormon Church or buy their way in. Joseph Smith set up the church in a manner that does not allow a person to simply believe or desire that he can be in the leadership of the church. Joseph Smith taught that one does not go to college to become one of the ministers or Bishops of the Mormon Church. These positions, to include the priesthood office of a high priest, is a calling that comes from inspired church leaders who themselves have been called by another church leader who has been called by a prophet.

In the original church the apostle Paul was very clear about the way to become a high priest. Paul taught:

*Hebrews 5:1&4 – 1. **For every high priest taken from among men is ordained for men in things pertaining to God,** that he may offer both gifts and sacrifices for sins:*

*4. **And no man taketh this honour unto himself, but he that is called of God, as was Aaron.***

It is very clear that Paul taught that no man should take this honour of being a high priest, or leader of a church congregation, unless he *"is called of God, as was Aaron."*

Question: How was Aaron called of God?

*Exodus 28:1 – **And take thou unto thee Aaron thy brother,** and his sons with him, from among the children of Israel, **that he may minister unto me in the priest's office,** even Aaron, Nadab and Abihu, Eleazar, and Ithamar, Aaron's sons.*

Exodus 40:12-15 – And thou shalt bring Aaron and his sons unto the door of the tabernacle of the congregation, and wash them with water. 13. And thou shalt put upon Aaron the holy garments, and anoint him, and sanctify him; that he may minister unto me in the priest's office. 14. And thou shalt bring his sons, and clothe them with coats: 15. **And thou shalt anoint them, as thou didst anoint their father, that they may minister unto me in the priest's office: for their anointing shall surely be an everlasting priesthood throughout their generations. 16. Thus did Moses: according to all that the Lord commanded him, so did he.**

This was God telling Moses, who was a prophet, to call Aaron to the office of priest. This is a strong example of Aaron not choosing the way he wanted to serve God. This is an example of God calling people to the offices that He wants them in, using His servants, the prophets! Moses then went and did as the Lord commanded.

The apostle Timothy also taught that these priesthood positions were a divine calling and given through prophecy.

1 Timothy 4:14 – Neglect not the gift that is in thee, **which was given thee by prophecy, with the laying on of the hands of the presbytery.**

The Restoration of All Things. Returning to the central theme of the restoration of the fullness of the original Church of Jesus Christ, Christ himself said:

Matthew 17:11 – And Jesus answered and said unto them, **Elias truly shall first come, and restore all things.**

After having studied the Bible in what it teaches about the two different priesthoods that have been on the earth in the past (Bible times), one must ask him/herself the following questions:

Question: If Jesus Christ was to "restore all things" would it not have to include both of the biblical priesthoods that were in existence—the Aaronic and the Melchizedek priesthoods?

Question: Was Joseph Smith inspired when he instituted the two different levels of priesthood?

The Biblical Support Chart. Joseph Smith taught that it is critical to one's salvation that he or she have the proper priesthood power and authority to perform the saving ordinances of salvation, the first being baptism. In addition to this, Joseph Smith also complicated the doctrine of priesthood by dividing the priesthood up and naming them the Aaronic and the Melchizedek Priesthoods. Having reviewed the two divisions of the priesthood in the Bible, the answers to the Biblical Support Chart are as follows:

THE BIBLICAL SUPPORT CHART

Is the following topic supported in the Bible?	Yes or No
Does the Bible support the existence of the Aaronic Priesthood? (Num 3:3,8-10; 18:1,7,8; Joshua 18:7)	Yes
Does the Bible support the existence of the Melchisedek Priesthood? (Gen 14:18; Psalms 110:4; Heb 5:6; 5:10)	Yes
Does the Bible support the division of the two priesthoods as one being a lesser than the other? (2 Kings 23:4; Heb 7:1,2,4; 7:11,12; 5:5,6; 5:8-10)	Yes
Does the Bible support Joseph Smith's claim that one needs to have the "power" given to him to be a church leader? (John 3:5-7; Acts 19:1-6; Matt 28:18; 1 Cor 4:20; Matt 10:1; Luke 10:19; Acts 6:8; Heb 5:1,4; Exo 28:1; 40:12-15)	Yes
Does the Bible support Joseph Smith's teaching that one must be baptized in order to enter into the kingdom of God? (John 3:5-7)	Yes

NOTES

CHAPTER 6

THE HOLY GHOST

As was discussed in the preceding chapter, Joseph Smith taught that the Holy Ghost is the third member of the Godhead, God the Father and His son Jesus Christ being the other two members. The Holy Ghost is a separate personage from the Father and Jesus Christ but does not have a glorified body of flesh and bone. The purpose of the Holy Ghost not having a body of flesh and bone is so that He can dwell in our hearts. So that He can testify of the truthfulness of the Father and Son. So that He can guide those who have chosen to take Jesus Christ into their lives.

All Christian churches believe in the Holy Ghost, but they differ in concept on how to believe in the Holy Ghost. Joseph Smith was quite explicit in his teachings of the Holy Ghost. The main points that Joseph Smith taught were:

- In some ways the Holy Ghost is one of the most important Gods of the Godhead.

- Each person on earth needs to be baptized by fire, which is the Holy Ghost.

- In order to enter into the Kingdom of God, each person on earth needs to receive the actual gift of the Holy Ghost by the laying on of hands by those who have the authority.

- That the Holy Ghost is where one learns of spiritual things, and the source of our testimonies of the divinity of Christ.

- The Holy Ghost is the avenue to a "higher spiritual plane" that includes the second comforter, the Holy Spirit of Promise, and the "calling and election made sure."

Each one of these teachings will be compared to the Bible for support. The first being, the Holy Ghost may be one of the most important members of the Godhead.

The Unpardonable Sin Against the Holy Ghost. Joseph Smith and every LDS prophet since Joseph Smith, have taught of the importance of the Holy Ghost. The LDS prophets always impress the utmost reference that should be taken when speaking of or dealing with spiritual matters. This importance is highly stressed with the LDS missionaries who are taught to be free of sin and from questionable situations that would detract from very sensitive spiritual feelings.

The reasons for this are that the missionaries are introducing what Joseph Smith claims to be "the restoration of the fullness of the gospel of Jesus Christ". Joseph Smith would send these missionaries out to teach, not by common sense, but teach by the Spirit of the Holy Ghost. The critical nature of these missionaries teaching people who may be "anti-Mormon," may place these "anti-Mormons" in a situation where they make light of the Holy Ghost or even blasphemy against the Holy Ghost.

The definition of blasphemy is important in order to understand the importance of the reference that the Holy Ghost is due. Although there are various degrees and types of blasphemy, the basic dictionary defines blasphemy as:

> 1. a. The act of insulting or showing contempt or lack of reverence for God. b. the act of claiming the attributes of deity. 2. Irreverence toward something considered sacred or inviolable.[6]

This is what Jesus Christ taught about people who "blasphemy" against the Holy Ghost.

> *Matthew 12:31 – Wherefore I say unto you,* **All manner of sin and blasphemy shall be forgiven unto men: but the blasphemy against the Holy Ghost shall not be forgiven unto men.**

> *Mark 3:29 –* **But he that shall blaspheme against the Holy Ghost hath never forgiveness, but is in danger of eternal damnation:**

> *Luke 12:10 –* **And whosoever shall speak a word against the Son of man, it shall be forgiven him: but unto him that blasphemeth against the Holy Ghost it shall not be forgiven.**

Knowing that one can commit some minor blasphemy against the Father and the Son—and be forgiven, but blasphemy against the Holy Ghost—and not be forgiven, is a serious doctrine. This chapter in itself is a serious and critical subject that neither the author nor the readers can take lightly.

Warning: It is the author's suggestion, that if the reader thinks lightly of the subject of the Holy Ghost, that he/she should skip this chapter.

The Baptism By Fire. Most Christian religions believe that a person must be spiritually reborn. That is where a particular emotional or spiritual feeling overcomes a person and that person basically changes his/her life to follow the teachings and commandments of Jesus Christ. This spiritual feeling is also called the "baptism by fire."

> *Matthew 3:11 – I indeed baptize you with water unto repentance: but he that cometh after me is mightier than I, whose shoes I am not worthy to bear:* **he shall baptize you with the Holy Ghost, and with fire:**

> *John 1:33 – And I knew him not: but he that sent me to baptize with water, the same said unto me, Upon whom thou shalt see the Spirit descending, and remaining on him,* **the same is he which baptizeth with the Holy Ghost.**

> *Acts 1:5 – For John truly baptized with water; but* **ye shall be baptized with the Holy Ghost not many days hence.**

The apostle Peter referred to it as being "born again."

> *1 Peter 1:22,23 – 22. Seeing ye have purified your souls in obeying the truth through the Spirit unto unfeigned love of the brethren, see that ye love one another with a pure heart fervently: 23.* **Being born again,** *not of corruptible seed, but of incorruptible, by the word of God, which liveth and abideth for ever.*

The apostle Paul described it as a person being "filled with the Holy Ghost."

> *Acts 2:4 –* **And they were all filled with the Holy Ghost,** *and began to speak with other tongues, as the Spirit gave them utterance.*

The important factor here that is taught by most Christian churches and Joseph Smith is that this feeling overcomes a person and changes his/her life for the good. This good includes following and getting to know the divinity of the Lord Jesus Christ and what He did for us by atoning for our sins. This atonement was accomplished through the death and resurrection of the Lord Jesus Christ, our eldest brother.

The Holy Ghost as a Gift. Most Christians believe that a person must be spiritually "born again" or "baptized by fire." Joseph Smith takes this basic principle a step further and taught that this "baptism by fire" is another physical ordinance that man must receive in addition to the ordinance of baptism by water.

The apostle John talked about it as something that must be given at a certain time.

> *John 7:39 – (**But this spake he of the Spirit, which they that believe on him should receive: for the Holy Ghost was not yet given;** because that Jesus was not yet glorified.)*

John described it as a particular action that Christ did after He resurrected from the tomb. Christ gave the Holy Ghost to the disciples by breathing on them.

> *John 20:22 – And when he had said this, he breathed on them, and saith unto them, **Receive ye the Holy Ghost:***

One reason Christ did not lay His hands on the apostles heads to give the Gift of the Holy Ghost may be because in verse 17, He told Mary not to touch Him because "He had not yet ascended unto His Father."

> *Matthew 20:17 – Jesus saith unto her, **Touch me not; for I am not yet ascended to my Father:** but go to my brethren, and say unto them, I ascend unto my Father, and your Father; and to my God, and your God.*

Peter and Paul also taught that the Holy Ghost was a "gift."

> *Acts 2:38 – Then Peter said unto them, Repent, and be baptized every one of you in the name of Jesus Christ for the remission of sins, **and ye shall receive the gift of the Holy Ghost.***

> *Acts 10:45 – And they of the circumcision which believed were astonished, as many as came with Peter, **because that on the Gentiles also was poured out the gift of the Holy Ghost.***

The Gift of the Holy Ghost by the Laying on of Hands. Joseph Smith taught that this "gift of the Holy Ghost" is an ordinance that comes after baptism. The ordinance entails one who has the priesthood authority to place his hands on the new members head, and addressing the person by name, he actually says similar words like "receive the gift of the Holy Ghost." After the gift is transferred to the member, a prayer is given to the person, and then all this is done by the authority of the Holy Melchizedek priesthood. Timothy taught that this gift was given by the laying on of the hands of the priesthood.

> *1 Timothy 4:14 – **Neglect not the gift that is in thee, which was given thee by prophecy, with the laying on of the hands of the presbytery.***

> *2 Timothy 1:6 – **Wherefore I put thee in remembrance that thou stir up the gift of God, which is in thee by the putting on of my hands.***

Paul taught that this ordinance was actually a doctrine of the church and the ordinance of baptism was different than that of the laying on of hands to give the gift of the Holy Ghost.

> *Hebrews 6:2 – **Of the doctrines of baptisms, and of laying on of hands,** and of resurrection of the dead, and of eternal judgment.*

The Mission of the Holy Ghost. Joseph Smith taught that the main mission of the Holy Ghost is to reveal to man the divinity of Jesus Christ. This is also taught by the apostle Paul.

> *1 Cor 12:3,4 – Wherefore I give you to understand, that no man speaking by the Spirit of God calleth Jesus accursed: and that **no man can say that Jesus is the Lord, but by the Holy Ghost. 4. Now there are diversities of gifts, but the same Spirit.***

Many people in the Christian religion believe that the wisdom and common sense of man is important in establishing religious beliefs and doctrines. On the contrary, Joseph Smith taught, and all the current members base their belief on the spiritual. Many times the teachings of Joseph Smith do not make sense and seem ridiculous to most people. But Joseph Smith always told one to pray about the things that were being taught. This practice continues today.

It is the Holy Ghost that will overcome all common sense and earthly wisdom that is taught by man.

> *1 Cor 2:4, 5 – **And my speech and my preaching was not with enticing words of man's wisdom, but in demonstration of the Spirit and of power: 5. That your faith should not stand in the wisdom of men, but in the power of God.***

> *2 Cor 1:12 – For our rejoicing is this, **the testimony of our conscience, that in simplicity and godly sincerity, not with fleshly wisdom,** but by the grace of God, we have had our conversation in the world, and more abundantly to you-ward.*

> *1 Cor 2:10-16 – **But God hath revealed them unto us by his Spirit: for the Spirit searcheth all things, yea, the deep things of God.** 11. For what man knoweth the things of a man, save the spirit of man which is in him? Even so the things of God knoweth no man, but the Spirit of God. 12. Now we have received, not the spirit of the world, but the spirit which is of God; that we might know the things that are freely given to us of God. 13. **Which things also we speak, not in the words which man's wisdom teacheth, but which the Holy Ghost teacheth; comparing spiritual things with spiritual. 14. But the natural man receiveth not the things of the Spirit of God: for they are foolishness unto him:** neither can he know them, because they are spiritually discerned. 15. But he that is spiritual judgeth all things, yet he himself is judged of no man. 16. For who hath known the mind of the Lord, that he may instruct him? But we have the mind of Christ.*

It is in this spirit, catering to "the wisdom of man," that this book contains the "Biblical Support Chart." This chart, when completed with all the many doctrines and teachings of Joseph Smith, will reveal how close Joseph Smith came to the Bible in organizing the LDS Church and establishing doctrine.

The men who are inclined to require the wisdom and common sense approach to religion will be able to count the number of doctrines and teachings, compare them to the Bible, and then produce the percentages or ratios that they want to figure out what is logical within the LDS prophet's teachings.

Question: Is it considered 'blasphemy against the Holy Ghost" when a Christian prefers to rely on the wisdom and common sense of man to justify spiritual things?

In addition to revealing the divinity of Jesus Christ, the Holy Ghost performs several other purposes. Among these are to teach people of all things, guide people to truth, show people of things to come, and witnesses to people. Biblical support for these purposes are:

> *Luke 12:12 – **For the Holy Ghost shall teach you in the same hour what ye ought to say.***

> *John 14:26 – **But the Comforter, which is the Holy Ghost,** whom the Father will send in my name, **he shall teach you all things, and bring all things to your remembrance,** whatsoever I have said unto you.*

> *John 16:13 – Howbeit when he, the Spirit of truth, is come, **he will guide you into all truth:** for he shall not speak of himself; **but whatsoever he shall hear, that shall he speak: and he will shew you things to come.***

1 Corinthians 2:13 – Which things also we speak, **not in the words which man's wisdom teacheth, but which the Holy Ghost teacheth; comparing spiritual things with spiritual.**

Romans 5:5 – And hope maketh not ashamed; **because the love of God is shed abroad in our hearts by the Holy Ghost which is given unto us.**

Romans 8:27 – **And he that searcheth the hearts knoweth what is the mind of the Spirit, because he maketh intercession for the saints according to the will of God.**

Hebrews 10:15 – **Whereof the Holy Ghost also is a witness to us:** *for after that he had said before,*

One of the basic teachings of Joseph Smith is how one may know the *Book of Mormon* is true. Joseph Smith and his missionary effort does not try to beat the *Book of Mormon* into people's heads through brain washing—like many churches.

What Joseph Smith does is to refer a person to a certain promise in the *Book of Mormon*. This promise follows the actual mission "to teach" through the Holy Ghost. This promise is given by what Joseph Smith describes as an ancient prophet of the Americas named Moroni. It is the same angel who Joseph Smith claims appeared to him and gave him the golden plates. Moroni writes:

Moroni 10:3-5 – 3. Behold, I would exhort you that when ye shall read these things, if it be wisdom in God that ye should read them, that ye would remember how merciful the Lord hath been unto the children of men, from the creation of Adam even down until the time that ye shall receive these things, and ponder it in your hearts.

4. And when ye shall receive these things, **I would exhort you that ye would ask God, the Eternal Father, in the name of Christ, if these things are not true; and if ye shall ask with a sincere heart, with real intent, having faith in Christ, he will manifest the truth of it unto you, by the power of the Holy Ghost. 5. And by the power of the Holy Ghost ye may know the truth of all things.**

Testimonies. Joseph Smith taught that once a person knows, through the Holy Ghost, that the *Book of Mormon* is true, this person now has a "testimony." Joseph Smith always taught that a member of the LDS Church, who has received the Gift of the Holy Ghost, has the companionship of the Holy Ghost on a daily basis to teach and to reveal truth to that member. Joseph Smith taught that the members should continue to grow spiritually and receive testimonies of every major and every little doctrine and teaching of Joseph Smith.

In essence, Joseph Smith taught that once a person receives the Gift of the Holy Ghost by the laying on of hands by someone who has authority, this person would continue to grow in testimony of all things spiritual. This is what the Bible has to say about the Holy Ghost and testimonies.

John 15:26 – **But when the Comforter is come, whom I will send unto you from the Father, even the Spirit of truth, which proceedeth from the Father, he shall testify of me:**

1 John 5:6 – This is he that came by water and blood, even Jesus Christ; not by water only, but by water and blood. And **it is the Spirit that beareth witness, because the Spirit is truth.**

John 5:34 – **But I receive not testimony from man:** *but these things I say, that ye* *might be saved.*

*John 8:32 – **And ye shall know the truth,** and the truth shall make you free.*

*John 21:24 – This is the disciple which testifieth of these things, and wrote these things: **and we know that his testimony is true.***

*1 Corinthians 1:6 – **Even the testimony of Christ was confirmed in you:***

*2 Timothy 1:8 – **Be not thou therefore ashamed of the testimony of our Lord,** nor of me his prisoner: but be thou partaker of the afflictions of the gospel according to the power of God;*

Joseph never laid claim to being the only church that has the right to the Holy Ghost. Joseph Smith taught that man may know, through the Holy Ghost, that Jesus Christ is Lord. Many people not affiliated with the church that Joseph Smith founded has received the witness of the divinity of Jesus Christ. This witness is from the Holy Ghost as the apostle Paul taught

*1 Corinthians 12:3 – Wherefore I give you to understand, that no man speaking by the Spirit of God calleth Jesus accursed: and **that no man can say that Jesus is the Lord, but by the Holy Ghost.***

Paul gave examples of where people received a testimony of Jesus Christ, through the Holy Ghost, but these people did not automatically have the Gift of the Holy Ghost. That was a separate ordinance. This example is in Acts.

*Acts 2:37, 38 – 37. **Now when they heard this, they were pricked in their heart,** and said unto Peter and to the rest of the apostles, men and brethren, what shall we do? 38. Then Peter said unto them, **Repent, and be baptized every one of you in the name of Jesus Christ for the remission of sins, and ye shall receive the gift of the Holy Ghost.***

This is what Joseph Smith taught, from the start in the early 1820's, and all his followers today teach—read the *Book of Mormon*, follow the promise, and if your heart is pricked by the Holy Ghost that these things are true, then you should repent, be baptized, and receive the Gift of the Holy Ghost.

Be Ye Therefore Perfect. Joseph Smith took the following commandment of Jesus Christ literally:

*Matthew 5:48 – **Be ye therefore perfect, even as your Father which is in heaven is perfect.***

*Colosians 4:12 – Epaphras, who is one of you, a servant of Christ, saluteth you, always labouring fervently for you in prayers, **that ye may stand perfect and complete in all the will of God.***

Joseph Smith knew that a person might become perfect while living in this life. Noah and Job were examples of this commandment to become perfect.

*Genesis 6:9 – These are the generations of Noah: **Noah was a just man and perfect in his generations, and Noah walked with God.***

*Job 1:8 – And the Lord said unto Satan, Hast thou considered my servant Job, that there is none like him in the earth, **a perfect and an upright man,** one that feareth God, and escheweth evil?*

The apostles of the New Testament also taught the teaching of Joseph Smith—that all men should literally strive to become perfect. Luke taught about perfection when he said that those who become perfect will as his master, Jesus Christ.

> *Luke 6:40 –The disciple is not above his master: but **every one that is perfect shall be as his master.***

John taught that we could all be perfect in one, as God and Christ were one.

> *John 17:23 – I in them, and thou in me, **that they may be made perfect in one; and that the world may know that thou hast sent me, and hast loved them, as thou hast loved me.***

Paul taught that the apostles and prophets were given "for the perfecting of the saints."

> *Ephesians 4:11,12 – 11. And he gave some, apostles; and some, prophets; and some, evangelists: and some, pastors and teachers; 12. **For the perfecting of the saints, for the work of the ministry, for the edifying of the body of Christ.***

Paul continued teaching the Colosians that it was his duty to "*present every man perfect in Christ.*"

> *Colosians 1:28 – Whom we preach, warning every man, and teaching every man in all wisdom; **that we may present every man perfect in Christ Jesus.***

The apostle Timothy also taught the doctrine that man might become perfect.

> *2 Timothy 3:17 – **That the man of God may be perfect,** thoroughly furnished unto all good works.*

Paul also taught that the "spirits of just men" were made perfect.

> *Hebrews 12:23 – To the general assembly and church of the firstborn, which are written in heaven, and to God the Judge of all, **and to the spirits of just men made perfect.***

The Holy Ghost-A Higher Spiritual Plane. Joseph Smith was the first and may be the only religious leader that has taught this doctrine that "man may become perfect" and that we should always be striving to become "perfect." If a prophet of God teaches that man may become perfect, he must also teach how to become perfect. Joseph Smith taught that there are many things of God that help man become perfect. Joseph Smith taught that the entire or "fullness" of the gospel of Jesus Christ, or The Church of Jesus Christ of Latter Day Saints, is set up and prepared to teach every "saint" or member the way to gain this perfection.

One of the main principles that Joseph Smith taught on how to obtain perfection is through the Gift of the Holy Ghost. Joseph Smith did not stop with just the Gift of the Holy Ghost, he also taught about the "Holy Spirit of Promise," one's "calling and election made sure," and the "second comforter." After one realizes that Jesus Christ is our Savior, he/she must be baptized and receive the Gift of the Holy Ghost. This spiritual progress does not stop at this point; he/she must continue to progress spiritually.

The Holy Spirit of Promise.

Joseph Smith's Teachings on the *"Holy Spirit of Promise."* After receiving the Gift of the Holy Ghost the next spiritual plane that one should strive for is the "*Holy Spirit of Promise.*" This promise was revealed to Joseph Smith on February 16, 1832 during a revelation that taught Joseph Smith of the glories of God in the celestial, terrestrial, and telestial kingdoms. Jesus Christ taught that those who receive the "*Holy Spirit of Promise*" will be those that go into the celestial kingdom.

> *D&C 76:53 – And who overcome by faith, and are **sealed by the Holy Spirit of promise,** which the Father sheds forth upon all those who are just and true.*

On December 27, 1832, Jesus Christ taught more about the "*Holy Spirit of Promise.*"

> *D&C 88:3-5 – 3. Wherefore, I now send upon you another Comforter, even upon you my friends, that it may abide in your hearts, **even the Holy Spirit of promise; which other Comforter is the same that I promised unto my disciples,** as is recorded in the testimony of John. 4. **The Comforter is the promise which I give unto you of eternal life, even the glory of the celestial kingdom;** 5. Which glory is that of the church of the Firstborn, even of God, the holiest of all, through Jesus Christ his Son –*

Jesus Christ taught that this "*Holy Spirit of Promise*" is actually a promise to the faithful members, that if they prove themselves in the faith, they will receive eternal life in the celestial kingdom of God.

On January 19, 1841, the Lord gave this "*Holy Spirit of Promise*" to Hyrum Smith.

> *D&C 124:124 – First, I give unto you Hyrum Smith to be a patriarch unto you, to hold the sealing blessings of my church, **even the Holy Spirit of promise, whereby ye are sealed up unto the day of redemption,** that ye may not fall notwithstanding the hour of temptation that may come upon you.*

The New Testament's Teachings on the "*Holy Spirit of Promise.*" Joseph Smith's teachings on this subject are very new and very far from the teachings of all the other Christian church's in his time and to the author's knowledge, to the Christian churches of our time. Being such a different teaching and such a critical subject as the Holy Ghost, there must be some type of support in the Bible. There is mention of the "*Holy Spirit of Promise*" in Ephesians.

Paul calls this "*Holy Spirit of Promise*" a sealing that is "*the earnest of our inheritance*" (Eph 1:14). "*Earnest*" is used here in exactly the same sense as payment received with the assurance that the remainder will also be given—or, being guaranteed a place in the kingdom of God.

> *Ephesians 1:13,14 – 13. In whom ye also trusted, after that ye heard the word of truth, the gospel of your salvation: in whom also after that ye believed, **ye were sealed with that Holy Spirit of promise. 14. Which is the earnest of our inheritance** until the redemption of the purchased possession, unto the praise of his glory.*

Paul continues to talk about the saints in Ephesus being sealed by the holy Spirit of God.

> *Ephesians 4:30 – **And grieve not the holy Spirit of God, whereby ye are sealed unto the day of redemption.***

In the same letter, Paul talks about those who did not have Christ being "*strangers from the covenants of promise.*"

> *Ephesians 2:12 – That at that time ye were without Christ, being aliens from the commonwealth of Israel, **and strangers from the covenants of promise,** having no hope, and without God in the world:*

In the same chapter and conversation, Paul tells the saints in Ephesus that those who are sealed in these promises are "*built upon the foundations of the apostles and prophets, Jesus Christ himself being the chief cornerstone.*"

> *Ephesians 2:19-22 – Now therefore ye are no more strangers and foreigners, but fellowcitizens with the saints, and of the household of God; 20. **And are built upon the foundation of the apostles and prophets, Jesus Christ himself being the chief corner stone;** 21. In whom ye also are builded together for an habitation of God through the Spirit.*

Your Calling and Election Made Sure. Joseph Smith quoted Ephesians chapter 1, verses

13 and 14 and stated that this sealing power of the "*Holy Spirit of Promise*" was the same as having one's "*calling and election made sure.*" (See Teachings of the Prophet Joseph Smith, p. 149). Joseph Smith taught that the "*calling and election made sure*" was a guarantee of obtaining a place in "*the everlasting kingdom of our Lord and Saviour Jesus Christ.*" The apostle Peter taught the same thing.

> *2 Peter 1:10,11 – 10. Wherefore the rather, brethren,* **give diligence to make your calling and election sure:** *for if ye do these things, ye shall never fall: 11.* **For so an entrance shall be ministered unto you abundantly into the everlasting kingdom of our Lord and Saviour Jesus Christ.**

Joseph Smith taught that the "*second comforter*" which is Jesus Christ himself gave this "*calling and election made sure*".

> *D&C 67:10 – And again, verily I say unto you that it is your privilege, and a promise I give you that have been ordained unto this ministry, that inasmuch as you strip yourselves from jealousies and fears, and humble yourselves before me, for ye are not sufficiently humble,* **the veil shall be rent and you shall see me and know that I am** *– not with the carnal neither natural mind, but with the spiritual.*

The apostle John taught that there was to be another comforter that would come and visit you. It was asked how would Christ manifest himself unto them, and not the world. There was an answer.

> *John 14:16 – And I will pray the Father, and he shall give you another Comforter, that he may abide with you for ever;*

> *John 14:21-23 – 21. He that hath my commandments, and keepeth them, he it is that loveth me: and he that loveth me shall be loved of my Father,* **and I will love him, and will manifest myself to him.** *22. Judas saith unto him, not Iscariot,* **Lord, how is it that thou wilt manifest thyself unto us, and not unto the world?** *23. Jesus answered and said unto him,* **If a man love me, he will keep my words: and my Father will love him, and we will come unto him, and make our abode with him,**

This appearing of Heavenly Father and Jesus Christ to the people was confirmed to Joseph Smith on April 2, 1843.

> *D&C 130:3 – John 14:23 – The appearing of the Father and the Son, in that verse,* **is a personal appearance;** *and the idea that the Father and the Son dwell in a man's heart is an old sectarian notion, and is false.*

The Biblical Support Chart. As with the teachings of Joseph Smith where it is critical to have the proper authority to administer the ordinances of Jesus Christ, bestowing the "gift of the Holy Ghost" by the laying on of hands to a newly baptized member is also critical. Joseph Smith's teachings about the Holy Ghost as the Comforter, the "*Holy Spirit of Promise*," and one's "*calling and election made sure*" goes far beyond the teachings of all the other Christian churches. There is definite Biblical support for all of Joseph Smith's teachings concerning the Holy Ghost.

THE BIBLICAL SUPPORT CHART

Is the following topic supported in the Bible?	Yes or No
Does the Bible support Joseph Smith's teaching that one must be spiritually reborn—or baptized by fire? (Matt 3:11; John 1:33; Acts 1:5; 1 Peter 1:22,23; Acts 2:4)	Yes
Does the Bible support Joseph Smith's teaching that receiving the Holy Ghost is a gift, after baptism? (John 7:39; John 20:22; Acts 2:38; Acts 10:45)	Yes
Does the Bible support Joseph Smith's teaching that the gift of the Holy Ghost is given by the "laying on of hands?" (1 Tim 4:14; 2 Tim 1:6; Hebrews 6:2)	Yes
Does the Bible support Joseph Smith's teaching that the gift of the Holy Ghost overcomes all common sense and earthly wisdom? (1 Cor 2:4,5; 2 Cor 1:12; 1 Cor 2:10-16)	Yes
Does the Bible support Joseph Smith's teaching that the members receive testimony through the Holy Ghost? (John 15:26; 1 John 5:6; John 5:34; John 8:32; John 21:24; 1 Cor 1:6; 2 Tim 1:8)	Yes
Does the Bible support Joseph Smith's teaching that one may become perfect? (Matt 5:48; Col 4:12; Gen 6:9; Job 1:8; Luke 6:40; John 17:23; Eph 4:11,12; Col 1:28; 2 Tim 3:17; Heb 112:23)	Yes
Does the Bible support Joseph Smith's teaching that the members receive testimony through the Holy Ghost? (John 15:26; 1 John 5:6; John 5:34; John 8:32; John 21:24; 1 Cor 1:6; 2 Tim 1:8)	Yes
Does the Bible support Joseph Smith's teaching that one may become perfect? (Matt 5:48; Col 4:12; Gen 6:9; Job 1:8; Luke 6:40; John 17:23; Eph 4:11,12; Col 1:28; 2 Tim 3:17; Heb 12:23)	Yes
Does the Bible support Joseph Smith's teaching about the Holy Spirit of Promise? (Eph 1:13,14; Eph 4:30; Eph 2:12, 19-22)	Yes
Does the Bible support Joseph Smith's teaching about one's "calling and election made sure?" (2 Peter 1:10,11; John 14:16; John 14:21-23; D&C 130:3; 67:10)	Yes

Author's Note. Joseph Smith's teaching that a person may become perfect during this life and receive the "*Holy Spirit of Promise*" and one's "*calling and election made sure*"—is a personal guarantee that one will be in the kingdom of God after this life. This knowledge is a great comfort for a person in this life!

A comparison to other great Christian leader's teachings may reveal the fruits of those leaders. A specific example is the teaching of Doctor Billy Graham. Doctor Graham has accomplished many wonderful things in the name of God and Christ. He has brought many people to Christ and is constantly witnessing for Christ. Doctor Graham also has a syndicated newspaper column where he answers people's religious questions. One particular question and answer follows:

> **Woman wants guarantee she'll go to heaven. Dear Dr. Graham:** *How can I be sure I'm going to heaven when I die? My aunt died not long ago, and it got me thinking about life after death. I've always tried to be a good person, but if someone were to ask me if I knew for sure that I am going to heaven, I'd have to say no, I'm not sure. – Mrs. L.K.*

> **Dear Mrs. L.K.:** *We can never be saved because of what we do; we can only be saved because of what Jesus Christ has already done for us. Let me explain.*

> *Our greatest problem can be put in one word: sin. Sin cuts us off from God, and sin also keeps us out of heaven. But how can we get rid of our sins? We can't erase them or cause them to disappear by ourselves; we don't have the power. The only way we can get rid of our sins is for someone to come along and take them away for us.*

> *And that is exactly what Jesus Christ did for us. We are weighed down by the burden of our sins – but Jesus took that burden upon himself when he died on the cross for us. To put it another way, he took the punishment we deserve when he went to the cross in our place. The Bible says, "For Christ died for sins once for all, the righteous for the unrighteous, to bring you to God." (1 Peter 3:18)*

> *What must you do? Simply believe that Christ has taken away your sins, and then receive him into your heart and life. The Bible's promise is for you: "To all who received him, to those who believed in his name, he gave the right to become children of God" (John 1:12). Become God's child today by asking Christ to come into your life.*[7]

Without criticizing the response to Mrs. L. K., one must compare the answer given, (which did not answer the actual question), with one that Joseph Smith would answer, knowing that with the "*Gift of the Holy Ghost*," the "*Holy Spirit of Promise*," and the "*calling and election made sure*," a person may receive, in this life, a guarantee to be in the Kingdom of God with Heavenly Father and Jesus Christ. In comparing the quality of answer given to this sister's question could be considered one of the "*fruits*" of a living prophet or the "*fruits*" of a righteous man.

> Matthew 10:41 – **He that receiveth a prophet in the name of a prophet shall receive a prophet's reward; and he that receiveth a righteous man in the name of a righteous man shall receive a righteous man's reward.**

When one knows the "law", it clearly states in the Bible that a person in this life can have a guarantee that he or she will make it to the kingdom of God.

NOTES

PART II: THE SCRIPTURES

CHAPTER 7

THE BIBLE: PERFECT AND COMPLETE?

There are many Christian religions and their leaders believe that the Mormon Church does not believe in the Bible. Many believe that:

"The Bible is the only word of God, it is complete and perfect. It contains no errors."

Many of these Christian leaders teach their followers that the Mormons believe that:

"The Bible is corrupted, all texts are essentially flawed, inaccurate, and cannot be trusted. At best, it is incomplete, at worst, it is tainted beyond reliability. It plays a small part in the religion, and little or no LDS theology is really derived from it."

Joseph Smith actually believed the following when it came to the Bible:

"We believe the Bible to be the word of God as far as it is translated correctly; we also believe the Book of Mormon to be the word of God" [8]

According to many of the Christian position, the Bible should support all of their own beliefs, teachings, admonitions to their followers, and all their accusations against the Mormons. Whereas, the Mormons understand that the Bible does have a few contradictions, that there are scriptures mentioned in the Bible that are not included, and that there is support to believe more scripture may come forth.

As we have learned in the previous chapters, the Bible does support Joseph Smith's teachings on the topics of the apostasy, the restoration, the organization of the Church of Jesus Christ of Latter Day Saints, the priesthood organization, the Holy Ghost, and the church being one. The Biblical Support Chart, so far has Joseph Smith being 100% on the topics discussed.

A detailed look at Joseph Smith's position on the Bible will shed light as to how close his belief is to the Bible.

Bible Contradictions. The following passages are examples of potential contradictions in the Bible. If these contradictions actually do exist, then Joseph Smith's belief that the Bible is the word of God as long as it has been translated correctly is closer to the truth than some of the Christian positions of the Bible being the perfect and complete word of God.

Example 1: The next two scriptures are two that need to have the whole chapter studied in order to understand what is going on. This subject is when Saul was converted to the Lord. In Acts, it is taught that the men journeying with Saul heard a voice, but again in another account, they did not hear the voice.

*Acts 9:7 – And the men which journeyed with him stood speechless, **hearing a voice, but seeing no man.***

*Acts 22:9 – And they that were with me saw indeed the light, and were afraid; **but they heard not the voice** of him that spake to me.*

Question: Which verse is correct?

Question: Did the men journeying with Saul hear the voice of the Lord or not?

Question: Which verse is wrong?

Most Christian responses on this contradiction is that "this does not pertain" to our salvation and does not "affect the word of God" from the Bible. These responses are both true, but these Christians are not addressing the real topic. The first topic is to find out if the Joseph Smith position that "*the Bible is the word of God as long as it is translated correctly*" is valid. A second purpose is to find out if the Christian position that "*the Bible is complete and perfect.*" The verses quoted above are contradictions.

Question: How does this contradiction support the contradiction between Joseph Smith's position and that of the Christian's position that the Bible is perfect?

Example 2: The next scripture is from the **First** Epistle of Paul to the Corinthians. This is supposed to be the first time Paul wrote to the Saints (members) in Corinth.

> *I Cor 5:9 – I wrote unto you in an epistle not to company with fornicators:*

Question: How can this be the first epistle to the Corinthians when he has already written to them?

Again, the Christian response is that it does not affect the word of God. Again, they avoid the real topic of the subject. According to their teachings to their followers, the Bible is perfect and complete; the followers do not need more scripture. In reality, this verse is another contradiction and reveals a missing epistle to the Corinthians. Again alluding to Joseph Smith's position that the Bible is not perfect and complete.

Example 3: In Matthew, the actual account of Judas's death, after the betrayal of Christ, is that he "hanged himself." But when compared to another account in Acts, we find that he died from "all his bowels gushed out."

> *Matt 27:5 – And he cast down the pieces of silver in the temple, and departed, **and went and hanged himself.***

> *Acts 1:18 – Now this man purchased a field with the reward of iniquity; and falling headlong, **he burst asunder in the midst, and all his bowels gushed out.***

Question: Is this another contradiction in the Bible?

Question: Which account is correct?

Question: How did Judas really die?

Again, it is agreed that this contradiction does not affect the word of God to mankind. But it is another contradiction, which again, undermines the official position of some Christian doctrine that the Bible is perfect.

Example 4: These next passages, unlike the first three examples, do affect a follower's salvation because the scriptures talk about real doctrine of Jesus Christ. This next potential contradiction is concerning the "saved Christian's" basic scripture for their entire religious philosophy. Paul taught:

> *Ephesians 2:5-9 – 5. Even when we were dead in sins, hath quickened us together with Christ, (by grace ye are saved;) 6. And hath raised us up together, and made us sit together in heavenly places in Christ Jesus: 7. That in the ages to come he might shew the exceeding riches of his grace in his kindness toward us through Christ Jesus. 8. **For by grace are ye saved through faith; and that not of yourselves: it is the gift of God: 9. Not of works, lest any man should boast.***

Yet, when compared to other teachings, not only Paul but also other apostles taught the opposite. They stated:

> *Galatians 6:7,8 – Be not deceived; God is not mocked: **for whatsoever a man***

soweth, that shall he also reap. 8. *For he that soweth to his flesh shall of the flesh reap corruption; but he that soweth to the Spirit shall of the Spirit reap life everlasting.*

James 1:22 – But be ye doers of the word, and not hearers only, deceiving your own selves.

James 2:14-20 – 14. What doth it profit, my brethren, though a man say he hath faith, and have not works? Can faith save him? 15. If a brother or sister be naked, and destitute of daily food, 16. And one of you say unto them, Depart in peace, be ye warmed and filled; notwithstanding ye give them not those things which are needful to the body; what doth it profit? 17. Even so faith, if it hath not works, is dead, being alone. 18. Yea, a man may say, Thou hast faith, and I have works: shew me thy faith without thy works, and I will shew thee my faith by my works. 19. Thou believest that there is one God; thou doest well; the devils also believe, and tremble. 20. But wilt thou know, O vain man, that faith without works is dead?

Question: Are these teachings contradictory?

Question: If they are in contradiction, could a misunderstanding of the meaning affect a person's salvation?

Details of this apparent contradiction can be found in Chapter 10, on "Saved by Grace." In Chapter 10 we will find that this "Saved Christian" interpretation is indeed a major contradiction and will definitely affect the salvation of the followers who embrace these teachings. Also in the chapter "Saved by Grace," Joseph Smith's interpretation of these passages will be discussed.

Example 5: The Personality of God the Father, Jesus Christ, and the Holy Ghost. Most Christian churches believe that God the Father, his Son Jesus Christ, and the Holy Ghost are all one entity and they do not have a body of flesh and bone. There are several passages that mention the oneness theory. One example is:

John 10:30 – I and my Father are one.

Other passages in the Bible teach that man was actually created in the image of God and that God has a body. A few scriptures that teach this doctrine are:

Genesis 1:26,27 – And God said, Let us make man in our image, after our likeness: and let them have dominion over the fish of the sea, and over the fowl of the air, and over the cattle, and over all the earth, and over every creeping thing that creepeth upon the earth. 27. So God created man in his own image, in the image of God created he him; male and female created he them.

Genesis 32:30 – And Jacob called the name of the place Peniel: for I have seen God face to face, and my life is preserved.

Acts 7:55,56 – 55. But he, being full of the Holy Ghost, looked up stedfastly into heaven, and saw the glory of God, and Jesus standing on the right hand of God, 56. And said, Behold, I see the heavens opened, and the Son of man standing on the right hand of God.

Here we have God creating man in His own image. The image of man is man, a person with a body. We also have an account of Jacob seeing God face to face. So, God has a face. We also have an account of the apostle Steven seeing Jesus standing on the right hand of God. Now, Jesus is standing on the right hand of God. So Christ has feet and legs to stand on. If God has a right hand, he must also have a left hand and arms attached to those hands! If one believes that God and Christ are both one in the same, then there is a major contradiction in the Bible!

Question: How can the Bible be perfect when it teaches such conflicting doctrine?

Question: Is it the Bible that contains such conflicting doctrine or is it the teachings of men that teach such conflicting doctrine?

Question: Would a mistaken belief in the actual personality of God and Jesus Christ be critical to one's salvation?

Question: How could knowing that God and Jesus Christ are two distinct persons with glorified bodies affect a person's life and salvation?

According to what Christ taught in John, a person must not mistaken their personality because knowing God and Jesus Christ is life eternal!

> *John 17:3 – And this is life eternal,* **that they might know thee the only true God; and Jesus Christ,** *whom thou hast sent.*

More details on this doctrine are presented in the Chapter 9 on the Personality of God.

Example 6: Another contradiction, one that is critical to ones salvation, is the concept of a person seeing God. The basic foundation of the **The Church of Jesus Christ of Latter Day Saints** is that Joseph Smith actually saw God the Father and Jesus Christ. The normal Christian position in reference to Joseph Smith's first vision where God the Father and Jesus Christ appeared to him, is that Joseph Smith could not have possibly seen what he claimed. That this vision of the prophet Joseph Smith is a contradiction to what the Bible teaches. The Christian reference the apostle John for this belief:

> *John 1:18 –* **"No man hath seen God at any time;** *the only begotten Son, which is in the bosom of the Father, he hath declared him."*

Much of the Christian principle belief depends on the correctness of this interpretation of this passage. Unfortunately, further study of the Bible reveals that this Christian interpretation is in conflict with other teachings of the Bible. The following passages are examples where other men in the Bible have actually seen God.

> *Genesis 12:7 –* **And the Lord appeared unto Abram,** *and said, Unto thy seed will I give this land: and there builded he an altar unto the Lord,* **who appeared unto him.**

> *Genesis 32:30 – And Jacob called the name of the place Peniel:* **for I have seen God face to face, and my life is preserved.**

> *Exodus 24:9-11 – 9. Then went up Moses, and Aaron, Nadab, and Abihu, and seventy of the elders of Israel: 10.* **And they saw the God of Israel:** *and there was under his feet as it were a paved work of a sapphire stone, and as it were the body of heaven in his clearness. 11. And upon the nobles of the children of Israel he laid not his hand:* **also they saw God,** *and did eat and drink.*

These three passages name Abram, Jacob, Moses, Aaron, Nadab, Abihu, and seventy of the elders of Israel have all seen God and lived! There are now seventy-seven witnesses, including Joseph Smith that have seen God and lived.

Question: Does the Christian doctrine of "no one can see God" contradict the doctrine that people have seen God?

Question: Does the first Joseph Smith vision of God the Father and Jesus Christ conflict with the Bible?

The answers to these questions are detailed in **Chapter 9 – The Personality of God.**

Missing Scriptures. A major concern about the Christian's position that "the Bible is the complete word of God," is the mention of approximately nineteen other potential writings of prophets that are not included in the Bible.

From 1 Corinthians 5:9, we find that there was at least one other epistle to the Corinthians that is not included in the Bible. Is it possible that there are other lost scripture out there like the Book of the Covenant, the Book of the Wars of the Lord, the Book of Jasher, the *Book of Mormon*? How could there be all of these missing scriptures if the Bible were perfect and complete? Here are a few scriptures that are mentioned that are not included in the Bible.

> **Example 1:** *Exo. 24:4, 7 – 4. And Moses wrote all the words of the Lord, and rose up early in the morning, and builded an altar under the hill, and twelve pillars, according to the twelve tribes of Israel... 7. And he took the **book of the covenant**, and read in the audience of the people: and they said, All that the Lord hath said will we do, and be obedient.*

> **Example 2:** *Numbers 21:14 – Wherefore it is said in the **book of the wars of the Lord**, What he did in the Red Sea, and in the **books of Arnon**.*

> **Example 3:** *Josh. 10:13 – And the sun stood still, and the moon stayed, until the people had avenged themselves upon their enemies. Is not his written in the **book of Jasher?** So the sun stood still in the midst of heaven, and hasted not to go down about a whole day.*

> **Example 4:** *2 Sam. 1:18 – (Also he bade them teach the children of Judah the use of the bow; behold, it is written in the **book of Jasher**.)*

> **Example 5:** *Ezekiel 37:15-17 – 15. The word of the Lord came again unto me, saying, 16. Moreover, thou son of man, take thee one stick, and write upon it, For Judah, and for the children of Israel his companions: then take another stick, and write upon it, For Joseph, the stick of Ephraim, and for all the house of Israel his companions: 17. And join them one to another into one stick; and they shall become one in thine hand.*

According to Joseph Smith's interpretation, this passage is where Ezekiel prophesies the coming forth of the Bible (the stick of Judah) and the *Book of Mormon* (the stick of Ephraim). In ancient times, according to Joseph Smith's teachings, the prophets wrote on scrolls with sticks on the top and bottom. These ancient scrolls were nicknamed "sticks."

These sticks mentioned by Ezekiel are actual scriptures that contain the inspired word of God. Mormons believe the Bible or *"stick of Judah,"* is the history of the tribe of Judah, and the *Book of Mormon* or *"stick of Ephraim,"* is a history of the tribe of Ephraim. Both are testimonies of the resurrection of Jesus Christ! More can be learned of the *Book of Mormon* and if there is any biblical support in the next chapter.

> **Example 6:** Additional writings of prophets that are mentioned in the Bible, but are not included in the Bible, are the Book of Statutes, Book of the Acts of Solomon, Books of Nathan and Gad, Prophecy of Ahijah and Visions of Iddo, Book of Shemaiah, Book of Jehu, Acts of Uzziah, Written by Isaiah, Saying of the Seers, other missing epistles of Paul, missing epistle of Jude, and the Prophecies of Enoch.

> **Example 7:** Another important missing scripture that is not included in the Bible is the **book of the prophet Esaias!** This book is important in that Jesus himself read out of it!

*Luke 4:17-20 – 17. And there was delivered unto him the **book of the prophet Esaias,** and when he had opened the book, he found the place where it was written, 18. The Spirit of the Lord is upon me, because he hath anointed me to preach the gospel to the poor; he hath sent me to heal the broken-hearted, to preach deliverance to the captives, and recovering of sight to the blind, to set at liberty them that are bruised, 19. To preach the acceptable year of the Lord.*

Question: How can the Bible be complete when there are so many missing scriptures that were used by the religious leaders, prophets, and even Christ?

Question: Where in the Bible does it state that the Bible is complete?

All Scriptures Are Acceptable. The apostle Timothy taught a very important concept about "all scripture." One must understand that when Timothy made this statement, the Bible was not yet in existence. The religious leaders of the time taught out of the writings of the prophets. Many of those writings are contained in the Bible, and many are mentioned here in **Examples 1- 7.** Therefore, from Timothy's teachings we learn the following:

*2 Tim 3:15-17 – 15. And that from a child thou hast known **the holy scriptures,** which are able to **make thee wise unto salvation** through faith which is in Christ Jesus. 16. **All scripture is given by inspiration of God, and is profitable for doctrine, for reproof, for correction, for instruction in righteousness:** 17. That the man of God may be perfect, thoroughly furnished unto all good works.*

According to Timothy "all scripture" is given by inspiration of God. Therefore, "the stick of Judah" and "the stick of Ephraim", or the **Bible** and the **Book of Mormon,** would be included as scripture and *"is profitable for doctrine, for reproof, for correction, for instruction in righteousness."*

The Biblical Support Chart. With the Christian stated position, pertaining to the perfection and completeness of the Bible one must ask him/herself:

Question: Is the Christian position that "the Bible is perfect and complete" in contradiction with the actual circumstance with the Bible?

Question: Is the Mormon position that "the Bible is the word of God, as far as it is translated correctly" in contradiction with above passages?

THE BIBLICAL SUPPORT CHART

Is the following topic supported in the Bible?	Yes or No
Does the Bible support Joseph Smith's teaching that we believe that "the Bible is the word of God as long as it is translated correctly?"	Yes
Do the six Biblical contradictions listed in this chapter support Joseph Smith's teaching that there are contradictions in the Bible? (Acts 9:7 & Acts 22:9; 1 Cor 5:9; Matt 27:5 & Acts 1:18; Eph 2:5-9 & Gal 6:7-20; John 10:30 & Gen 1:26,27, Gen 32:30, Acts 7:55,56; John 1:18 & Gen 12:7, Gen 32:30, Ex 24:9-11)	Yes
Do the Bible support Joseph Smith's teaching that there are missing scriptures from the Bible? (Exo 24:4,7; Num 21:14; Josh 10:13; 2 Sam 1:18; Ezek 37:15-17; Luke 4:17-20)	Yes

Author's Note: As of this writing, there has not been a firm scripture presented by the Christian position that states the Bible is perfect and complete, or that the Mormons are incorrect to believe that there can be more scripture. The closest scripture quoted that would suggest that there were to be no more scripture, is John's final statement in Revelation.

> *Rev 22:18 – For I testify unto every man that heareth the words of the prophecy of this book,* ***If any man shall add unto these things, God shall add unto him the plagues that are written in this book:***

Many Christians use this statement by John to dispel the existence of any new scripture like the ***Book of Mormon.*** In reality, the meaning of this passage is taken out of context and misinterpreted by the Christian leaders. The setting for the Book of Revelation was when the apostle John was on the island Patmos. He received this revelation long before the Bible was compiled. Therefore, John warned against adding to the "words of the prophecy of this book" meaning that it pertains to the Book of Revelation only. Not the Bible.

To support Joseph Smith's interpretation of this a similar statement was made by Moses in Deuteronomy.

> *Deuteronomy 4:2 –* ***Ye shall not add unto the word which I command you,*** *neither shall ye diminish ought from it, that ye may keep the commandments of the Lord your God which I command you.*

If the same Christian interpretation of John's Revelation passage is applied to this passage, then every word between Deuteronomy and the end of Revelation would have to be discounted from the Bible and not used. If these teachings are from man, then one must be aware of the following teachings of Paul. In explaining the organization of the church to the Ephesians, he said:

> *Ephesians 4:11-14 – 11.* ***And he gave some, apostles, and some, prophets;*** *and some evangelists; and some, pastors and teachers; 12.* ***For the perfecting of the saints, for the work of the ministry, for the edifying of the body of Christ: 13. Till we all come in the unity of the faith, and of the knowledge of the Son of God,*** *unto a perfect man, unto the measure of the stature of the* ***fullness of Christ.*** *14. That we henceforth be no more children, tossed to and fro, and carried about with every wind of doctrine,* ***by the sleight of men, and cunning craftiness, whereby they lie in wait to deceive;***

Paul was very clear that apostles and prophets were given for the specific purpose of perfecting the saints "*til we all come in the unity of the faith, and the knowledge of the Son of God.*"

NOTES

CHAPTER 8

THE BOOK OF MORMON

According to the Mormons, one of the major accomplishments of the Prophet Joseph Smith was the bringing forth of *The Book of Mormon.* After the visit of God the Father and his Son Jesus Christ to Joseph Smith, an angel named Moroni, was sent to Joseph Smith. This angel Moroni showed Joseph Smith where a set of "golden plates" was buried in a stone box. Each year for four years, Joseph Smith went to the place where the "golden plates" were buried. Each visit the angel Moroni would teach Joseph Smith more about the "golden plates" and his mission in bringing these plates to the world.

During the fourth visit, the angel Moroni gave Joseph Smith the plates to be translated. With the power of God Joseph Smith translated the plates and eventually published them. During these years, Joseph Smith learned that Moroni was a prophet from the period around 521 AD. It was Moroni's father, Mormon, who had compiled the writings of many American prophets from approximately 600 BC to his time in approximately 500 AD on this particular set of "gold plates."

The Book of Mormon is the history of an ancient civilization in the Central American region. It contains the major writings of the prophets and kings that lived through this thousand-year period. It relates the history of how several different white races from the Middle East came from Jerusalem to live in the Americas. *The Book of Mormon* includes their religious beliefs, their wars, trials, and tribulations. It also tells of how Jesus Christ, as a resurrected being, visited the people in the Americas and established His church. This history also includes the total demise of the white population by the Indian population.

The angel Moroni, Mormon's son, was the last person to write on the gold plates and Moroni hid them up in the ground until he came back, approximately 1,300 years later, as a messenger from God to give them to Joseph Smith for translation and publication.

The Mormons believe *The Book of Mormon* is a second divine witness of Jesus Christ our Saviour. The first witness being the Holy Bible. They believe *The Book of Mormon* is the word of God as is the Bible. Before *The Book of Mormon,* there had never been the idea that Jesus Christ had visited the Americas or set up his church in another area besides the Middle East.

The Christian Stand on *The Book of Mormon*. The general consensus in the Christian world is quite contrary to what Joseph Smith claims. These positions are:

>**Position 1:** There is no biblical support for *The Book of Mormon*. The belief stems from one passage by the apostle John in Revelation.

>*Revelation 22:18 – For I testify unto every man that heareth the words of the prophecy of this book, **If any man shall add unto these things, God shall add unto him the plagues that are written in this book:***

Biblical Support for *The Book of Mormon*. In the Bible it was taught by the apostle Paul that more than one witness would establish everything pertaining to God's word and Christ's gospel.

>*II Corinthians 13:1 – This is the third time I am coming to you. **In the mouth of two or three witnesses shall every word be established.***

The Mormons believe *The Book of Mormon* is a second witness of Jesus Christ, His death, His resurrection, and His role as our savior. An important Biblical passage that supports the coming forth of the *Book of Mormon* is in Ezekiel.

Ezekiel 37:15-18 – 15. The word of the Lord came again unto me saying, 16. Moreover, thou son of man, take thee one stick, and write upon it, for Judah, and for the children of Israel his companions: then take another stick, and write upon it, **for Joseph, the stick of Ephraim, and for all the house of Israel his companions: 17. And join them one to another into one stick; and they shall become one in thine hand.**

According to the Mormons, this is a prophecy come true. *The Book of Mormon* is the history of the linage of Ephraim, the second son of Joseph and the Bible is the history of Judah, also a tribe of Israel. With realization of *The Bible* and *The Book of Mormon,* they are two witnesses—both in our hands, testifying of Christ's divinity!

Another prophecy from *The Bible* is when Isaiah was talking about the descendants of Ephraim and that they shall speak out of the dust. Ephraim was the second son of Joseph.

Isaiah 29:1-4 – 4. And thou shalt be brought down, **and shalt speak out of the ground, and thy speech shall be low out of the dust,** *and thy voice shall be, as of one that hath a familiar spirit, out of the ground, and thy speech shall whisper out of the dust.*

The plates of gold that Joseph Smith was given were buried in the ground. Joseph Smith was given those plates and by the power of God fulfilled this prophecy of Isaiah – the lineage of Ephraim "spoke out of the dust." The spirit from *The Book of Mormon* is "one that has a familiar spirit" to *The Bible* – they both testify of Jesus Christ's role as our Saviour!

Supporting Isaiah's prophecy of "speaking out of the dust", the following passage is found in Psalm.

Psalms 85:11 – **Truth shall spring out of the earth;** *and righteousness shall look down from heaven.*

Shortly before His crucifixion, Jesus Christ himself told us that he has other sheep, which were not of the lineage of Israel that he must go and teach his gospel. Then He would have these two cultures as one fold, under His leadership.

John 10:16 – **And other sheep I have, which are not of this fold:** *them also I must bring, and they shall hear my voice; and there shall be one fold, and one shepherd.*

Question: Who are these other sheep?

From *The Book of Mormon* we learn that the people in the Americas were the **"other sheep"** that Christ spoke about in John. After Christ's ascension into heaven, Christ came to the people in the Americas and set up His church to be one fold. This is what Christ told His sheep in the Americas.

3 Nephi 15:21 – 21. And verily I say unto you, that **ye are they of whom I said: Other sheep I have which are not of this fold; them also I must bring, and they shall hear my voice; and there shall be one fold, and one shepherd.**

Towards the end of His visit to the people of *The Book of Mormon,* Christ again stated that He had even "other sheep" that He must take His word to and teach.

3 Nephi 16:1-3 – And verily, verily, I say unto you that **I have other sheep which are not of this land, neither of the land of Jerusalem,** *neither in any parts of that land round about whither I have been to minister. 2. For they of whom I speak are they who have not as yet heard my voice; neither have I at any time manifested myself unto them. 3.* **But I have received a commandment of the Father that I shall go unto them,** *and that they shall hear my voice, and shall be numbered*

> *among my sheep, that there may be one fold and one shepherd; therefore I go to show myself unto them.*

Referring back to ***The Bible,*** Christ again spoke about how He was not just sent to "the lost sheep of Israel."

> *Matthew 15:24 – But he answered and said, **I am not sent but unto the lost sheep of the house of Israel.***

Here, Christ infers that he has other sheep that he must visit.

Question: Did Jesus Christ go and visit other lost tribes on this earth?

Other Biblical Support for "lost sheep." Additional Biblical support for the "lost sheep" theory begins in Genesis.

> *Genesis 11:8 – **So the Lord scattered them abroad from thence upon the face of all the earth…***

This is when the God of the Old Testament scattered His children over all the continents. This passage supports the need for Christ having to go to other *"lost sheep, not of the fold of Israel"* and establishing His gospel.

The Bible also supports the fact that the lineage of Ephraim will become greater than his older brother's lineage.

> *Genesis 48:15-19 – 15. And he blessed Joseph, and said…19. And his father refused, and said, I know it, my son, I know it; he also shall become a people, and he shall be great: **but truly his younger brother shall be greater than he, and his seed shall become a multitude of nations.***

Again, Joseph lineage is prophesied to become great.

> *Genesis 49:22-26 – Joseph is a fruitful bough, even a fruitful bough by a well; **whose branches run over the wall:** …*

In Deuteronomy, the land of Joseph is also be blessed.

> *Deuteronomy 33:13-16 – **And of Joseph he said, Blessed of the Lord be his land,** for the precious things of heaven, for the dew, and for the deep that coucheth beneath, 14. And for the precious fruits brought forth by the sun, and for the precious things put forth by the moon, 15. And for the chief things of the ancient mountains, and for the precious things of the lasting hills, 16. And for the precious things of the earth and fullness thereof, and for the good will of him that dwelt in the bush: let the blessing come upon the head of Joseph, and upon the top of the head of him that was separated from his brethren.*

It is common knowledge that the land of the Americas is a very blessed land!

1. Not only did ***The Bible*** testify that the posterity of Joseph and the land that they inhabited would be great, it also testified that this land would be overseas!

> *Isaiah 16:8 – For the fields of Heshbon languish, and the vine of Sibmah: the lords of the heathen have broken down the principal plants thereof, they are come even unto Jazer, **they wandered through the wilderness: her branches are stretched out, they are gone over the sea.***

The Book of Mormon relates the history of a family out of Israel going into the wilderness, building a boat and sailing to a new land that was *"over the sea."*

2. According to Joseph Smith, another prophecy came true from Isaiah.

> Isaiah 29:11,12 – *11. And the vision of all is become unto you as the words of a book that is sealed, which men deliver to one that is learned, saying, **Read this, I pray thee: and he saith, I cannot; for it is sealed:** 12. And the book is delivered to him that is not learned, saying, Read this, I pray thee: and he saith, I am not learned.*

Joseph Smith had a very similar occurrence while he had possession of the gold plates. Approximately two thirds of the gold plates were sealed, prompting a scholar to repeat the words from Isaiah.

3. Another biblical passage that supports the importance of ***The Book of Mormon*** is in Timothy.

> 2 Timothy 3:15-17 – *15. And that from a child thou hast known the holy scriptures, which are able to make thee wise unto salvation through faith which is in Christ Jesus. 16. **All scripture is given by inspiration of God, and is profitable for doctrine, for reproof, for correction, for instruction in righteousness:** 17. That the man of God may be perfect, thoroughly furnished unto all good works.*

At the time this was written by Timothy there was no *Bible*. The religious leaders read from the individual writings of prophets. Timothy is stating that all these sacred writings were given by inspiration of God. A list of other scriptures included in Timothy's statement are found in the first chapter, "The Bible – Perfect and Complete?" Nowhere in these writings does it state that there cannot be any more sacred scriptures come forth, except in Revelation 22:18.

The Mormon Position on Revelation 22:18.

> Revelation 22:18 – *For I testify unto every man that heareth the words of the prophecy of this book, **If any man shall add unto these things, God shall add unto him the plagues that are written in this book:***

4. The Mormon's believe that John's statement was speaking specifically for the book of Revelation, not the Bible in its entirety. John was on the island of Patmos when this was written. After the Revelation was written, John wrote other epistles and letters as did the other apostles that are included in the *Bible*. If the Christian interpretation is used, all epistles written after the Book of Revelation, should not be included into the Bible.

The Mormon interpretation of John's statement is also supported in Deuteronomy. Moses is speaking about his writings.

> Deuteronomy 4:2 – *Ye shall not add unto the word which I command you, neither shall ye diminish ought from it, that ye may keep the commandments of the Lord your God which I command you.*

Saying basically the same thing as John, Moses commanded that nothing "*shall*" be added to his commandments. If the Christian interpretation were to be used, then the statement by Moses would prevail and nothing past the book of Deuteronomy would be allowed to be used as scripture! Therefore, the *Bible* would only contain the books of Genesis, Exodus, Leviticus, Numbers, and Deuteronomy.

The Biblical Support Chart. The Christian position is that there can be no other scripture other than the current *Bible* and that there is no biblical support for the *Book of Mormon*.

Question: Other than Revelation 22:18—Where is the Christian biblical support that denies the existence of the Book of Mormon and that Jesus Christ did not visit other people after His crucifixion?

The claims of Joseph Smith in relation to the *Book of Mormon* do have the support of the *Bible*.

THE BIBLICAL SUPPORT CHART	
Is the following topic supported in the Bible?	**Yes or No**
Does the Bible support Joseph Smith's claim that the Book of Mormon came out of the ground? (Isa 29:1-4; Psalms 85:11)	Yes
Does the Bible support Joseph Smith's claim that the Book of Mormon could have been sealed? (Isa 29:11,12)	Yes
Does the Bible support Joseph Smith's claim that the Book of Mormon could be another scripture? (2 Tim 3:15-17)	Yes
Does the Bible support the claim that a book will be written that contains the history of the tribe of Judah, one of the twelve tribes of Israel? (Ezk 37:15-18)	Yes
Does the Bible support Joseph Smith's claim that the Book of Mormon is the history of tribe of Ephraim, one of the twelve tribes of Israel? (Ezk 37:15-18)	Yes
Does the Bible support the claim of the Book of Mormon that it contains the history of a family from Jerusalem that went across the ocean to another land? (Gen 11:8; Gen 48:15-19; Gen 49:22-26; Deut 33:13-16; Isa 16:8)	Yes
Does the Bible support the Book of Mormon's account of Jesus Christ visiting the people in the Americas? (Matt 15:24; John 10:16)	Yes

Author's Note: This note is especially made to the non-members of the Church of Jesus Christ of Latter Day Saints. As much as I wish that the explanations of the teachings in this particular book would be enough to sway a person's desire to know by wisdom and common sense that these things are spiritually true, I do not kid myself into believing that these writings will spiritually convert a wise man/woman. What is true is what the Lord and the angel Moroni have said about the *Book of Mormon*. The Lord testifies:

> *D&C 17:5,6 – 5. And ye shall testify that you have seen them (golden plates), even as my servant Joseph Smith, Jun., has seen them; for it is by my power that he has seen them, and it is because he had faith. 6. And he has translated the book, even that part which I have commanded him,* **and as your Lord and your God liveth it is true.**

> *D&C 20:8-12 – 8. And gave him power from on high, by the means which were before prepared, to translate the Book of Mormon; 9.* **Which contains a record of a fallen people, and the fullness of the gospel of Jesus Christ to the Gentiles and to the Jews also; 10. Which was given by inspiration, and is confirmed to others by the ministering of angels, and is declared unto the world by them—11. Proving to the world that the holy scriptures are true, and that God does inspire men and call them to his holy work in this age and generation, as well as in generations of old; 12. Thereby showing that he is the same God yesterday, today, and forever. Amen.**

The angel Moroni gives a promise to those who are sincere in knowing if the *Book of Mormon* and "the fullness of the gospel of Jesus Christ" are true.

> *Moroni 10:3-5 – 3. Behold, I would exhort you that when ye shall read these things, if it be wisdom in God that ye should read them, that ye would remember how merciful the Lord hath been unto the children of men, from the creation of Adam even down until the time that ye shall receive these things, and ponder it in your hearts. 4.* **And when ye shall receive these things, I would exhort you that ye would ask God, the Eternal Father, in the name of Christ, if these things are not true; and if ye shall ask with a sincere heart, with real intent, having faith in Christ, he will manifest the truth of it unto your, by the power of the Holy Ghost. 5. And by the power of the Holy Ghost ye may know the truth of all things.**

For those who actually follow Moroni's promise the Lord has said:

> *D&C 20:14,15 – 14.* **And those who receive it in faith, and work righteousness, shall receive a crown of eternal life.**

NOTES

PART III: GOD AND SALVATION

CHAPTER 9

THE PERSONALITY OF GOD THE FATHER AND JESUS CHRIST

In **Chapter 7 – The Bible,** one of the errors that exist in the Bible, Example 5, revealed that the personality of God the Father, Jesus Christ, and the Holy Ghost as interpreted by several different churches was a contradiction. The chapter brought up the possibility that knowing the real personality of our Heavenly Father and His son Jesus Christ is critical to ones own eternal salvation. John taught that:

> *John 17:3 – And this is life eternal, that they might know thee the only true God; and Jesus Christ, whom thou hast sent.*

Question: How could misunderstanding the actual personality of God and Jesus Christ affect a person's eternal salvation?

> *Matthew 7:13,14 – 13. **Enter ye in at the strait gate:** for wide is the gate, and broad is the way, that leadeth to destruction, and many there be which go in thereat: 14. **Because strait is the gate, and narrow is the way, which leadeth unto life, and few there be that find it.***

> *Matthew 7:21 – Not every one that saith unto me, Lord, Lord, shall enter into the kingdom of heaven; **but he that doeth the will of my Father which is in heaven.***

It is clear that the gate that leads to eternal life is *"straight and narrow"* and few are going to find it. Therefore, knowing the real God the Father and Jesus Christ and how they actually exist is a deciding factor as to one's opportunity to enter into eternal life. It is critical to a person's eternal salvation to know the real God the Father and Jesus Christ.

Recognizing the fact that a person's knowledge of God the Father and Jesus Christ is eternally important, a comparative study will be made into who is the real God the Father and who is Jesus Christ. The various topics studied will be:

1. What is the personality of God and Jesus Christ?
2. Are God and Jesus Christ one God, or are they two separate Gods?
3. Can man actually see God and Jesus Christ?
4. What is Christ's role?

From this study, one will learn both the general Christian belief and the LDS position on "who are the real God the Father and Jesus Christ." The general Christian position is that they believe in the real God and Jesus of the Bible. Many Christian religion's position is that Joseph Smith and the Mormons actually believe in a different God from the *Bible*—that the Mormons worship "Satan," the "God" of the *Book of Mormon.*

This chapter will be more of a comparative study that will compare the general Christian and the LDS positions on who is God the Father and Jesus Christ. The Biblical Support Chart will help each reader to visualize just how close Joseph Smith teachings are to the real God and Jesus Christ according to the Bible. The chart will help each person to begin to "know" God the Father and Jesus Christ.

1. What is the personality of God and Jesus Christ?

The General Christian Position. Many Christians believe that the personality of God, Jesus Christ, and the Holy Ghost is the following:

> God is not a man. There is only one God. God is an immaterial spirit and invisible. The Father, Son, and Holy Ghost are three uncreated, eternal Persons existing in the same divine nature and sharing all the same divine attributes. The Son is the only Person in the godhead who has joined himself with a created human nature but without undergoing any changes in his divine nature.

Scriptural support for this belief is:

> *Numbers 23:19 –* **God is not a man,** *that he should lie; neither the son of man, that he should repent: hath he said, and shall he not do it? Or hath he spoken, and shall he not make it good:*

> *John 4:24 –* **God is a Spirit:** *and they that worship him must worship him in spirit and truth.*

> *1 Timothy 1:17 – Now unto the King eternal, immortal,* **invisible,** *the only wise God, be honour and glory for ever and ever. Amen.*

The LDS Position. This is Joseph Smith's testimony of whom God the Father and Jesus Christ are:

> *16. …I saw a pillar of light exactly over my head, above the brightness of the sun, which descended gradually until it fell upon me. 17. It no sooner appeared than I found myself delivered from the enemy which held me bound.* **When the light rested upon me I saw two Personages, whose brightness and glory defy all description, standing above me in the air. One of them spake unto me, calling me by name and said, pointing to the other – This is My Beloved Son. Hear Him!** [9]

It is the position of the LDS church that God the Father is a person with a glorified body of flesh and bone, Jesus Christ is a separate person with a glorified body of flesh and bone, and the Holy Ghost is a separate third person that is a spirit, without a body of flesh and bone.

Man Created in the Image of God. One of the **Bible's** first lessons is that man was "*Created in the Image of God.*"

> *Genesis 1:26,27 – And God said,* **Let us** *make man* **in our image, after our likeness:** *and let them have dominion over the fish of the sea, and over the fowl of the air, and over the cattle, and over all the earth, and over every creeping thing that creepeth upon the earth. 27.* **So God created man in his own image,** *in the image of God created he him; male and female created he them.*

In order to consider the fact that God the Father and Jesus Christ are two separate beings, one must listen carefully to what the writer of Genesis was saying: "*Let us make man in our image.*" This passage is definitely stating there is more than one God creating man.

The Random House College Dictionary defines "image" in the following manner:

> **1. a physical likeness or representation of a person,** animal, or thing, photographed, painted, sculptured, or otherwise produced. 2. an optical counterpart or appearance of an object, such as is produced by reflection from a mirror. 3. a mental representation; idea; conception. 4. **form; appearance; semblance;** *God created man in his own image.* **5. counterpart; copy:** *That child is the image of his mother.*

According to the Random House College Dictionary, man, being created in the image of God, would have a physical likeness, be a representation and a copy of God. The general Christian position on this "image" interpretation is that it is "symbolic" and it wasn't what God intended when the passage was written.

Question: If this passage is only symbolic and wasn't intended to mean that God actually looks like man, then what was the author of the book of Genesis speaking of when he said the following, just several chapters after the first chapter of Genesis?

*Genesis 5:1,3 – This is the book of generations of Adam. In the day that **God created man, in the likeness of God** made he him; 3. And Adam lived an hundred and thirty years, **and begat a son in his own likeness, after his image;** and called his name Seth:*

Question: If God did not intend for us to understand that man was created in the image of God, then why did He use the exact same language for describing Adam's son Seth?

Question: Knowing that if Seth was begat after Adam's image, and Seth had a body like Adam, isn't it logical to believe that man was created after God's image, and man has a body like God?

Then again, it is stated that God created man in his image.

*Genesis 9:6 – Whoso sheddeth man's blood, by man shall his blood be shed: **for in the image of God made he man.***

Another scripture that supports the fact that God has a body of flesh and bone is:

*Genesis 6:3 – And the Lord said, My spirit shall not always strive with man, **for that he also is flesh:** yet his days shall be an hundred and twenty years.*

The Lord is stating that his spirit will not also be with man because he is "**also flesh.**"

Question: Who are the players in this passage?

There is only the *"more than one"* God, and Adam and Eve. There are no other players at this time.

Answer: It can only be the God's who created man – are "also" flesh!

The teaching of James also confirmed the fact that man is made in the similitude of God:

*James 3:9 – Therewith bless we God, even the Father; and therewith curse we men, **which are made after the similitude of God.***

Similitude[10], as defined in The Random House College Dictionary means:

1. likeness; resemblance. 2. a person or thing that is like or the match or counterpart of another. 3. a semblance: a similitude of the truth. 4. a likening or comparison; parable or allegory.

Question: Does being created in the image and being made after the similitude of God mean that God has a body of flesh and bone also?

God's Body of Flesh and Bone. The following scriptures are passages supporting the fact that God does indeed have a body.

*Genesis 32:30 – And Jacob called the name of the place Peniel: **for I have seen God face to face, and my life is preserved.***

*Exodus 24:10 – And they saw the God of Israel: and there was **under his feet** as it* *were a paved work of a sapphire stone, and as it were the body of heaven in his clearness.*

*Exodus 33:11 – And **the Lord spake unto Moses face to face,** as a man speaketh unto his friend....*

*Exodus 31:18 – And he gave unto Moses, when he had made an end of communing with him upon mount Sinai, two tables of testimony, tables of stone, written with **the finger of God.***

*Exodus 33:21-23 – And the Lord said, Behold, there is a place by me, and thou shalt stand upon a rock: 22. – And it shall come to pass, while my glory passeth by, that I will put thee in a clift of the rock, and will cover thee with **my hand** while I pass by: 23. And I will take away **mine hand,** and thou shalt see **my back parts:** but **my face** shall not be seen.*

*Numbers 12:7-8 – 7. My servant Moses is not so, who is faithful in all mine house. 8. With him will **I speak mouth to mouth,** even apparently, and not in dark speeches; and the similitude of the Lord shall he behold: wherefore then were ye not afraid to speak against my servant Moses?*

*Deuteronomy 9:10 – And the Lord delivered unto me two tables of stone **written with the finger of God;** and on them was written according to all the words, which the Lord spake with you in the mount out of the midst of the fire in the day of the assembly.*

*Mark 16:19 – So then after the Lord had spoken unto them, he was received up into heaven, and **sat on the right hand of God.***

*Acts 7:55-56 – 55. But he, being full of the Holy Ghost, looked up stedfastly into heaven, and **saw the glory of God, and Jesus standing on the right hand of God,** 56. And said, Behold, I see the heavens opened, **and the Son of man standing on the right hand of God.***

*Matthew 3:16, 17 – And Jesus, when he was baptized, went up straightway out of the water: and, lo, the heavens were opened unto him, and he saw the Spirit of God descending like a dove, and lighting upon him: 17. And lo **a voice from heaven,** saying, This is my beloved Son, in whom I am well pleased.*

*Matthew 4:4 – But he answered and said, It is written, Man shall not live by bread alone, but by every word that proceedeth out of **the mouth of God.***

*Matthew 17:5 – While he yet spake, behold, a bright cloud overshadowed them: and behold **a voice out of the cloud,** which said, This is my beloved Son, in whom I am well pleased; hear ye him.*

*Hebrews 1:3 – Who being the brightness of his glory, and the express image of his person, and upholding all things by the word of his power, when he had by himself purged our sins, **sat down on the right hand of the Majesty on high;***

*Revelations 22:4 – **And they shall see his face;** and his name shall be in their foreheads.*

From these passages, we learn that God has at least one finger, hands, back parts, face, mouth, a right hand, and a derriere (needed for sitting).

Luke 24:36-40 – And as they thus spake, Jesus himself stood in the midst of them, and saith unto them, Peace be unto you. 37. But they were terrified and affrighted, and supposed that they had seen a spirit. 38. And he said unto them, Why are ye

> *troubled: and why do thoughts arise in your hearts: 39. Behold my hands and my*
> *feet, that it is I myself: **handle me, and see; for a spirit hath not flesh and***
> ***bones, as ye see me have.** 40. And when he had thus spoken, he shewed them his*
> *hands and his feet.*

From Christ's resurrected visit to the apostles, we learn that he has his entire body. When the apostles were "supposing" they had seen a spirit, Christ quickly corrected those thoughts by having them "handle him, his body of flesh and bone" and said **"handle me, and see; for a spirit hath not flesh and bones, as ye see me have."**

   Question: If Christ is a spirit, as some Christians believe, would have Christ so quickly corrected the apostle's thoughts of having seen a spirit?

Then Paul taught that when the Savior comes, He will change our vile bodies to be like His new glorious body which is a glorified resurrected body.

> *Philippians 3:20, 21 – For our conversation is in heaven; from whence also we look*
> *for the Saviour, the Lord Jesus Christ: 21. **Who shall change our vile body, that***
> ***it may be fashioned like unto his glorious body,** according to the working*
> *whereby he is able even to subdue all things unto himself.*

> *1 John 3:2 – Beloved, now are we the sons of God, and it doth not yet appear what*
> *we shall be: but we know that, when he shall appear, **we shall be like him;** for we*
> *shall see him as he is.*

We learn that after the coming of Christ, we will be like Christ. This also means that we will be like God the Father. After Christ was resurrected, the apostle Paul taught that Christ was also in the image of our Heavenly Father.

> *2 Cor 4:4 – In whom the god of this world hath blinded the minds of them which*
> *believe not, lest the light of the glorious gospel of Christ, **who is the image of God,***
> *should shine unto them.*

> *Philippians 2:6 – **Who, being in the form of God,** thought it not robbery to be*
> *equal with God:*

> *Colossians 1:14, 15 – In whom we have redemption through his blood, even the*
> *forgiveness of sins; 15. **Who is the image of the invisible God,** the firstborn of*
> *every creature:*

The Christian's position that God, Jesus Christ, and the Holy Ghost are all one God and do not have bodies of flesh and bone contradicts what is taught elsewhere in the Bible. Joseph Smith, having seen God the Father and Jesus Christ has found to be "in unity with the Bible."

2. Are God and Jesus Christ one God, or are they two separate Gods?

The General Christian Position. Many Christians believe that the personality of God, Jesus Christ, and the Holy Ghost is the following:

There is only one God. The Father, Son, and Holy Ghost are three uncreated, eternal Persons existing in the same divine nature and sharing all the same divine attributes. The Son is the only Person in the godhead who has joined himself with a created human nature but without undergoing any changes in his divine nature.

The scriptural support for this interpretation is:

> *John 10:30 – **I and my Father are one.***

> *Isaiah 43:10-11 – Ye are my witnesses, saith the Lord, and my servant whom I have*
> *chosen: that ye may know and believe me, and understand that I am he: **before me***

there was no God formed, neither shall there be after me. 11. I, even I, am
the Lord; and beside me there is no saviour.

Isaiah 44:6 – Thus saith the Lord the King of Israel, and his redeemer the Lord of
hosts; I am the first, and I am the last; and beside me there is no God.

Isaiah 45:21-23 – Tell ye, and bring them near; yea, let them take counsel together:
who hath declared this from ancient time? Who hath told it from that time? have
not I the Lord? And there is no God else beside me; a just God and a Saviour;
there is none beside me. 22. Look unto me, and be ye saved, all the ends of the
earth: for I am God, and there is none else. 23. I have sworn by myself, the
word is gone out of my mouth in righteousness, and shall not return, That unto me
every knee shall bow, every tongue shall swear.

The LDS Position. This is Joseph Smith's testimony of who God the Father and Jesus
Christ are:

> *16. …I saw a pillar of light exactly over my head, above the brightness of the sun,*
> *which descended gradually until it fell upon me. 17. It no sooner appeared than I*
> *found myself delivered from the enemy which held me bound. When the light rested*
> *upon me I saw two Personages, whose brightness and glory defy all description,*
> *standing above me in the air. One of them spake unto me, calling me by name and*
> *said, pointing to the other – This is My Beloved Son.. Hear Him!*[11]

It is the position of the LDS church that God the Father, Jesus Christ, and the Holy Ghost
are three separate and distinct persons. Joseph Smith's testimony is that he saw and talked
to God the Father and Jesus Christ, and that they are two distinct persons, each having their
own glorified bodies of flesh and bone.

> **Question: Having these two entirely different opinions about God, which interpre-**
> **tation is correct?**

> **Question: Which interpretation does the Bible support?**

> **Question: Knowing now that the Bible is not complete and perfect, how will this**
> **affect the two conflicting beliefs?**

> **Question: Is the Christian teaching of "God is not a man…an immaterial spirit and**
> **invisible" another contradiction in the Bible?**

Interpretation Discussion. With the two different interpretations from the Christians and
the Mormons, there is biblical support for both beliefs. This support for both creates a biblical
contradiction with a doctrine that could be eternally critical for many. A closer look at what
John and many other prophets have said about God the Father and Jesus Christ being one
will reveal that, according to the Bible, there is no contradiction. John explains the concept
of being one in the following passages.

> *John 17:11 – And now I am no more in the world, but these are in the world, and*
> *I come to thee, Holy Father, keep through thine own name those whom thou hast*
> *given me, that they may be one, as we are.*

> *John 17:20-22 – Neither pray I for these alone, for them also which shall believe on*
> *me through their word; 21. That they all may be one; as thou, Father, art in*
> *me, and I in thee, that they also may be one in us: that the world may believe*
> *that thou hast sent me. 22. And the glory which thou gavest me I have given them;*
> *that they may be one, even as we are one: 23. I in them, and thou in me,*
> *that they may be made perfect in one; and that the world may know that thou*
> *hast sent me, and hast loved them, as thou hast loved me.*

It is clear that Christ wants all his disciples to be one like He and the Father are one.

Question: How can all of us be one?

Paul also teaches that everyone who is joined unto Christ is one.

> *1 Cor. 6:17 – **But he that is joined unto the Lord is one spirit.***

To understand what John meant when he said the following:

> *John 10:30 – **I and my Father are one.***

One must understand who He was talking about. Christ, throughout chapter 10, was speaking about His sheep, how the sheep listen to His voice, how He knew them, and how He gives them eternal life. Then in chapter 17, John is relating Christ's prayer to his Father. In this prayer, Christ is telling His Father of the faithfulness of His servants here, the apostles and other members of his church. He asks his Holy Father to *"keep through his own name those whom He hast given to Christ, **that they may be one, as they are one.***"

Not only once did Christ pray for his special followers "to be one like He and the Father are one", He requested it four different times.

Question: Why, if the Father and Christ were one, would Christ being praying to the Father, requesting that his special followers to be one with them?

Question: How, according to the Christians, can all of Christ's special followers be one with the Father and Christ, when we know that at the time of this request, they were living beings?

Question: How are God and Christ one?

The LDS interpretation of this concept is that God the Father and Jesus Christ are "one in purpose." This purpose is to:

> *Moses 1:39 – For behold, this is my work and my glory—**to bring to pass the immortality and eternal life of man.***

Question: How can we be one with the Father and Jesus Christ?

As in John chapters 10 and 17, Christ was talking about His sheep doing His will. It is in essence, missionary work. The spreading the gospel of Jesus Christ to the entire world is how we can become one with the Father and Jesus Christ.

Another passage in the Bible that portrays the Godhead as three distinct personages is the actual baptism of Jesus Christ.

> *Matt 3:16, 17 – **And Jesus, when he was baptized, went up straightway out of the water:** and, lo, the heavens were opened unto him, and he saw the **Spirit of God descending like a dove,** and lighting upon him: 17. And lo a voice from heaven, saying, **This is my beloved Son, in whom I am well pleased.***

Here is Jesus Christ himself, coming out of the water, the Spirit of God (which is the Holy Ghost) descending from heaven in the form of a dove, and God the Father, speaking from heaven saying, "This is my beloved Son, in whom I am well pleased."

Question: How can God, Jesus Christ, and the Holy Ghost all be one Spirit, and have all of these bodily parts, be in three different locations, and always have Jesus Christ standing on the right hand of God?

The following passages are quoted because of the distinct separation of our Heavenly Father and his son Jesus Christ:

> *Acts 7:55-56 – 55. But he, being full of the Holy Ghost, looked up stedfastly into heaven, **and saw the glory of God, and Jesus standing on the right hand of God,** 56. And said, Behold, I see the heavens opened, **and the Son of man standing on the right hand of God.***

Peter distinctly saw Jesus Christ standing on the right hand of God.

Question: How can God and Jesus Christ be one, when Peter actually sees two personages?

When Christ prays to His Father, He states the following:

> *John 17:1-5 – These words spake Jesus, and lifted up his eyes to heaven, and said, Father, the hour is come; glorify thy Son, that thy Son also may glorify thee: 2. As thou hast given him power over all flesh, that he should give eternal life to as many as thou hast given him. 3. And this is life eternal, that they might know thee the only true God, and Jesus Christ, whom thou hast sent. 4. I have glorified thee on the earth: I have finished the work which thou gavest me to do. 5. And now, O Father, glorify thou me with thine own self with the glory which I had with thee before the world was.*

Question: Why would Jesus pray to Himself?

Question: Why would Jesus ask the Father to glorify Himself?

Question: If they were one, why would the Father give Christ power over all flesh?

Question: Why would life eternal be to know the only true God, and Jesus Christ?

Question: If they were one, why would the Father send Christ?

Question: Why would the Father give Christ work to do?

Question: Why would Christ be asking God to glorify Him with the glory that He had when he was with God before the world was?

Question: After reading Christ's own words, is God the Father and Jesus Christ one person or two personages?

Paul taught the Hebrews that God spoke to us by his Son, God appointed His Son heir of all things, and by His Son God made the worlds.

> *Hebrews 1:1-2 – 1. God,who at sundry times and in divers manners spake in time past unto the fathers by the prophets, 2. **Hath in these last days spoken unto us by his Son, whom he hath appointed heir of all things, by whom also he made the worlds.***

Paul continues to teach that God was indeed the Father of Christ, and Christ was the Son of the Father.

> *Hebrews 1:5 – For unto which of the angels said he at any time, Thou are my Son, this day have I begotten thee? And again, **I will be to him a Father, and he shall be to me a Son?***

The Christian's position that God, Jesus Christ, and the Holy Ghost are all one God is brought on from Isaiah's teaching that *"there is no other God beside him."* Searching the scriptures even further reveals the multiplicity of Gods is possible.

> *Psalm 136:2 – O give thanks unto **the God of gods:** for his mercy endureth for ever.*

The Christian's believe that they are referring to the Gods made by man, the graven images, the Greek Gods and etc.. This is not particularly so because nowhere in the scriptures has God acknowledged that He even accepts these gods of man. In fact, God is always condemning these graven image gods.

Moses, a prophet who was directly taught *"face to face"* by the God of the Old Testament, also taught the same concept.

> *Deut 10:17 –* **For the Lord your God is God of gods, and Lord of lords,** *a great God, a mighty, and a terrible, which regardeth not persons, nor taketh reward:*

One of the most revealing passages that supports the multiple God theory is:

> *Psalm 82:1,6 –* **God standeth in the congregation of the mighty; he judgeth among the gods.**

This passage is very clear that our God *"stands in the congregation of the mighty and he judgeth among the gods."*

Question: How big is a congregation?

Question: Is there more than one God?

The apostle Paul answers these questions!

> *1 Cor 8:5 – For though there be that are called gods, whether in heaven or in earth,* **(as there be gods many, and lords many,)**

There are many gods, congregations of Gods, but to us, here on earth, there is only one God. The Christian's belief that these gods are the gods made by man, it is seriously doubtful that the God of the Old Testament would *"stand in a congregation of almighties"* and judge with a bunch of pagan, man made gods!

When comparing the Christian's interpretation of there being only one God with what the Bible teaches in other areas, they have a clear contradiction with the Bible.

3. Can Man See God?

The General Christian Position. Many Christians believe that:

> "God is not a man. God is an immaterial spirit and invisible. No man can see God."

Scriptural support for this belief is:

> *John 1:18 –* "**No man hath seen God at any time; the only begotten Son,** *which is in the bosom of the Father, he hath declared him".*

> *1 John 4:12 –* **No man hath seen God at any time.** *If we love one another, God dwelleth in us, and his love is perfected in us.*

> *Colossians 1:15 – Who is the image of the* **invisible God,** *the firstborn of every creature:*

> *Hebrews 11:27 –* **By faith** *he forsook Egypt, not fearing the wrath of the king: for* **he endured, as seeing him who is invisible.**

> *Exodus 33:20 – And he said,* **Thou canst not see my face:** *for there shall no man see me, and live.*

> *1 Timothy 1:17 – Now unto the King eternal, immortal,* **invisible,** *the only wise God, be honour and glory for ever and ever. Amen.*

The LDS Position. This is Joseph Smith's testimony of whom God the Father and Jesus

Christ are:

> 16. ...I saw a pillar of light exactly over my head, above the brightness of the sun, which descended gradually until it fell upon me. 17. It no sooner appeared than I found myself delivered from the enemy which held me bound. When the light rested upon me I saw two Personages, whose brightness and glory defy all description, standing above me in the air. One of them spake unto me, calling me by name and said, pointing to the other – This is My Beloved Son.. Hear Him![12]

It is the position of the LDS church that Joseph Smith actually saw God the Father and his Son, Jesus Christ.

Scriptural Comparison of Interpretations. In the passages that the Christians use to deny the possibility of Joseph Smith's first vision, where God the Father and Jesus Christ appeared to him, John is interpreted as saying *"that no man has seen God."* If this passage was interpreted correctly, then Joseph Smith could not have seen God.

In order to determine the correct interpretation of this passage, a closer study of the Bible will be necessary. This closer look will reveal that over seventy other people on the earth have seen God. A review of the following passages will support this fact:

> *Genesis 12:7 – **And the Lord appeared unto Abram,** and said, Unto thy seed will I give this land: and there builded he an altar unto the Lord, **who appeared unto him.***

> *Genesis 32:30 – And Jacob called the name of the place Peniel: **for I have seen God face to face, and my life is preserved.** (Another witness of seeing God face to face.)*

> *Exodus 24:9-11 – Then went up Moses, and Aaron, Nadab, and Abihu, and seventy of the elders of Israel: 10. **And they saw the God of Israel:** and there was under his feet as it were a paved work of a sapphire stone, and as it were the body of heaven in his clearness. 11. And upon the nobles of the children of Israel he laid not his hand: **also they saw God,** and did eat and drink.*

> *Exodus 33:11 – **And the Lord spake unto Moses face to face,** as a man speaketh unto his friend.*

> *1 Kings 3:5 – In Gibeon **the Lord appeared to Solomon in a dream** by night: and God said, Ask what I shall give thee.*

> *1King 9:2 – **That the Lord appeared to Solomon the second time,** as he had appeared unto him at Gibeon.*

> *Isaiah 6:1-5 – 1. In the year that king Uzziah died **I saw also the Lord sitting upon a throne,** high and lifted up, and his train filled the temple.......5. Then said I, Woe is me! For I am undone; because I am a man of unclean lips, and I dwell in the midst of a people of unclean lips: **for mine eyes have seen the King, the Lord of hosts.***

> *Job 42:5 – I have heard of thee by the hearing of the ear: but **now mine eye seeth thee.***

> *Amos 9:1 – **I saw the Lord standing upon the altar:...***

A common Christian interpretation of these appearances of God to man is that these are all symbolic.

Question: If these appearances were symbolic, then why is Stephen teaching the very

fact that God did appear to Abraham?

> *Acts 7:2 – And he said, Men, brethren, and fathers, hearken;* **The God of glory appeared unto our father Abraham,** *when he was in Mesopotamia, before he dwelt in Charran,*

The apostle Stephen not only saw God and Jesus, he testified that he saw Jesus on the right hand of God, in heaven. Another witness.

> *Acts 7:55-56 – But he, being full of the Holy Ghost, looked up stedfastly into heaven, and* **saw the glory of God, and Jesus standing on the right hand of God,** *56. And said, Behold, I see the heavens opened,* **and the Son of man standing on the right hand of God.**

Question: If the appearances of God to all of these "men of God" are symbolic, then why would the apostles teach that "the God of glory appeared unto our father Abraham?"

Question: If man can not see God, then why did Stephen see Christ on the right hand of God?

John continues to prophesy, in the Book of Revelation, that people in the last days will "see the face of God.

> *Rev 22:3-5 – 4.* **And they shall see his face;** *and his name shall be in their foreheads.*

Question: Is the Christian interpretation of John 1:18 a conflict in the Bible?

Question: How can the Christian interpretation lead one to qualify for "life eternal"?

> *John 17:3 –* **And this is life eternal, that they might know thee the only true God; and Jesus Christ,** *whom thou hast sent.*

Question: With this further Biblical evidence, how does the visit of God the Father and His Son Jesus Christ to Joseph Smith conflict with the *Bible?*

We have the testimonies of over seventy-five "men of God," that they have seen God. Another important account of "men" seeing God is the very appearance of the resurrected Jesus Christ to the Mary Magdalene, the other Mary, and the eleven apostles.

> *John 20:18 – Mary Magdalene came and told the* **disciples that she had seen the Lord,** *and that he had spoken these things unto her.*

> *Matthew 28:9 – And as they went to tell his disciples, behold, Jesus met them, saying, All hail.* **And they came and held him by the feet, and worshipped him.**

> *Luke 24:15-16 – And it came to pass, that, while they communed together and reasoned, Jesus himself drew near, and went with them. 16. But their eyes were holden that they should not know him.*

> *Luke 24:34 – Saying, The Lord is risen indeed, and* **hath appeared to Simon.**

> *1 Corinthians 15:6 – After that, he was seen of above five hundred brethren at once; of whom the greater part remain unto this present, but some are fallen asleep.*

> *1 Corinthians 15:7 – After that, he was seen of James; then of all the apostles.*

> *Acts 26:13-16 – 13. At midday, O king, I saw in the way a light from heaven, above the brightness of the sun, shining round about me and them which journeyed with me. 14. And when we were all fallen to the earth, I heard a voice speaking*

*unto me, and saying in the Hebrew tongue, Saul, Saul, why persecutest thou me: it is hard for thee to kick against the pricks. 15. And I said, Who art thou, Lord? And he said, I am Jesus whom thou persecutest. 16. But rise, and stand upon thy feet: for **I have appeared unto thee** for this purpose, to make thee a minister and a witness both of these things which thou hast seen, and of those things in the which I will appear unto thee;*

*John 20:24-29 – 24. But Thomas, one of the twelve, called Didymus, was not with them when Jesus came. 25. The other disciples therefore said unto him, **We have seen the Lord.** But he said unto them, Except I shall see in his hands the print of the nails, and put my finger into the print of the nails, and thrust my hand into his side, I will not believe. 26. And after eight days again his disciples were within, and Thomas with them: **then came Jesus,** the doors being shut, and **stood in the midst,** and said, Peace be unto you. 27. Then saith he to Thomas, Reach hither thy finger, and behold my hands; and reach hither thy hand, and thrust it into my side: and **be not faithless, but believing.** 28. And Thomas answered and said unto him, My Lord and my God. 29. Jesus saith unto him, **Thomas, because thou hast seen me,** thou hast believed: **blessed are they that have not seen, and yet have believed.***

*Luke 24:36-40 – 36. And as they thus spake, **Jesus himself stood in the midst of them** and saith unto them, Peace be unto you. 37. But they were terrified and affrighted, and supposed that they had seen a spirit. 38. And he said unto them, Why are ye troubled? And why do thoughts arise in your hearts: 39. Behold my hands and my feet, that it is I myself: **handle me, and see; for a spirit hath not flesh and bones, as ye see me have.** 40. And when he had thus spoken, **he shewed them his hands and his feet.***

Here we have the people closest to Jesus Christ seeing him and touching him. Jesus Christ himself declaring that he was not a spirit *"for a spirit hath not flesh and bones, as ye see me have."*

The Christian definition of who is Jesus Christ, is that he is a "spirit" the same as "God" and the Holy Ghost, that they are all one.

This interpretation of God and Christ is a definite contradiction in the Bible.

4. Does Jesus Christ have a body of flesh and bones, or is he just a spirit?

The LDS Position. The LDS church believes that if a person is "Quickened by the Spirit" he can see God. Through the modern day prophet, Joseph Smith, we have learned what the passage in John 1:18 means.

*D&C 67:11,12 – For no man has seen God at any time in the flesh, **except quickened by the Spirit of God.** 12. Neither can any natural man abide the presence of God, neither after the carnal mind.*

We learn here that a natural man cannot see God, but if God wants us to see him, he can quicken us in the spirit to see him. After all, God is *"all powerful!"* This concept is also taught in the Bible!

*John 6:46 – "Not that any man hath seen the Father, **save he which is of God, he hath seen the Father."***

John states here that a *"man of God"* can see the Father, thus making Joseph Smith's first vision and the experiences of over 70 men of God in the Bible in unity with the Bible.

When comparing the Christian's interpretation of "no man being able to see God" with what the Bible teaches in other areas, they again have a clear contradiction with the Bible.

5. What is Christ's Role?

The General Christian Position. Many Christian interpret that God the Father and Jesus Christ, and the Holy Ghost are all one. Therefore, God, Jesus Christ, and the Holy Ghost are:

- The creators of the earth and heaven.
- The God of the Old Testament.
- The saviour of all mankind.
- The judge of all mankind.

Joseph Smith's Position. From the personal teachings from Jesus Christ, Joseph Smith learned that:

- Christ created this earth.
- Christ was the God of the Old Testament.
- Christ is the saviour of all mankind.
- Christ is to be our judge.

Scriptural Comparison of Interpretations.

Christ as the Creator. One of the strongest scriptural passages that shows that Christ is the creator of this world is in John.

> John 1:1-3, 14 – In the beginning was the **Word, and the Word was with God, and the Word was God. 2. The same was in the beginning with God.** 3. All things were made by him; and without him was not any thing made that was made.

John teaches three important principles that we have discussed in this chapter. These are:

1. The Word was with God.
2. The Word was God.
3. The Word was in the beginning with God.
4. All things were made by Him.

An important factor in this passage is that the Word spoken of by John was actually Jesus Christ. In order to understand this passage better, replace the **"the Word"** with **"Christ."**

> John 1:1-3, 14 – In the beginning was **"Christ,"** and **"Christ"** was with God, and **"Christ"** was God. 2. The same (**Christ**) was in the beginning with God. 3. All things were made by him (**Christ**); and without him (**Christ**) was not any thing made that was made.

If there is still some doubt that Christ was the "Word," and that Christ was with God, and Christ was God, and Christ was in the beginning with God, and Christ created all things, then the following passage should clarify who the "Word" really is:

> John 1:14 – **And the Word was made flesh, and dwelt among us,** (and we beheld his glory, the glory as of the only begotten of the Father), full of grace and truth.

Question: Who was made flesh and dwelt among us?

Question: Who is the only begotten of the Father?

Question: Who is the creator of all things?

The answer is Jesus Christ! Jesus Christ was with God! In order to better visualize this concept, take this same passage and replace *"the Word"* with *"Christ:"*

> *John 1:14 – And **Christ** was made flesh, and dwelt among us, (and we beheld his (Christ's) glory, the glory as of the only begotten (Christ) of the Father,) full of grace and truth.*

Since the *"Word"* is *"Jesus Christ"* then we also have two separate Gods – Christ was with God and Christ was God, and we have Christ being the creator of all things.

Not only did John teach this concept to the Saints, Paul also understood the same concept when he taught the Hebrews:

> *Hebrews 1:1-3 – God, who at sundry times and in divers manners spake in time past unto the fathers by the prophets, 2. Hath in these last days spoken unto us by his Son, whom he hath appointed heir of all things, **by whom also he made the worlds;***

Here we have a second apostle stating that through Christ, God made the worlds. Not only did Paul teach this concept here, he also mentioned it again to the Hebrews, the Colossians, and to the Ephesians:

> *Hebrews 11:3 – Through faith we understand that **the worlds** were framed by the word of God, so that things which are seen were not made of things which do appear.*

> *Colossians 1:16 – **For by him were all things created,** that are in heaven, and that are in earth, visible and invisible, whether they be thrones, or dominions, or principalities, or powers: all things were created by him, and for him:*

> *Ephesians 3:21 – Unto him be glory in the church by Christ Jesus throughout all ages, **world without end.** Amen.*

A change of the subject: But we see mention that the Son "Made the Worlds" and Jesus Christ is "world without end."

Question: Is this concept "world without end" one of the secrets that God talks about that He will reveal to His prophets?

With apostles and prophets, the LDS church knows the meaning of these plural "Worlds" that Christ created.

Question: If one does not know the concept of who created the earth and how many worlds did he actually create, then, is this person being tossed to and fro by deceitful people and churches?

The Bible clearly distinguishes that Jesus Christ made the worlds. Thus far, there has been no scriptural mention of the Holy Ghost being involved in the creation of the World. Since the Christians clearly believe that God, Jesus Christ, and the Holy Ghost are one and they all made the world, then their belief is again in contradiction to the Bible.

6. Who is our Saviour and who is the God of the Old Testament?

The General Christian Position. Many Christians believe that God the Father, Jesus Christ, and the Holy Ghost are the Saviour of the World and also the God of the Old Testament. The Christians use Isaiah as one of their biggest supporters of the "three in one God theory".

> *Isaiah 43:10,11 – 10. Ye are my witnesses, saith the Lord, and my servant whom I have chosen: that ye may know and believe me, and understand that I am he: before me there was not God formed, neither shall there be after me. 11. **I, even I, am the Lord; and beside me there is no saviour.***

Isaiah 44:6 – Thus saith the Lord the King of Israel, and his redeemer the Lord of hosts; **I am the first, and I am the last; and beside me there is no God.**

Isaiah 45:21-23 – 21. Tell ye, and bring them near; yea, let them take counsel together: who hath declared this from ancient time: who hath told it from that time? Have not I the Lord? **And there is no God else beside me; a just God and a Saviour; there is none beside me.** *22. Look unto me, and be ye saved, all the ends of the earth: for I am God, and there is none else. 23. I have sworn by myself, the word is gone out of my mouth in righteousness, and shall not return, That unto me every knee shall bow, and every tongue shall swear.*

Joseph Smith's Position. Again, through personal training from Jesus Christ, Joseph Smith learned that Jesus Christ is our Saviour and was the God of the Old Testament. Jesus Christ was or is Jehovah.

Scriptural Comparison of Interpretations. From the previous passages given in this chapter on the Personality of God the Father and Jesus Christ, we learned that:

1. We were made in the image of God.
2. That God and Jesus Christ have their own glorious bodies.
3. That God and Jesus Christ are two distinct persons, both Gods.
4. That Jesus Christ, not God the Father, made the world.
5. That a man of God can see God.

Question: If these things are true, then how can the statement of Isaiah be true. These doctrines are in conflict with what Isaiah taught?

If you read Isaiah's statement again and compare it with what the Bible teaches elsewhere, then a better understanding comes to light.

Isaiah 43:11 – **I, even I, am the Lord; and beside me there is no saviour.**

Isaiah 45:21 – And there is no God else beside me; a just God and **a Saviour;** *there is none beside me.*

Isaiah teaches here that God is a just God and a Saviour, and *"there is no Saviour beside him."*

The apostles and other prophets have also taught about this subject.

Acts 4:10-12 – 10. Be it known unto you all, and to all the people of Israel, that by the name of Jesus Christ of Nazareth, whom ye crucified, whom God raised from the dead, even by him doth this man stand here before you whole. 11. This is the stone which was set at nought of you builders, which is become the head of the corner. 12. **Neither is there salvation in any other: for there is none other name under heaven given among men, whereby we must be saved.**

Acts 13:23 – Of this man's seed hath God according to his **promise raised unto Israel a Saviour, Jesus:**

Philippians 3:20 – For our conversation is in heaven; from whence also **we look for the Saviour, the Lord Jesus Christ.**

Titus 2:13 – **Looking for that blessed hope, and the glorious appearing of the great God and our Saviour Jesus Christ;**

1 Timothy 4:10 – For therefore we both labour and suffer reproach, because **we trust in the living God, who is the Saviour of all men,** *specially of those that believe.*

From these teachings of the apostles and many more not included here, we learn that Jesus

Christ is the just God who is our Saviour. It is clearly stated in Isaiah that the God of Israel is our Saviour. Our Heavenly Father, who begat Jesus Christ, is neither the Saviour, neither the creator of the world, nor the God of the Old Testament.

Therefore, the Christian position of the combined Godhead, is again contradicting much of the Bible's teachings on the subjects of Jesus Christ as our Saviour and Jesus Christ being the God of Israel.

Christ is to be our judge. Many Christians believe that God the Father, Jesus Christ, and the Holy Ghost as one God is the judge of all mankind. Again, this is much like the past topics of who is our Saviour, who is the God of Israel, and who created this world. The following verse is very explanatory of God the Father's involvement with the judgment and Jesus Christ's involvement with the judgment.

> *John 5:21, 22 – 21. For as the Father raiseth up the dead, and quickeneth them; even so the Son quickeneth whom he will. 22. **For the Father judgeth no man, but hath committed all judgment unto the Son:***

> *John 5:27 – **And hath given him authority to execute judgment also,** because he is the Son of man.*

Question: Why would one God have to establish the fact that he is giving the judgement to his other third?

Question: Where in all the Bible does it state that the Holy Ghost had a part in the creation of the world, being the Saviour, or being our judge?

Again, like in the previous three topics, the Christian belief that God the Father, His Son Jesus Christ, and the Holy Ghost are to be our judge creates a contradiction in the Bible.

Joseph Smith's Interpretation of the Christian's Quoted Scriptures.

The Isaiah quotes used by the Christians for their belief that "God the Father, Jesus Christ, and the Holy Ghost are one" and there is no other God, could support this interpretation when taken out of context of Isaiah and when used alone, without any other passages in the Bible. When put in context with the subject at hand, and other support from the Bible, the Joseph Smith interpretation is clearer. The first scripture to place in full context is Isaiah 43:10,11. A closer look at the real subject is:

> *Isaiah 43:6-9 – 6. I will say to the north, Give up; and to the south, Keep not back: bring my sons from far, and my daughters from the ends of the earth; 7. **Even every one that is called by my name: for I have created him for my glory, I have formed him; yea, I have made him.** 8. Bring forth the blind people that have eyes, and the deaf that have ears. 9. Let all the nations be gathered together, and let the people be assembled: who among them can declare this, and shew us former things: let them bring forth their witnesses, that they may be justified: or let them hear, and say, It is truth.*

The quoted scripture continues as follows:

> *Isaiah 43:10,11 – 10. Ye are my witnesses, saith the Lord, and my servant whom I have chosen: that ye may know and believe me, and understand that I am he: before me there was not God formed, neither shall there be after me. 11. **I, even I, am the Lord; and beside me there is no saviour.***

When placed into true context, the Lord is talking to the people He made, on this earth. To these people the Lord is the only God and Saviour, there is no other God for them. With this interpretation, Joseph Smith is in unity of the Bible.

> *1 Corinthians 8:5, 6 – 5. For though there be that are called Gods, whether in heaven or in earth, (as there be gods many, and lords many,) 6. **But to us there is but one God,** the Father, of whom are all things, and we in him; and one Lord Jesus Christ, by whom are all things, and we by him.*

Knowing that Jesus Christ, the God that created this world and created us, satisfies all potential contradictions that are involved with the three Gods of the Christian's Godhead. This leaves the possibility of other gods out in the universe that have nothing to do with Christ's creations or us.

As these topics are always discussed in the Bible, there are always at least two Gods involved, God the Father and God the only begotten Son of the Father.

The next Isaiah quote used for there being only one God is Isaiah 44:6.

> *Isaiah 44:6 – Thus saith the Lord the King of Israel, and his redeemer the Lord of hosts; **I am the first, and I am the last; and beside me there is no God.***

A look at the full context of the subject is God (Jesus Christ, the Son of God) is talking to Jacob and telling him that the graven images being made by man are all in vain, that he is the only God. Again, this is putting this in direct context to the people on this earth.

> *Isaiah 44:8-10 – 8. Fear ye not, neither be afraid: have not I told thee rom that time, and have declared it: ye are even my witnesses. Is there a God beside me? Yea, there is not God; I know not any. 9. **They that make a graven image are all of them vanity;** and their delectable things shall not profit; and they are their own witnesses; they see not, nor know; that they may be ashamed. 10. **Who hath formed a god, or molten a graven image that is profitable for nothing?***

When Jesus Christ, as the God of the Old Testament, speaks of being the God of the Jews he is speaking with power and authority from God the Father. God the Father gave all that authority to his Son, Jesus Christ.

With the Isaiah quote from Isaiah 45:12, we have the same circumstance as in Isaiah chapter 44. God is talking about his position with the people here on this earth, and their making graven images.

> *Isaiah 45 20 – Assemble yourselves and come; draw near together, ye that are escaped of the nations: **they have not knowledge that set up the wood of their graven image,** and pray unto a god that cannot save.*

Jesus Christ, as the God of the Old Testament, tells these image worshippers that:

> *Isaiah 45:21 – …And there is no God else beside me; a just God and **a Saviour;** there is none beside me.*

The Christian interpretation of three Gods being one God creates a contradiction throughout the *Bible.* If one concept is true then there are many other concepts that are false. This in itself makes the Christian's belief that the Bible is the "perfect and complete" word of God a contradiction.

The Biblical Support Chart. As the Bible teaches – it is critical to one's eternal life to *"**know God and Jesus Christ."***

> *John 17:3 – **And this is life eternal, that they might know thee the only true God; and Jesus Christ,** whom thou hast sent.*

There are some very significant doctrines that Joseph Smith taught that are critical to one's eternal life. It is important to know what kinds of support of these teachings are there in the Bible. The Biblical Support Chart details these different teachings.

THE BIBLICAL SUPPORT CHART

Is the following topic supported in the Bible?	Yes or No
Does the Bible support the teaching that God the Father and His son Jesus Christ each have a body of flesh and bone? (Gen 5:1,3; Gen 9:6; Gen 6:3; James 3:9; Gen 32:30; Exo 24:10; Exo 33:11; Exo 31:18; Exo 33:21-23; Num 12:7,8; Deu 9:10; Mark 16:19; Act 7:55-56; Matt 3:16,17; Matt 4:4; Matt 17:5; Heb 1:3; Heb 1:3; Rev 22:4; Luke 24:36-40; Phil 3:20,21; 1 John 3:2; 2 Cor 4:4; Phil 2:6; Col 1:14,15;)	Yes
Does the Bible support the teaching that God the Father and His son Jesus Christ are two different personages? (John 17:11,20-22, 1 Cor 6:17; John 10:30; Matt 3:16,17; Acts 7:55,56; Heb 1:1,2,5; Psalm 136:2; Deu 10:17; Psalm 82:1,6; 1 Cor 8:5)	Yes
Does the Bible support the teaching of Joseph Smith that man can see God? (Gen 12:7; 32:30; Exo 24:9-11; 33:11; 1 King 3:2; 9:2; Isa 6:1-5; Job 42:5; Amos 9:1; Acts 7:2; 7:55,56; Rev 22:3-5; John 20:18; Matt 28:9; Luke 24:15,16,34; 1 Cor 15:6,7, Acts 26:13-16; John 20:24-29; Luke 24:36-40; John 6:46)	Yes
Does the Bible support Joseph Smith's teaching that Christ created the world? (John 1:1-3,14; Heb 1:1-3; Col 1:16; Heb 11:3; Eph 3:21)	Yes
Does the Bible support Joseph Smith's teaching that Jesus Christ is the God of the Old Testament? (Isa 43:11; 45:21; Acts 4:10-12; 13:23; Phil 3:20; Titus 2:13; 1 Tim 4:10;)	Yes
Does the Bible support Joseph Smith's claim that Jesus Christ will be the judge? (John 5:21,22; John 5:27)	Yes

NOTES

CHAPTER 10

SAVED BY GRACE

Many Christian religions follow the philosophy that "those who believe in Christ" are "saved by grace." In order to not be confrontational and demeaning in this chapter, no particular religion will be mentioned. Knowing that there are many denominational and nondenominational churches that profess the *"saved by grace"* doctrine, the term "saved Christian" will be used to identify those Christians who follow this particular doctrine.

The apostle Paul's teaching on *"saved by grace"* is the primary support for this "saved Christian" belief. Paul stated:

> *Ephesians 2:5-9 – Even when we were dead in sins, hath quickened us together with Christ, (by grace ye are saved;) 6. And hath raised us up together, and made us sit together in heavenly places in Christ Jesus: 7. That in the ages to come he might shew the exceeding riches of his grace in his kindness toward us through Christ Jesus. 8. **For by grace are ye saved through faith; and that not of yourselves: it is the gift of God: 9. Not of works, lest any man should boast.***

Peter's warning about Paul's teachings. The first point that must be made here is Peter's warning to all saints that Paul was hard to understand when teaching about the topic of salvation. If we listen to the apostle Peter's teachings, we learn that Paul is hard to understand—specifically when speaking about the subject of salvation. And, when people that are *"unlearned"* and *"unstable"* follow Paul's teaching, it could lead to their own destruction. Peter's warning states:

> *2 Peter 3:15-17 – And account that the longsuffering of our Lord is salvation; even as our beloved brother Paul also according to the wisdom given unto him hath written unto you;*
> *16. As also in all his epistles, speaking in them of these things; **in which are some things hard to be understood, which they that are unlearned and unstable wrest**, as they do also the other scriptures, **unto their own destruction.** 17. Ye therefore, beloved, seeing ye know these things before, beware lest ye also, being led away with the error of the wicked, fall from your own steadfastness.*

Peter consciously gives the saints of Christ a very strong and specific warning that if they are not careful in correctly understanding Paul's teachings about salvation, they will then *"be let away with the error of the wicked,"* and *"fall from their own steadfastness," "unto their own destruction!"* Therefore it is critical that everybody understand this warning before studying about salvation and specifically the "saved by grace" philosophy.

Terms Defined. In order to ensure that we are not falling into the *"error of the wicked"* it is important to define several of the Biblical terms when dealing with "salvation." These terms that we will define are salvation, faith, "salvation from sin," and "eternal salvation."

Salvation Defined.
The "Saved Christian's" Definition. The "Saved Christian's" define salvation in this manner:

> *"Salvation is where every believer will dwell in the same heaven in the presence of the Father, Son, and Holy Spirit.*[13] *"Salvation is not universal but received by an individual's exercise of faith in the person and work of Christ alone-through grace—not works. Salvation delivers believers from their sinful nature, particular sins, and the ultimate consequences of sin-*

physical death and everlasting torment."[14]

Scriptural support for this belief are:

> *Romans 1:16 – For I am not ashamed of the gospel of Christ: for it is the power of God unto salvation to every one that believeth; to the Jew first, and also the Greek.*

> *Hebrews 9:28 – So Christ was once offered to bear the sins of many; and unto them that look for him shall he appear the second time without sin unto salvation.*

> *Ephesians 2:8-9 – 8. For by grace are ye saved through faith; and that not of yourselves: it is the gift of God; 9. Not of works, lest any man should boast.*

> *Galatians 3:10-14 – For as many as are of the works of the law are under the curse: for it is written, Cursed is every one that continueth not in all things which are written in the book of the law to do them. 11. But that no man is justified by the law in the sight of God, it is evident: for, **The just shall live by faith.** 12. And the **law is not of faith:** but, The man that doeth them shall live in them. 13. **Christ hath redeemed us from the curse of the law,** being made a curse for us: for it is written, Cursed is every one that hangeth on a tree: 14. That the blessing of Abraham might come on the Gentiles through Jesus Christ; **that we might receive the promise of the Spirit through faith.***

The Bible Definition. The Bible actually talks about faith and salvation in several different contexts. So what does the word "faith" and "salvation" actually mean in the different contexts?

Faith. Faith is used in several different contexts. The Random House Dictionary defines "faith" in the following manner:

> 2. belief that is not based on proof. 3. belief in God or in the doctrines or teachings of religion. 5. a system of religious belief: the *Jewish faith.* 8. Christian Theology. The trust in God and in His promises as made through Christ and the Scriptures by which man is justified or saved.[15]

Faith is defined in two different ways here. The first is "one's belief, that is not based on proof, in God or in the doctrines and teachings of a religion." As in the specific Christian religion, it is the trust in God and Christ.

The second definition that is important here is "the system of religious belief: *the Jewish faith.*" It is the actual religion or formal institution (i.e., Catholic, LDS, Baptist, and Jewish) that is faith.

The Bible teachings support both definitions.

Faith as ones "belief." A good example of this type of faith is Ephesians 2:8-9. There are many more passages that talk about a person's faith.

> *Ephesians 2:8-9 – 8. For by grace are ye saved through faith; and that not of yourselves: it is the gift of God; 9. Not of works, lest any man should boast.*

Faith as a religious institution. This definition of faith is harder to recognize in the passages. It is also the cause of much misunderstanding and misinterpretation of the passages concerning faith. Here are references that are referring to the faith, as in Christ's church.

> *1 Corinthians 16:13 – Watch ye, **stand fast in the faith,** quit you like men, be strong.*

"Stand fast in the faith" is referring to Christ's church.

> *Ephesians 4:5 – **One Lord, one faith, one baptism,***

Paul is very clear when he states that there is only *"one Lord, one faith"* (or Christ's church), and only *"one baptism"* (into Christ's church). Any other church or baptisms are not part of the true *"faith"* or the actual Church of Jesus Christ. More will be spoken on this in **Chapter 3 – The Organization of the Original Church of Jesus Christ** and **Chapter 4 –The Priesthood.**

> *Galatians 2:20 – I am crucified with Christ: nevertheless I live; yet not I, but Christ liveth in me: **and the life which I now live in the flesh I live by the faith of the Son of God,** who loved me, and gave himself for me.*

Here, Paul is commenting how he *"lives by the faith (or church) of the Son of God,"* not by his own faith, or belief in Christ.

> *Galatians 3:2 – This only would I learn of you, Received ye the Spirit by the works of the law, or **by the hearing of faith?***

Paul is continuing his epistle to the Galatians and he asked them if they received the Spirit by the *"works of the law"* (Mosaic Law, or Jewish church), or if they received it through *"the hearing of faith"* (or did they hear it through Christ's church). Knowing that once a person believes in Christ, has faith in Christ, then repents and is baptized, they receive the Gift of the Holy Ghost by the *"laying on of hands."* This is what Paul was referring to when he asked how they received the Spirit. See **Chapter 5 – The Holy Ghost** for more details on this topic.

Faith Defined.

Faith as a personal belief. For this books purposes, a personal faith is a belief in Jesus Christ as our Savior.

Faith as a religious institution. For this books purposes the religious institution is Jesus Christ's church, the Jewish faith after Christ, and the Jewish faith before Christ which was also called "the Mosaic Law" or "the law."

Salvation from Sin. The next definition that is defined will be the most basic of the term. It is that of *"salvation from sin"* as described by the apostle Matthew.

> *Matthew 1:21 – And she shall bring forth a son, and thou shalt call his name JESUS: **for he shall save his people from their sins.***

Here is a specific definition of "saved," that is "people are being saved from their sins." Luke also supports this definition in the following passage:

> *Luke 1:77-79 – 77. To give **knowledge of salvation** unto his people **by the remission of their sins,** 78. Through the tender mercy of our God; whereby the dayspring from on high hath visited us, 79. To give light to them that sit in darkness and in the shadow of death, to guide our feet into the way of peace.*

Luke is explaining that people, who are *"sitting in darkness"* and in the *"shadow of death"* are given salvation through the remission of their sins. Therefore, we have Christ "saving His people from their sins and from death."

Question: Who receives Salvation from sin?

Matthew and Luke actually do not specify who all are *"saved from sin and death."* In order to learn who all is included in being "saved from sin and death" we must listen to the teachings of Jesus Christ and His other apostles. Paul is specific about who is saved from death when he stated:

*1 Corinthians 15:22 – **For as in Adam all die, even so in Christ shall all be made alive.***

The statement here, is where "Christ shall make **all** alive again." It is through Christ's mercy and grace that "all men shall live" eternally. Paul even goes on and speaks that every man will be made alive in his own order.

*1 Corinthians 15:23 – **But every man in his own order: Christ the firstfruits; afterward they that are Christ's at his coming.***

Question: Is this a prejudiced judgement in the resurrection, where one person may receive more than another person?

Question: Is Paul hinting that, *with the first fruits,* there is a hierarchy in the resurrection?

Under the Christian definition of *"saved by grace,"* this statement of Paul's, that *"all men shall live,"* is also an actual contradiction to Paul's statement, "all who believe will be saved." This is one of the things Peter was alluding to when he said *"Paul was hard to understand!"*

Some of the other apostle's teachings will also shed some light on this "saved by grace" concept. Luke taught that *"all flesh shall see the salvation of God."* Again, this is in total contradiction to the "saved Christian" definition of *"saved by grace."*

*Luke 3:6 – **And all flesh shall see the salvation of God.***

Reading John's teaching will also shed more light on "salvation." John teaches about how God sent His Son to "save the world."

Question: Does this mean the entire population of the world will "see the salvation of God," as it obviously states, or does it mean only a portion of the population will "see the salvation of God?"

It is interpreted by some of the "saved Christians" to mean *"only those that believe."* But when compared to the teachings of Matthew, Luke, John, and Paul, it does take on the inclusion of the entire population of the world, since it was created.

*John 3:17 – For God sent not his Son into the world to condemn the world; but that **the world through him might be saved.***

John puts the final clarification on the Christian's misunderstanding of the "saved by grace" theory for believers only when he teaches about who will be resurrected.

*John 5:25 – Verily, verily, I say unto you, The hour is coming, and now is, when **the dead shall hear the voice of the Son of God: and they that hear shall live.***

*John 5:28,29 – 28. Marvel not at this: for the hour is coming, in the which all **that are in the graves shall hear his voice,** 29. And shall come forth; **they that have done good, unto the resurrection of life; and they that have done evil, unto the resurrection of damnation.***

John is very clear about all the dead *"will hear the voice,"* and *"they that have done good will be resurrected unto life,"* and *"they that have done evil will be resurrected unto damnation."* It does state that all people will be resurrected and will live some kind of eternal life!

John also says *"those who hear his voice will live."* Here we have a specific definition of the "saved by grace" misinterpretation. All persons, living on earth will be resurrected. This means their spirits will be reunited with their bodies. All persons will live eternally, some in the presence of God and Christ, and some not in the presence of God and Christ, which is a form of eternal damnation.

To confirm what Peter, Paul, Luke, and John have taught about both believers and unbelievers being *"saved,"* Peter again mentions the occasion that Christ actually went and preached His Word to the *"spirits in prison."* Thereby giving the *"unjust"* and *"disobedient"* a chance *"to live according to God in the spirit."*

> *1 Peter 3:18-20 – 18. For Christ also hath once suffered for sins, the just for the unjust, that he might bring us to God, being put to death in the flesh, but quickened by the Spirit: 19. By which also **he went and preached unto the spirits in prison;** 20. Which sometime were disobedient, when once the longsuffering of God waited in the days of Noah, while the ark was a preparing, wherein few, that is, eight souls were saved by water.*

> *1 Peter 4:6 – For for this cause was **the gospel preached also to them that are dead,** that they might be judged according to men in the flesh, **but live according to God in the spirit.***

After reading that Christ will teach His gospel to the dead, we can understand how *"every knee will bow and every tongue confess,"* that Christ is our savior.

> *Isaiah 45:23 – I have sworn by myself, the word is gone out of my mouth in righteousness, and shall not return, **That unto me every knee shall bow, every tongue shall swear.***

> *Romans 14:11 – For it is written, As I live, saith the Lord, **every knee shall bow to me, and every tongue shall confess to God.***

> *Philippians 2:10,11 – 10. That **at the name of Jesus every knee should bow,** of things in heaven, and things in earth, and things under the earth; 11. And that every tongue **should confess that Jesus Christ is Lord,** to the glory of God the Father.*

It is evident from these teachings that every person born on this earth, whether in this life or after this life, will hear the gospel of Christ. In the end, all will bow and confess that Christ is Lord and they will live eternally as a resurrected being. Therefore, they will all obtain *"salvation from sin."*

From these teachings of Christ and the apostles, we will use the following definition to describe *"salvation from sin."*

> **"Salvation from Sin" Defined** – *Through Christ's grace, sacrifice, and atonement all people that have been born on the earth and received a body of flesh and bone will live eternally.*

Eternal Salvation. The next definition is one that more closely suits the Christian belief – *"Salvation is where every believer will dwell in the same heaven in the presence of the Father, Son, and Holy Spirit."* But according to Joseph Smith's interpretation and understanding, we will find that this definition is not totally true, complete, and understood by its authors.

John expounds on the definition of "eternal life" as:

> *John 17:3 – And this is life eternal, **that they might know thee the only true God, and Jesus Christ,** whom thou hast sent.*

"Life eternal" is where we actually get to *"know the only true God and Jesus Christ!"* It is very similar to the "saved Christian" definition, except it goes one step further in stating that we will actually get to know "God and Christ!" How well a person gets to know God and Christ depends on how you believe they actually are. The "saved Christian" definition of the Godhead is that they are not personages, but that they are spirits and hence are everywhere.

Question: How well can a person get to know a God that is a spirit and is everywhere?

With the Joseph Smith definition of God and Christ, being persons with a perfected body of flesh and bone, we can theoretically get to know God and Christ as we can know our own earthly father here on earth!

Question: Which denominational definition of God supports John's meaning of *"eternal life is getting to know the only true God and Jesus Christ,"* and which one is in conflict?

Much more is written on the subjects of the *"kingdom of God"* in **Chapter 12 – The Plan of Salvation – Post-Mortal Life** and the *"personality of God"* in **Chapter 9 – The Personality of God.** Joseph Smith defines the term "Eternal Salvation" as:

> **Eternal Salvation Defined:** *"Eternal Salvation" is where man may live in the presence of God the Father and his Son, Jesus Christ, in the actual kingdom of God.*

Requirements for Eternal Salvation.

Who receives Eternal Salvation? Now that we have defined two important levels of salvation, "salvation from sin" and "eternal salvation," one can better discuss the "saved Christian's" doctrine versus Joseph Smith's doctrine. According to the "Saved Christian's" belief, from two scriptures in the Bible, "all who have faith and believe in Christ will be saved in heaven." According to Joseph Smith's doctrine, much more is taught by Christ and His apostles on who actually will be entering into the kingdom of God, and who actually "will know God and Christ." Paul wrote:

> *Hebrews 5:9 – And being made perfect, he became the author of **eternal salvation unto all them that obey him;***

Paul taught here that once Christ was made perfect, he became the author of *"eternal salvation."* This *"eternal salvation"* is only for those that *"obey him!"*

Question: Is this teaching of Paul's, where we must "obey him," a contradiction to the one in Paul's epistle to the Ephesians, where he tells us that "we only need to have faith" to be saved?

In continuing to define the difference between *"saved by grace"* and *"eternal salvation in the kingdom of God,"* the apostles taught that there are several different requirements to receive the *"eternal salvation in the kingdom of God."* These are the different requirements.

Requirements for "Eternal Salvation in the kingdom of God!"

1. We must obey him.

> *Hebrews 5:9 – And being made perfect, he became the author of **eternal salvation unto all them that obey him;***

2. Be born of water (baptized). John and Matthew added a few more requirements to enable our entry into the *"kingdom of God."*

> *Mark 16:15, 16 – 15. And he said unto them, Go ye into all the world, and preach the gospel to every creature. 16. **He that believeth and is baptized shall be saved;** but he that believeth not shall be damned.*

3. Be born of spirit (receive the Gift of the Holy Ghost).

> *John 3:5 – Jesus answered, Verily, verily, I say unto thee, **Except a man be born of water and of the Spirit, he cannot enter into the kingdom of God.***

4. Endure to the end. Matthew puts an additional requirement into the list!

> *Matthew 10:22 – And ye shall be hated of all men for my name's sake:* **but he that shall endure to the end shall be saved.**

> *Matthew 24:11-13 – And many false prophets shall rise, and shall deceive many. 12. And because iniquity shall abound, the love of many shall wax cold. 13.* **But he that shall endure unto the end, the same shall be saved.**

> *Mark 13:13 – And ye shall be hated of all men for my name's sake: but* **he that shall endure unto the end, the same shall be saved.**

According to the Joseph Smith's interpretation, *"endure to the end"* means that everyone has to continue their entire lives having faith in Christ, living God's commandments, staying strong in the "faith" (both personal faith and in the faith as in the organized Church of Jesus Christ).

Question: How does the "saved Christian's" definition of *"saved by grace"* relate to this requirement of "enduring to the end?"

Another two requirements added to the list of requirements for "eternal salvation in the kingdom of God!

5. Love God with all our heart, soul, and mind.

6. Love our neighbor as our self.

These two requirements fall under *"obey Him"* are the first and second greatest commandments of all. Christ himself taught these two commandments.

> *Matthew 22:36-40 – 36. Master, which is the great commandment in the law? 37. Jesus said unto him,* **Thou shalt love the Lord thy God with all thy heart, and with all thy soul, and with all thy mind.** *38. This is the first and great commandment. 39. And the second is like unto it,* **Thou shalt love thy neighbor as thyself.** *40. On these two commandments hang all the law and the prophets.*

Question: Does living the first requirement for eternal salvation, "we must obey Him", include any and all commandments?

Christ continues and teaches us that we must be perfect, even as Father in heaven is perfect.

> *Matthew 5:48 –* **Be ye therefore perfect,** *even as your Father which is in heaven is perfect.*

7. Be perfect, like Father in heaven!

Question: What does it mean to become perfect like our Father in heaven?

The details of our requirement of "being perfect" are in **Chapter 6 – The Holy Ghost, Chapter 13 – The Plan of Salvation: The Mortal Earth Life, and Chapter 16 – The "God-Makers."**

One could continue on and on with requirements that meet the *"we must obey Him"* commandment, but one question must be asked!

Question: Is the requirement to receive "eternal salvation in the kingdom of God," by having "faith" only or by "faith and works?"

Mormon doctrine states that faith is important and a person must have it, but works is an essential part to it. As listed there are already seven requirements listed in order to achieve *"Eternal Salvation in the kingdom of God."* This does not include the 10 commandments given to Moses and many of the other directives given by Christ and his apostles.

When considering the *"Saved Christian's"* definition of being *"saved by grace,"* we must take into context what the Bible teaches about a saint's performance, after beginning the salvation process. First, we will study the actual teachings of Jesus Christ, then we will see what the apostles teach.

Enter into the "strait gate." Agreeing that Christ was full of grace towards all mankind…

> **Question: Does the *"saved by grace"* doctrine for *"those that believe"* contradict or conflict in anyway with what Christ taught in Matthew?**

> **Question: What did Christ mean when he stated:**

>> *Matthew 7:13,14 – 13. **Enter ye in at the strait gate: for wide is the gate,** and broad is the way, that leadeth to destruction, and many there be which go in thereat: 14. **Because strait is the gate, and narrow is the way, which leadeth unto life, and few there be that find it.***

It is very apparent that Christ taught that the way to *"eternal salvation"* or to *"eternal life"* is ***"very narrow, and few be there that find It!"*** This teaching of Christ does conflict with the 'Saved Christian" definition of *"saved by grace"* for whosoever believes. Because under the "Saved Christian" definition—all Christians who "only believe" will enter into God's kingdom. The "Saved Christian" definition does not sound in any way close to what is taught under the requirements to enter into the kingdom of God, or that very few will actually enter.

Requirements to enter into the kingdom of God!
1. **We must obey him.**
2. **Be born of water (baptized).**
3. **Be born of spirit (receive the Gift of the Holy Ghost).**
4. **Endure to the end.**
5. **Love God with all our heart, soul, and mind.**
6. **Love our neighbor as our self.**
7. **Be perfect, like our Father in heaven!**

> **Question: With the strict requirements and the knowledge of very few entering into the kingdom of God, then who will enter?**

Not only here, but again the Lord teaches that all those Christians who believe in Christ, only the Christians who *"do the will of my Father"* will *"enter into the kingdom of heaven."*

>> *Matthew 7:21 – **Not every one that saith unto me, Lord, Lord, shall enter into the kingdom of heaven; but he that doeth the will of my Father which is in heaven.***

It is clearer in the next passage that Christ will *"reward every man according to his works."*

>> *Matthew 16:27 – For the Son of man shall come in the glory of his Father with his angels; and then **he shall reward every man according to his works.***

> **Question: Which group of followers is Christ talking about here, the Christians who only have to "believe" in Christ or the Christians who "doeth his will?"**

The Christians who Christ is talking about in these past scriptures are those Christians who actually believe in Christ, for they are crying *"Lord, Lord."* But Christ definitely divides the followers, into those who *"doeth the will of his Father"* and those who *"do not do the will of the Father."* Not only does He divide them but He qualifies them into two groups, those who *"shall enter into the kingdom of heaven"* and those who *"will not enter into the kingdom of heaven."* Christ is talking about all the people who believe in Him!

Question: Which group does the "saved Christians," those that only have to believe, fall into?

This is where the definitions of *"salvation"* become important. The definition of *"salvation from sins,"* that all mankind will be resurrected and live eternally, receives *"salvation"* through the *"grace of God and Christ."* Even those who will suffer the *"spiritual death"* will live eternally, just not in the presence of God and Christ, which fulfills the requirement for the definition of *"eternal salvation."* Those who **"doeth the will of the Father"** will **"enter into the kingdom of heaven."**

Christ supports this concept in His parable of the wise man.

> *Matthew 7:24-27 – 24. Therefore whosoever heareth these sayings of mine, and doeth them, I will liken him unto a wise man, which built his house upon a rock; 25. And the rain descended, and the floods came, and the winds blew, and beat upon that house; and it fell not: for it was founded upon a rock. 26. **And every one that heareth these sayings of mine, and doeth them not, shall be likened unto a foolish man, which built his house upon the sand:** 27. And the rain descended, and the floods came, and the winds blew, and beat upon that house; and it fell: **and great was the fall of it.***

Question: Does this parable support the interpretation of Christ's own words when He stated that "strait is the gate?"

Question: Does it sound like Christ favors those who "doeth his will" as "wise" men?

Question: Is a "saved Christian" who "only has to believe" building his house on rock or sand?

Further teachings of Christ will expound on this concept in the "parable of the talents! Again, Christ teaches some hard facts that are in direct contradiction to the "saved by grace" doctrine.

> *Matthew 25:14-30 – 14. For the **kingdom of heaven** is as a man traveling into a far country, who called his own servants, and delivered unto them his goods. 15. An unto one he gave five talents, to another two, and to another one; to every man according to his several ability; and straightway took his journey.*
>
> *16. Then he that had received the five talents went and traded with the same, and made them other five talents. 17. And likewise he that had received two, he also gained other two. 18. But he that had received one went and digged in the earth, and hid his lord's money.*
>
> *19. After a long time the lord of those servants cometh, and reckoneth with them. 20. And so he that had received five talents came and brought other five talents, saying, Lord, thou deliveredst unto me five talents: behold, I have gained beside them five talents more.*
>
> *21. His lord said unto him, Well done, thou good and faithful servant: thou hast been faithful over a few things, I will make thee ruler over many things: enter thou into the joy of thy lord.*
>
> *22. He also that had received two talents came and said, Lord, thou deliveredst unto me two talents: behold, I have gained two other talents beside them. 23. His lord said unto him, Well done, good and faithful servant; thou hast been faithful over a few things, I will make thee ruler over many things: enter thou into the joy of thy lord.*
>
> *24. Then he which had received the one talent came and said, Lord **I knew thee***

> *that thou art an hard man, reaping where thou hast not sown, and gathering where thou hast not strawed: 25. And I was afraid, and went and hid thy talent in the earth: lo, there thou hast that is thine.*
>
> *26. His lord answered and said unto him, Thou wicked and slothful servant, thou knewest that I reap where I sowed not, and gathered where I have not strawed: 27. Thou oughtest therefore to have put my money to the exchangers, and then at my coming I should have received mine own with usury.*
>
> *28. Take therefore the talent from him , and give it unto him which hath ten talents. 29. For unto every one that hath shall be given, and he shall have abundance: but from him that hast not shall be taken away even that which he hath. 30. **And cast ye the unprofitable servant into outer darkness:** there shall be weeping and gnashing of teeth.*

In this parable all believers and followers of Christ are given talents. Those who worked at increasing their talents were allowed to enter into the ***"joy of the Lord."*** He who did not work at increasing his talent, who was slough full, lost everything and was ***"cast into outer darkness!"*** He was not necessarily a bad person; he just did not work at increasing the Lord's talent.

Christ continued to teach about works in the "parable of the sower." Using the agrarian example of what happens to a farmer who sows their crops, we all know what a farmer will harvest if he has a lot of faith but doesn't quite get out the door on a daily basis to do the work required. Christ uses this well known fact in order to express his feelings about ***"seeds that were planted in good ground and brought forth fruit."***

> *Matthew 13:3-9 – 3. And he spake many things unto them in parables, saying, Behold, a sower went forth to sow; 4. And when he sowed, some seeds fell by the way side, and the fowls came and devoured them up: 5. Some fell upon stony places, where they had not much earth: and forthwith they sprung up, because they had no deepness of earth: 6. And when the sun was up, they were scorched; and because they had no root, they withered away. 7. And some fell among thorns; and the thorns sprung up, and choked them: 8. **But other fell into good ground, and brought forth fruit, some an hundredfold, some sixty fold, some thirtyfold.** 9. Who hath ears to hear, let him hear.*

Question: How do these parables apply the teaching of "by faith alone, ye are saved?"

Let us use a down-to-earth comparison of three different men that we can relate to. The first is an example of a great man, the crusader Reverend Billy Graham. Billy Graham has really worked his whole life to bring the words and works of Christ into the lives of people worldwide. The second man can be a local church leader or volunteer who works on Sunday and maybe one or two other nights of the week, to make sure the Sunday services go off well. The third example is one of a member of a congregation, who believes that he is *"saved in Christ"* but only goes to church on most Sundays. According to the "saved Christians" if we are *"saved by faith in Christ alone"* then all three men will receive the same reward in heaven.

Question: What incentive do the children of men have to serve Christ in the building of His kingdom here on earth?

Actually, under the *"Saved by Grace"* teachings, there is no heavenly incentive at all. In fact, this doctrine teaches each person the utmost desires for mediocrity. It is contrary to the require-ments for *"eternal salvation in the kingdom of God."*

In the next few passages, Paul teaches us the opposite of what the "saved Christians" believe he taught to the Ephesians. In Paul's epistles to the Galatians, he expounds the teachings of *"works beget rewards."*

> *Galatians 6:7,8 – 7. Be not deceived; God is not mocked:* **for whatsoever a man soweth, that shall he also reap.** *8. For he that soweth to his flesh shall of the flesh reap corruption; but* **he that soweth to the Spirit shall of the Spirit reap life everlasting.**

Question: How does Paul's *"saved by grace, not by works"* support or coincide with Paul's teachings of *"for whatsoever a man soweth, that shall he also reap?"*

Answer, the two different teachings do not support each other. They are again, a contradiction in the Bible, for the *"saved by Grace"* believers, who also in most cases, believe the Bible to be perfect and complete. This contradiction in the "Saved Christian" interpretation of Paul's teachings on salvation is exactly what Peter was warning us about in 2 Peter 3:15.

James' teachings on faith and works. A look at what the apostle James taught on the subject of "faith versus works" sheds more light on the subject of "saved by grace." James could not be any clearer when he taught the following:

> *James 1:22 – But* **be ye doers of the word, and not hearers only,** *deceiving your own selves.*

> *James 2:14-20 – 14.* **What doth it profit, my brethren, though a man say he hath faith, and have not works? Can faith save him?** *15. If a brother or sister be naked, and destitute of daily food, 16. And one of you say unto them, Depart in peace, be ye warmed and filled; notwithstanding ye give them not those things which are needful to the body; what doth it profit? 17.* **Even so faith, if it hath not works, is dead, being alone.** *18. Yea, a man may say, Thou hast faith, and I have works:* **shew me thy faith without thy works, and I will shew thee my faith by my works.** *19. Thou believest that there is one God; thou doest well; the devils also believe, and tremble. 20.* **But wilt thou know, O vain man, that faith without works is dead?**

> *James 2:21,22 – 21. Was not Abraham our father justified by works, when he had offered Isaac his son upon the altar? 22. Seest thou how faith wrought with his works,* **and by works was faith made perfect?**

Again, we go back to the basics that Christ and the apostles taught, first we must believe, have faith, and then progress to perfection. It is through the scriptures and work, building the kingdom of God on earth, that a person's faith can achieve perfection. It is within every man and woman on earth, the ability to achieve perfection! Christians, working on living by faith only, reaps only a partial reward.

> *James 2:23,24 – 23. And the scripture was fulfilled which saith, Abraham believed God, and it was imputed unto him for righteousness: and he was called the Friend of God. 24.* **Ye see then how that by works a man is justified, and not by faith only.**

> *James 2:25,26 – 25. Likewise also was not Rahab the harlot justified by works, when she had received the messengers, and had sent them out another way? 26.* **For as the body without the spirit is dead, so faith without works is dead also.**

Question: What is hard to understand about "faith without works is dead also?"

It is easy to state that "once we believe and have faith in Christ, we are saved"—then works are a result of faith. But even this statement conflicts with itself. If all we need is faith, then why do we need works? The apostle John did more than just teach on this subject. John actually saw in Revelations a vision as to what would happen come judgment day!

> *Revelations 20:12,13 – 12. And I saw the dead, small and great, stand before God; and the books were opened: and another book was opened, which is the book of life: and **the dead were judged out of those things which were written in the books, according to their works.** 13. And the sea gave up the dead which were in it; and death and hell delivered up the dead which were in them: and **they were judged every man according to their works.***

John, not once, but twice stated that the dead were **"judged every man according to their works!"**

Question: What happened to the Christians who had faith but did not have many works?

Christ again answers this question and supports what Paul, Peter, James and John taught.

> *Matthew 16:27 – For the Son of man shall come in the glory of his Father with his angels; **and then he shall reward every man according to his works.***

All of the teachings presented here, except the three initial scriptures that the "saved Christians" base their belief, lead one to think "that one without works will not be entering into the kingdom of God."

Joseph Smith's Interpretation of the "saved Christian's" Quoted Scriptures. The "saved Christians" used Romans 1:16, Hebrews 9:28, Ephesians 2:8-9, and Galatians 3:10-14 for their interpretation of the "saved by faith only" theology. The interpretations of these passages, according to the Joseph Smith, are as follows:

> 1. *Romans 1:16 – For I am not ashamed of the gospel of Christ: **for it is the power of God unto salvation to every one that believeth;** to the Jew first, and also the Greek.*

The situation surrounding this quote is after Christ was crucified, Paul was teaching the already converted members of Christ's church. Paul is commenting here that the gospel of Christ and the salvation that comes through it is offered to the Jews first and also the Greeks. When Paul or any of the apostles taught they did not write every requirement for salvation. The apostles assumed the saints knew that there were requirements, like baptism, that one needed to enter into the kingdom of God.

The Mormons support the fact that one must believe in Christ for eternal salvation. But, this scripture does not state in any way that it is the only requirement for salvation. Mormons believe that belief in Christ is the first step, of many, in the eternal salvation perspective. As explained in this chapter, there are many requirements that Christ gives in order to achieve eternal salvation in the kingdom of God.

> 2. *Hebrews 9:28 – So Christ was once offered to bear the sins of many; and unto them that look for him shall he appear the second time without sin unto salvation.*

Nowhere in this epistle to the Hebrews does it say or infer that only those that believe will be saved, without any works. According to Joseph Smith, this chapter is explaining about the blood sacrifices made in Moses' time as compared to Christ's own blood sacrifice. In verse 27, it states that men will die once, but after that the judgement will come—through Christ's atonement. As we know from what was learned earlier, the salvation will come to all men who lived on the earth. This verse gives more support for universal "salvation from sin" than it does for "saved by faith only, not by works."

> 3. *Ephesians 2:8-9 – 8. For by grace are ye saved through faith; and that not of your-selves: it is the gift of God; 9. Not of works, lest any man should boast.*

Joseph Smith's interpretation of this is that this "saved by grace through faith…not of works" is actually "salvation from sin." It is not the ***"eternal salvation in the kingdom of God."*** All men who lived on earth will be saved from mortal death, will be resurrected, judged, and then will live for the rest of eternity.

> 4. *Galatians 3:10-14 – 10.For as many as are of the works of the law are under the curse: for it is written, Cursed is every one that continueth not in all things which are written in the book of the law to do them. 11. But that no man is justified by the law in the sight of God, it is evident: for,* **The just shall live by faith.** *12. And the* **law is not of faith:** *but, The man that doeth them shall live in them. 13.* **Christ hath redeemed us from the curse of the law,** *being made a curse for us: for it is written, Cursed is every one that hangeth on a tree: 14. That the blessing of Abraham might come on the Gentiles through Jesus Christ;* **that we might receive the promise of the Spirit through faith.**

Some "saved Christians" misinterpret this passage to mean that anybody living *"the law is cursed,"* therefore, they justify *"only believing"* or *"having faith in Christ"* will get them eternal salvation.

The Mormon stand on this passage is that the "Saved Christians" have taken this concept out of context and have misinterpreted it. In verse 2, Paul asks the saints if they *"received the Spirit through the works of the law or by the hearing of faith."*

> *Galatians 3:2 – This only would I learn of you,* **Received ye the Spirit by the works of the law, or by the hearing of faith?**

With the *"works of the law"* meaning the Mosaic law given to the descendants of Abraham, or the Jewish faith at that time. Faith meaning, Christ's gospel or church, not ones own personal belief in Christ. Paul was asking the church members in Galatians where they received the Spirit. He asks them again in chapter 5 that the people who minister to them in the Spirit, works miracles among them, do they do it by works of the law (Jewish faith) or did they do it first by hearing of faith, or hearing of the Church of Jesus Christ.

Many "Saved Christians" still must profess that this "by hearing of faith" is their own personal belief in Jesus Christ. People do not first "hear their faith." They first hear the words of Jesus Christ, and then their faith in Christ begins to grow as they learn more.

Question: Where, specifically in Paul's time to the Galatians, did they learn of Jesus Christ?

It was from the apostles and other members of the Church of Jesus Christ that were called of God to go out and preach the gospel of Jesus Christ.

The teachings continue. The topic in this Galatians chapter 3, is the difference of the Mosaic law or Christ's church. There was apparently some confusion among the membership in Galatians about who were to be the children or heirs of Abraham. Some members, being raised as very good members of the Jewish faith or "the law," needed reassurance that becoming members of the Church of Jesus Christ would still give them their inheritance as children of Abraham. That is why Paul told them the following:

> *Galatians 3:7 – Know ye therefore that they which are of faith the same are the children of Abraham.*

Paul explains to the saints in Galatians that the promise by faith of Jesus Christ, or the promise by the Church of Jesus Christ might be given to them that believe.

> *Galatians 3:22 – But the scripture hath concluded all under sin, that the promise by faith of Jesus Christ might be given to them that believe.*

He further explains that before the Church of Jesus Christ came the Jews were kept under the law, or the Mosaic law, waiting for the gospel of salvation to come forth.

> *Galatians 3:23 – But before faith came, we were kept under the law, shut up unto the faith which should afterwards be revealed.*

Question: What faith was always prophesied to be revealed?

The faith to be revealed was "Christ's gospel of salvation that man may be justified." The Mosaic law or Jewish religion with all of their rules, that was to prepare them for Christ's gospel.

> *Galatians 3:24 – Wherefore the law was our schoolmaster to bring us unto Christ, that we might be justified by faith.*

It is through *"faith"* that is *"baptism into Christ"* that one becomes the seed of Abraham, and heirs according to the promise made to Abraham.

> *Galatians 3:27-29 – 27. **For as many of you as have been baptized into Christ** have put on Christ. 28. There is neither Jew nor Greek, there is neither bond nor free, there is neither male nor female: **for ye are all one in Christ Jesus.** 29. And if ye be Christ's, then are ye Abraham's seed, and heirs according to the promise.*

The Biblical Support Chart. The apostle Peter taught that it is critical to one's salvation that he or she has the proper understanding of the apostle Paul's teachings on salvation.

> *2 Peter 3:15-17 – 15. And account that the longsuffering of our Lord is salvation; even as our beloved brother Paul also according to the wisdom given unto him hath written unto you; 16. As also in all his epistles, speaking in them of these things; **in which are some things hard to be understood, which they that are unlearned and unstable wrest,** as they do also the other scriptures, **unto their own destruction.** 17. Ye therefore, beloved, seeing ye know these things before, beware lest ye also, being led away with the error of the wicked, fall from your own steadfastness.*

With the great division among the Christian religions today in regards to the definition of salvation and who actually receives it, Joseph Smith's teachings on salvation and works does a lot in clarifying who actually receives "salvation from sin" and who receives "eternal life in the kingdom of God." The actual teachings of Joseph Smith on the "kingdom of God" are detailed in **Chapters 12 – The Plan of Salvation – The Pre-Mortal Life,** and **Chapter 13 – The Plan of Salvation – The Post-Mortal Life.**

Having studied the teachings of Joseph Smith on "saved by grace" in the Bible, the answers to the Biblical Support Chart are as follows:

THE BIBLICAL SUPPORT CHART	
Is the following topic supported in the Bible?	**Yes or No**
Does the Bible support Joseph Smith's teaching that "saved by grace" is defined as – "salvation from sin is given to all men and women who are born on earth?" (1 Cor 15:22,23; Luke 3:6; John 3:17; 3:17; 1 Peter 3:18-20; 1 Peter 4:6; Isa 45:23; Rom 14:11; Phil 2:10,11)	Yes
Does the Bible support Joseph Smith teaching that "eternal salvation" is where only certain men and women may live in the presence of God the Father and Jesus Christ, in the actual kingdom of God? (John 17:3; Heb 5:9; John 3:5; Mark 16:15,16; Matt 7:13; 7:21; 16:27; 7:24-27; 25:14-30; 13:3-9; Gal 6:7,8)	Yes
Does the Bible support Joseph Smith's teaching that one's religious "works" here on earth is critical to entering into the kingdom of God? (James 1:22; 2:14-25; Gal 6:7,8; Rev 20:12,13; Matt 16:27)	Yes

Author's Note: Now that Joseph Smith has defined the difference between "saved by grace" and "eternal salvation in the kingdom of God," it is important to learn about the Plan of Salvation. Joseph Smith's teachings on the Plan of Salvation is the most detailed and comprehensive description of who we are, where we came from, where we are going after this life, and why we are here on earth. In the next three chapters, Joseph Smith will answer all of these questions, according to the revelations that he received from Jesus Christ.

The most important answer will be the defining the "kingdom of God," which can be vague and confusing for many Christians. The next chapter will discuss **The Plan of Salvation: the Pre-mortal Life,** or where did we come from? This will be the first step in understanding the kingdom of God.

NOTES

CHAPTER 11

THE PLAN OF SALVATION: THE PRE-MORTAL LIFE

The majority of the Christian religions are in general agreement that the heaven, where God's kingdom is located, is the same heaven where the good people go when they die. The differences between the Christian religions begins when identifying when we, mankind, began to exist. There are some churches that teach that the spirit of man existed before this life, but there are many who believe that mankind's existence begins when we are born on this earth.

As for a complete Christian "Plan of Salvation" that answers the following questions, most religions cannot sufficiently answer them all without contradicting the Bible. Some of the most frequently asked questions are:

- **Where did we come from?**
- **Why are we here on earth?**
- **Where are we going after this life?**
- **What happens to our family after this life?**
- **What happens to the many people who lived on this earth and never heard of Jesus Christ?**

One of the most controversial teachings of Joseph Smith is his complete "Plan of Salvation." It is the purpose of these next three chapters to find out just how Joseph Smith's "Plan of Salvation" will stand up to the Bible. These next chapters are:

Chapter 11: The Plan of Salvation – The Pre-Mortal Life
Chapter 12: The Plan of Salvation – The Post-Mortal Life
Chapter 13: The Plan of Salvation – The Earth Life

Joseph Smith, the self proclaimed prophet of God taught his "Plan of Salvation" from the beginning of his ministry. Some of these teachings were and still are called blasphemous by many other Christian religious leaders.

As quoted earlier in this book, Jesus Christ warned of false prophets and wicked teachers.

> *Matthew 7:15 – 15. **Beware of false prophets,** which come to you in sheep's clothing, but inwardly they are ravening wolves. 16. **Ye shall know them by their fruits.** Do men gather grapes of thorns, or figs of thistles?*

Christ also gave prophets for the *"perfecting of the saints"* and *"for the work of the ministry."*

> *Ephesians 4:11-14 – 11. **And he gave some, apostles; and some, prophets;** and some, evangelists; and some, pastors and teachers; 12. **For the perfecting of the saints, for the work of the ministry, for the edifying of the body of Christ: 13. Till we all come in the unity of the faith, and of the knowledge of the Son of God,** unto a perfect man, unto the measure of the stature of the fullness of Christ: 14. **That we henceforth be no more children, tossed to and fro, and carried about with every wind of doctrine, by the sleight of men, and cunning craftiness, whereby they lie in wait to deceive;***

By calling true prophets, God also gave a way for Christians to know the difference between a false prophet and a true prophet or perhaps to make clear the confusion in the *Bible.*

> *Matthew 7:20 – **Wherefore by their fruits ye shall know them.***

Joseph Smith, in regards to his "Plan of Salvation" taught some real controversial teachings that contradict, in many ways, all other Christian religious teachings. Many religious leaders have charged that Joseph Smith and the Mormons do not believe in the Bible. It is the author's position that if Joseph Smith were a true prophet of God, then there would be support in the Bible for all of his "Plan of Salvation" teachings. These controversial teachings of Joseph Smith are:

1. Joseph Smith's teaching that all mankind existed before this earth life in the kingdom of God as children of God.

2. Joseph Smith's teaching that the purpose of this life "is a trial period for eternal progression."

3. Joseph Smith's teaching that there are multiple heavens that include the "spirit prison," paradise, the celestial kingdom, the terrestrial kingdom, and the telestial kingdom.

4. Joseph Smith's teaching that the three different kingdoms mentioned previously will be the kingdoms that all mankind will be sent to after the resurrection and judgment day according to their works and faith.

The Pre-Mortal Existence of Spirits.

1. Joseph Smith's teaching that all mankind existed before this earth life in the kingdom of God as children of God.

It is the view of most Christians that only Christ pre-existed, not human beings or any other creatures. The scriptures used for this interpretation are:

> *John 8:58 – Jesus said unto them, Verily, verily, I say unto you, Before Abraham was, I am.*

> *Colossians 1:17 – And he is before all things; and by him all things consist.*

> *1 Corinthians 15:46 – Howbeit that was not first which is spiritual, but that which is natural; and afterward that which is spiritual.*

From these passages, many Christians believe that before this earth life began, there was only God, which includes Jesus Christ and the Holy Ghost (all one being), and there were no others. A human being's spirit is created or started at birth.

Although both the Mormons and most Christians believe that Christ lived in the pre-existence, in order to establish a basis for the pre-existence of man a close look at Christ and His position is presented. The following verses all testify that Christ was with God the Father before the world was. Again John and Peter both testified of this truth.

> *John 1:1-3, 14 – **In the beginning was the Word** (Christ), **and the Word (Christ) was with God,** and the Word (Christ) was God. 2. **The same (Christ) was in the beginning with God.** 3. All things were made by him (Christ); and without him (Christ) was not any thing made that was made.*

> *John 6:38 – **For I came down from heaven,** not to do mine own will, but the will of him that sent me.*

> *John 6:51 – **I am the living bread which came down from heaven:** if any man eat of this bread, he shall live for ever: and the bread that I will give is my flesh, which I will give for the life of the world.*

> *John 6:62 – What and if ye shall see the Son of man ascend up **where he was before?***

> *John 8:58 – Jesus said unto them, Verily, verily, I say unto you, **Before Abraham was, I am.***

*John 16:28-33 – **I came forth from the Father,** and am come into the world: again, **I leave the world, and go to the Father.***

*John 17:4,5 – I have glorified thee on the earth; I have finished the work which thou gavest me to do. 5. And now, O Father, glorify thou me with thine own self **with the glory which I had with thee before the world was.***

*I Peter 1: 18-20 – Forasmuch as ye know that ye were not redeemed with corruptible things, as silver and gold, from your vain conversation received by tradition from your fathers; 19. But with the precious blood of Christ, as of a lamb without blemish and without spot: 20. **Who verily was foreordained before the foundation of the world,** but was manifest in these last times for you,*

These scriptures teach us the following about Christ:

1. Christ was in the beginning with God.
2. Christ was a God.
3. Christ created all things.
4. Christ came down from heaven.
5. Christ ascended up to where he was before.
6. *"Before Abraham, Christ was."*
7. Christ came forth from the Father and returned to the Father.
8. Christ was going to receive the glory that he had *"before the world was."*
9. Christ was foreordained before the foundation of the world.

Jesus Christ-The Son of God. Having placed Christ in the pre-existence with God, what was Christ's relationship to God? The following scriptures are just a few that testify that Christ was the literal Son of God.

*Matthew 3:17 – And lo a voice from heaven, saying, **This is my beloved Son,** In whom I am well pleased.*

*Matthew 17:5 – While he yet spake, behold, a bright cloud overshadowed them: and behold a voice out of the cloud, which said, **This is my beloved Son,** in whom I am well pleased; hear ye him.*

*Mark 9:7 – And there was a cloud that overshadowed them: and a voice came out of the cloud, saying, **This is my beloved Son:** hear him.*

*Luke 9:35 – And there came a voice out of the cloud, saying, **This is my beloved Son:** hear him.*

*2 Peter 1:17 – For he received from God the Father honour and glory, when there came such a voice to him from the excellent glory, **This is my beloved Son,** in whom I am well pleased.*

Now that we know that Jesus Christ was the Son of God, which Son was he?

*Psalms 89:27 – **Also I will make him my firstborn,** higher than the kings of the earth.*

*Romans 8:29 – For whom he did foreknow, he also did predestinate to be conformed to the image of his Son, **that he might be the firstborn among many brethren.***

*Colosians 1:15 – Who is the image of the invisible God, **the firstborn of every creature:***

*Hebrews 1:6 – And again, **when he bringeth in the firstbegotten into the*** *world,* he saith, *And let all the angels of God worship him.*

Having learned that Jesus Christ is the Son of God, we now know that He is the first Son of God.

Question: If there is a first Son of God, who would be the second Son of God? And the third Son of God, and so forth?

The answer to this question is found in the following scriptures.

> *Psalms 82:6 – I have said, Ye are gods;* **and all of you are children of the most High.**

> *Hosea 1:10 – Yet the number of the children of Israel shall be as the sand of the sea, which cannot be measured nor numbered; and it shall come to pass, that in the place where it was said unto them, Ye are not my people, there it shall be said unto them,* **Ye are the sons of the living God.**

> *Malachi 2:10 –* **Have we not all one father? Hath not one God created us?** *Why do we deal treacherously every man against his brother, by profaning the covenant of our fathers?*

> *Matthew 5:48 – Be ye therefore perfect,* **even as your Father which is in heaven** *is perfect.*

> *Acts 17:28, 29 – For in him we live, and move, and have our being; as certain also of your own poets have said,* **For we are also his offspring. 29. Forasmuch then as we are the offspring of God,** *we ought not to think that the Godhead is like unto gold, or silver, or stone, graven by art and man's device.*

> *Romans 8:16 – The Spirit itself beareth witness with our spirit,* **that we are the children of God:**

> *Ephesians 4:6 –* **One God and Father of all,** *who is above all, and through all, and in you all.*

> *Hebrews 12:9 – Furthermore we have had fathers of our flesh which corrected us, and we gave them reverence:* **shall we not much rather be in subjection unto the Father of spirits,** *and live?*

> *Job 32:8 –* **But there is a spirit in man:** *and the inspiration of the Almighty giveth them understanding.*

We not only learn that all humans are the sons of God, we also learn that He is the Father of our Spirits. The main controversy here is:

Question: When does our spirit begin?

According to some Christians, the spirit begins to exist at birth.

Question: What scriptural evidence is there for this teaching?

> *1 Corinthians 15:45,46 – 45. And so it is written, The first man Adam was made a living soul; the last Adam was made a quickening spirit. 46. Howbeit that was not first which is spiritual, but that which is natural; and afterward that which is spiritual.*

Per the teachings of Joseph Smith, our Father in Heaven formed Christ's spirit first then he created many other spirits which includes all those spirits who have been born here on the earth. The following scriptures testify of mortal man's existence before the world was created, this includes everybody born on this earth and even Lucifer and his angels.

*Job 38:4-7 – **Where wast thou when I laid the foundations of the earth?
Declare, if thou hast understanding….7. When the morning stars sang
together, and all the sons of God shouted for joy?***

When God made the final plans for the creation of the earth, all of us, the sons of God, shouted for joy.

*Ecclesiastes 12:7 – **Then shall the dust return to the earth as it was; and the
spirit shall return unto God who gave it.***

The spirit *"returns unto God,"* who first gave it to us. So if we return, we must have been there before.

*John 3:13 – **And no man hath ascended up to heaven, but he that came
down from heaven, even the Son of man which is in heaven.***

As Christ came down from heaven, no man can ascend up to heaven unless we came down from heaven. Some claim that John was talking only about Christ, but with the previous three scriptures quoted, this can include all men. Therefore, all men will also go back to heaven, as did Jesus Christ.

*Jeremiah 1:4,5 – **Then the word of the Lord came unto me, saying, 5. Before I
formed thee in the belly I knew thee; and before thou camest forth out of the
womb I sanctified thee, and I ordained thee a prophet unto the nations.***

This is another scripture revealing the fact that the Lord actually knew Jeremiah before Jeremiah was born. Then after Jeremiah was born, God ordained him a prophet.

*Job 1:6 – **Now there was a day when the sons of God came to present themselves before the Lord, and Satan came also among them.***

While in the pre-existence, all of the sons of God presented themselves before the Lord, which included Satan.

We now have five scriptures that support Joseph Smith's teachings that we as spirits lived in heaven before the earth was created and that we must *"return"* to God.

There is even mention of Satan living in heaven before the earth.

The War in Heaven. Joseph Smith taught that all humans were living as spirits with God in heaven and that there was a war in heaven.

*Job 1:6 – **Now there was a day when the sons of God came to present themselves before the Lord, and Satan came also among them.***

Joseph Smith continues to teach that in the pre-existence we all presented ourselves before God, to include Satan. God the Father requested a plan that all his spirit children will be able to come to earth, receive a body of flesh and bone and have our faith tested so we can return to Him and inherit all that He has. Christ gave a plan where mankind would have their own free agency to choose between right and wrong. Satan gave a plan that would force all mankind to be good so that all would return to Heavenly Father. Heavenly Father chose Christ's plan. Lucifer rebelled. There was then a war in heaven where Lucifer, the morning star, and his angels were cast out of heaven and onto the earth. Joseph Smith received these additional teachings on this subject from the Book of Moses and the Book of Abraham.

*Moses 4:1-5 – And I, the Lord God, spake unto Moses, saying: That Satan, whom
thou hast commanded in the name of mine Only Begotten, is the same which was
from the beginning, and he came before me, saying—Behold, here am I, send me, I
will be thy son, and I will redeem all mankind, that one soul shall not be lost, and*

surely I will do it; wherefore give me thine honor. 2. But, behold, my Beloved Son, which was my Beloved and Chosen from the beginning, said unto me—Father, thy will be done, and the glory be thine forever. 3. Wherefore, because that Satan rebelled against me, and sought to destroy the agency of man, which I, the Lord God, had given him, and mine own power; by the power of mine Only Begotten, I caused that he should be cast down; 4. And he became Satan, yea, even the devil, the father of all lies, to deceive and to blind men, and to lead them captive at his will, even as many as would not hearken unto my voice. 5. And now the serpent was more subtle than any beast of the field which I, the Lord God, had made.

Abraham 3:22-28 – Now the Lord had shown unto me, Abraham, the intelligences that were organized before the world was; and among all these, there were many of the noble and great ones; 23. And God saw these souls that they were good, and he stood in the midst of them, and he said: These I will make my rulers; for he stood among those that were spirits, and he saw that they were good; and he said unto me: Abraham, thou art one of them; thou wast chosen before thou wast born. 24. And there stood one among them that was like unto God, and he said unto those who were with him: We will go down, for there is space there, and we will take of these materials, and we will make an earth whereon these may dwell; 25. And we will prove them herewith, to see if they will do all things whatsoever the Lord their God shall command them; 26. And they who keep their first estate shall be added upon; and they who keep not their first estate shall not have glory in the same kingdom with those who keep their first estate; and they who keep their second estate shall have glory added upon their heads for ever and ever. 27. And the Lord said: Whom shall I send? And one answered like unto the Son of Man: Here am I, send me. And another answered and said: Here am I, send me. And the Lord said: I will send the first. 28. And the second was angry, and kept not his first estate; and, at that day, many followed after him.

From these passages Joseph Smith teaches us many great mysteries of our Heavenly Father. We learn that:

1. We lived as spirit children of our Heavenly Father, in heaven.

2. Our Heavenly Father requested a plan that would allow all His spirit children to come to earth to receive a body of flesh and bone, like His, and test our faith in Him.

3. Two spirit children of Heavenly Father gave their rendition of His plan. One a plan of free agency for all mankind, and the other where all mankind will obey His will and all would return to the kingdom of God.

4. Heavenly Father chose the first plan that was given by Jesus Christ.

5. Lucifer, who submitted the second plan, became angry and rebelled.

6. There was a war in heaven and Lucifer and one third of the host of heaven was kicked out of heaven and sent to earth, where they immediately began tempting Adam and Eve.

These teachings are from revealed scriptures and revelations that Joseph Smith received and are not from the Bible. The important factor here is that the Bible supports all of these new teachings. The war in heaven is supported in The Book of Revelation.

*Revelation 12:7-9 – **And there was war in heaven: Michael and his angels fought against the dragon; and the dragon fought and his angels.** 8. And prevailed not; neither was their place found any more in heaven. 9. **And the great dragon was cast out, that old serpent, called the Devil, and Satan, which deceiveth the whole world: he was cast out into the earth, and his angels*** *were cast out with him.*

In this passage from Revelation, John teaches the fact that Satan was living in heaven before the world was created. He rebelled against God the Father and Jesus Christ and was cast out with his angels or spirit children of God.

> *Revelation 8:10-12 – And the third angel sounded, and **there fell a great star from heaven,** burning as it were a lamp, and it fell upon the third part of the rivers, and upon the fountains of waters; 11. **And the name of the star is called Wormwood: and the third part of the waters became wormwood;** and many men died of the waters, because they were made bitter. 12.And the fourth angel sounded, and the third part of the sun was smitten, and the third part of the moon, and the third part of the stars; so as the third part of them was darkened, and the day shone not for a third part of it, and the night likewise.*

From Revelation, chapter 8, we learn that a *"great star"* from heaven fell, which was Lucifer. That star fell on one third of the waters, the sun, the moon, and the stars. Which the Mormons believe to be one third of the host of heaven, or one third of Heavenly Father's spirit children.

> *Isaiah 14:12-16 – 12. **How art thou fallen from heaven, O Lucifer, son of the morning! How art thou cut down to the ground, which didst weaken the nations!** 13. For thou hast said in thine heart, I will ascend into heaven, I will exalt my throne above the stars of God: I will sit also upon the mount of the congregation, in the sides of the north: 14. I will ascend above the heights of the clouds; I will be like the most High. 15. Yet thou shalt be brought down to hell, to the sides of the pit. 16. They that see thee shall narrowly look upon thee, and consider thee, saying, Is this the man that made the earth to tremble, that did shake kingdoms;*

Here, Isaiah saw Lucifer as "the son of the morning." He saw Lucifer wanting to exalt himself above everything and make himself equal to our Heavenly Father. He saw Lucifer, because of his pride, fall from heaven. We also read that the apostle Luke saw Lucifer, or Satan, fall from heaven.

> *Luke 10:18 – And he said unto them, **I beheld Satan as lightning fall from heaven.***

The Biblical Support Chart. When Joseph Smith saw God the Father and His son Jesus Christ, Joseph Smith learned that they were two separate beings and God the Father introduced Jesus Christ as His "beloved son". As Joseph Smith continued to be taught by Jesus Christ, he learned that we are all spirit children of our Heavenly Father. Jesus Christ was the first-born and then we all came afterwards, to include Lucifer, commonly known as Satan. The Bible supports all Joseph Smith's teachings on the pre-mortal life.

THE BIBLICAL SUPPORT CHART

Is the following topic supported in the Bible?	Yes or No
Does the Bible support Joseph Smith's teaching that Jesus Christ existed before this life? (John 1:1-3,14; 6:38; 6:51,62; 8:58; 16:28-30; 17:4,5; 1 Pet 1:18-20; Col 1:17)	Yes
Does the Bible support Joseph Smith's teaching that Jesus Christ is the literal son of God? (Matt 3:17; 17:5; Mark 9:7; Luke 9:35; 2 Pet 1:17)	Yes
Does the Bible support Joseph Smith's teaching that Jesus Christ is literally God's first born? (Psm 89:27; Rom 8:29; Col 1:15; Heb 1:6)	Yes
Does the Bible support Joseph Smith's teaching that we are all sons of God? (Psm 82:6; Hos 1:10; Mal 2:10; Matt 5:48; Acts 17:28,29; Rom 8:16; Eph 4:6; Heb 12:9; Job 32:8)	Yes
Does the Bible support Joseph Smith's teaching that our spirits were first in heaven with God before this life? (1 Cor 15:45,46; Job 38:4-7; Eccl 12:7; John 3:13; Jer 1:4,5; Job 1:6)	Yes
Does the Bible support Joseph Smith's teaching that there was a war in heaven that included Lucifer and all men who are born on earth? (Job 1:6; Rev 12:7-9; 8:10-12; Isa 14:12-16; Luke 10:18)	Yes

Author's Note. Expounding on one Christian belief that has seemingly become popular these days is that the spirit and earthly body life of man begins at birth. Never has anybody produced a scripture out of the Bible to support this theory. I would like to Invite anybody who is learned in the "beginning of life" to produce the scripture or scriptures that are the foundation of this belief.

In order to visually describe the different places in heaven that Joseph Smith revealed I have started a map of the sequence of happenings and locations of the Plan of Salvation below. The plan begins with the kingdom of god where we all lived before we came to this earth. Joseph Smith taught that there was a veil of forgetfulness that all humans pass through before we are born on the earth. Once we are born on this earth we should fulfill the items that are described in **Chapter 13: The Plan of Salvation – The Earth Life.** The final stages of the Plan of Salvation are found in **Chapter 12: The Plan of Salvation – The Post-Mortal Life.** As we progress in the Plan of Salvation more of the map will be added.

Map of the Plan of Salvation

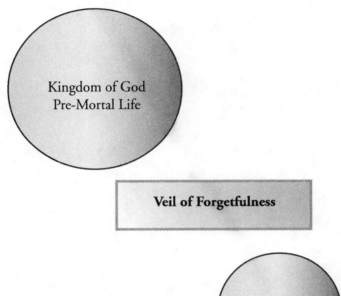

NOTES

CHAPTER 12

THE PLAN OF SALVATION: POST-MORTAL LIFE

Now, were do people go when they die? Most churches believe in the basic Christian doctrine of one heaven and one hell. Good people go to heaven and bad people go to hell. There are several Bible passages that speak of the different places where we go and the different time that we go there.

Some Christians believe that heaven, where God and Jesus came from and still now dwell is an actual location somewhere. This heaven is sometimes referred to as the Kingdom of God. It is in this Kingdom of God where God the Father resides that one must be baptized by water and the Spirit to be able to enter into it.

> *John 3:5 – Jesus answered, Verily, verily, I say unto thee,* ***Except a man be born of water and of the Spirit, he cannot enter into the kingdom of God.***

Now that it is understood that there is a heaven, an actual place where God and Christ exist, we will see how that location relates to other locations that are in "heaven."

Multiple Heavens. Most Christians believe there is only one heaven and one hell. The Prophet Joseph Smith taught that heaven was a series of different locations that people went to as a reward for their works. Here are some of the biblical references that refer to multiple heaven teachings:

> *Psalms 33:6 –* ***By the word of the Lord were the heavens made;*** *and all the host of them by the breath of his mouth.*

> *Psalms 102:25 – Of old hast thou laid the foundation of the earth: and the heavens* ***are the work of thy hands.***

> *Hebrews 1:10 – And, Thou, Lord, in the beginning hast laid the foundation of the earth;* ***and the heavens are the works of thine hands:*** *11. They shall perish; but thou remainest; and they all shall wax old as doth a garment.*

> *Psalms 104:2 – Who coverest thyself with light as with a garment:* ***who stretchest out the heavens like a curtain:***

> *Isaiah 40:22 – It is he that sitteth upon the circle of the earth, and the inhabitants thereof are as grasshoppers;* ***that stretcheth out the heavens as a curtain,*** *and spreadeth them out as a tent to dwell in:*

> *Isaiah 55:9 –* ***For as the heavens are higher than the earth,*** *so are my ways higher than your ways, and my thoughts than your thoughts.*

> *Joel 2:30 –* ***And I will shew wonders in the heavens and in the earth,*** *blood, and fire, and pillars of smoke.*

> *2 Corinthians 12: 2 – I knew a man in Christ above fourteen years ago, (whether in the body, I cannot tell; or whether out of the body, I cannot tell: God knoweth;)* ***such an one caught up to the third heaven.***

Most religious leaders refer to the plural heavens as the sky and/or atmosphere. A simple test can be administered to test this theory. In each passage, replace the word *"heavens"* with the word "skies" or "atmospheres" and see if the passage makes sense.

Paradise and Prison. In establishing the actual existence of several heavens the crucifixion of Jesus Christ will be used as an example. While hanging on the cross, Christ refers to a place where He and the thief hanging next to Him, will be the same day that they die. Christ tells the thief the following:

> Luke 23:42,43 – 42. and he said unto Jesus, lord, remember me when thou comest into thy kingdom. 43. And Jesus said unto him, verily I say unto thee, **To day shalt thou be with me in paradise.**

A lot of people understand *"paradise"* as a place in heaven with Heavenly Father or the kingdom of God. But a deeper look of Christ's crucifixion reveals something different. The day of the crucifixion, Jesus was to be in paradise. At the first day of the week after the crucifixion, early in the morning, Mary went to the sepulcher where they had laid Jesus and Jesus was not there. Jesus then appeared to Mary and when Mary went to touch Him and He said:

> John 20:17 – Jesus saith unto her, touch me not; **for I am not yet ascended to my Father:** but go to my brethren, and say unto them, I ascend unto my Father, and your Father; and to my God, and your God.

This is three days after Jesus died and He still had not yet ascended up to his father, which was in heaven. But Christ, while hanging on the cross stated that *"Today shalt thou be with me in paradise."* This reveals that paradise is not in the same location that our Heavenly Father resides...thus identifying two different places in heaven.

There are other Bible passages that reveal that there is actually another location in heaven in addition to the Kingdom of God and Paradise.

In 1 Peter 3:18-20 Peter talks of Christ going and teaching the spirits in prison.

> I Peter 3:18,19 – 18. For Christ also hath once suffered for sins, the just for the unjust, that he might bring us to God, being put to death in the flesh, but quickened by the spirit: 19. **By which also he went and preached unto the spirits in prison;**

Christ went and preached to the spirits in prison. Who were these spirits? The next verse tells us!

> 1 Peter 3:20 – **Which sometime were disobedient,** when once the longsuffering of god waited in the days of Noah, while the ark was a preparing, wherein few, that is eight souls were saved by water.

Now we know that the disobedient people on the earth at the time of the great flood are some of the ones in the "spirit prison." But we also learn that Christ included all the dead.

> 1 Peter 4:6 – For **for this cause was the gospel preached also to them that are dead,** that they might be judged according to men in the flesh, but live according to god in the spirit.

Understanding better this doctrine of the *"spirits in prison"* as a place where the bad people are sent after they die sheds some light as to what Isaiah prophesied.

> Isaiah 24:21-22 – 21. And it shall come to pass in that day, that the Lord shall punish the host of the high ones that are on high, and the kings of the earth upon the earth. 22. **And they shall be gathered together, as prisoners are gathered in the pit, and shall be shut up in the prison, and after many days shall they be visited.**

This visit to the prison was Jesus Christ, after His crucifixion and before He ascended to His Father in Heaven. Christ himself said:

> John 5:25 – verily, verily, I say unto you, **the hour is coming, and now is, when**

the dead shall hear the voice of the Son of God: and they that hear shall live.

*John 5:28 – Marvel not at this: **for the hour is coming, in the which all that are in the graves shall hear his voice,***

*John 5:29 – **And shall come forth; they that have done good, unto the resurrection of life; and they that have done evil, unto the resurrection of damnation.***

In Luke, Christ also taught about the spirits and the two different places they can go.

*Luke 16:19-23 – 19. There was a certain rich man, which was clothed in purple and fine linen, and fared sumptuously every day: 20. And there was a certain beggar named Lazarus, which was laid at his gate, full of sores, 21. And desiring to be fed with the crumbs which fell from the rich man's table: moreover the dogs came and licked his sores. 22. And it came to pass, that **the beggar died, and was carried by the angels into Abraham's bosom: the rich man also died, and was buried; 23. And in hell he lifted up his eyes, being in torments,** and seeth Abraham afar off, and Lazarus in his bosom.*

This rich man was in hell or what is also called the *"spirit prison."* As he looked at Lazarus who was in a place that, while hanging on the cross, Christ called *"paradise,"* the rich man wanted out of that torment. He asked that Lazarus be sent to dip his finger in water and cool his tongue.

*Luke 16:24 – And he cried and said, Father Abraham, have mercy on me, **and send Lazarus, that he may dip the tip of his finger in water, and cool my tongue; for I am tormented in this flame.***

Father Abraham answers the rich man that he request cannot be fulfilled because there is a *"great gulf"* between the *"prison"* and *"paradise."* At this time, before the sacrifice of Jesus Christ, this *"great gulf"* could not be passed.

*Luke 16:25,26 — 25. But Abraham said, Son, remember that thou in thy lifetime receivedst thy good things, and likewise Lazarus evil things: but now he is comforted, and thou are tormented. 26. And beside all this, **between us and you there is a great gulf fixed: so that they which would pass from hence to you cannot; neither can they pass to us, that would come from thence.***

Once the rich man understood there could be nothing done for himself, he requested that Lazarus, being from the dead, be sent to his brothers so that they would believe in Jesus Christ and not have to suffer the torment in the *"spirit prison"* or hell.

Luke 16:27,28 – 27 Then he said, I pray thee therefore, father, that thou wouldest send him to my father's house: 28. For I have five brethren; that he may testify unto them, lest they also come into this place of torment.

Father Abraham's answer is sore, so very sore, to all who refuse to accept the words of the prophets, both early biblical and latter day prophets!

*Luke 16:29-31 – 29. **Abraham saith unto him, They have Moses and the prophets; let them hear them.** 30. And he said, Nay, father Abraham: but if one went unto them from the dead, they will repent. 31. **And he said unto him, If they hear not Moses and the prophets, neither will they be persuaded, though one rose from the dead.***

Abraham states very clearly, that if a person does not accept the gospel and teachings of the living prophets, they will not accept the gospel if an angel or a resurrected being from the dead appeared to them.

Judgment Day. Now that we identified the spirits in *"paradise"* and *"spirits in prison"* (or hell), we have Christ going and teaching His gospel to the *"spirits in prison"* and all the dead, which includes the spirits in *"paradise."* The next step in the eternities is the *"judgment day"* where all who have lived on this earth will be judged for their works. John has the most famous teaching about this *"judgment day."*

> *Rev 20:12,13 – 12. and I saw the dead, small and great, stand before god; and the books were opened: and another book was opened, which is the book of life: and **the dead were judged out of those things which were written in the books, according to their works.***

> *13. And the sea gave up the dead which were in it; **and death and hell delivered up the dead which were in them:** and they were judged every man according to their works.*

John mentions here twice, that all the dead will be "judged according to their works." John also states another time in the Book of Revelations that men will be judged according to their works.

> *Revelations 22:12 – And behold, I come quickly; **and my reward is with me, to give everyman according as his work shall be.***

Peter also taught that man would be judged by his works.

> *1 Peter 1:17 – And if ye call on the Father who without respect of **persons judgeth according to every man's work,** pass the time of your sojourning here in fear.*

Paul also taught of the judgment.

> *Romans 14:10 – But why dost thou judge thy brother? Or why dost thou set at nought thy brother? **For we shall all stand before the judgment seat of Christ.***

Christ also taught that He would judge every man according their works.

> *Matthew 16:27 – For the Son of man shall come in the glory of his Father with his angels; **and then he shall reward every man according to his works.***

God is Just. If all the dead will hear the gospel of Jesus Christ in the *"spirit paradise"* and *"spirit prison"* or *"hell,"* and if they accept the gospel, how can they receive salvation, or a place in the *"kingdom of God,"* if they have not been baptized by *"the water and the spirit?"*

> *John 5:25 – verily, verily, I say unto you, **the hour is coming, and now is, when the dead shall hear the voice of the Son of God:** and they that hear shall live.*

> *John 5:28 – Marvel not at this: **for the hour is coming, in the which all that are in the graves shall hear his voice,***

> *John 5:29 – And shall come forth; **they that have done good, unto the resurrection of life; and they that have done evil, unto the resurrection of damnation.***

Knowing that it is a requirement to be baptized by the proper authority to enter into the kingdom of God…

> *John 3:5 – Jesus answered, Verily, verily, I say unto thee, **Except a man be born of water and of the Spirit, he cannot enter into the kingdom of God.***

God the Father and Jesus Christ, being just Gods, did provide a way for these people to receive the gospel in the *"spirit paradise"* and the *"spirit prison"* and still receive the ordinance of baptism by water and by the spirit. Isaiah also prophesied of the prisoners in prison will be freed.

> *Isaiah 42:6,7 – 6. I the Lord have called thee in righteousness, and will hold thine hand, and will keep thee, and give thee for a covenant of the people, for a light of the Gentiles; 7. To open the blind eyes,* **to bring out the prisoners from the prison, and them that sit in darkness out of the prison house.**

Isaiah taught that it would be the Lord God, Jesus Christ that would go to the "spirit prison" and proclaim liberty, which is the gospel of Jesus Christ, to the captives and actually open the prison to those who are bound.

> *Isaiah 61:1 – The Spirit of the Lord God is upon me; because the Lord hath anointed me to preach good tidings unto the meek; he hath sent me to bind up the brokenhearted,* **to proclaim liberty to the captives, and the opening of the prison to them that are bound;**

Isaiah even went into further detail as to stating that the *"gentiles"* will be the ones that will be the *"salvation"* of these *"spirits in prison."*

> *Isaiah 49:6 – And he said, It is a light thing that thou shouldest be my servant to raise up the tribes of Jacob, and to restore the preserved of Israel:* **I will also give thee for a light to the Gentiles, that thou mayest be my salvation unto the end of the earth.**

> *Isaiah 49:9,10 – 9.* **That thou mayest say to the prisoners, Go forth; to them that are in darkness, Shew yourselves. They shall feed in the ways, and their pastures shall be in all high places.** *10. They shall not hunger nor thirst; neither shall the heat nor sun smite them: for he that hath mercy on them shall lead them, even by the springs of water shall he guide them.*

Author's Note: For completing the *"jot and tittle,"* Heavenly Father restored the fullness of the Gospel of Jesus Christ through a gentile, Joseph Smith. Thus fulfilling the prophesy of Isaiah in 49:6.

Not only did Isaiah teach the salvation to the *"spirits in prison,"* Zechariah also taught that Jesus Christ would release the prisoners out of the *"pit."*

> *Zechariah 9:9,11 – 9. Rejoice greatly, O daughter of Zion; shout, O daughter of Jerusalem: behold,* **thy King cometh unto thee: he is just, and having salvation; lowly, and riding upon an ass, and upon a colt the foal of an ass.**

> *11.* **As for thee also, by the blood of thy covenant I have sent forth thy prisoners out of the pit wherein is no water.**

Question: How is it that Jesus Christ, through the "gentiles," can provide salvation to the "spirits in prison?"

As we will learn in **Chapter 13 – The Plan of Salvation – The Mortal Life,** we are sent here to become perfect.

> *Matthew 5:48 –* **Be ye therefore perfect, even as your Father which is in heaven is perfect.**

Paul taught that our ancestors could not be made perfect without us.

> *Hebrews 11:40 – God having provided some better thing for us,* **that they without us should not be made perfect.**

Malachi prophesied of Elijah being sent to the earth to turn the hearts of the fathers to the children and the heart of the children to their father.

*Malachi 4:5,6 – 5. Behold, I will send you Elijah the prophet before the coming of the great and dreadful day of the Lord: 6. **And he shall turn the heart of the fathers to the children, and the heart of the children to their father,** lest I come and smite the earth with a curse.*

Elijah actually visited the Prophet Joseph Smith on April 3, 1836 and gave him the authority and power to provide the ordinances of salvation that will give these spirits in *"paradise"* and *"prison"* that never have had the saving ordinance of baptism. This visit occurred in the Kirtland temple and is recorded in the Doctrine and Covenants.

*D&C 110:13-16 – 13. After this vision had closed, another great and glorious vision burst upon us; for **Elijah the prophet, who was taken to heaven without tasting death, stood before us, and said: 14. Behold, the time has fully come, which was spoken of by the mouth of Malachi—testifying that he [Elijah] should be sent,** before the great and dreadful day of the Lord come—15. **To turn the hearts of the fathers to the children, and the children to the fathers, lest the whole earth be smitten with a curse**—16. Therefore, **the keys of this dispensation are committed into your hands;** and by this ye may know that the great and dreadful day of the Lord is near, even at the doors.*

One of the several ordinances *"restored"* to the earth by Elijah is the saving ordinance of *"**baptism for the dead.**"* In the sacred Houses of the Lord, or temples, baptisms are performed by proxy, using the name of the deceased person. The prophet Joseph Smith taught that a person in the *"spirit paradise"* or *"spirit prison"* who accepted the gospel there, could accept the proxy baptism from earth and receive the saving ordinance of baptism and the blessings that come with it. This *"**baptism for the dead**"* ordinance was in effect during the time of the apostles, otherwise Paul, would have never used this ordinance as an example in his letter to the Corinthians.

*1 Corinthians 15:29 – **Else what shall they do which are baptized for the dead, if the dead rise not at all? Why are they then baptized for the dead?***

Today, there are over one hundred temples providing baptisms in the names of the dead, who while on the earth, may not have had the opportunity to accept the gospel of Jesus Christ. Now the *"spirits in prison"* have this opportunity to receive the salvation that Christ promised them. This perfect plan certainly sheds light on how Christ is the *"**Lord both of the dead and living.**"*

*Romans 14:9 – For to this end Christ both died, and rose, and revived, **that he might be Lord both of the dead and living.***

This plan to offer salvation to those who have already died and may never have had the opportunity to accept Jesus Christ as their savior reveals the *"just"* God that the Bible teaches. This plan also offers man *"hope"* for our own eternal salvation as well as those who have passed on before us. Paul understood this "hope" as being the saving temple ordinances as *"**baptism for the dead**"* when he wrote:

*1 Corinthians 15:19 – **If in this life only we have hope in Christ, we are of all men most miserable.***

Genealogy. It is this *"hope"* and *"knowledge"* for our ancestors that the latter day prophets since Joseph Smith have put so much money and effort into the collection of birth, marriage, death, and other historical records. The prophet Joseph Smith taught that once our ancestors have accepted the gospel in the *"**spirit prison**"* and their *"saving ordinances"* are completed in the temples here on earth, the ancestor may join in the salvation of Christ and even move from the *"spirit prison"* into the *"spirit paradise."* The Prophet Joseph Smith stated:

> *...Every man that has been baptized and belongs to the kingdom has a right to be baptized for those who have gone before; and **as soon as the law of the Gospel is obeyed here by their friends who act as proxy for them, the Lord has administrators there to set them free.**[16]*

It is this *"hope"* that our ancestors may be released from the *"spirit prison"* or the *"bonds of hell"* when the LDS membership researches the names of their ancestors and takes those names into the temples and performs these sacred ordinances. Doing genealogy work for our ancestors is explained in more detail in Chapter 13: The Mortal Life.

Judgement Day and Eternal Rewards.

New Heavens. Referring back to the beginning of this chapter and the topic of multiple heavens, once the earth as we know it ends, and Christ comes, He changes the heavens and the earth. The following passages clearly state that the *"heavens"* will change!

> *Isaiah 65:17 – For, behold, **I create new heavens and a new earth:** and the former shall not be remembered, nor come into mind.*

> *Isaiah 66:22 – **For as the new heavens and the new earth,** which I will make, shall remain before me, saith the Lord, so shall your seed and your name remain.*

> *2 Peter 3:13 – Nevertheless we, according to his promise, **look for new heavens** and a new earth, wherein dwelleth righteousness.*

> *Revelation 21:1 – **And I saw a new heaven and a new earth: for the first heaven and the first earth were passed away;** and there was no more sea.*

Glory. To talk about man's rewards in heaven, one must understand the reward of *"glory."* Webster's New World dictionary defines glory as:

> **Glory.** 1. Great honor or fame, or its source 2. adoration 3. **great splendor, prosperity** 4. **heavenly bliss**[17]

From this definition, it includes the "honor" given to a person, it includes "great splendor and/or prosperity, and it includes "heavenly bliss" which can be concluded as a place in heaven where all this honor and glory is given to a person.

While studying the scriptures, one can read that there are varying decrees or levels of glory. It is important to understand that while reading these passages, *"glory"* is usually a gift given to a person for what he has done.

The Earth and Glory. In the following passages, the earth is referred to as being filled with glory and being glory.

> *Isaiah 6:3 – And one cried unto another, and said, Holy, holy, holy, is the Lord of hosts: **the whole earth is full of his glory.***

> *Matthew 4:8 – Again, the devil taketh him up into an exceeding high mountain, and sheweth him all the kingdoms of the world, **and the glory of them;***

Being human beings on this earth at this time is, according to these passages, we are partaking of a level of God's *"glory."* Referring back to **Chapter 11: The Plan of Salvation – the Pre-Mortal Life,** the "Pre-mortal Existence" is where there was a war in heaven over the plan of salvation. Those who chose Lucifer's plan were kicked out of the kingdom of God, and those who chose Christ's plan were rewarded...were rewarded with the opportunity to come to the earth and receive a body of flesh and bone. In simpler terms, for choosing Christ's plan, we are being rewarded with a level of Heavenly Father's glory.

As we continue in the scriptures there are more levels and degrees of glory.

Christ and His Glory. For everything that Christ did for us, he was *"rewarded"* or *"crowned"* with *"glory."*

> *Psalm 8:4-8 – 4. What is man, that thou art mindful of him? And the son of man, that thou visitest him? 5. For thou hast made him a little lower than the angels, **and hast crowned him with glory and honour.** 6. Thou madest him to have dominion over the works of thy hands; thou hast put all things under his feet: 7. All sheep and oxen, yea, and the beasts of the field; 8. The fowl of the air, and the fish of the sea, and whatsoever passeth through the paths of the seas.*

Paul spoke of Christ being crowned with *"glory and honour"* in the same way in his letter to the Hebrews.

> *Hebrews 2:6,7 – 6. But one in a certain place testified, saying, What is man, that thou art mindful of him? **Or the son of man, that thou visitest him? 7. Thou madest him a little lower than the angels; thou crownedst him with glory and honour, and didst set him over the works of thy hands:***

Paul, emphasizing the importance of Christ's reward, again mentions in the same passage that Christ was *"crowned with glory."*

> *Hebrews 2:8,9 – Thou hast put all things in subjection under his feet. For in that he put all in subjection under him, he left nothing that is not put under him. But now we see not yet all things put under him. 9. **But we see Jesus, who was made a little lower than the angels for the suffering of death, crowned with glory and honour;** that he by the grace of God should taste death for every man.*

Paul continues with the rewarding of Christ with *"glory"* was because Christ was able to bring *"many"* sons of Heavenly Father *"unto glory."*

> *Hebrews 2:10 – For it became him, for whom are all things, and by whom are all things, **in bringing many sons unto glory,** to make the captain of their salvation perfect through sufferings.*

And in the famous prayer that is quoted often, *"glory"* is *"forever."*

> *Matthew 6:13 – And lead us not into temptation, but deliver us from evil: **For thine is the kingdom, and the power, and the glory,** for ever. Amen.*

Noting that there is a higher degree of *"glory"* than here on earth, the apostle Timothy taught that Christ was *"received up into glory"* which was Heavenly Father's kingdom.

> *1 Timothy 3:16 – And without controversy great is the mystery of godliness: God was manifest in the flesh, justified in the Spirit, seen of angels, preached unto the Gentiles, believed on in the world, **received up into glory.***

Continuing on the subject of Christ's reward, Peter speaks of it as *"the excellent glory."*

> *2 Peter 1:17 – For he received from God the Father **honour and glory,** when there came such a voice to him from **the excellent glory,** This is my beloved Son, in whom I am well pleased.*

Having Heavenly Father's kingdom, where He resides, being the *"excellent glory"* strongly infers that there may be other levels of glory that are not "excellent" that a person who did not obey Heavenly Father's will go.

Man and His Rewards and Glory. In speaking in terms of "man's rewards" for following Heavenly Father's commandments, receiving a certain level of *"glory"* is definitely one of the rewards.

> *Psalm 62:7 –* **In God is my salvation and my glory:** *the rock of my strength, and my refuge, is in God.*

> *Psalm 84:11 – For the Lord God is a sun and shield:* **the Lord will give grace and glory:** *no good thing will he withheld from them that walk uprightly.*

> *Proverbs 4:9 – She shall give to thine head an ornament of grace:* **a crown of glory** *shall she deliver to thee.*

In speaking of a righteous people Jeremiah talked about those righteous people *"changing their glory"* because they changed the gods they believed in.

> *Jeremiah 2:11 – Hath a nation changed their gods, which are yet no gods? But* **my people have changed their glory** *for that which doth not profit.*

This passage of Jeremiah's introduces the concept of different levels of *"glory"* that is man's reward for our obedience here on earth. Paul follows with a passage that describes our bodies after the resurrection and the varying types of degrees of *"glory"* that our bodies will be.

> *1 Corinthians 15:40-43 – 40. There are also celestial bodies, and bodies terrestrial: but* **the glory of the celestial is one,** *and* **the glory of the terrestrial is another. 41.** **There is one glory of the sun, and another glory of the moon, and another glory of the stars: for one star differeth from another star in glory.** *42. So also is the resurrection of the dead. It is sown in corruption; it is raised in incorruption: 43. It is sown in dishonour;* **it is raised in glory:** *it is sown in weakness; it is raised in power:*

It is important to carefully read the entire 15th chapter of 1 Corinthians because it is all about the resurrection and what happens after this life. This concept of our resurrected bodies receiving a *"glory"* status is confirmed in Paul's writings to the Philippians.

> *Philippians 3:20, 21 – 20. For our conversation is in heaven; from whence also we look for the Saviour, the Lord Jesus Christ: 21.* **Who shall change our vile body, that it may be fashioned like unto his glorious body,** *according to the working whereby he is able even to subdue all things unto himself.*

Paul is specific when he tells how *"our vile body"* will *"be fashioned"* like Christ's *"glorious"* body. From these passages it is evident that our bodies will have the form of one of several basic types of glory. The first being a glorious body fashioned like Christ's glorious body similar to the sun. Then another type of body that is a terrestrial glory similar to the moon. The last type of body mentioned by Paul was a body with the glory like the stars.

The Celestial Glory. To continue on the subject of "glory" and our bodies, the teachings of Joseph Smith will be explained in detail with support from the *Bible*. The first is a celestial glory, like the sun.

Question: Could this glory be the "excellent glory" spoken of by Peter in 2 Peter 1:17?

> *2 Peter 1:17 – For he received from God the Father* **honour and glory,** *when there came such a voice to him from* **the excellent glory,** *This is my beloved Son, in whom I am well pleased.*

Other scriptures talking about the *"glory"* that man may receive are as follows.

> *2 Corinthians 3:7-11 – 7. But if the ministration of death, written and engraven in stones, was* **glorious,** *so that the children of Israel could not stedfastly behold the face of Moses for the* **glory** *of his countenance; which* **glory** *was to bedone away: 8.*

How shall not the ministration of the spirit be rather glorious? 9. For if the ministration of righteousness exceed in glory. 10. For even that which was made glorious had no glory in this respect, by reason of the glory that excelleth. 11. For if that which is done away was glorious, much more that which remaineth is glorious.

2 Corinthians 3:18 – But we all, with open face beholding as in a glass the glory of the Lord, are changed into the same image from glory to glory, even as by the Spirit of the Lord.

2 Corinthians 4:17 – For our light affliction, which is but for a moment, worketh for us a far more exceeding and eternal weight of glory;

Colossians 1:26-28 – 26. Even the mystery which hath been hid from ages and from generations, but now is made manifest to his saints: 27. To whom God would make known what is the riches of the glory of this mystery among the Gentiles; which is Christ in you, the hope of glory: 28. Whom we preach, warning every man, and teaching every man in all wisdom; that we may present every man perfect in Christ Jesus:

1 Peter 5:1 – The elders which are among you I exhort, who am also an elder, and a witness of the sufferings of Christ, and also a partaker of the glory that shall be revealed.

1 Peter 5:4 – And when the chief Shepherd shall appear, ye shall receive a crown of glory that fadeth not away.

1 Peter 5:10 – But the God of all grace, who hath called us unto his eternal glory by Christ Jesus, after that ye have suffered a while, make you perfect, stablish, strengthen, settle you.

The second and third *"glory,"* the *"terrestrial"* and *"telestial **glories**,"* are compared to like the moon and the stars in brightness. They are definitely not as *"glorious"* as the *"Celestial glory"* or the *"excellent glory".* They do qualify for what the prophet Jeremiah was speaking of when he talked about his people having *"changed their glory for that which doth not profit."*

*Jeremiah 2:11 – Hath a nation changed their gods, which are yet no gods? But **my people have changed their glory** for that which doth not profit.*

Joseph Smith's teaching on the different degrees of glories were actual revelations from Jesus Christ that Joseph Smith received on February 16, 1832 and is found in the Doctrine and Covenants (D & C) Section 76. The first is a detailed explanation of who goes to the "excellent glory" or the Celestial Kingdom of God and what blessings they will receive for their works.

D&C 76:50-70 – 50. And again we bear record—for we saw and heard, and this is the testimony of the gospel of Christ concerning them who shall come forth in the resurrection of the just—51. They are they who received the testimony of Jesus, and believed on his name and were baptized after the manner of his burial, being buried in the water in his name, and this according to the commandment which he has given—52. That by keeping the commandments they might be washed and cleansed from all their sins, and receive the Holy Spirit by the laying on of the hands of him who is ordained and sealed unto the power; 53. And who overcome by faith, and are sealed by the Holy Spirit of promise, which the Father sheds forth upon all those who are just and true. 54. They are they who are the church of the Firstborn. 55. They are they into whose hands the Father has given all things—56. They are they who are priests and kings, who have received of his fullness, and of his glory; 57. And are priests of the Most High, after the order of Melchizedek, which was after

*the order of Enoch, which was after the order of the Only Begotten Son. 58.
Wherefore, as it is written, they are gods, even the sons of God—59. Wherefore, all
things are theirs, whether life or death, or things present, or things to come, all are
theirs and they are Christ's, and Christ is God's. 60. And they shall overcome all
things. 61. Wherefore, let no man glory in man, but rather let him glory in God,
who shall subdue all enemies under his feet. 62. These shall dwell in the presence of
God and his Christ forever and ever. 63. These are they whom he shall bring with
him, when he shall come in the clouds of heaven to reign on the earth over his
people. 64. These are they who shall have part in the first resurrection. 65. These are
they who shall come forth in the resurrection of the just. 66. These are they who are
come unto Mount Zion, and unto the city of the living God, the heavenly place, the
holiest of all. 67. These are they who have come to an innumerable company of
angels, to the general assembly and church of Enoch, and of the Firstborn. 68. These
are they whose names are written in heaven, where God and Christ are the judge of
all. 69. These are they who are just men made perfect through Jesus the mediator of
the new covenant, who wrought out this perfect atonement through the shedding of
his own blood. 70.* **These are they whose bodies are celestial, whose glory is
that of the sun, even the glory of God, the highest of all, whose glory the sun
of the firmament is written of as being typical.**

The Terrestrial Glory. The next portion of this vision was about the *"glory of the terrestrial
world"* and those who go there and the blessing that they will receive for their obedience
and works.

> *D&C 76:71-80 – 71. And again,* **we saw the terrestrial world,** *and behold and
> lo,* **these are they who are of the terrestrial, whose glory differs from that of
> the church of the Firstborn who have received the fullness of the Father, even
> as that of the moon differs from the sun in the firmament.** *72. Behold, these
> are they who died without law; 73.* **And also they who are the spirits of men
> kept in prison, whom the Son visited, and preached the gospel unto them,
> that they might be judged according to men in the flesh; 74. Who received
> not the testimony of Jesus in the flesh, but afterwards received it. 75. These
> are they who are honorable men of the earth, who were blinded by the
> craftiness of men. 76. These are they who receive of his glory, but not of his
> fullness. 77. These are they who receive of the presence of the Son, but not of
> the fullness of the Father. 78. Wherefore, they are bodies terrestrial, and not
> bodies celestial, and differ in glory as the moon differs from the sun. 79.**
> *These are they who are not valiant in the testimony of Jesus; wherefore, they obtain
> not the crown over the kingdom of our God. 80. And now this is the end of the
> vision which we saw of the terrestrial, that the Lord commanded us to write while
> we were yet in the Spirit.*

The Telestial Glory. The last portion of this vision is about the *"glory of the stars"* or the
Telestial Kingdom.

> *D&C 76:81-113 – 81. And again, we saw the glory of the telestial, which glory is
> that of the lesser, even as the glory of the stars differs from that of the glory of the
> moon in the firmament. 82.* **There are they who received not the gospel of
> Christ, neither the testimony of Jesus. 83. These are they who deny not the
> Holy Spirit. 84. These are they who are thrust down to hell. 85. These are
> they who shall not be redeemed from the devil until the last resurrection,
> until the Lord, even Christ the Lamb, shall have finished his work. 86. These
> are they who receive not of his fullness in the eternal world, but of the Holy Spirit
> through the ministration of the terrestrial; 87. And the terrestrial through the minis-*

tration of the celestial. 88. And also the telestial receive it of the administering of angels who are appointed to minister for them, or who are appointed to be ministering spirits for them; for they shall be heirs of salvation. 89. And thus we saw, in the heavenly vision, the glory of the telestial, which surpasses all understanding; 90. And no man knows it except him to whom God has revealed it. 91. And thus we saw the glory of the terrestrial which excels in all things the glory of the telestial, even in glory, and in power, and in might, and in dominion. 92. And thus we saw the glory of the celestial, which excels in all things—where God, even the Father, reigns upon his throne forever and ever; 93. Before whose throne all things bow in humble reverence, and give him glory forever and ever. 94. They who dwell in his presence are the church of the Firstborn; and they see as they are seen, and know as they are known, having received of his fullness and of his grace; 95. And he makes them equal in power, and in might, and in dominion. 96. And the glory of the celestial is one, even as the glory of the sun is one. 97. And the glory of the terrestrial is one, even as the glory of the moon is one. 98. And the glory of the telestial is one, even as the glory of the stars is one; for as one star differs from another star in glory, even so differs one from another in glory in the telestial world; 99. For these are they who are of Paul, and of Apollos, and of Cephas. 100. These are they who say they are some of one and some of another—some of Christ and some of John, and some of Moses, and some of Elias, and some of Isaiah, and some of Enoch; 101. **But received not the gospel, neither the testimony of Jesus, neither the prophets, neither the everlasting covenant. 102. Last of all, these are they who will not be gathered with the saints, to be caught up unto the church of the Firstborn, and received into the cloud. 103. These are they who are liars, and sorcerers, and adulterers, and whoremongers, and whosoever loves and makes a lie. 104. These are they who suffer the vengeance of eternal fire. 106. These are they who are cast down to hell and suffer the wrath of Almighty God, until the fullness of times, when Christ shall have subdued all enemies under his feet, and shall have perfected his work;** *107. When he shall deliver up the kingdom, and present it unto the Father, spotless, saying: I have overcome and have trodden the wine-press alone, even the winepress of the fierceness of the wrathe of Almighty God. 108. Then shall he be crowned with the crown of his glory, to sit on the throne of his power to reign forever and ever. 109.* **But behold, and lo, we saw the glory and the inhabitants of the telestial world, that they were as innumerable as the stars in the firmament of heaven, or as the sand upon the seashore;** *110. And heard the voice of the Lord saying: These all shall bow the knee, and every tongue shall confess to him who sits upon the throne forever and ever; 111.* **For they shall be judged according to their works, and every man shall receive according to his own works, his own dominion, in the mansions which are prepared;** *112. And they shall be servants of the Most High; but where God and Christ dwell they cannot come, worlds without end. 113. This is the end of the vision which we saw, which we were commanded to write while we were yet in the Spirit.*

Biblical Support for the Different Kingdoms of God. The *"celestial," "terrestrial,"* and *"telestial glories"* are the rewards for most of the children of God who have been born on this earth. When we receive one of these *"glories,"* we will then have a resurrected body that matches the *"glory"* for which we earned. Read the apostle Paul's teachings on our resurrected bodies again:

1 Corinthians 15:40-43 – 40. There are also celestial bodies, and bodies terrestrial: **but the glory of the celestial is one, and the glory of the terrestrial is another. 41. There is one glory of the sun, and another glory of the moon, and**

another glory of the stars: for one star differeth from another star in glory.
42. So also is the resurrection of the dead. It is sown in corruption; it is raised in
*incorruption: 43. It is sown in dishonour; **it is raised in glory:** it is sown in*
weakness; it is raised in power:

The Lake of Fire and Brimstone. There is still another location that some may go to. This place is the *"lake of fire and brimstone"* that Satan, his angels, and some people who have lived on the earth will be sent. In the same vision that Joseph Smith saw the *"glories"* of the *"celestial,"* *"terrestrial,"* and *"telestial kingdoms,"* he saw the condemnation of the wicked and who goes there.

> *D&C 76:25-39 – 25. And this we saw also, and bear record, that an angel of God who was in authority in the presence of God, who rebelled against the Only Begotten Son whom the Father loved and who was in the bosom of the Father, was thrust down from the presence of God and the Son, 26. And was called Perdition, for the heavens wept over him—he was Lucifer, a son of the morning. 27. And we beheld, and lo, he is fallen! Is fallen, even a son of the morning! 28. And while we were yet in the Spirit, the Lord commanded us that we should write the vision; for we beheld Satan, that old serpent, even the devil, who rebelled against God, and sought to take the kingdom of our God and his Christ—29. Wherefore, he maketh war with the saints of God, and encompasseth them round about. 30. And we saw a vision of the sufferings of those with whom he made war and overcame, for thus came the voice of the Lord unto us: 31. **Thus saith the Lord concerning all those who know my power, and have been made partakers thereof, and suffered themselves through the power of the devil to be overcome, and to deny the truth and defy my power—32. The are they who are the sons of perdition, of whom I say that it had been better for them never to have been born; 33. For they are vessels of wrath, doomed to suffer the wrath of God, with the devil and his angels in eternity; 34. Concerning whom I have said there is no forgiveness in this world nor in the world to come—35. Having denied the Holy Spirit after having received it, and having denied the Only Begotten Son of the Father, having crucified him unto themselves and put him to an open shame. 36. These are they who shall go away into the lake of fire and brimstone, with the devil and his angels—37. And the only ones on whom the** second death shall have any power; 38. Yea, verily, the only ones who shall not be redeemed in the due time of the Lord, after the sufferings of his wrath. 39. For all the rest shall be brought forth by the resurrection of the dead, through the triumph and the glory of the Lamb, who was slain, who was in the bosom of the Father before the worlds were made.*

The Judgment of Christ. The judgment of Christ is a simple doctrine in the Bible that is also a misunderstood and a misrepresented throughout the many different Christian sects. In actuality there are several different judgments at different times of our progression in the mortal and post-mortal lives.

The first real judgment is when we were in the pre-mortal life living with our Heavenly Father. When one third of the host of heaven took Lucifer's side and rebelled against Heavenly Father, that one third of the spirit children of God plus the other two thirds, which includes all who were born on earth, were judged. The one third who rebelled, were kicked out of heaven and sent to earth. The remaining two thirds were judged as worthy to continue on in the eternal progression plan and to be born down here on earth.

A second judgment is when our mortal bodies die. Our spirits are then sent to the *"spirit paradise"* or the *"spirit prison"* or *"hell."* An interesting scripture about this second judgment is found in Luke.

> *Luke 12:4, 5 – 4. And I say unto you my friends, Be not afraid of them that kill the body, and after that have no more that they can do. 5. But I will forewarn you whom ye shall fear:* **Fear him, which after he hath killed hath the power to cast into hell;** *yea, I say unto you, Fear him.*

A third judgment takes place when Jesus Christ comes in all His glory. Many righteous people, who have died, will be raised on the morning of the first resurrection to live through the thousand-year period known as the millennium. The last and final judgment will take place at the end of the thousand-year millennium where Christ reigns on the earth. The following scriptures depict this final judgment not as a mean and cruel type of judgment where Christ cast all the wicked into hell. As the scripture stated in Revelation, that tough judgment was made at the time of our death. In this final judgment, *"hell will give up its dead."*

> *Rev 20:12,13 – 12. and I saw the dead, small and great, stand before god; and the books were opened: and another book was opened, which is the book of life: and the dead were judged out of those things which were written in the books, according to their works. 13. And the sea gave up the dead which were in it;* **and death and hell delivered up the dead which were in them:** *and they were judged every man according to their works.*

This final judgment is a judgment of love and kindness where Christ will be handing out our ***"rewards"*** for the work that we did here on earth. Jeremiah spoke of the loving kindness that Christ will have when He judges us.

> *Jeremiah 9:24 – But let him that glorieth glory in this, that he understandeth and knoweth me,* **that I am the Lord which exercise loving kindness, judgment, and righteousness,** *in the earth: for in these things I delight, saith the Lord.*

John the Beloved spoke of Christ giving out rewards according to the work done by us.

> *Revelations 22:12 – And behold, I come quickly;* **and my reward is with me, to give everyman according as his work shall be.**

Matthew also spoke of Christ giving out rewards according to our works.

> *Matthew 16:27 – For the Son of man shall come in the glory of his Father with his angels;* **and then he shall reward every man according to his works.**

Question: How, at the final judgment, can Christ give out rewards, when there were many wicked people who lived on the earth?

The answer is that all people will have received the gospel of Jesus Christ either here on earth or in the *"spirit paradise"* or *"spirit prison,"* and will have confessed that Jesus Christ is the Lord.

> *Isaiah 45:23 – I have sworn by myself, the word is gone out of my mouth in righteousness, and shall not return,* **That unto me every knee shall bow, every tongue shall swear.**

> *Roman 14:11 – For it is written, As I live, saith the Lord,* **every knee shall bow to me, and every tongue shall confess to God.**

> *Philipians 2:10 –* **That at the name of Jesus every knee should bow,** *of things in heaven, and things in earth, and things under the earth; 11.* **And that every tongue should confess that Jesus Christ is Lord, to the glory of God the Father.**

It will be only Lucifer, his angels, and the few souls who are described as the sons of perdition that will be sent to outer darkness as stated in Doctrine and Covenants,

D&C 76:34 – Concerning whom I have said there is no forgiveness in this world nor in the world to come—35. **Having denied the Holy Spirit after having received it, and having denied the Only Begotten Son of the Father, having crucified him unto themselves and put him to an open shame.**

All the other people who have lived on the earth and who have received the gospel of Christ on the earth, or in the *"spirit paradise"* or in the *"spirit prison"* will be given a reward.

Question: How can the major sinners, whoremongers, murderers, and etc. be given a "reward" when they will be sent to the telestial kingdom where they will not have the presence of Heavenly Father or Jesus Christ?

The answer is that the *"telestial kingdom"* is a better place than earth is now. The *"telestial kingdom"* will be a place similar to the Garden of Eden where there is no sin. Then, if the major sinners receive a better place or kingdom than what we are experiencing now, it is a reward!

The major question that we have to ask ourselves is:

Question: Since, eventually, every knee will bow and every tongue confess, do we want to wait until the *"spirit prison"* or the *"spirit paradise"* to accept this gospel, or do we want to do it now, while we have a chance to do many great works?

The way each one of us answers this question, will determine the *"reward"* or *"glory"* that we will receive.

Question: Do you want a glory that is like the brightness of the sun, or a glory that is like the brightness of the moon, or a glory that is like the brightness of the stars?

This question is for you, and you only, to answer!

The Biblical Support Chart. It must be mentioned here that Joseph Smith did not get any formal religious training that prepared him for organizing the Church of Jesus Christ of Latter Day Saints. In this organization, Joseph Smith established these teachings in the first few years that it existed. Since that time in the 1830's, these basic doctrines in this chapter have stood the test of time and have not changed.

In teaching such controversial doctrine, a true prophet would have biblical support for the doctrine. In the many Christian churches that exist, there are not any that have the extensive teachings of what happens after this life as Joseph Smith taught. There are not any that teach the fact that the people who have died, will still have an opportunity to accept the fullness of the gospel of Jesus Christ and receive the ordinances that will allow them to enter into the kingdom of God.

THE BIBLICAL SUPPORT CHART

Is the following topic supported in the Bible?	Yes or No
Does the Bible support Joseph Smith's teaching on the existence of multiple heavens? (Psm 33:6; 102:25; Heb 1:10; Psm 104:2; Isa 40:22; 55:9; Joel 2:30; 2 Cor 12:2)	Yes
Does the Bible support Joseph Smith's teaching on Paradise? (Luke 23:42,43)	Yes
Does the Bible support Joseph Smith's teaching on the spirit prison? (1 Pet 3:18-20; 4:6; Isa 24:21-22)	Yes
Does the Bible support Joseph Smith's teaching on the location of Paradise and Prison being a separate location from the kingdom of God? (Luke 23:42,43; John 20:7; Luke 16:19-31)	Yes
Does the Bible support Joseph Smith's teaching that Jesus Christ went to the Spirit World to preach the gospel ? (John5:25,28,29; 1 Pet 3:18-20; 1 Pet 4:6)	Yes
Does the Bible support Joseph Smith's teaching that all who are in the spirit world (paradise and prison) will be judged by Jesus Christ? (Rev 20:12,13; Rev 22:12; 1 Pet 1:17; Rom 14:10; Matt 16:27)	Yes
Does the Bible support Joseph Smith's teaching that the people in the spirit world can accept the gospel of Jesus Christ and receive the ordinances required to enter into the kingdom of God? (John 5:25,28,29; John 3:5; Isa 42:6,7; Isa 61:1; Isa 49:6; 49:9,10; Zech (9:9,11; Heb 11:40; Mal 4:5,6; 1 Cor 15:29; Rom 14:9; 1 Cor 15:19)	Yes
Does the Bible support Joseph Smith's teaching that there will be new heavens? (Isa 65:17; 66:22; 2 Pet 3:13; Rev 21:1)	Yes
Does the Bible support Joseph Smith's teaching that God deals in "glory" as to His kingdom and rewards? (Isa 6:3; Matt 4:8; Psm 8:4-8; Heb 2:6-10; Matt 6:13; 1 Tim 3:16; 2 Pet 1:17)	Yes
Does the Bible support Joseph Smith's teaching that we will receive a "glory" depending on our works here in this life? (Psm 62:7; 84:11; Prov 4:9; Jer 2:11; 1 Cor 15:40,41; Phil 3:20,21)	Yes
Does the Bible support Joseph Smith's teaching of the existence of a Celestial glory being the highest glory man can receive? (2 Pet 1:17; 2 Cor 3:7-11; 2 Cor 4:17; Col 1:26-28; 1 Pet 5:1; 5:4; 5:10; Jer 2:11)	Yes
Does the Bible support Joseph Smith's teaching that Jesus Christ will be our judge? (Luke 12:4,5; Rev 20:12,13; Jer 9:24; Rev 22:12; Matt 16:27)	Yes

Author's Note: Having gone through the Plan of Salvation the following map shows the entire plan of salvation. The map now includes the addition of the Spirit World where Paradise and the Spirit Prison is located. It then depicts the final resurrection and judgment day where all men and women will be judged according to their faith and works during mortality.

In the next chapter we will learn the purpose of this mortal life. A very beautiful passage will be introduced that explains the *"purpose of God."* The reality of that passage is staggering! To be able to know why God exists and what He does—is very humbling in one way but very exhilarating in another way!

Having just learned that we will receive a *"glory"* according to our faith and works on this earth, we will learn that if we just do the requirements in the next chapter, we will be able to receive the *"excellent glory"* which will give us the opportunity to live in that *"excellent glory"* with our Heavenly Father, Jesus Christ, and our earthly family who, hopefully, we have grown to know and love.

This is the map of the **The Plan of Salvation** as Joseph Smith taught—according to the Bible!

Map of the Plan of Salvation

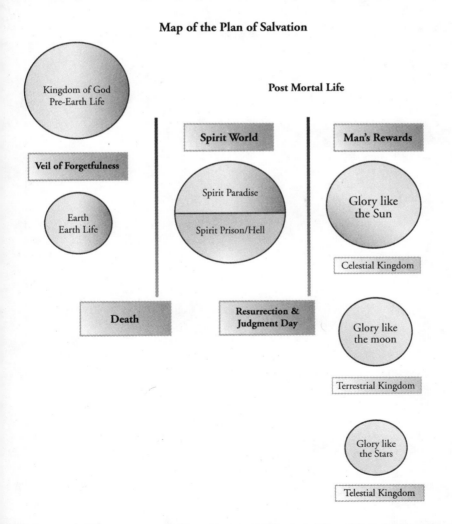

NOTES

CHAPTER 13

THE PLAN OF SALVATION:
THE MORTAL EARTH LIFE.

Question: Why are we here on this earth?

After translating some ancient papyri, Joseph Smith learned the purpose of God was *"to bring to pass the immortality and eternal life of man."*

> *Moses 1:39 – For behold, this is my work and my glory—to bring to pass the immortality and eternal life of man.*

When Joseph Smith received his first visit from Heavenly Father and Jesus Christ, he saw that they were two distinct personages, both with glorified bodies of flesh and bone. In **Chapter 9** we discussed the personality of God the Father and Jesus Christ. The scriptures attesting to Heavenly Father and Jesus Christ having bodies overwhelm the few scriptures that describe them as one spirit.

Joseph Smith, through teachings from God the Father and Jesus Christ, learned that while we were living as spirits in the pre-existence, we saw that Heavenly Father had a glorified body of flesh and bone. As all good fathers want the best for their children, our Heavenly Father wants the best for us, and even wants us to be like Him.

Having set His plan for us, our Heavenly Father made this earth life a very critical part of the plan to *"bring to pass the immortality and eternal life of man."* Most of the requirements (but not limited to these requirements) are what each person must fulfill while on this earth. These requirements are:

1. To be born on this earth with a body.
2. To demonstrate our faith in God the Father and Jesus Christ.
3. To repent of our sins.
4. To be baptized and receive the Gift of the Holy Ghost.
5. To live His commandments.
6. To receive other ordinances.
7. To receive the Ordinance of Eternal Marriage.
8. To endure to the end.
9. To become perfect!
10. To ensure our ancestors receive the ordinances of salvation.

The last chapter on **"The Plan of Salvation – The Post-Mortal Life"** explains in detail what happens when we fail to accomplish these requirements. Those who fail miserably end up in the Telestial kingdom, a glory that does not have the presence of Heavenly Father or Jesus Christ. Those on this earth who are basically mediocre in their performance will be assigned to the Terrestrial kingdom and have the presence of Jesus Christ. Both of these kingdoms will be better than this current earth life, but both are in a state of being cast out of the presence of God the Father and the actual kingdom of God, or Celestial kingdom.

While these two "lesser glories" are not a place of eternal fire and brimstone, they are a form of "eternal damnation." These two "lesser glories" and Christ's judgment of all who are assigned to them do reveal a Heavenly Father who is a loving God but also a just God.

Each of the above stated requirements to enter into the Celestial Glory will now be discussed in detail.

Step 1. To be born on this earth with a body.

This requirement to receive a body is fulfilled for all who are born on this earth. As discussed in **Chapter 11 – *The Plan of Salvation–The Pre-Mortal Life,*** each person born on this earth chose Christ's plan in the pre-mortal life with Heavenly Father. Creating man in the image of God was the first step in Heavenly Father's Plan of Salvation as evidenced in the first chapter of the Bible.

> *Genesis 1:26, 27 – 26. And God said,* **Let us make man in our image, after our likeness:** *and let them have dominion over the fish of the sea, and over the fowl of the air, and over the cattle, and over all the earth, and over every creeping thing that creepeth upon the earth. 17.* **So God created man in his own image, in the image of God created he him;** *male and female created he them.*

To show us the importance of our bodies Christ told us how Heavenly Father felt towards our bodies.

> *1 Corinthians 3:16 –* **Know ye not that ye are the temple of God,** *and that the Spirit of God dwelleth in you?*

> *1 Corinthians 6:19 – What?* **Know ye not that your body is the temple of the Holy Ghost which is in you,** *which ye have of God, and ye are not your own? 20. For ye are bought with a price:* **therefore glorify God in your body, and in your spirit, which are God's.**

Paul understood the importance of having this body and it being *"fashioned like unto his glorious body"* when he wrote to the Philippians.

> *Philippians 3:20, 21 – For our conversation is in heaven; from whence also we look for the Saviour, the Lord Jesus Christ: 21.* **Who shall change our vile body, that it may be fashioned like unto his glorious body,** *according to the working whereby he is able even to subdue all things unto himself.*

It is important to note that Paul was talking to the saints in Philippi. Those saints who understood all of Christ's teachings and were following the commandments. To receive a glorious body like Christ's, one must attain a *"body celestial,"* as was also taught to the Corinthians.

> *1 Corinthians 15:40,41 – 40. There are also celestial bodies, and bodies terrestrial:* **but the glory of the celestial is one, and the glory of the terrestrial is another. 41. There is one glory of the sun, and another glory of the moon, and another glory of the stars: for one star differeth from another star in glory.** *42. So also is the resurrection of the dead. It is sown in corruption; it is raised in incorruption: 43. It is sown in dishonour;* **it is raised in glory:** *it is sown in weakness; it is raised in power:*

To continue, Matthew testified of seeing many bodies of the dead saints, or members of Christ's church, be resurrected with a new immortal body.

> *Matthew 27:52,53 – 52. And the graves were opened; and* **many bodies of the saints which slept arose, 53. And came out of the graves after his resurrection,** *and went into the holy city, and appeared unto many.*

Paul then told the saints in Rome that we, while on earth, wait for the time when our bodies are redeemed.

> *Romans 8:23 – And not only they, but ourselves also, which have the firstfruits of The Spirit, even we ourselves groan within ourselves,* **waiting for the adoption, to wit, the redemption of our body.**

Many fables, modern movies, and TV shows glamorize the thought of being "immortal" and living forever. It is Heavenly Father's plan for everybody that is born on earth—to someday be "immortal," and will live forever with a body that will not die. This is part of the "grace" of God that no matter how good, bad, or indifferent a person is here on this earth; all will receive an immortal body!

> *Acts 24:15 – And have hope toward God, which they themselves also allow,* **that there shall be a resurrection of the dead, both of the just and unjust.**

> *1 Corinthians 15:21,22 – 21. For since by man came death,* **by man came also the resurrection of the dead. 22. For as in Adam all die, even so in Christ shall all be made alive.**

Author's Note: Receiving a body of flesh and bone is a pertinent requirement and a pre-earthly desire of everybody who has been born on this earth. The importance of being resurrected and receiving an immortal body is also great to each one of us. One example to demonstrate how important this body is to us—eternally, is given in the Doctrine and Covenants section 138. This was a revelation given to President Joseph F. Smith (the prophet of the church at that time) on October 3, 1918. It is generally referred to as the "vision of the redemption of the dead" given to President Joseph F. Smith.

In this vision President Joseph F. Smith saw all the righteous dead to include the great leaders and the members of the church through the ages waiting for Christ to come to the spirit world and redeem them. This was at the time of Christ's crucifixion. Included in this list of leaders were all the righteous people of the Old Testament which included Father Adam, Mother Eve, Abel the first martyr, Seth, Noah, Shem, Abraham, Isaac, Jacob, Moses, Isaiah, Ezekiel, Daniel, Elias, Malachi, Elijah, and even the prophets from the *Book of Mormon* and all the other righteous individuals from their time.

In this vision, President Joseph F. Smith saw how these spirits felt about being spirits that were separated from their bodies. This is what he said:

> *Doctrine & Covenants 138:50 – **For the dead had looked upon the long absence of their spirits from their bodies as a bondage.***

The separation of our spirits and our bodies was perceived as "bondage!" These good people who are in the spirit paradise felt this way! Receiving this body on earth, then dying and then being resurrected is a great part of the Plan of Salvation. This brings to my mind the great scriptural passage just mentioned:

> *Moses 1:39 – **For behold, this is my work and my glory—to bring to pass the immortality and eternal life of man.***

This one profound statement gives the whole purpose and goal of our Heavenly Father. One half of it is to give us immortal bodies and the second half is explained **Chapter 16 – The God-Makers.**

Step 2. To demonstrate our faith in God the Father and Jesus Christ.

The prophet Joseph Smith also learned that we are here to prove ourselves by doing what the Lord our God has commanded us. They who do what is commanded will have a different glory in a different kingdom than those who do not prove themselves—thus the three different degrees of glory—the Celestial Glory, the Terrestrial Glory, and the Telestial glory.

> *Abraham 3: 25, 26 – 25. **And we will prove them herewith, to see if they will do all things whatsoever the Lord their God shall command them; 26. And they who keep their first estate shall be added upon; and they who keep not***

> *their first estate shall not have glory in the same kingdom with those who keep their first estate;*

The first step in proving ourselves is well understood by most Christian religions.

> *Mark 11:22 – And Jesus answering saith unto them,* **Have faith in God.**

We must have faith in Heavenly Father and Jesus Christ. Some of the biblical teachings on faith are:

> *Habakkuk 2:4 – Behold, his soul which is lifted up is not upright in him:* **but the just shall live by his faith.**

> *Romans 1:17 – For therein is the righteousness of God revealed from faith to faith:* **as it is written, The just shall live by faith.**

> *Galatians 3:11 – But that no man is justified by the law in the sight of God, it is evident: for,* **The just shall live by faith.**

> *Hebrews 10:38 –* **Now the just shall live by faith:** *but if any man draw back, my soul shall have no pleasure in him.*

> *2 Corinthians 5:6,7 – 6. Therefore we are always confident, knowing that, whilst we are at home in the body, we are absent from the Lord: 7.* **(For we walk by faith, not by sight)**

Question: What is faith?

Paul defined faith as:

> *Hebrews 11:1 –* **Now faith is the substance of things hoped for, the evidence of things not seen.**

Webster's Ninth New Collegiate Dictionary[18] defines faith as:

> 2 a (1) belief and trust in and loyalty to God (2) belief in the traditional doctrines of a religion b. (1) firm belief in something for which there is no proof (2) complete trust.

Being that most Christian religions are faith based, where the people must "believe in something for which there is no proof," they are exercising or practicing this second step. For those who exercise this faith in Jesus Christ, His atonement, His resurrection, and His redemption for all mankind, it will abode well for them. This is what Christ said about the people who have faith after the apostle Thomas did not believe Christ was resurrected until he actually saw Him for himself.

> *John 20:29 – Jesus saith unto him, Thomas, because thou hast seen me, thou hast believed:* **blessed are they that have not seen, and yet have believed.**

Some Christian churches have this "faith" requirement step as the only requirement to be "saved". As was explained in Chapter 10 – Saved By Grace, Joseph Smith taught that having "faith" was important, but it is only the second step.

Step 3. To repent of our sins.

The third step is to repent of our sins. John the Baptist was clear when he preached repentance saying:

> *Matthew 3:2 – And saying,* **Repent ye: for the kingdom of heaven is at hand.**

Christ taught the same saying:

> *Mark 1:15 – And saying, The time is fulfilled, and the kingdom of God is at hand;* **repent ye, and believe the gospel.**

When the twelve apostles were first sent out to preach, they preached repentance.

> *Mark 6:12 –* **And they went out, and preached that men should repent.**

> *Acts 17:30 – And the times of this ignorance God winked at;* **but now commandeth all men every where to repent:**

> *2 Peter 3:9 – The Lord is not slack concerning his promise, as some men count slackness; but is longsuffering to us-ward,* **not willing that any should perish, but that all should come to repentance.**

The importance of repentance is great. Once a person repents, his sins may be blotted out.

> *Acts 3:19 –* **Repent ye therefore, and be converted, that your sins may be blotted out,** *when the times of refreshing shall come from the presence of the Lord.*

Having our sins forgiven is a requirement to enter into the presence of God, or in layman's terms, if one does not repent, he/she will not enter into "the kingdom of Christ and God."

> *Ephesians 5:5 – For this ye know, that no whoremonger,* **nor unclean person,** *nor covetous man, who is an idolater,* **hath any inheritance in the kingdom of Christ and of God.**

To continue in layman's terms, Christ was very clear as to what happens to the people who do not repent.

> *Luke 13:3 – I tell you, Nay: but,* **except ye repent, ye shall all likewise perish.**

Repentance defined. Webster defines the term to "repent" as:

> Repent – 1. to turn from sin and dedicate oneself to the amendment of one's life 2. a. to feel regret or contrition b. to changes one's mind.

In order to repent one must recognize what he/she is doing is wrong, feel guilty for one's bad deeds, turn from that sin and never do it again. These people who do not have faith and do not repent will end up in the Terrestrial or Telestial kingdoms.

Step 4. To be baptized and receive the Gift of the Holy Ghost.

Jesus Christ, the literal Son of God, who was also God was baptized and received the Holy Ghost.

> *Matthew 3:13-17 – 13. Then cometh Jesus from Galilee to Jordan unto John, to be baptized of him. 14. But John forbad him, saying, I have need to be baptized of thee, and comest thou to me? 15. And Jesus answering said unto him, Suffer it to be so now: for thus it becometh us to fulfill all righteousness. Then he suffered him. 16.* **And Jesus, when he was baptized, went up straightway out of the water:** *and, lo, the heavens were opened unto him, and he saw the Spirit of God descending like a dove, and lighting upon him: 17. And lo a voice from heaven, saying, This is my beloved Son, in whom I am well pleased.*

Question: Why was Jesus Christ baptized?

> *John 3:5,6 – 5.* **Jesus answered, Verily, verily, I say unto thee, Except a man be born of water and of the Spirit, he cannot enter into the kingdom of God.**

> *Mark 16:15,16 – 15. And he said unto them, Go ye unto all the world, and preach*

the gospel to every creature. 16. **He that believeth and is baptized shall be saved; but he that believeth not shall be damned.**

Answer: Because proper baptism is a requirement for a man or woman to enter into the kingdom of God. Jesus Christ, being a man, also needed the ordinance of baptism.

Even Jesus Christ needed the ordinance of baptism and receive the Gift of the Holy Ghost to get into the kingdom of God. Everybody needs to follow His example.

Acts 2:38 – Then Peter said unto them, **Repent, and be baptized every one of you in the name of Jesus Christ for the remission of sins, and ye shall receive the gift of the Holy Ghost.**

Acts 19:4-6 – 4. Then said Paul, John verily baptized with the baptism of repentance, saying unto the people, that they should believe on him which should come after him, that is, on Christ Jesus. 5. When they heard this, **they were baptized in the name of the Lord Jesus.** *6. And when Paul had laid his hands upon them,* **the Holy Ghost came on them;** *and they spake with tongues, and prophesied.*

As Joseph Smith taught in Chapter 4-The Priesthood, it is a requirement to have the proper priesthood to perform the ordinances of the church of Jesus Christ. These priesthoods are the Aaronic Priesthood and the Melchizedek Priesthood. The original twelve apostles were given the power and authority to go out and perform the necessary ordinances. It is important to be baptized by the proper authority, because if not, the ordinance does not count as valid. There is an example of this when Paul came upon some men who thought that "they were baptized unto John's baptism." But after close scrutiny by Paul, he determined that it was not the proper baptism because the gift of the Holy Ghost was not also given to them, Paul immediately went and baptized them again.

Acts 19:1-6 – 1. And it came to pass, that, while Apollos was at Corinth, Paul having passed through the upper coasts came to Ephesus: and finding certain disciples, 2. He said unto them, **Have ye received the Holy Ghost since ye believed?** *And they said unto him,* **We have not so much as heard whether there be any Holy Ghost.** *3. And he said unto them, Unto what then were ye baptized? And they said, Unto John's baptism. 4. Then said Paul,* **John verily baptized with the baptism of repentance, saying unto the people, that they should believe on him which should come after him, that is, on Christ Jesus. 5. When they heard this, they were baptized in the name of the Lord Jesus. 6. And when Paul had laid his hands upon them, the Holy Ghost came on them; and they spake with tongues, and prophesied.**

This *"one baptism"* requirement is confirmed in the apostle Paul's teachings to the Ephesians.

Ephesians 4:5 – One Lord, one faith, **one baptism,**

Question: What happens to those Christians who do not receive the correct baptism?

Answer: They go into the Terrestrial Kingdom in the presence of Jesus Christ. They do not get to enter into the Celestial Kingdom where Heavenly Father dwells.

The following scriptures may shed some light on this very important requirement.

Matthew 7:13,14 – 13. **Enter ye in at the strait gate: for wide is the gate, and broad is the way, that leadeth to destruction, and many there be which go in thereat:** *14.* **Because strait is the gate, and narrow is the way, which leadeth unto life, and few there be that find it.**

Matthew 7:21-23 – 21. **Not every one that saith unto me, Lord, Lord, shall** *enter into the kingdom of heaven;* but he that doeth the will of my Father which is in heaven. 22. ***Many will say to me in that day, Lord, Lord, have we not prophesied in thy name: and in thy name have cast out devils? And in thy name done many wonderful works? 23. And then will I profess unto them, I never knew you: depart from me, ye that work iniquity.***

No matter what anybody says or teaches, the proper baptism and receiving of the Gift of the Holy Ghost is a requirement to enter into the kingdom of our Heavenly Father.

Question: How does one know if he/she has received the proper ordinance of baptism?

The answer lies in what Christ stated in between the two statements above.

> Matthew 7:15,16,20 – 15. ***Beware of false prophets, which come to you in sheep's clothing, but inwardly they are ravening wolves. 16. Ye shall know them by their fruits. Do men gather grapes of thorns, or figs of thistles?***

> 20. ***Wherefore by their fruits ye shall know them.***

It is the theme of this book to reveal who is a real prophet of God! Once a person finds out who a real prophet is, he/she will find out which baptism is the proper baptism.

Step 5. To live His commandments.

Unlike most other Christian churches that have wavered on many of the commandments of God, Joseph Smith and the prophets who have followed him, have maintained a strong stance on living all the commandments of God. More is explained as to why we must live the commandments in the **Chapter 14 – The Mormon Temples** and **Chapter 15 – The Covenant People.** The basics of living the commandments start with the very basic and simple teachings of Jesus Christ. The apostle John taught a lot in his writings on keeping the commandments. John first quoted Jesus Christ.

> John 14:2 – *In my Father's house are many mansions: if it were not so, I would have told you. I go to prepare a place for you.*

Referring back to the post mortal ***"glories"*** that Christ will give us are the Celestial kingdom, the Terrestrial kingdom, and the Telestial kingdom. The Celestial kingdom is the place where Christ talks about now, where our Heavenly Father is and where Christ went to—the actual kingdom of our Heavenly Father.

Talking to His apostles Christ continued:

> John 14:3 – ***And if I go and prepare a place for you,*** *I will come again, and receive you unto myself; that where I am, there ye may be also.*

The apostle Thomas questioned Him about not knowing the way. Christ answered him:

> John 14:5 – *Thomas saith unto him, Lord, we know not whither thou goest; and how can we know the way?*

Christ answered him:

> John 14:6 – ***Jesus saith unto him, I am the way, the truth, and the life: no man cometh unto the Father, but by me. 7. If ye had known me, ye should have known my Father also: and from henceforth ye know him, and have seen him.***

Christ continues teaching Thomas and the other apostles:

> John 14:12 – *Verily, verily, I say unto you,* **He that believeth on me, the works**

that I do shall he do also; and greater works than these shall he do; because I go unto my Father.

Christ was very plain—those who believeth in Christ will do even greater works than Christ. These works include teaching the gospel, healing the sick, raising the dead, and being an example to all in living a good life or keeping the commandments of God. Then Christ on this same topic as works states this very simple statement:

> *John 14:15 – If ye love me, keep my commandments.*

Christ continues to teach that He will manifest Himself to those who love Him and keep the commandments.

> *John 14:21-23 – 21. He that hath my commandments, and keepeth them, he it is that loveth me: and he that loveth me shall be loved of my Father, and I will love him, and will manifest myself to him. 22. Judas saith unto him, not Iscariot, Lord, how is it that thou wilt manifest thyself unto us, and not unto the world? 23. Jesus answered and said unto him, If a man love me, he will keep my words: and my Father will love him, and we will come unto him, and make our abode with him.*

More is spoken on these topics of keeping the commandments, being loved by the Father, and Christ manifesting Himself to us in the following chapters **Chapter 14 – The Mormon Temples and Chapter 15 – The Covenant People** and **Chapter 16 – The God-Makers.** What is important to learn now—is to keep God's commandments—NOW!

The Ten Commandments. For one to keep God's commandments, he/she needs to know what the commandments are. The basic place to start is when Moses received the Ten Commandments from the God of the Old Testament.

> *Exodus 34:28 – And he was there with the Lord forty days and forty nights; he did neither eat bread, nor drink water. And he wrote upon the tables the words of the covenant, the ten commandments.*

These are the Ten Commandments given through Moses.

The First Commandment.

> *Exodus 20:3-17 – 3. Thou shalt have no other gods before me.*

The Second Commandment.

> *4. Thou shalt not make unto thee any graven image, or any likeness of any thing that is in heaven above, or that is in the earth beneath, or that is in the water under the earth: 5. Thou shalt not bow down thyself to them nor serve them: for I the Lord thy god am a jealous God, visiting the iniquity of the fathers upon the children unto the third and fourth generation of them that hate me; 6. And shewing mercy unto thousands of them that love me, and keep my commandments.*

The Third Commandment.

> *7. Thou shalt not take the name of the Lord thy God in vain; for the Lord will not hold him guiltless that taketh his name in vain.*

The Fourth Commandment.

> *8. Remember the sabbath day, to keep it holy. 9. Six days shalt thou labour, and do all thy work: 10. But the seventh day is the Sabbath of the Lord thy God: in it thou shalt no do any work, thou, nor thy son, nor they daughter, thy manservant, nor thy maidservant, nor thy cattle, nor thy stranger that is within thy gates: 11. For in six days the Lord made heaven and earth, the sea, and all that in them is, and rested*

the seventh day: wherefore the Lord blessed the Sabbath day, and hallowed it.

The Fifth Commandment.

12. Honour thy father and thy mother: that thy days may be long upon the land which the Lord thy God giveth thee.

The Sixth Commandment.

13. Thou shalt not kill.

The Seventh Commandment.

14. Thou shalt not commit adultery.

The Eighth Commandment.

15. Thou shalt not steal.

The Ninth Commandment.

16. Thou shalt not bear false witness against thy neighbor.

The Tenth Commandment.

17. Thou shalt not covet thy neighbour's house, thou shalt not covet thy neighbour's wife, nor his manservant, nor his maidservant, nor his ox, nor his ass, nor any thing that is thy neighbour's.

There are some Christians who believe that when Christ fulfilled the Law of Moses, Christ did away with the original Ten Commandments. Those who feel this way need to read the words of the original apostles in the New Testament and they will find that not only did they support all the original Ten Commandments; they also expanded on those with several new commandments. Two of these commandments that Joseph Smith stressed, when other churches were not stressing them, are tithing and the Word of Wisdom. Another commandment that is currently very controversial has to do with homosexuality.

Here is what the Bible has to say about these commandments.

Tithing. The law of tithing, defined as paying one-tenth of all ones increases to God, was an old biblical practice. It is confirmed in the following Old Testament passages:

*Genesis 14:20 – And blessed be the most high God, which hath delivered thine enemies into thy hand. **And he gave him tithes of all.***

*Hebrews 7:1,2 – 1. For this Melchizedek, king of Salem, priest of the most high God, who met Abraham returning from the slaughter of the kings, and blessed him; 2. **To whom also Abraham gave a tenth part of all;** first being by interpretation King of righteousness, and after that also King of Salem, which is, King of peace.*

*Genesis 28:22 – And this stone, which I have set for a pillar, shall be God's house: **and of all that thou shalt give me I will surely give the tenth unto thee.***

*Leviticus 27:30 – **And all the tithe of the land, whether of the seed of the land, or of the fruit of the tree, is the Lord's: it is holy unto the Lord.***

*Numbers 18:26 – Thus speak unto the Levites, and say unto them, When ye take of the children of Israel **the tithes which I have given you from them for your inheritance, then ye shall offer up an heave offering of it for the Lord, even a tenth part of the tithe.***

*Deuteronomy 12:6 – And thither ye shall bring your burnt offerings, and your sacrifices, **and your tithes,** and heave offerings of your hand, and your vows, and your freewill offerings, and the firstlings of your herds and of your flocks:*

> *Deuteronomy 14:22 – **Thou shalt truly tithe all the increase of thy seed,** that the field bringeth forth year by year.*
>
> *2 Chronicles 31:5 – And as soon as the commandment came abroad, the children of Israel brought in abundance the firstfruits of corn, wine, and oil, and honey, and of all the increase of the field; **and the tithe of all things brought they in abundantly.***

Seeing that there was a tithe in the Old Testament times, there is not much said about it in the New Testament. Although there was a form of donations to the original Church of Jesus Christ, it carried on through the years to today. Most Christian churches have offerings of some type to support them.

With the claim of Joseph Smith that *"Elias truly shall first come, and restore all things…"*

> *Matthew 17:11 – And Jesus answered and said unto them, **Elias truly shall first come, and restore all things.***

…and Christ's statement that *"one jot or one tittle shall in no wise pass from the law, till all be fulfilled…"*

> *Matthew 5:17-18 – 17. Think not that I am come to destroy the law, or the prophets: I am not come to destroy, but to fulfill. 18. For verily I say unto you, Till heaven and earth pass, **one jot or one tittle shall in no wise pass from the law, till all be fulfilled.***

…that tithing should be one of the laws that should be restored!

The prophet Malachi was very clear on the law of tithing. He quoted God as saying that when we did not pay a full tithing, or a full tenth of our increases, that God looked at it as actually "robbing God." Then God commanded us to pay tithing.

> *Malachi 3:8-10 – 8. Will a man rob God? Yet ye have robbed me. But ye say, **Wherein have we robbed thee? In tithes and offerings.** 9. Ye are cursed with a curse: for ye have robbed me, even this whole nation. 10. **Bring ye all the tithes into the storehouse,** that there may be meat in mine house, and prove me now herewith, saith the Lord of hosts, if I will not open you the windows of heaven, and pour you out a blessing, that there shall not be room enough to receive it.*

Yes, tithing is one of the laws that should be restored! A revelation given to Joseph Smith on September 11, 1831 that restored the law of tithing. It also came with a blessing for doing so. That blessing was that those people who paid a full tithing *"shall not be burned at his coming!"*

> *D&C 64:23 – Behold, now it is called today until the coming of the Son of Man, **and verily it is a day of sacrifice, and a day for the tithing of my people; for he that is tithed shall not be burned at his coming.***

The Word of Wisdom. One of the most controversial teachings of Joseph Smith was his new commandment called the Word of Wisdom. This commandment is more a health law than a moral law but is very specific in what we should and should not eat or drink and when we should eat certain items. The following are the excerpts of the specific instructions that were given as direct revelation to Joseph Smith from the Lord on February 27, 1833.

> *D&C 89:4 – 4. Behold, verily, thus saith the Lord unto you: In consequence of evils and designs which do and will exist in the hearts of conspiring men in the last days, I have warned you, and forewarn you, **by giving unto you this word of wisdom by revelation—5. That inasmuch as any man drinketh wine or strong drink***

among you, behold it is not good, neither meet in the sight of your Father, only in assembling yourselves together to offer up your sacraments before him.

7. And, again, strong drinks are not for the belly, but for the washing of your bodies. *8. And again, tobacco is not for the body, neither for the belly, and is not good for man,* but is an herb for bruises and all sick cattle, to be used with judgment and skill. *9. And again, hot drinks are not for the body or belly.*

12. Yea, flesh also of beasts and of the fowls of the air, I, the Lord, have ordained for the use of man with thanksgiving; nevertheless they are to be used sparingly; 13. And it is pleasing unto me that they should not be used, only in times of winter, or of cold, or famine.

Joseph Smith, having received the Word of Wisdom from the Lord, being a prophet of God, and considering the fact that the Lord stated that Elias will come and *"restore all things"* should have some support in the Bible on a health law of what one should and should not eat or drink. This is what the Old Testament of the Bible has to say about the health laws. It is very clear that liquor and strong drinks were forbidden.

Leviticus 10:9-11 – 9. Do drink wine nor strong drink, thou, nor thy sons with thee, when ye go into the tabernacle of the congregation, *lest ye die: it shall be a statute for ever throughout your generations: 10. And that ye may put differ-ence between holy and unholy, and between unclean and clean.* 11. And that ye may teach the children of Israel all the statutes which the Lord hath spoken unto them by the hand of Moses.

Numbers 6:2,3 – 2. Speak unto the children of Israel, and say unto them, When either man or woman shall separate themselves to vow a vow of a Nazarite, to separate themselves unto the Lord: 3. *He shall separate himself from wine and strong drink, and shall drink no vinegar of wine, or vinegar of strong drink, neither shall he drink any liquor of grapes, nor eat moist grapes, or dried.*

Eccl 10:17 – Blessed art thou, O land, when thy king is the son of nobles, and thy princes *eat in due season, for strength, and not for drunkenness!*

Isaiah 5:22 – Woe unto them that are mighty to drink wine, and men of strength to mingle strong drink:

In the Old Testament, it was very plain and laid out for the people of Moses. The Lord gave them specific instructions on what was to be eaten and what wasn't to be eaten.

Deuteronomy 14:2-21 – 2. For thou art an holy people unto the Lord thy God, and the Lord hath chosen thee to be a peculiar people unto himself, above all the nations that are upon the earth. 3. *Thou shalt not eat any abom-inable thing. 4. These are the beasts which ye shall eat: the ox, the sheep, and the goat,* 5. The hart, and the roebuck, and the fallow deer, and the wild goat, and the pygarg, and the wild ox, and the chamois. 6. And every beast that parteth the hoof, and cleaveth the cleft into two claws, and cheweth the cud among the beasts, that ye shall eat. 7. *Nevertheless these ye shall not eat of them that chew the cud, or of them that divide the cloven hoof;* as the camel , and the hare, and the coney: for they chew the cud, but divide not the hoof; therefore they are unclean unto you. 8. *And the swine, because it divideth the hoof, yet cheweth not the cud, it is unclean unto you: ye shall not eat of their flesh,* nor touch their dead carcase. 9. These ye shall eat of all that are in the waters: al that have fins and scales shall ye eat: 10. *And whatsoever hath not fins and scales ye may not eat; it is unclean unto you.* 11. Of all clean birds ye shall eat. 12. *But these are they of which ye shall not eat: the eagle, and the ossifrage, and the ospray,* 13. And

> *the glede, and the kite, and the vulture after his kind, 14. And every raven after his kind, 15. And the owl, and the night hawk, and the cuckow, and the hawk after his kind, 16. The little owl, and the great owl, and the swan, 17. And the pelican, and the gier eagle, and the cormorant, 18. And the stork, and the heron after her kind, and the lapwing, and the bat. 19. And every creeping thing that flieth is unclean unto you: they shall not be eaten. 20. But of all clean fowls ye may eat. 21. **Ye shall not eat of any thing that dieth of itself:** thou shalt give it unto the stranger that is in thy gates, that he may eat it; or thou mayest sell it unto an alien: for thou art an holy people unto the Lord thy God. Thou shalt not seethe a kid in his mother's milk. 22. Thou shalt truly tithe all the increase of thy seed, that the field bringeth forth year by year.*

Notice that in the last verse (verse 22), that along with the commandment on what was to be eaten was the commandment to pay tithing on the increase of their crops.

The New Testament also has a few things to say about the commandment of abstaining from the different substances.

> *Ephesians 5:17,18 – 17. Wherefore be ye not unwise, but understanding what the will of the Lord is. 18. **And be not drunk with wine,** wherein is excess; but be filled with the Spirit;*

> *Col 2:16 – Let no man therefore judge you in meat, or in drink, **or in respect of an holyday, or of the new moon, or of the Sabbath days:***

> *1 Timothy 3:1-3 – 1. This is a true saying, If a man desire the office of a bishop, he desireth a good work. 2. A bishop then must be blameless, the husband of one wife, vigilant, **sober,** of good behaviour, given to hospitality, apt to teach; 3. **Not given to wine,** no striker, not greedy of filthy lucre; but patient, not a brawler, not covetous;*

These commandments of the Lord to abstain from these substances is very clear and direct. The importance of living His health commandments is revealed in the next two passages.

> *1 Corinthians 6:10 – Nor thieves, nor covetous, **nor drunkards,** nor revilers, nor extortioners, **shall inherit the kingdom of God.***

> *Daniel 1:8 – But **Daniel purposed in his heart that he would not defile himself with the portion of the king's meat, nor with the wine which he drank: therefore he requested of the prince of the eunuchs that he might not defile himself.***

It is clear that a "drunkard" will not enter into the kingdom of God and the last passage about Daniel is clear that he did not want to defile himself with *"the king's meat nor with the wine."*

Question: What happens when one defiles himself with these restricted substances?

> *1 Cor 3:16,17 – 16. Know ye not that ye are the temple of God, and that the Spirit of God dwelleth in you? 17. **If any man defile the temple of God, him shall God destroy; for the temple of God is holy, which temple ye are.***

It is clear that if a person defiles his body, he/she will be "destroyed!"

Word of Wisdom Blessings. As usual, when the Lord gives a commandment, there is a blessing that comes from the obedience to the commandment. These are the blessings that come with obeying the Word of Wisdom.

> *D&C 89:18-21 – 18. And all saints who remember to keep and do these sayings, walking in obedience to the commandments, shall receive health in their navel and*

marrow to their bones; 19. And shall find wisdom and great treasures of knowledge, even hidden treasures; 20. And shall run and not be weary, and shall walk and not faint. 21. And I, the Lord, give unto them a promise, that the destroying angel shall pass by them, as the children of Israel, and not slay them. Amen.

Homosexuality. This topic or commandment is growing to be a very big controversy amongst the Christian religions. Many religions are accommodating the "gay movement" by ordaining both men and women as ministers in their churches who openly profess that they are gay or lesbian. There is high pressure for the church leadership to cave into the pressures of accepting a homosexual relationship as something natural and definitely not sinful—in the eyes of God.

Question: What does the Bible have to say about homosexual relationships?

It is hard to understand the churches that have accepted homosexual relations into their church leadership. The Bible is very clear that these types of relationships are an abomination!

> *Leviticus 18:22 –* ***Thou shalt not lie with mankind, as with womankind: it is abomination.***

> *Leviticus 20:13 –* ***If a man also lie with mankind, as he lieth with a woman, both of them have committed an abomination:*** *they shall surely be put to death; their blood shall be upon them.*

Not only the Old Testament condemns these homosexual or "gay" relationships, the New Testament also comments on them.

> *Romans 1:18,26,27 – 18.* ***For the wrath of God is revealed from heaven against all ungodliness and unrighteousness of men, who hold the truth in unrighteousness;...26. For this cause God gave them up unto vile affections: for even their women did change the natural use into that which is against nature: 27. And likewise also the men, leaving the natural use of the woman, burned in their lust one toward another; men with men working that which is unseemly,*** *and receiving in themselves that recompence of their error which was meet.*

> *1 Timothy 1:9,10 – 9. Knowing this, that the law is not made for a righteous man, but for the lawless and disobedient, for the ungodly and for sinners, for unholy and profane, for murderers of fathers and murderers of mothers, for manslayers, 10. For whoremongers,* ***for them that defile themselves with mankind,*** *for menstealers, for liars, for perjured persons, and if there be any other thing that is contrary to sound doctrine;*

> *Jude 1:7 – Even as Sodom and Gomorrha, and the cities about them in like manner, giving themselves over to fornication,* ***and going after strange flesh,*** *are set forth for an example, suffering the vengeance of eternal fire.*

Paul was very clear as to what reward the "gays" will receive—they will definitely not inherit the kingdom of God!

> *1 Corinthians 6:9,10 – 9.* ***Know ye not that the unrighteous shall not inherit the kingdom of God?*** *Be not deceived: neither fornicators, nor idolaters,* ***nor adulterers, nor effeminate, nor abusers of themselves with mankind,*** *10. Nor thieves, nor covetous, nor drunkards, nor revilers, nor extortioners, shall inherit the kingdom of God.*

The LDS Church continues to stand strong against the "gay" lifestyle. The general policy for "gays" is to love them, help them as any other sinner to repent of their sins, overcome their weaknesses, and accept them back into the fold! If a "gay" refuses to try and overcome their weaknesses, he/she then may be excommunicated from the church. The LDS Church will definitely not ordain an open "gay" person into the priesthood or make them a leader in the Church.

The first and second greatest commandments. Two of these are the all-familiar greatest commandment and the second greatest commandment that Christ revealed. These two great commandments were *"Thou shalt love the Lord thy God with all thy heart, and with all thy soul, and with all thy mind"* and *"Thou shalt love thy neighbour as thyself."*

> *Matthew 22:36-40 – 36. Master, which is the great commandment in the law? 37. Jesus said unto him,* ***Thou shalt love the Lord thy God with all thy heart, and with all thy soul, and with all thy mind.*** *38. This is the first and great commandment. 39. And the second is like unto it,* ***Thou shalt love thy neighbour as thyself.*** *40. On these two commandments hang all the law and the prophets.*

When Moses received the Ten Commandments, God mentioned a covenant.

> *Deuteronomy 4:13 –* ***And he declared unto you his covenant, which he commanded you to perform, even ten commandments;*** *and he wrote them upon two tables of stone.*

Question. What is the covenant that is made with the Lord when one keeps the commandments of the Lord?

> *Deuteronomy 6:17-19 – 17. Ye shall diligently keep the commandments of the Lord your God, and his testimonies, and his statutes, which he hath commanded thee. 18. And thou shalt do that which is right and good in the sight of the Lord:* ***that it may be well with thee, and that thou mayest go in and possess the good land which the Lord sware unto thy fathers, 19. To cast out all thine enemies from before thee, as the Lord hath spoken.***

Answer: In addition to what was promised here to Moses, Chapter 15 – The Covenant People will explain in detail about the covenants we may make with the Lord and His promises to us, once we do fulfill our covenants with Him.

Here are some other passages from the Bible that comment on keeping the commandments of God.

> *Deuteronomy 5:32,33 – 32.* ***Ye shall observe to do therefore as the Lord your God hath commanded you: ye shall not turn aside to the right hand or to the left. 33. Ye shall walk in all the ways which the Lord your God hath commanded you, that ye may live,*** *and that it may be well with you, and that ye may prolong your days in the land which ye shall possess.*

> *Deuteronomy 6:1-3 – 1.* ***Now these are the commandments, the statutes, and the judgments, which the Lord your God commanded to teach you,*** *that ye might do them in the land whither ye go to possess it: 2. That thou mightest fear the Lord thy God, to keep all his statutes and his commandments, which I command thee, thou, and thy son, and thy son's son, all the days of thy life; and that thy days may be prolonged. 3. Hear therefore, O Israel, and observe to do it; that it may be well with thee, and that ye may increase mightily, as the Lord God of thy fathers hath promised thee, in the land that floweth with milk and honey.*

> *Proverbs 4:4 –* ***He taught me also, and said unto me, Let thine heart retain my words: keep my commandments, and live.***

> *Proverbs 7:2 –* ***Keep my commandments, and live;*** *and my law as the apple of*

thine eye.

*1 John 2:3,4 – 3. **And hereby we do know that we know him, if we keep his commandments.** 4. He that saith, I know him, and keepeth not his commandments, is a liar, and the truth is not in him.*

*Revelation 22:14 – **Blessed are they that do his commandments, that they may have right to the tree of life, and may enter in through the gates into the city.***

*1 Timothy 1:5 – **Now the end of the commandment is charity out of a pure heart,** and of a good conscience, and of faith unfeigned:*

*Exodus 20:6 – **And shewing mercy unto thousands of them that love me, and keep my commandments.***

Author's Note: After learning about the celestial, terrestrial, and telestial glories that are the rewards that will be given to us (once Christ comes for the final judgment), each of us should ponder and meditate about this section on keeping the commandments of God. God is very clear and concise as to what He expects of us. He is also giving us our free agency to keep His commandments or not. Through a latter-day prophet, God has given us the knowledge of what our rewards will be if we should decide to keep a portion of the commandments that we feel comfortable with following, or not keeping them at all. This is the beauty of God's plan—it is fair and just!

> **Question: Why should somebody who has dedicated his/her whole life to serving God and keeping His commandments receive the same reward as somebody who has only declared his faith in Jesus Christ and then followed just the commandments that were convenient?**

Step 6. To receive other ordinances.

The Endowment Ordinance. While organizing the restored Church of Jesus Christ of Latter Day Saints, Joseph Smith established a special ordinance called the "endowment." At this writing, the author has not heard of any other Christian church offering or even mentioning an ordinance closely relating to the "endowment." Joseph Smith received the ordinance from God in the following revelations that were recorded over one hundred and fifty years ago. These are the passages:

> *D&C 38:32 – Wherefore, for this cause I gave unto you the commandment that ye should go to the Ohio; **and there I will give unto you my law; and there you shall be endowed with power from on high;***

> *D&C 95:8 – Yea, verily I say unto you, I gave unto you a commandment that you should build a house, **in the which house I design to endow those whom I have chosen with power from on high;***

> *D&C 105:33 – Verily I say unto you, **it is expedient in me that the first elders of my church should receive their endowment from on high in my house,** which I have commanded to be built unto my name in the land of Kirtland.*

Although there is no mention of an "endowment" ordinance in the Bible, the apostle Luke did touch on the subject. He spoke of being *"endued with power from on high"*.

> *Luke 24:49 – And, behold, I send the promise of my Father upon you: but tarry ye in the city of Jerusalem, **until ye be endued with power from on high.***

The Anointing. While restoring the temple and temple ordinances through Joseph Smith, Jesus Christ also restored the "anointing" ordinance. Although there is very little said about the "anointing" that goes on in the LDS temples, there is more said about the "anointing" in the Old and New Testaments than the "endowment." Most of the references were by Moses.

> *Exodus 28:41 – And thou shalt put them upon Aaron thy brother, and his sons with him;* **and shalt anoint them, and consecrate them, and sanctify them,** *that they may minister unto me in the priest's office.*

> *Exodus 30:25 –* **And thou shalt make it an oil of holy ointment, an ointment compound** *after the art of the apothecary:* **it shall be an holy anointing oil.**

> *Exodus 30:29-31 – 29. And thou shalt sanctify them, that they may be most holy: whatsoever toucheth them shall be holy. 30.* **And thou shalt anoint Aaron and his sons, and consecrate them,** *that they may minister unto me in the priest's office. 31. And thou shalt speak unto the children of Israel, saying,* **This shall be an holy anointing oil unto me throughout your generations.**

> *Leviticus 8:10 –* **And Moses took the anointing oil, and anointed the tabernacle and all that was therein, and sanctified them.**

Notice that in this ordinance, the anointing was with oil. Currently, the LDS anointing is performed using olive oil.

Some may not have made the connection with the "anointing ordinance" and who are called "the Lord's anointed, as mentioned in 2 Samuel.

> *2 Samuel 1:14 – And David said unto him, How wast thou not afraid to stretch forth thine hand* **to destroy the Lord's anointed?**

Not only did God perform "the anointing" ordinance in the Old Testament, He also was performing "the anointing" in the New Testament, as Paul mentioned.

> *2 Corinthians 1:21 – Now he which stablisheth us with you in Christ,* **and hath anointed us, is God.**

John the Beloved also mentioned that the members of the church in his time actually received an "anointing" from "the Holy One".

> *1 John 2:20 – But ye have an unction from the Holy One, and ye know all things.*

> *1 John 2:27 – But the* **anointing which ye have received of him** *abideth in you, and ye need not that any man teach you:* **but as the same anointing teacheth you of all things, and is truth, and is no lie,** *and even as it hath taught you, ye shall abide in him.*

Step 7. The Ordinance of Eternal Marriage.

This particular teaching of Joseph Smith, the fact that couples can be "sealed" together "for time and all eternity" has caused a very big conflict among many different Christian religions. It was and still is common for many churches to marry their members "until death do you part." With great pressure from the LDS church and their teaching that couples can be married for time and all eternity, many Christian churches have changed their marriage vows. Some have taken the "until death do you part" out of their ceremonies and tell the couples "believing in Christ will keep you together after this life."

Then, on the other hand, they teach that there is no marriage in the resurrection. The scriptures used to teach "there is no marriage in the resurrection" are as follows. These passages are Luke's, Matthew's, and Mark's version of the same incident where the Sadducees ask Christ about the woman who married seven different brothers, and whom will she belong to in the resurrection. These are the specific passages:

*Luke 20:27-33 – 27. Then came to him certain of the Sadducees, which deny that there is any resurrection; and they asked him, 28. Saying, Master, Moses wrote unto us, If any man's brother die, having a wife, and he die without children, that his brother should take his wife, and raise up seed unto his brother. 29. There were therefore seven brethren: and the first took a wife, and died without children. 30. And the second took her to wife, and he died childless. 31. And the third took her; and in like manner the seven also: and they left no children, and died. 32. Last of all the woman died also. 33. **Therefore in the resurrection whose wife of them is she? For seven had her to wife.** 34. And Jesus answering said unto them, **The children of this world marry, and are given in marriage; 35. But they which shall be accounted worthy to obtain that world, and the resurrection from the dead, neither marry, nor are given in marriage: 36.** Neither can they die any more: for they are equal unto the angels; and are the children of God, being the children of the resurrection.*

*Matthew 22:23-30 – 23. The same day came to him the Sadducees, which say that there is no resurrection, and asked him, 24. Saying, Master, Moses said, If a man die, having no children, his brother shall marry his wife, and raise up seed unto his brother. 25. Now there were with us seven brethren: and the first, when he had married a wife, deceased, and, having no issue, left his wife unto his brother: 26. Likewise the second also, and the third, unto the seventh. 27. And last of all the woman died also. 28. Therefore in the resurrection whose wife shall she be of the seven? For they all had her. 29. Jesus answered and said unto them, **Ye do err, not knowing the scriptures, nor the power of God. 30. For in the resurrection they neither marry, nor are given in marriage, but are as the angels of God in heaven.***

*Mark 12:23-25 – In the resurrection therefore, when they shall rise, whose wife shall she be of them? For the seven had her to wife, 24. And Jesus answering said unto them, **Do ye not therefore err, because ye know not the scriptures, neither the power of God? 25. For when they shall rise from the dead, they neither marry, nor are given in marriage; but are as the angels which are in heaven.***

The Christian ministers, leaders, and teachers who claim there is no marriage after this life use these specific words of Christ as their backing:

*Luke 20:35 – **But they which shall be accounted worthy to obtain that world, and the resurrection from the dead, neither marry, nor are given in marriage:***

*Matthew 23:30. **For in the resurrection they neither marry, nor are given in marriage, but are as the angels of God in heaven.***

*Mark 12:30 – **For in the resurrection they neither marry, nor are given in marriage, but are as the angels of God in heaven.***

Something very difficult to say concerning these Christian ministers, leaders, and teachers can only be said using Christ's own words in the same passages:

*Matthew 23:29 – Jesus answered and said unto them, **Ye do err, not knowing the scriptures, nor the power of God.***

*Mark 12:24 – And Jesus answering said unto them, **Do ye not therefore err, because ye know not the scriptures, neither the power of God?***

Christ told these leaders that they were in err! Calling all these Christian ministers, leaders, and teachers wrong is quite bold. It is here that we must again be reminded of Christ's own teachings about marriage.

The first point to be made is that if there were no eternal marriage

Question: Why would these Sadducees be asking whom this woman would belong to?

If, from the beginning, there were no eternal marriage this question, "Which brother would this woman belong to after they all died?" would not have come up.

The second point to be made is that if there were no eternal marriage…

Question: Why would Christ tell them that they do not know the scriptures nor the power of God?

The answer to both these questions is that there is "eternal marriage" and under the example that the Sadducees used, this woman was only married "until death do you part" to each of the seven brothers. Not knowing "the scriptures nor the power of God," the Sadducees were told, *"when they shall rise from the dead, they neither marry, nor are given in marriage."* Which is a true statement and is not a conflict with Joseph Smith's teaching of eternal marriage.

The main reason for this chapter on **The Plan of Salvation – The Mortal Life** being placed after the chapter on **The Plan of Salvation – The Post-mortal Life** is so that you the reader, will understand Joseph Smith's teaching on the three different kingdoms that every person born on earth will be awarded—after the final resurrection of all mankind. It is God's teachings that to reach His kingdom, the highest degree of glory, where God dwells, one must receive the correct ordinances of baptism, the Gift of the Holy Ghost, and the other temple ordinances mentioned previously in this chapter.

It is important to note that Joseph Smith taught that if one does not *"know the scriptures nor the power of God"* he or she will not *"when they shall rise from the dead, they neither marry, nor are given in marriage."*

This is because **NOW, the time that we have on earth, and the time after we die**—before the great judgment day, **is when we need to be married for time and all eternity!** If one fails to accept the fullness of the gospel of Jesus Christ and be "sealed" to his/her spouse and family in this life and the life in the spirit world, then after the last resurrection and great judgment day, then **"they will neither marry, nor are given in marriage."**

Question: Why is it that we have time in the spirit world to accept the gospel and be sealed to our spouses?

The answer to this question will be explained in the last section of this chapter.

The teaching of Jesus Christ, the teachings of the apostles, and the teachings of the Old Testament prophets support these teachings of Joseph Smith on eternal marriage.

Christ's Teachings on Eternal Marriage. Jesus Christ's teachings on eternal marriage were very simple and easy to understand. Christ gave to Peter the "power of God" that most Christian religions "do not know." This "power of God" gave Peter the power to "what he binds on earth will be bound in heaven."

> *Matthew 16:19 – And I will give unto thee the keys of the kingdom of heaven: and whatsoever thou shalt bind on earth shall be bound in heaven: and whatsoever thou shalt loose on earth shall be loosed in heaven.*

Before Christ was crucified, he turned over the keys of the kingdom to Peter. Or in simple terms, Christ made Peter the head of Christ's church on the earth. Christ specifically told Peter *"whatsoever thou shalt bind on earth shall be bound in heaven."*

Question: What is it that a religious leader in the Christian religion binds?

The answer for all Christian religions excluding the LDS church, are two things:

1. Religious leaders bind people to Heavenly Father through the ordinance of baptism, and

2. Religious leaders bind people together through the marriage ordinances that they perform.

The first ordinance of baptism, is a requirement to enter into the Kingdom of God.

> *John 3:5,6 – 5.* ***Jesus answered, Verily, verily, I say unto thee, Except a man be born of water and of the Spirit, he cannot enter into the kingdom of God.***

The second ordinance is the ordinance of marriage—"until death do you part." All Christian churches taught that marriage is for this life only until began Joseph Smith teaching that marriage could be for eternity. Joseph Smith taught that "eternal marriage" is a requirement for one to achieve the highest degree of glory in the Kingdom of God.

> *D&C 131:2 –* ***And in order to obtain the highest, a man must enter into this order of the priesthood [meaning the new and everlasting covenant of marriage];***

Jesus Christ did not just mention this eternal binding power once He also said it again.

> *Matthew 18:18 – Verily I say unto you,* ***Whatsoever ye shall bind on earth shall be bound in heaven: and whatsoever ye shall loose on earth shall be loosed in heaven.***

Paul's Teachings on Eternal Marriage. The apostle Paul also spoke of eternal marriage. He wrote to the saints in Corinth that **"in the Lord"**—man and woman should not be without each other.

> *1 Corinthians 11:11 –* ***Nevertheless neither is the man without the woman, neither the woman without the man, in the Lord.***

This passage supports the fact that those true followers of Christ, will be able to be "bound on earth" and "bound in heaven."

Paul also said that a man and a woman shall be joined together and they will become one flesh.

> *Ephesians 5:31,32 – 31.* ***For this cause shall a man leave his father and mother, and shall be joined unto his wife, and they two shall be one flesh.*** *32. This is a great mystery: but I speak concerning Christ and the church.*

Question: How can man and woman become one flesh?

The answer is the same as God the Father and Jesus Christ "are one," as explained in **Chapter 9 – The Personality of God.**

> *John 17:11 – And now I am no more in the world, but these are in the world, and I come to thee.* ***Holy Father, keep through thine own name those whom thou hast given me, that they may be one, as we are.***

One element of Heavenly Father and Jesus Christ being one, is being together forever in Heavenly Father's kingdom. Like Heavenly Father and Jesus Christ are one, you with your spouse can be one also.

Peter's Teachings on Eternal Marriage. Peter taught very clearly that a man and woman could be together forever.

> *1 Peter 3:7 – Likewise, ye husbands, dwell with them according to knowledge, giving honour unto the wife, as unto the weaker vessel,* **and as being heirs together of the grace of life; that your prayers be not hindered.**

This husband and wife **"being heirs together of the grace of life"** does support the teaching of Joseph Smith that a man and woman can be *"sealed"* together for all time and eternity. Joseph Smith always referred to the "eternal marriage" as the couple being *"sealed"* together. This *"sealing"* is also supported in the Bible. Paul spoke of being "sealed" to the saints in Corinth.

> *2 Corinthians 1:22 –* **Who hath also sealed us,** *and given the earnest of the Spirit in our hearts.*

Not only were the saints in the New Testament sealed together, there were also *"sealings"* performed in the Old Testament.

> *Nehemiah 9:38 –* **And because of all this we make a sure covenant, and write it; and our princes, Levites, and priests, seal unto it.**

> *Nehemiah 10:1-27,29 – 1.* **Now those that sealed were,** *Nehemiah, the Tirshatha, the son of Hachaliah, and Zidkijah, 2. Seraiah, Azariah, Jeremiah. 3. Pashur, Amariah, Malchijah, 4. Hattush, Shebaniah, Malluch, 5. Harim, Meremoth, Obadiah, 6. Daniel, Ginnethon, Baruch, 7. Meshullam, Abijah, Mijamin, 8. Maaziah, Bilgai, Shemaiah: these were priests. 9. And the Levites: both Jeshua the son of Azaniah, Binnui of the sons of Henadad, Kadmiel; 10. And their brethren, Shebaniah, Hodijah, Kelita, Pelaiah, Hanan, 11. Micha, Rehob, Hashabiah, 12. Zaccur, Sherebiah, Shebaniah, 13. Hodijah, Bani, Beninu. 14. The chief of the people; Parosh, Pahath-moab, Elam, Zatthu, Bani, 15. Bunni, Azgad, Bebai, 16. Adonijah, Bigvai, Adin, 17. Ater, Hizkijah, Azzur, 18. Hodijah, Hashum, Bezai, 19. Hariph, Anathoth, Nebai, 20. Magpiash, Meshullam, Hezir, 21. Meshezabeel, Zadok, Jaddua, 22. Pelatiah, Hanan, Anaiah, 23. Hoshea, Hananiah, Hashub, 24. Hallohesh, Pileha, Shobek, 25. Rehum, Hashabnah, Maaseiah, 26. And Ahijah, Hanan, Anan, 27. Malluch, Harim, Baanah. 28. And the rest of the people, the priests, the Levites, the porters, the singers, the Nethinims, and all they that had separated themselves from the people of the lands unto the law of God, their wives, their sons, and their daughters, every one having knowledge, and having understanding; 29.* **They clave to their brethren, their nobles, and entered into a curse, and into an oath, to walk in God's law, which was given by Moses the servant of god, and to observe and do all the commandments of the Lord our Lord, and his judgments and his statues;**

Joseph Smith taught that with this "eternal marriage sealing" was a special covenant that couples make with the Lord in order to be *"joints heirs"* in the Kingdom of God. These people mentioned in Nehemiah made the *"special covenants"* with God, and thus received the *"sealing"*—of eternal marriage. Isaiah even spoke of the *"covenant."*

> *Isaiah 49:8 – Thus saith the Lord, In an acceptable time have I heard thee, and in a day of salvation have I helped thee: and* **I will preserve thee, and give thee for a covenant of the people,** *to establish the earth, to cause to inherit the desolate heritages;*

Not only did Isaiah speak on this topic, other Old Testament prophets had something to say on marriages. Moses spoke of marriage in the creation of the earth and man. He quotes God as saying that *"it is not good for man to be alone."*

> *Genesis 2:18 – And the Lord God said, It is not good that the man should be alone; I will make him an help meet for him.*

Question: With the supporting passages in the Bible on eternal marriage, do you not think that this advice could be not only good on this earth, but also for the eternities?

Moses also spoke of man and woman leaving their parents and "becoming one flesh" with each other.

> *Genesis 2:24 – Therefore shall a man leave his father and his mother, and shall cleave unto his wife: **and they shall be one flesh.***

In the famous speech in Ecclesiastes about "To every thing there is a season" (Ecclesiastes 3:1-8), it states that *"whatsoever God doeth, it shall be forever!"*

> *Ecclesiastes – 3:14 – I know that, **whatsoever God doeth, it shall be for ever:** nothing can be put to it, nor any thing taken from it: and God doeth it, that men should fear before him.*

Question: If husband and wife shall *"become one flesh"* and *"be joint heirs together of the grace of life,"* and the fact that Christ gave Peter the power *"to bind on earth will be bound in heaven,"* is it not also possible that marriage *"shall be forever?"*

Joseph Smith taught that now, the mortal life, is the time to do all of God's will, which includes receiving the "sealing" which will bind us to our spouse and family for eternity. If we do not receive this in this life, or during the life after death while in the Spirit World, then we will "neither marry nor are given in marriage; but are appointed angels in heaven."

> *D&C 132:16 – Therefore, **when they are out of the world they neither marry nor are given in marriage; but are appointed angels in heaven,** which angels are ministering servants, to minister for those who are worthy of a far more, and an exceeding, and an eternal weight of glory.*

This was Christ's teachings to Joseph Smith, the same teaching that Christ taught to the Sadducees.

> *Matthew 23:30 – **For in the resurrection they neither marry, nor are given in marriage, but are as the angels of God in heaven.***

> *Mark 12:30 – **For in the resurrection they neither marry, nor are given in marriage, but are as the angels of God in heaven.***

> *Luke 20:35, 36 – **But they which shall be accounted worthy to obtain that world, and the resurrection from the dead, neither marry, nor are given in marriage:** 36. Neither can they die any more: **for they are equal unto the angels;** and are the children of God, being the children of the resurrection.*

Returning to the subject of the Sadducees *"not knowing the scriptures nor the power of God,"* all of the Christian religions and religious leaders who teach "there is no marriage in the resurrection" have a conflict with the Bible. This conflict is easily explained in **Chapter 1 – The Apostasy.** There was a *"falling away"* from the pure truths of Christ's church and teachings.

> *2 Thessalonians 2:3 – **Let no man deceive you by any means: for that day shall not come, except there come a falling away first, and that man of sin be revealed, the son of perdition;***

The number one example of having this conflict with the Bible is teaching on marriage in the Catholic Church. The Catholic Church professes to have the priesthood authority, handed down through all the Popes who received the authority from Peter. The Catholics do not perform "eternal marriage" or "sealing" ordinances. Other examples of erroneous doctrines on marriage are the churches that branched off from the Catholic Church, i.e., the Lutherans, the Presbyterians, the Baptists, none of which teach or perform the "eternal marriage" or "sealing" ordinances.

Referring back to the teachings of the prophet Amos:

> *Amos 3:7 –* **Surely the Lord God will do nothing, but he revealeth his secret unto his servants the prophets.**

Christ taught:

> *Matthew 10:41 –* **He that receiveth a prophet in the name of a prophet shall receive a prophet's reward; and he that receiveth a righteous man in the name of a righteous man shall receive a righteous man's reward.**

The prophet Joseph Smith clearly taught the doctrine of "eternal marriage" where we can be "sealed" for all time and eternity to our spouse and children. This is where we can receive the guarantee that we will be with our families forever. This is truly a *"prophets reward!"*

Those children of God who choose to follow a *"righteous man's"* teachings, in this case— there is no marriage after the resurrection, will receive a *"righteous man's"* reward. Having learned the different glories that are Christ's rewards for man, the terrestrial glory will most likely be the *"righteous man's"* reward. This will include being in the presence of Jesus Christ.

Author's Note: I would like to share something that I have understood for many years. This is the knowledge that all the Christian leaders and their followers who sincerely believe what they think is best from the Bible will actually receive the eternal blessings that they believe they will receive. These Christians who do not believe there is no marriage in the resurrection will receive exactly that—no eternal partnership with their families. In the previous chapter we read about the different glories that we receive after this life. Those good Christians who do not accept the fullness of Christ's gospel will receive an eternal life in the terrestrial kingdom that includes the presence of Christ—without their families. Without the *"special covenants,"* *"ordinances",* and *"promises"* of God, they will not receive a guarantee to be with their families.

A review of the previous chapter on **The Plan of Salvation – The Post-mortal Life** may be beneficial to remind us of the different glories that will be available to us when Christ comes to reward us our glory.

> *Matthew 16:27 –* For the Son of man shall come in the glory of his Father with his angels; **and then he shall reward every man according to his works.**

Another important element to the "eternal marriage" will be taught in the next chapter **The Mormon Temples.**

Step 8. To Endure to the End

There are many Christian churches that believe and teach that once a person takes Christ into their hearts and confess that Christ is our savior—they are saved, whether or not they continue in the faith. There are other Christian churches that believe that one must stay the course and live the commandments for the rest of their lives in order to be saved. Joseph Smith taught much like the second example—that one must stay the course and continue to live the commandments and build the kingdom of God until we are physically incapable of doing so or until we die. Joseph Smith taught that, in order to enter into the kingdom of God, we must all repent, be baptized, receive the Gift of the Holy Ghost, and then *"endure to the end."* If by chance one fell by the wayside and left the teachings of the gospel, the commandments, and general activity, he/she would probably not make it to the highest degree of glory—the kingdom of God.

The Bible backs up the requirement to endure to the end. The Savior Himself taught on several different occasions that in order to be saved we must *"endure to the end."*

> *Matthew 10:22 – And ye shall be hated of all men for my name's sake: **but he that endureth to the end shall be saved.***

> *Matthew 24:13 – **But he that shall endure unto the end, the same shall be saved.***

> *Mark 13:13 – And ye shall be hated of all men for my name's sake: **but he that shall endure unto the end, the same shall be saved.***

Christ also taught the doctrine "endure to the end" in a parable that Mark wrote about. It is the parable of the sower.

> *Mark 4:11-17 – 13. And he said unto them, Know ye not this parable? And how then will ye know all parables? 14. The sower soweth the word. 15. And these are they by the way side, where the word is sown; but when they have heard, Satan cometh immediately, and taketh away the word that was sown in their hearts. 16. And these are they likewise which are sown on stony ground; who, when they have heard the word, immediately receive it with gladness; 17. **And have no root in themselves, and so endure but for a time:** afterward, when affliction or persecution ariseth for the word's sake, immediately they are offended. 18. And these are they which are sown among thorns; such as hear the word, 19. And the cares of this world, and the deceitfulness of riches, and the lusts of other things entering in, choke the word, and it becometh unfruitful.*

It is important to recognize the importance of the doctrine *"to endure to the end."* Those that "hear not" the word and those that "fall wayward" are included in the followers of Christ that are not accepted into the kingdom of God or Celestial Kingdom. It is clear from Christ's teaching that *"what you sow you will also reap"*—or *"with what measure ye mete, it shall be measured to you, and unto you that hear shall more be given."*

> *Mark 4:24, 25 – 24. And he said unto them, Take heed what ye hear: **with what measure ye mete, it shall be measured to you: and unto you that hear shall more be given.** 25. For he that hath, to him shall be given: and he that hath not, from him shall be taken even that which he hath.*

The Christian churches that believe in "one heaven and one hell" have a conflict with this biblical statement of Christ's. This belief in "one heaven and one hell" has no relationship to living by degrees of faith or the amount of works one demonstrates.

Question: How can Christ measure out your reward from what you sow, if there is only one Heaven and one Hell?

Author's Note: While contemplating this doctrinal conflict, keep in mind the following scripture that is actually a prophecy.

> *2 Timothy 4:3, 4 – 3. **For the time will come when they will not endure sound doctrine;** but after their own lusts shall they heap to themselves teachers, having itching ears; 4. And they shall turn away their ears from the truth, and shall be turned unto fables.*

The beautiful part of Mark's quote of Christ on endurance is the part that states— ***"and unto you that hear shall more be given."*** From what has been written thus far in this book and what will come in the following chapters will explain what *"is more to be given!"* The *"promise"* from God and Christ that binds us to our spouses and families, which no other churches practice, is an example of what *"more"* can be given to us.

> *Hebrews 6:15 – **And so, after he had patiently endured, he obtained the promise.***

> *James 5:11 – **Behold, we count them happy which endure.** Ye have heard of the patience of Job, and have seen the end of the Lord; that the Lord is very pitiful, and of tender mercy.*

Another important element of endurance is the fact that it is part of charity—or the pure love of Christ. Paul included "endurance" when he defined "charity". Charity is best described in Corinthians:

> *1 Corinthians 13:7 – **Beareth all things, believeth all things, hopeth all things, endureth all things.***

Step 9. To Become Perfect!

In **Chapter 5 – The Holy Ghost** we learned that Joseph literally taught that *"man may become perfect,"* as was taught by Jesus Christ.

> *Matthew 5:48 – **Be ye therefore perfect, even as your Father which is in heaven is perfect.***

> *Colosians 4:12 – Epaphras, who is one of you, a servant of Christ, saluteth you, always labouring fervently for you in prayers, **that ye may stand perfect and complete in all the will of God.***

While most Christian religious leaders claim that there was only one perfect man and that was Jesus Christ—none of these leaders that I know of teach that perfection is a possibility for each man or woman who live on this earth. In the LDS Church, it is a common doctrine that *"man may become perfect."* There are steps to becoming perfect. Each one of these purposes for being on this earth that are mentioned in this chapter is a step to becoming perfect.

A few examples of people who may become perfect in this life are Noah and Job. In the eyes of God—they were perfect!

> *Genesis 6:9 – These are the generations of Noah: **Noah was a just man and perfect in his generations, and Noah walked with God.***

> *Job 1:8 – And the Lord said unto Satan, Hast thou considered my servant Job, that there is none like him in the earth, **a perfect and an upright man,** one that feareth God, and escheweth evil?*

It is important to understand that those people who become perfect in this life will be as our master, Jesus Christ.

> *Luke 6:40 –The disciple is not above his master: but **every one that is perfect shall be as his master.***

As congregations of the Church of Jesus Christ we can all be perfect in one, as God and Christ were one.

> *John 17:23 – I in them, and thou in me, **that they may be make perfect in one; and that the world may know that thou hast sent me, and hast loved them, as thou hast loved me.***

Those churches who do not have a living prophet and apostles at the head of their church will not reach perfection.

> *Ephesians 4:11,12 – 11. And he gave some, apostles; and some, prophets; and some, evangelists: and some, pastors and teachers; 12. **For the perfecting of the saints,** for the work of the ministry, for the edifying of the body of Christ.*

It is the responsibility of these prophets and apostles to *"present every man perfect in Christ."*

> *Colossians 1:28 – Whom we preach, warning every man, and teaching every man in all wisdom; **that we may present every man perfect in Christ Jesus.***

Author's Note: Almost all churches ignore the commandment to become perfect. They ask "How can man become perfect—Christ was the only perfect person on the earth." As we learn here, man may become perfect and it is through our works, as was taught by Paul:

> *2 Timothy 3:17 – **That the man of God may be perfect,** thoroughly furnished unto all good works.*

It is through our works, the ordinances we receive while on earth, living the commandments, and the charity that we have that we may become perfect. While growing up I always questioned how Christ was perfect when He made so many people mad. It was taught to me that Christ was perfect in that he was "free from sin." It is in this same manner that we can become perfect also.

If we literally take the commandments, write them on a calendar chart and then everyday evaluate our behavior, we can see that there are those commandments that we can become perfect in. For example:

Keeping the Sabbath day holy. If, on every Sunday, we go to church, we visit the sick, we help the needy, we study the scriptures, we spend time with the family, we can become perfect. It is possible to maintain a chart of "did-nots." We "did-not" go shopping on Sunday…we "did-not" go to a movie…we "did-not" participate in sports…we "did-not" work on Sunday and etc. Once we avoid the "did-nots" and accomplished the works of God on every Sunday we are "perfect" in living that commandment.

Tithing. It is fairly easy to be able to know our total financial increases each month. If, each and every month we pay one tenth of our increases to the church, we are "perfect" in living that commandment.

Adultery. If we only have sexual relations with our married spouse…then we are "perfect" in living this commandment.

Stealing. If we never steal anything from another person…then we are "perfect" in this commandment.

Killing. If we never kill anybody…then we are perfect in this commandment.

Taking the Lord's name in vain. If we never use the Lord's name in vain…then we are "perfect" in that commandment.

The Word of Wisdom. If we never partake of alcoholic beverages, tobacco, tea, coffee, and etc.…then we can become "perfect" in living this commandment.

Coveting our neighbor's wife. This is where becoming "perfect" begins to be challenging. The challenge is controlling one's thoughts. Christ said:

> *Matthew 5:27, 28 – 27. Ye have heard that it was said by them of old time, Thou shalt not commit adultery: 28. But I say unto you, **That whosoever looketh on a woman to lust after her hath committed adultery with her already in***

his heart.

The greatest commandment. Loving God with all our heart, might, mind, and soul is really challenging, especially when He says:

> *John 14:15 – If ye love me, keep my commandments.*

The second greatest commandment. Loving our neighbors as ourselves is also very challenging.

Question: How many times do we pass by the poor without helping them?

Question: How many times do we pass by somebody in need on the side of the highway without stopping to help?

Receive the ordinances. God expects us to receive the required ordinances that were spoken of in this chapter. Once we have received those ordinances, we are "perfect" in those particular works.

Genealogy Work. The counsel of the current prophet and apostles is to have five generations of our ancestors identified and the work in the temples performed.

Question: How many generations have you completed?

Once a person completes the work for five generations of ancestors, then he/she is perfect in this work!

Although many commandments are fairly easy to become "perfect" in living and some of the Lord's work we are expected to complete is defined, it is difficult on the intangible commandments and works. This is where the challenge to become "perfect" is rewarding. Once we are "perfect" in the easy ones, we are more likely to achieve the harder ones. The important fact to remember is that it is a commandment to *"become perfect even as our Heavenly Father is perfect."*

> *Matthew 5:48 – **Be ye therefore perfect, even as your Father which is in heaven is perfect.***

To show the importance of *"becoming perfect"* it is written in Psalms of the Second Coming of Christ. It is quite clear who will be preserved when the *"fire comes to devour!"*

> *Psalms 50:1-5 – 1. **The mighty God, even the Lord, hath spoken, and called the earth from the rising of the sun unto the going down thereof.** 2. Out of Zion, the perfection of beauty, God hath shined. 3. **Our God shall come, and shall not keep silence:** a fire shall devour before him, and it shall be very tempestuous round about him. 4. **He shall call to the heavens from above, and to the earth, that he may judge his people.** 5. Gather my saints together unto me; those that have made a covenant with me by sacrifice.*

There are four important points to this passage:

1. *"The perfection of beauty, God hath shined"* are the members of the Church that Christ has restored on the earth that are striving to become perfect.

2. There will be a fire that *"comes to devour."*

3. The Lord will *"gather His saints"* to be protected. These "saints" are the members of Christ's church.

4. These *"saints"* are those who have *"made a covenant with the Lord by sacrifice."*

The meaning of this message is that the people who are striving to become perfect, are *"saints"* (or members of the Church of Jesus Christ), who have *"made a covenant with the Lord"* will be gathered and protected from the great *"fire"* of the last days.

Question: Are you one of the ones who will be gathered and protected from the great fire in the last days?

More is written on the "covenant" in **Chapter 14 – The Mormon Temples** and **Chapter 15 – The Covenant People.**

Step 10. Do the Genealogy Work for Our Ancestors.

Genealogy. With the LDS Church being the leaders in genealogy research worldwide, many Christians quote the following passage to counter the necessity of this genealogy research.

> *1 Timothy 1:3-7 – 3. As I besought thee to abide still at Ephesus, when I went into Macedonia, that thou mightest charge some that they teach no other doctrine, 4.* ***Neither give heed to fables and endless genealogies, which minister questions, rather than godly edifying which is in faith: so do.*** *5. Now the end of the commandment is charity out of a pure heart, and of a good conscience, and of faith unfeigned: 6. From which some having swerved have turned aside unto vain jangling; 7. Desiring to be teachers of the law; understanding neither what they say, nor whereof they affirm.*

This passage must be understood in its context *"neither give heed to fables and endless genealogies, which minister questions, rather than godly edifying which is in faith: so do."* This does not say "don't do your genealogy," it is saying to *"not get caught up in endless genealogies that don't edify the faith."* Since there are many places that list the genealogies of many people in the Bible there must be a reason for this.

The second chapter of Ezra in the Old Testament is a good example. It lists in the first 61 verses many people who lost their genealogies of their "seed" or ancestors. It is quite clear as to what happens to them—they loose the right to hold the priesthood!

> *Ezra 2:62 –* ***These sought their register among those that were reckoned by genealogy, but they were not found: therefore were they, as polluted, put from the priesthood.***

It is evident here that it was required to maintain your genealogy. Paul was speaking to *"avoid making your genealogy—a vain genealogy"*, worked up for pride.

Another important reference to having a genealogy of your family is mentioned in Malachi. He states that those who keep a "book of remembrance" "will be His", "will be spared", and "they will return."

> *Malachi 3:16-18 – 16. Then they that feared the Lord spake often one to another: and the Lord hearkened, and heard it,* ***and a book of remembrance was written before him for them that feared the Lord, and that thought upon his name.*** *17.* ***And they shall be mine,*** *saith the Lord of hosts, in that day when I make up my jewels;* ***and I will spare them,*** *as a man spareth his own son that serveth him. 18.* ***Then shall ye return,*** *and discern between the righteous and the wicked, between him that serveth God and him that serveth him not.*

It is also important to note here that it is a *"book of remembrance"* that is a discerning point between *"him that serveth God and him that serveth him not"*.

Question: Is it this, or lack of, this "book of remembrance" or a genealogy of your family that will be your oil in the ten virgins lamps when Christ comes—that keeps you from entering in with Christ?

Joseph Smith also taught on the importance of keeping your genealogy and doing the work for the dead.

> *And now as the great purposes of God are hastening to their accomplishment, and the things spoken of in the prophets are fulfilling, as the kingdom of God is established on the earth, and the ancient order of things restored, the Lord has manifested to us this day and privilege, and **we are commanded to be baptized for our dead,** thus fulfilling the words of Obadiah, when speaking of the glory of the latter-day: "And saviours shall come up on mount Zion to judge the remnant of Esau, and the kingdom shall be the Lord's". (Obad 1:21) A view of these things reconciles the scriptures of truth, justifies the ways of God to man, places the human family upon an equal footing, and harmonizes with every principle of righteousness, justice, and truth.*[19]

It is the genealogies of church members that keep the temples going. Once these saving ordinances mentioned earlier in this chapter are performed for each living individual, each time the individual enters afterwards and performs the ordinances, it is done in proxy for someone who has already died.

Temple work. As Joseph Smith progressed in the church and built a temple in Kirkland, Ohio, then again in Nauvoo, Illinois, Joseph Smith taught that the Lord revealed many of the secrets of the temple and the temple ordinances. As Joseph Smith taught, our dead ancestors who have not had the chance to accept Christ's fullness of the gospel, will be given the chance to receive the ordinances through the current living members acting as proxy for the dead ancestors.

Among these ordinances are "the baptism for the dead," "the anointings," "the endowment," and "the family sealings," which seal the marriages and children of those marriages together for all eternity.

Joseph Smith taught that what Christ was talking about when he spoke to Peter was the power to bind families together here on earth.

> *Matthew 16:19 – And I will give unto thee the keys of the kingdom of heaven: and whatsoever thou shalt bind on earth shall be bound in heaven: **and whatsoever thou shalt loose on earth shall be loosed in heaven.***

Christ not only told Peter this one time, but He told it a second time.

> *Matthew 18:18 – Verily I say unto you, Whatsoever ye shall bind on earth shall be bound in heaven: and whatsoever ye shall loose on earth shall be loosed in heaven.*

Having the understanding and teachings from Christ and angels, Joseph Smith taught that without us performing the temple ordinances for our dead ancestors, to include the sealing of families together, our ancestors were "nothing" without our generations performing these ordinances for them. Biblical support for this particular doctrine is found in Hebrews, chapter 11.

Paul is talking about some particular people that were identified by name. Paul said:

> *Hebrews 11:32,33 – 32. And what shall I more say? For the time would fail me to tell of Gedeon, and of Barak, and of Samson, and of Jephthae; of David also, and Samuel, and of the prophets: 33. Who through faith subdued kingdoms, wrought righteousness, **obtained promises,** stopped the mouths of lions,*

Paul was specific with these people that they received "the promises." Joseph Smith identifies one of these *"promises"* as being sealed together in the temple for time and all eternity.

Paul continues telling about these people and then switches to another people who were not as fortunate enough to have received the *"promises."*

> *Hebrews 11:36-39 – 36. And others had trial of cruel mockings and scourgings, yea moreover of bonds and imprisonment: 37. They were stoned, they were sawn asunder, were tempted, were slain with the sword: they wandered about in sheepskins and goatskins; being destitute, afflicted tormented; 38. (Of whom the world was not worthy:) they wandered in deserts, and in mountains, and in dens and caves of the earth. 39. And these all, having obtained a good report through faith,* **received not the promise:**

These people were identified as faithful people, but these people did not receive **"the promise."** They did not receive **"the promise"** of "the eternal sealing" with their families. It is interesting what Paul says about them in the very next verse.

> *Hebrews 11:40 –* **God having provided some better thing for us, that they without us should not be made perfect.**

Paul hints that without Paul and his generation, those people who did not have **"the promise"** of the eternal ordinances and sealing, they could not be made perfect.

Understanding what Christ told Peter that whatever *"he bound on earth was bound in heaven"* and what Joseph Smith taught that our ancestors could be sealed together through proxy ordinances, these people would not have the chance for the eternal sealing without Paul.

> **Question: How, under the current teachings of all churches, could Paul make a difference and give these people an opportunity to be made perfect?**

> **Question: Could that what "God having provided some better thing for us" be the temple sealing that would bind a family together on earth and in heaven, whether they are living or dead?**

To review the topic of baptism, Christ stated that "except a man be born of water and of the Spirit, he cannot enter into the kingdom of God"

> *John 3:5,6 – 5.* **Jesus answered, Verily, verily, I say unto thee, Except a man be born of water and of the Spirit, he cannot enter into the kingdom of God.**

> **Question: Is it just that a good man who had the opportunity to know and follow Christ be allowed in the Kingdom of God and when another equally good man, who did not have the chance to know and follow Christ is not given the chance to enter into the Kingdom of God?**

Christ gave to Peter the keys of the kingdom of heaven that included the power to whatever Peter would bind on earth would be bound in heaven.

> *Matthew 16:19 – And I will give unto thee the keys of the kingdom of heaven: and whatsoever thou shalt bind on earth shall be bound in heaven:* **and whatsoever thou shalt loose on earth shall be loosed in heaven.**

The God that the Mormons worship is a just God! This just God made a plan for everybody to have an equal chance *"to enter into the Kingdom of God."* This was given when Christ died on the cross and went to preach His gospel to the "spirits in prison."

> *I Peter 3:18,19 – 18. For Christ also hath once suffered for sins, the just for the unjust, that he might bring us to God, being put to death in the flesh, but quickened by the spirit: 19.* **By which also he went and preached unto the spirits in prison;**

> *John 5:25 – verily, verily, I say unto you,* **the hour is coming, and now is, when**

> *the dead shall hear the voice of the Son of God: and they that hear shall live.*

> *John 5:28,29 – Marvel not at this: **for the hour is coming, in the which all that are in the graves shall hear his voice,** 29. And shall come forth; they that have done good, unto the resurrection of life; and they that have done evil, unto the resurrection of damnation.*

It is important to understand that Christ went to the Spirit World and commenced the preaching of His gospel to those who were in the Spirit Prison—so that they too may be *"judged according to men in the flesh, but live according to God in the spirit."*

> *1 Peter 4:6 – For **for this cause was the gospel preached also to them that are dead,** that they might be judged according to men in the flesh, but live according to God in the spirit.*

If Christ was speaking truth that **"except a man be born of water and of the Spirit, he cannot enter into the kingdom of God,"** then He would also establish a way for these good people who lived on the earth but did not get a chance to receive the required ordinance of baptism. This is where the Apostle Paul's statement makes sense.

> *1 Corinthians 15:29 – **Else what shall they do which are baptized for the dead, if the dead rise not at all? Why are they then baptized for the dead?***

As Joseph Smith was given the special ordinances that were to be performed in the sacred temples for and in behalf of the deceased ancestors, it was also given to the saints, or members of Christ's original church. Receiving these special ordinances is one of the steps to becoming perfect. These ordinances performed in the sacred temples for our dead ancestors brings truth and meaning to the following passage:

> *Romans 14:9 – For to this end Christ both died, and rose, and revived, **that he might be Lord both of the dead and living.***

These saving ordinances for the dead also brings to light the following statement made by the apostle Paul:

> *1 Corinthians 15:19 – **If in this life only we have hope in Christ, we are of all men most miserable.***

Question: Being that there are millions of people who have lived on this earth who have never heard of Jesus Christ, do the Christians who believe that only the people who accept Christ in this life can be saved fall into the apostle Paul's "most miserable" category?

Joseph Smith taught:

> *...Again; if we can, by the authority of the Priesthood of the Son of God, baptize a man in the name of the Father, of the Son, and of the Holy Ghost, for the remission of sins, **it is just as much our privilege to act as an agent, and be baptized for the remission of sins for and in behalf of our dead kindred, who have not heard the Gospel, or the fullness of it.**[20]*

In the parable of the ten virgins who did not have oil in their lamps and who are left out of the marriage with Christ when He comes—may be most miserable. If these saving ordinances for our ancestors are not completed when Christ comes, then maybe the lack of doing these ordinances will be the oil that wasn't in the lamps, thus leaving these people *"most miserable"* and "left behind" at His coming.

> *Matthew 25:10-12 – 10. **And while they went to buy, the bridegroom came; and they that were ready went in with him to the marriage: and the door***

was shut. 11. Afterward came also the other virgins, saying, Lord, Lord, open to us. 12. But he answered and said, Verily I say unto you, I know you not.

Joseph Smith also stated:

"This doctrine presents in a clear light the wisdom and mercy of God in preparing an ordinance for the salvation of the dead, being baptized by proxy, their names recorded in heaven and they judged according to the deeds done in the body. This doctrine was the burden of the scriptures. **Those Saints who neglect it in behalf of their deceased relatives, do it at the peril of their own salvation.**[21]

This doctrine and practice of saving our ancestors is a practice that could not be described better than what Joseph Smith taught:

A view of these things reconciles the scriptures of truth, justifies the ways of God to man, places the human family upon an equal footing, and harmonizes with every principle of righteousness, justice, and truth.[22]

This doctrine of searching our ancestors and performing the life saving baptisms and sealing of our families together for eternity sheds a little light and understanding on the following passage in Proverbs.

Proverbs 17:6 – **Children's children are the crown of old men;** *and the glory of children are their fathers.*

Joseph Smith explains the reason why we become the "crown of old men."

…Every man that has been baptized and belongs to the kingdom has a right to be baptized for those who have gone before; **and as soon as the law of the Gospel is obeyed here by their friends who act as proxy for them, the Lord has administrators there to set them free.**[23]

We actually have the power to set our ancestors free from their bondage in the Spirit Prison or Hell! We have the power to seal our dead ancestors together for the rest of eternity so they can *"live according to God in the spirit."*

1 Peter 4:6 – *For* **for this cause was the gospel preached also to them that are dead,** *that they might be judged according to men in the flesh,* **but live according to God in the spirit.**

Summary:

From the teachings of the prophet Joseph Smith, we learn that we all lived in heaven with our Heavenly Father, we saw that Heavenly Father had a physical body of flesh and bone, glorified and perfected. It was Heavenly Father's desire to have His spirit children come to earth to:

1. Receive a body of flesh and bone, feel pain and joy.
2. Test our faith in God and Christ.
3. Repent of our sins.
4. Be baptized and receive the Gift of the Holy Ghost.
5. Live the commandments which includes being tempted by Satan.
6. Receive the important ordinances of the anointing and endowment.
7. Receive the eternal promise and ordinance from God that will bind us to our family for ever.
8. Test our endurance of living God's word for our entire life.
9. To become perfect.
10. To ensure our dead ancestors receive the required ordinances for them to live

eternally with their families.

Not only was it Heavenly Father's desire that we come to earth and accomplish these goals, it was also each of our own desire! As the foundation of the earth was laid for us to come here, we also shouted for joy!

> *Job 38:4-7 – **Where wast thou when I laid the foundations of the earth? Declare, if thou hast understanding....7. When the morning stars sang together, and all the sons of God shouted for joy?***

Author's Note: I would like to emphasize once again the importance of the following scriptures that state that only a few of the dedicated Christians will make it to the kingdom God. The parable of the ten virgins where only the half who are prepared and have the oil in their lamps are invited in with Christ.

> *Matthew 25:1-13 – 1. Then shall the kingdom of heaven be likened unto ten virgins, which took their lamps, and went forth to meet the bridegroom. 2. And five of them were wise, and five were foolish. 3. They that were foolish took their lamps, and took no oil with them: 4. But the wise took oil in their vessels with their lamps. 5. While the bridegroom tarried, they all slumbered and slept. 6. And at midnight there was a cry made, Behold, the bridegroom cometh; go ye out to meet him. 7. Then all those virgins arose, and trimmed their lamps. 8. And the foolish said unto the wise, Give us of your oil; for our lamps are gone out. 9. But the wise answered, saying, Not so; lest there be not enough for us and you: but go ye rather to them that sell, and buy for yourselves. 10. **And while they went to buy, the bridegroom came; and they that were ready went in with him to the marriage: and the door was shut. 11. Afterward came also the other virgins, saying, Lord, Lord, open to us. 12. But he answered and said, Verily I say unto you, I know you not.** 13. Watch therefore, for ye know neither the day nor the hour wherein the Son of man cometh.*

> *Revelation 19:7-10 – 7. Let us be glad and rejoice, and give honour to him: **for the marriage of the Lamb is come, and his wife hath made herself ready.** 8. And to her was granted that **she should be arrayed in fine linen, clean and white: for the fine linen is the righteousness of saints.** 9. And he saith unto me, Write, **Blessed are they which are called unto the marriage supper of the Lamb.** And he saith unto me, These are the true sayings of God. 10. And I fell at this feet to worship him. And he said unto me, See thou do it not: I am thy fellow servant, and of thy brethren that have the testimony of Jesus: worship God: **for the testimony of Jesus is the spirit of prophecy.***

Question: Could this oil that is lacking in half of the virgins lamps possibly be the "book of remembrance" spoken of by the prophet Malachi?

God was very clear when He said that having this *"book of remembrance,"* or in current terms, your genealogy completed, which *"discerns between the righteous and the wicked, between him that serveth God and him that serveth him not."*

> *Malachi 3:16-18 – 16. Then they that feared the Lord spake often one to another: and the Lord hearkened, and heard it, **and a book of remembrance was written before him for them that feared the Lord, and that thought upon his name.** 17. And they shall be mine, saith the Lord of hosts, in that day when I make up my jewels; and I will spare them, as a man spareth his own son that serveth him. 18. Then shall ye return, and **discern between the righteous and the wicked, between him that serveth God and him that serveth him not.***

Question: Have you completed your genealogy and have submitted your ancestor's

names to receive the required ordinances of baptism, anointing, endowment, and family sealings?

Question: If you are not a Mormon, does your church even encourage you to do this work for your ancestors?

Question: If not, then why not? It is the biblical way!

The Biblical Support Chart. As most agree, Joseph Smith stepped way out of the mainstream Christian bounds when he started teaching about the spirit prison and that we can be baptized for the dead. It was the same way when he taught about the specific reasons why we are here on this earth. No other Christian religion has outlined such a specific plan as Joseph Smith as to why we are here on this earth today. In the Biblical Support Chart, we will see just how many of these teachings are supported by the Bible.

THE BIBLICAL SUPPORT CHART

Is the following topic supported in the Bible?	Yes or No
Does the Bible support Joseph Smith's teaching on the importance of man being born with a body of flesh and bone? (Gen 1:26,27; Phil 3:20,21; 1 Cor 15:40,41; Matt 27:52,53; Rom 8:23; Act 24:15; 1 Cor 15:21,22)	Yes
Does the Bible support Joseph Smith's teaching on importance of demonstrating faith in God & Jesus Christ? (Mark 11:22; Habab 2:4; Rom 1:17; Gal 3:11; Heb 10:38; 2 Cor 5:6,7; Heb 11:1; John 20:29)	Yes
Does the Bible support Joseph Smith's teaching on the requirement of repenting for our sins? (Matt 3:2; Mark 1:15; Mark 6:12; Acts 17:30; 2 Pet 3:9; Acts 3:19; Eph 5:5; Luke 13:3)	Yes
Does the Bible support Joseph Smith's teaching on the requirement of the proper baptism and receiving the Gift of the Holy Ghost? (Matt 3:13-17; John 3:5,6; Mark 16:15,16; Acts 2:38; 19:1-6; Eph 4:5; Matt 7:13,14; 7:21-23; 7:15,16,20)	Yes
Does the Bible support Joseph Smith's teaching that we should follow strict adherence to God's commandments ? (John 14:15; 14:21-23; Exo 20:3-17; 34:28; Deut 4:13; Matt 22:36-40)	Yes
Does the Bible support Joseph Smith's teaching that all Christians should pay a full tithing to the Lord? (Gen 14:20; Heb 7:1,2; Gen 28:22; Lev 27:30; Num 18:26; Deut 12:6; 14:22; 2 Chron 31:5; Mal 3:8-10; Matt 17:11; Matt 5:17,18)	Yes
Does the Bible support Joseph Smith's teaching that there is a health commandment known as the Word of Wisdom? (Lev 10:9-11; Num 6:2,3; Eccl 10:17; Isa 5:22; Deu 14:2-21; Eph 5:17,18; Col 2:16; 1 Tim 3:1-3; 1 Cor 6:10; Dan 1:8; 1 Cor 3:16,17)	Yes
Does the Bible support Joseph Smith's teaching that homosexuality should not be an accepted practice? (Lev 18:22; 20:13; Rom 1:18,26,27; 1 Tim 1:9,10; Jude 1:7; 1 Cor 6:9,10)	Yes
Does the Bible support Joseph Smith's temple ordinances of the endowment and annointings? (Luke 24:49; Exo 28:41; 30:25; 30:29-31; Lev 8:10; 2 Sam 1:14; 2 Cor 1:21; 1 John 2:20; 2:27)	Yes
Does the Bible support Joseph Smith's teaching that we can receive the ordinance of eternal marriage? (Luke 20:27-33; Matt 22:23-30; Mark 12:23-25; Luke 20:35; Matt 16:19; John 3:5,6; Matt 18:18; 1 Cor 11:11; Eph 5:31,32; John 17:11; 1 Peter 3:7; 2 Cor 1:22; Neh 9:38; 10:1-27, 29; Isa 49:8; Gen 2:18; 2:24; Eccl 3:14; Matt 10:41)	Yes
Does the Bible support Joseph Smith's teaching that all Christians are required to endure to the end in living God's laws? (Matt 10:22; 24:13; Mark 13:13; 4:11-17; 4:24,25; 2 Tim 4:3,4; Heb 6:15; James 5:11; 1 Cor 13:7)	Yes
Does the Bible support Joseph Smith's teachings that we should keep a genealogy of our ancestors and perform the temple ordinances for them? (Ezra 2:62; Mal 3:16-18; Matt 16:19; 18:18; Heb 11:32,33; 11:36-40; John 3:5,6; 1 Pet 3:18,19; John 5:25,28,29; 1 Pet 4:6; 1 Cor 15:29; Rom 14:9; 1 Cor 15:19; Pro 17:6)	Yes

Author's Note:

It is beautiful to know that God's whole purpose is to give other spirits—us—the opportunity to live eternally with a glorified body of flesh and bone, with our families.

NOTES

NOTES

PART IV: SPECIAL TEACHINGS OF JOSEPH SMITH – ELECT OF GOD OR CULT?

CHAPTER 14

THE MORMON TEMPLES– "THE HOUSE OF THE LORD"

The Biblical Temples. Something that is very sacred to the *"Elect of God,"* throughout the Biblical ages has been the *"House of the Lord"* or the temples. Through certain generations of the Old Testament, the Lord has commanded His current prophet at that time to build a House through which His "elect" could worship Him. Examples of these temples or "Houses of the Lord" are:

The Tabernacle: With the freed Egyptian Jews, the Lord had Moses construct a portable Tabernacle that could be carried around with the Jews as they were guided through the wilderness.

Solomon's Temple: The Lord commanded David to build a Temple, which David's son, Solomon, built. This Temple was used, desecrated, and re-cleansed several times until it's destruction in about 600 B.C. by Nebuchadnezzar.

The Temple of Zerubbabel: The Temple of Zerubbabel was built on the same site about 100 years later. In about 168 B.C., Antiochus Epiphanes ransacked and polluted the Temple. After three years of sitting desolate, Judas Maccabaeus cleaned it up and rededicated the Temple. In 37 B.C., when Herod took the city of Jerusalem, a portion of the Temple again was burned and desecrated.

The Temple of Herod: In about 17 B.C., Herod, wanting to win popularity with the Jews, offered to rebuild the Temple of Zerubbabel. This reconstruction lasted through the life of Jesus Christ and up to about 64 A.D.. This is the Temple where Christ and His apostles taught during their ministries. In 70 A.D., on the night of the anniversary of the destruction of the first temple, the army of Titus totally destroyed the Temple of Herod.

The Temple on Mount Gerizim: In the time of Manasseh, the brother of Jaddua the high priest, the Temple on Mount Gerizim was constructed on Mount Gerizim. Manasseh was its first high priest. This Temple became the refuge of all the Jews who had violated the precepts of the Mosaic law. The Temple of Gerizim was taken over by the Samaritans and they consecrated it to Jupiter, the defender of strangers.

The Christian's Positions About Temples: Knowing that most of the Christian religions on earth have beautiful churches and chapels, these buildings are not comparable to the temples that the Mormons build. The Christian churches and chapels are basically opened to all members and non-members of their congregations. The Mormon also have nice buildings that are for al the members and visitors of the church. In addition to their chapels, the Mormons build what is thought as equal to the temples build in the Bible as mentioned above. These temples are considered to be The House of the Lord and so only the Mormon members who demonstrate strict adherence to the commandments of the Lord and who go through an interview process may enter into the temples. Most Christian religions are opposed to modern day Mormon temples of the Lord. The Christians believe the time for temples are over and there is no need for temples. The Christians have several positions against the Mormons and the Mormon's claim to temple use. These basic positions are:

Position 1: The Mormon Temples are not of God, because God does not go into

Temples built by the hands of man. Scriptural references to support this position are:

> *Acts 7:48, 49 – 48.* **Howbeit the most High dwelleth not in temples made with hands;** *as saith the prophet. 49. Heaven is my throne, and earth is my footstool: what house will ye build me? Saith the Lord: or what is the place of my rest?*

> *Acts 17:24 – God that made the world and all things therein, seeing that he is Lord of heaven and earth,* **dwelleth not in temples made with hands.**

Position 2: There is no reason for temples. God ended the need for temples with Christ. Scriptural support is:

> *Revelations 21:22 –* **And I saw no temple therein:** *for the Lord God Almighty and the Lamb are the temple of it.*

Position 3: The work for the dead that the Mormons do inside the temples is unnecessary and needless.

> *No scripture cited, only professional clerical opinion.*

Position 4: The Mormons are wrong to build a church or temple and then prevent everybody from entering into the temple except a member who has a temple recommend. This practice keeps all but only the best of Mormons out of the temple and is "un-Christ like". A building dedicated to the worship of God should allow any person who wants to worship God, into the buildings.

> *No scripture cited, only professional clerical opinion.*

Position 5: The Mormons who go through the Temple are "crazy" because they wear special undergarments.

No scripture cited, only professional clerical opinion.

Response to Position 1: The Mormon temples are not of God, because God does not dwell in temples built by the hands of man.

The manner in which the Christian's interpret the passages creates a contradiction. Because throughout the history of the Old Testament, the Lord directed several of the prophets to build a house where He could visit. Examples of these commandments to the ancient prophets are:

The Tabernacle: The Lord commanded Moses to make Him a sanctuary so that the Lord could dwell among them, where the He could meet them, where He could speak to them, and where the Lord could appear to them.

> *Exodus 25:8,9 – 8. And let them make me a sanctuary;* **that I may dwell among them.** *9. According to all that I shew thee, after the pattern of the tabernacle, and the pattern of all the instruments thereof, even so shall ye make it.*

> *Exodus 29:42-46 – 42. This shall be a continual burnt offering throughout your generations at the door of the tabernacle of the congregation before the Lord: where I will meet you, to speak there unto thee. 43.* **And there I will meet with the children of Israel, and the tabernacle shall be sanctified by; my glory.** *44. And I will sanctify the tabernacle of the congregation, and the altar: I will sanctify also both Aaron and his sons, to minister to me in the priest's office. 45.* **And I will dwell among the children of Israel, and will be their God.** *46. And they shall know that I am the Lord their God, that brought them forth out of the land of Egypt,* **that I may dwell among them:** *I am the Lord their God.*

Leviticus 1:1 – And the Lord called unto Moses, and **spake unto him out of the tabernacle of the congregation,** *saying,*

Deuteronomy 31:15 – **And the Lord appeared in the tabernacle in a pillar of a cloud:** *and the pillar of the cloud stood over the door of the tabernacle.*

2 Chronicles 1:6, 7 – 6. And Solomon went up thither to the brazen altar before the Lord, which was at the tabernacle of the congregation, and offered a thousand burnt offerings upon it. 7. **In that night did God appear unto Solomon,** *and said unto him, Ask what I shall give thee.*

After reading those passages, it is obvious the Christian interpretation on *"the Lord does not dwell in Temples made of hands"* passage, is a clear contradiction.

The Solomon Temple: Again, the Lord directs his prophet to build a house for the Lord to dwell in.

2 Sam 7:5-7, 13 – 5. Go and tell my servant David, Thus saith the Lord, **Shalt thou build me an house for me to dwell in?** *6. Whereas I have not dwelt in any house since the time that I brought up the children of Israel out of Egypt, even to this day, but have walked in a tent and in a tabernacle. 7. In all the places wherein I have walked with all the children of Israel spake I a word with any of the tribes of Israel, whom I commanded to feed my people of Israel, saying, Why build ye not me an house of cedar? 13.* **He shall build an house for my name,** *and I will stablish the throne of his kingdom for ever.*

I Kings 5:3-5 – 3. Thou knowest how that David my father could not build an house unto the name of the Lord his God for the wars which were about him on every side, until the Lord put them under the soles of his feet. 4. But now the Lord my God hath given me rest on every side, so that there is neither adversary nor evil occurrent. 5. **And, behold, I purpose to build an house unto the name of the Lord my God, as the Lord spake unto David my father, saying, Thy son, whom I will set upon thy throne in thy room, he shall build an house unto my name.**

Habakkuk 2:20 – **But the Lord is in his holy temple:** *let all the earth keep silence before him.*

Zechariah 1:16 – Therefore thus saith the Lord; I am returned to Jerusalem with mercies: **my house shall be built in it, saith the Lord of hosts,** *and a time shall be stretched forth upon Jerusalem.*

Zechariah 6:12,13 – 12. And speak unto him, saying, Thus speaketh the Lord of hosts, saying, Behold the man whose name is the BRANCH; and he shall grow up out of his place, **and he shall build the temple of the Lord:** *13.* **Even he shall build the temple of the Lord;** *and he shall bear the glory, and shall sit and rule upon his throne: and he shall be a priest upon his throne: and the counsel of peace shall be between them both.*

We learn from the past ten Biblical passages that the Lord commands His prophets to build temples so that He, the Lord, can dwell in them, appear to his prophets, and to His children.

Question: If the Lord was the same yesterday, today, and forever, do you not think that when the Lord restored His gospel to the earth, that He would also include the restoration of His Temples?

Response to Position 2: There is no need for Temples. God ended the need for temples with Christ.

The Need for Latter Day Temples. Having read in the Old Testament how the Lord had His elect "build an house for His name," one may want to ask the following question:

Question: What does the Bible say about what the Lord do for His people in His restored church in the last days?

Again, using only passages from the Bible, we learn that the Lord will have a house built for His people in the last days.

> *Isaiah 2:2-3 – 2. And it shall come to pass in the last days,* **that the mountain of the Lord's house shall be established in the top of the mountains,** *and shall be exalted above the hills; and all nations shall flow unto it. 3. And many people shall go and say, Come ye, and let us go up to the mountain of the Lord, to the house of the God of Jacob; and he will teach us of his ways, and we will walk in his paths: for out of Zion shall go forth the law, and the word of the Lord from Jerusalem.*

Joseph Smith's interpretation of this passage is that the *"Lord's house shall be established in the top of the mountains"* is the Mormon temple in Salt Lake City, Utah. The reasons for this interpretation are:

- It is very clear in this passage from Isaiah, that this *"House of the Lord"* will be established in the *"last days."* If Joseph Smith was indeed the prophet the Lord used to *"restore all things,"* then this restoration would have to include the "House of the Lord" as mentioned by Isaiah.

- Matthew 17:11 – And Jesus answered and said unto them, **Elias truly shall first come, and restore all things.**

- Acts 3:19-21 – 19. Repent ye therefore, and be converted, that your sins may be blotted out, **when the times of refreshing shall come from the presence of the Lord;** 20. And he shall send Jesus Christ, which before was preached unto you: 21. Whom the heavens must receive **until the times of restitution of all things,** which God hath spoken by the mouth of all his holy prophets since the world began.

- Brigham Young established this temple and city from the tops of the mountains when he first arrived in the valley. As Brigham Young came around from the tops of the mountains, he said "This is the place." "The place" meaning that Joseph Smith had prophesied that the Mormons would go west to the mountains and establish a society where they could build a "House of the Lord" and worship without the persecution that they had been receiving since before Joseph Smith even established the Church of Jesus Christ of Latter Day Saints.

- The strong missionary program of the church has been in many nations and those members from all over the world have come to Salt Lake City and have entered into the "House of the Lord" and "have been taught of His ways."

- It is from this "House of the Lord" that was completed in 1895 that Jesus Christ has been setting forth His law.

The importance of the Lord establishing His house in the "last days" is again re-established by another prophet of the Old Testament. The prophet Micah prophesizes almost the exact prophesy as Isaiah.

> *Micah 4:1, 2 – 1. But in the last days it shall come to pass,* **that the mountain of the house of the Lord shall be established in the top of the mountains,** *and it shall be exalted above the hills; and people shall flow unto it. 2. And many nations shall come, and say, Come, and let us go up to the mountain of the Lord, and to the house of the God of Jacob; and he will teach us of his ways, and we will walk in his paths: for the law shall go forth of Zion, and the word of the Lord from Jerusalem.*

Yet another prophet, Amos, prophesied of the House of the Lord being raised up for the remnant of Edom and all the heathens or gentiles that will accept the Lord's true gospel.

> *Amos 9:11, 12 – 11.* **In that day will I raise up the tabernacle of David that is fallen,** *and close up the breaches thereof; and I will raise up his ruins, and I will build it as in the days of old: 12.* **That they may possess the remnant of Edom, and of all the heathen,** *which are called by my name, saith the Lord that doeth this.*

The apostle Paul reiterates Amos' prophecy that the gentiles will be given the chance to "seek after the Lord" in a House of the Lord.

> *Acts 15:16, 17 – 16. After this I will return, and will build again the tabernacle of David, which is fallen down; and I will build again the ruins thereof, and I will set it up. 17.* **That the residue of men might seek after the Lord, and all the Gentiles,** *upon whom my name is called, saith the Lord, who doeth all these things.*

In John's writings in Revelation, it states that temples will be used.

> *Revelation 7:15 – 14. And I said unto him, Sir, thou knowest. And he said to me, These are they which came out of great tribulation, and have washed their robes, and made them white in the blood of the Lamb. 15.* **Therefore are they before the throne of God, and serve him day and night in his temple:** *and he that sitteth on the throne shall dwell among them.*

> *Revelation 11:1 – And there was given me a reed like unto a rod: and the angel stood, saying, Rise,* **and measure the temple of God, and the altar, and them that worship therein.**

Isaiah again spoke of a tabernacle that would be a refuge for the people in the last days.

> *Isaiah 4:6 –* **And there shall be a tabernacle** *for a shadow in the daytime from the heat, and* **for a place of refuge, and for a covert from storm and from rain.**

Another important reason the "House of the Lord" will be restored to the earth in the "last days" is the fact that before the Lord will come in all His glory, He will **"suddenly come to his temple."**

> *Malachi 3:1 – Behold, I will send my messenger, and he shall prepare the way before me:* **and the Lord, whom ye seek, shall suddenly come to his temple,** *even the messenger of the covenant, whom ye delight in: behold, he shall come. saith the Lord of hosts.*

The prophet Zechariah explains in detail what will happen after the Lord's second coming. He describes that many of the people who came up against Jerusalem will worship the King, the Lord of hosts, and keep the feast of tabernacles. Zechariah continues to describe people who refuse to go up and worship the King, will have plagues brought upon them.

> *Zechariah 14:16-19 – 16. And it shall come to pass, that every one that is left of all the nations which came against Jerusalem shall even go up from year to year* **to worship the King, the Lord of hosts, and to keep the feast of tabernacles.** *17. And it shall be, that whoso will not come up of all the families of the earth unto Jerusalem to worship the King, the Lord of hosts, even upon them shall be no rain. 18. And if the family of Egypt go not up, and come not, that have no rain; there shall be the plague,* **wherewith the Lord will smite the heathen that come not up to keep the feast of tabernacles.** *19. This shall be the punishment of Egypt, and the punishment of all nations that come not up to keep the feast of tabernacles.*

In the same passage, Zechariah continues that **HOLINESS UNTO THE LORD** will be found written somewhere in the temple.

> *Zechariah 14:20-21 – 20 . **In that day shall there be upon the bells of the horses, HOLINESS UNTO THE LORD;** and the pots in the Lord's house shall be like the bowls before the altar. 21. Yea, every pot in Jerusalem and in Judah shall be holiness unto the Lord of hosts: and all they that sacrifice shall come and take of them, and seethe therein: and in that day there shall be no more the Canaanite in the house of the Lord of hosts.*

This is similar to what was done in the tabernacle that Moses was commanded to build.

> *Exodus 39:29-33 – 29. And a girdle of fine twined linen, and blue, and purple, and scarlet, of needlework; as the Lord commanded Moses, 30. **And they made the plated of the holy crown of pure gold, and wrote upon it a writing, like to the engravings of a signet, HOLINESS TO THE LORD.** 31. And they tied unto it a lace of blue, to fasten it on high upon the mitre; as the Lord commanded Moses. 32. Thus was all the work of the tabernacle of the ten of the congregation finished: and the children of Israel did according to all that the Lord commanded Moses, so did they.*

Joseph Smith was inspired to place this phrase, *HOLINESS TO THE LORD,* above the door of every Mormon temple built. A person may go to any Mormon temple and he/she will see these words above the front door.

The past passages are ten scriptures that prophesy of the importance uses of the temples in the last days. It is necessary to note that the Lord will build a temple in the last days so that all nations will flow into it and that it is necessary for the Lord to *"come suddenly"* to His Temple.

Question: Does your church have a sacred temple with *"Holiness Unto The Lord"* written on it?

Question: Are you being taught the *"ways of the Lord"* in a temple?

Question: Will your church leadership be in the temple when the Lord *"comes suddenly"* to a temple?

Response to Position 3: The work for the dead that the Mormons do inside the Mormon temples is unnecessary.

Baptism for the Dead. As discussed in the chapter on the Plan of Salvation, the Christians, by their professional minister's opinion, do not believe in the necessity of being baptized for our ancestors who have died. It was taught by Joseph Smith and supported by the Bible, that the Lord restored the fullness of His gospel, which included a "just plan" which allows every son or daughter born on this earth the opportunity to achieve salvation and all ordinances required for salvation, whether they had the opportunity here on earth or not.

Again, the Bible will further support Joseph Smith's teachings about "baptisms for the dead." Paul taught the saints in Corinth the following:

> *1 Corinthians 15:29 – **Else what shall they do which are baptized for the dead, if the dead rise not at all? Why are they then baptized for the dead?***

The Bible describes a font, or a molten sea, sitting upon twelve oxen. Three of the oxen are looking toward the north, three are looking toward the west, three are looking toward the south, and three are looking toward the east. All twelve oxen's hinder parts are facing inward. In the book of Kings, Solomon builds the House of the Lord. There are some very detailed descriptions of how the temple was made. In this passage, is the description of what Joseph

Smith taught was a sacred baptismal font.

> *1 Kings 7:23-25 – **And he made a molten sea,** ten cubits from the one brim to the other: it was round all about, and his height was five cubits: and a line of thirty cubits did compass it round about. 24. And under the brim of it round about there were knops compassing it, ten in a cubit, compassing the sea round about: the knops were cast in two rows, when it was cast. 25. **It stood upon twelve oxen, three looking toward the north, and three looking toward the west, and three looking toward the south, and three looking toward the east: and the sea was set above upon them, and all their hinder parts were inward.***

A second description of the baptismal font in Solomon's temple is found in 2 Chronicles.

> *2 Chronicles 4:2-4 – **Also he made a molten sea** of ten cubits form brim to brim, round in compass, and five cubits the height thereof; and a line of thirty cubits did compass it round about. 3. And under it was the similitude of oxen, which did compass it round about: ten in a cubit, compassing the sea round about. Two rows of oxen were cast, when it was cast. 4. **It took upon twelve oxen, three looking toward the north, and three looking toward the west, and three looking toward the south, and three looking toward the east: and the sea was set above upon them, and all their hinder parts were inward.***

A third description of the "baptismal font" in the Solomon temple is found in Jeremiah. Jeremiah describes the destruction of the temple by the Chaldeans, who took over Jerusalem. In this siege, the Chaldeans carries off the precious parts of the temple.

> *Jeremiah 52:17, 20 – 17. Also the pillars of brass that were in the house of the Lord, and the bases, and **the brazen sea that was in the house of the Lord,** the Chaldeans brake, and carried all the brass of them to Babylon.*

> *20. The two pillars, **one sea, and twelve brazen bulls that were under the bases, which king Solomon had made in the house of the Lord:** the brass of all these vessels was without weight.*

The basic Christian belief on what this molten sea atop the backs of twelve oxen is different than that of Joseph Smith's belief. The basic Christian belief for these twelve oxen with a pool on their backs is it is a place where the priests who worked in the temple to wash themselves.

The Christian viewpoint that this baptismal font is a priest's bathtub comes from the following passage.

> *2 Chronicles 4:6 – He made also ten lavers, and put five on the right hand, and five on the left, to wash in them; such things as they offered for the burnt offering they washed in them; **but the sea was for the priests to wash in.***

Although this is a contradiction with Joseph Smith's use of the font to perform baptisms for the dead, latter day revelation to Joseph Smith has revealed that the font is to be used for baptisms for the dead.

Response to Position 4: The Mormons are wrong to build a church or temple and then prevent everybody from entering into the Temple except a member who has a Temple recommend.

The Law of Worthiness. The Christian position against Joseph Smith continues with the criticism that keeps all but only the best of Mormons out of the temple. The Christians believe a building dedicated to the worship of God should allow any person who wants to worship God, into the buildings. The Christians have no scriptural support for this interpretation. It is only their ecclesiastical opinion. This interpretation or opinion leaves the Christian followers without a temple for all nations to come into and without a temple for the Lord to *"suddenly come to."*

The response to these positions against the temples built by Joseph Smith and the following **prophets of God** is that the Christians are correct when it comes to the chapels or churches built for everyday usage. The Mormon chapels do indeed meet the expectations of the Christians, wherein everybody is allowed entrance into the Mormon chapels for worship services and other church related activities. But when it comes to the "House of the Lord" or the Mormon temples, the Christian's have a gross misunderstanding of the scriptures.

The Christians currently have no, and never have had in the past, any spiritual direction from God concerning the "House of the Lord" or the special temples. If they had some spiritual direction on temples they would have a better understanding of this law. For the purpose of this book only, this law will be called the "Law of Worthiness."

As the "Law of Worthiness" is interpreted by the Christians they have no scriptural support for this **Position 4** against the Prophet Joseph Smith or the rules established by the Lord who set the rules allowing people to enter or not enter into the "House of the Lord."

The Biblical support for the Prophet Joseph Smith's rules are many. One of the first rules of the Temple is the "Law of Worthiness" or who is worthy of building the temple. As we learned in response to **Position 1,** David was called of God to build the "House of the Lord."

> *2 Sam 7:5-7,13 – 5. Go and tell my servant David, Thus saith the Lord,* **Shalt thou build me an house for me to dwell in?**

That Position was given to David but was later transferred to his son, Solomon. We learn in **1 Kings 5:3-5** that because of the wars surrounding David, David was not able to build the temple.

> *I Kings 5:3-5 – 3. Thou knowest how that David my father could not build an house unto the name of the Lord his God for the wars which were about him on every side, until the Lord put them under the soles of his feet. 4. But now the Lord my God hath given me rest on every side, so that there is neither adversary nor evil occurrent. 5.* **And, behold, I purpose to build an house unto the name of the Lord my God, as the Lord spake unto David my father, saying, Thy son, whom I will set upon thy throne in thy room, he shall build an house unto my name.**

In **I Chronicles 22** we learn that it was because of the abundant blood that David shed during those wars that kept him from building the "House of the Lord."

> *I Chronicles 22:6-11 – 6. Then he called for Solomon his son, and charged him to build an house for the Lord God of Israel. 7. And David said to Solomon,* **My son, as for me, it was in my mind to build an house unto the name of the Lord my God:** *8. But the word of the Lord came to me, saying,* **Thou hast shed blood abundantly, and hast made great wars: thou shalt not build an house unto my name, because thou hast shed much blood upon the earth in my sight.** *9. Behold, a son shall be born to thee, who shall be a man of rest; and I will give him rest from all his enemies round about: for his name shall be Solomon, and I will give peace and quietness unto Israel in his days. 10.* **He shall build an house for my name;** *and he shall be my son, and I will be his father; and I will establish the throne of his kingdom over Israel for ever. 11. Now, my son, the Lord be with thee; and prosper thou, and build the house of the Lord thy God, as he hath said of thee.*

These passages clearly denote that David, because of his much bloodshed, was not to build the temple. It is apparent the Lord did not feel that David was worthy to build the temple so He called David's son Solomon to build the temple. Similar to Solomon, Joseph Smith was called of God to build the modern day temples.

A second principle that we learn from the Bible is—Who is worthy to enter into the House of the Lord? On August 2, 1833, Joseph Smith was given this direction from the Lord.

> *D&C 97:15-17 – And inasmuch as my people build a house unto me in the name of the Lord,* **and do not suffer any unclean thing to come into it, that it be not defiled, my glory shall rest upon it;** *16. Yea, and my presence shall be there, for I will come into it, and all the pure in heart that shall come into it shall see God. 17. But if it be defiled I will not come into it, and my glory shall not be there; for I will not come into unholy temples.*

The biblical support for the "Law of Worthiness" are the prophets of the Old Testament and the New Testament apostles. The first example is in Ezekiel. Apparently, the Jewish leadership was allowing strangers into the temple. The Lord's instruction was very clear to Ezekiel, **"No stranger, uncircumcised in heart or flesh shall enter into my sanctuary."**

> *Ezekiel 44:7-9 – 7. In that ye have brought into my sanctuary strangers, uncircumcised in heart, and uncircumcised in flesh, to be in my sanctuary, to pollute it, even my house, when ye offer my bread, the fat and the blood, and they have broken my covenant because of all your abominations. 8. And ye have not kept the charge of mine holy things: but ye have set keepers of my charge in my sanctuary for yourselves. 9.* **Thus saith the Lord God; No stranger, uncircumcised in heart, nor uncircumcised in flesh, shall enter into my sanctuary, of any stranger that is among the children of Israel.**

In Psalms, David asks the Lord who is allowed to abide in his tabernacle. The Lord set specific guidelines and requirements, that included people who were righteous, honest, worked righteousness, did not gossip, did not hurt their neighbors, had pure hearts, were not vain, nor deceived other people.

> *Psalms 15:1-3 – 1. Lord, who shall abide in thy tabernacle? Who shall dwell in thy holy hill? 2.* **He that walketh uprightly, and worketh righteousness, and speaketh the truth in his heart. 3. He that backbiteth not with his tongue, nor doeth evil to his neighbour, nor taketh up a reproach against his neighbour.**

> *Psalm 24:3-5 – 3. Who shall ascend into the hill of the Lord? Or who shall stand in his holy place? 4.* **He that hath clean hands, and a pure heart; who hath not lifted up his soul unto vanity, nor sworn deceitfully.** *5. He shall receive the blessing from the Lord, and righteousness from the God of his salvation.*

The Lord told Isaiah who could enter into the House of the Lord or His holy mountain. It included people who joined themselves to the Lord, or who joined His church. It included those who serve Him, and keep the Sabbath day holy. It includes those who are willing to make covenants with Him.

> *Isaiah 56:6, 7 – 6. Also the sons of the stranger, that join themselves to the Lord, to serve him, and to love the name of the Lord, to be his servants,* **every one that keepeth the Sabbath from polluting it, and taketh hold of my covenant; 7. Even them will I bring to my holy mountain, and make them joyful in my house of prayer:** *their burnt offerings and their sacrifices shall be accepted upon mine altar;* **for mine house shall be called an house of prayer for all people.**

Another example of the Lord setting up rules of worthiness was His command to Jeremiah. He told Jeremiah that the people had to thoroughly amend their ways and doings. In current terms, the people had to thoroughly repent of their sins before they could enter the House of the Lord. The thoroughly implies that they sin no more in the future.

> *Jeremiah 7:1-7 – 1. The word that came to Jeremiah from the Lord, saying, 2. Stand in the gate of the Lord's house, and proclaim there this word, and say, Hear the word of the Lord, all ye of Judah, that enter in at these gates to worship the Lord. 3. Thus saith the Lord of hosts, the God of Israel, **Amend your ways and your doings, and I will cause you to dwell in this place.** 4. Trust ye not in lying words, saying, The temple of the Lord, The temple of the Lord, The temple of the Lord, are these. 5. **For if ye thoroughly amend your ways and your doings; if ye thoroughly execute judgment between a man and his neighbour; 6. If ye oppress not the stranger, the fatherless, and the widow, and shed not innocent blood in this place, neither walk after other gods to your hurt: 7. Then will I cause you to dwell in this place,** in the land that I gave to your fathers, for ever and ever.*

Following the same pattern for the requirement of repentance, the Lord told Ezekiel that only when people who are genuinely repentant or ashamed of their iniquities, then they should be allowed to enter into the temple and receive the ordinances and covenants.

> *Ezekiel 43:10-12 – 10. Thou son of man, shew the house to the house of Israel, that they may be ashamed of their iniquities: and let them measure the pattern. 11. **And if they be ashamed of all that they have done,** shew them the form of the house, and the fashion thereof, and the goings out thereof, and the comings in thereof, and all the forms thereof, **and all the ordinances thereof, and all the laws thereof:** and write it in their sight, **that they may keep the whole form thereof, and all the ordinances thereof, and do them.** 12. **This is the law of the house;** Upon the top of the mountain the whole limit thereof round about shall be most holy. **Behold, this is the law of the house.***

Having just read six different Biblical passages that established very strict rules for the "Law of Worthiness" for entering into the temple a question must be asked:

Question: What was the consequence of disobeying the commandments of God and entering into the temple unworthily?

The Penalty. The Lord told Moses that the penalty for an unworthy person or stranger who entered into the tabernacle was death.

> *Numbers 1:51 – And when the tabernacle setteth forward, the Levites shall take it down: and when the tabernacle is to be pitched, the Levites shall set it up: **and the stranger that cometh nigh shall be put to death.***

This penalty of death was handed down through all the ages, up to Christ and beyond. This "death penalty" is supported in Acts, where Paul took Greek Christian converts, who were non-Jews, into the temple. The Jews, still following the Mosaic laws, saw the Greeks as strangers, shut the doors of the temple and proceeded to implement this death penalty by trying to kill Paul.

> *Acts 21:26-31 – Then Paul took the men, and the next day purifying himself with them **entered into the temple, to signify the accomplishment of the days of purification,** until that an offering should be offered for every one of them. 27. And when the seven days were almost ended, the Jews which were of Asia, when they saw him in the temple, stirred up all the people, and laid hands on him, 28. Crying out, Men of Israel, help: This is the man, that teacheth all men every where against the people, and the law, and this place: **and further brought Greeks also into the temple, and hath polluted this holy place.** 29. (For they had seen before with*

*him in the city Trophimus an Ephesian, **whom they supposed that Paul had brought into the temple.**) 30. And all the city was moved, and the people ran together: and they took Paul, **and drew him out of the temple:** and forthwith the doors were shut. 31. **And as they went about to kill him,** tidings came unto the chief captain of the band, that all Jerusalem was in an uproar.*

Christ's Anger. Another aspect of the importance of the sanctity of the temples to our Heavenly Father is the example of Jesus Christ. Jesus Christ, a perfect man on earth, was loving and accepting of most men, even those that condemned Him and nailed Him to the cross.

The one time that Christ showed anger at somebody on the earth was when He was in our Heavenly Father's House and the Jews were desecrating it. This is Jesus Christ's reaction.

> *Matthew 21:12,13 – 12. And Jesus went into the temple of God, **and cast out all them that sold and bought in the temple, and overthrew the tables of the moneychangers, and the seats of them that sold doves,** 13. And said unto them, It is written, My house shall be called the house of prayer; but ye have made it a den of thieves.*

> *Mark 11:15-18 – 15. **And they come to Jerusalem: and Jesus went into the temple,** and began to cast out them that sold and bought in the temple, and overthrew the table of the moneychangers, and the seats of them that sold doves: 16. **And would not suffer that any man should carry any vessel through the temple.** 17. **And he taught, saying unto them, Is it not written, My house shall be called of all nations the house of prayer? But ye have made it a den of thieves.** 18. **And the scribes and chief priests heard it, and sought how they might destroy him: for they feared him, because all the people was astonished at his doctrine.***

> *Luke 19:45,46 – And he went into the temple, **and began to cast out them that sold therein, and them that bought;** 46. Saying unto them, It is written, My house is the house of prayer: but ye have made it a den of thieves.*

> *John 2:14-16 – 14. And found in the temple those that sold oxen and sheep and doves, and the changers of money sitting: 15. **And when he had made a scourge of small cords, he drove them all out of the temple, and the sheep, and the oxen; and poured out the changers money, and overthrew the tables;** 16. And said unto them that sold doves, Take these things hence; make not my Father's house an house of merchandise.*

Christ's example of how sacred He believes the "House of the Lord" to be should send a message to all those who have anything to do with the temples, whether positive or negative. "The Law of Worthiness" is very clear! The Lord wants no unworthy member of the Jewish faith or Christian faith in the House of the Lord.

Understanding how the Lord is the same yesterday, today, and forever, the "Law of Worthiness" would also stand in the times of "the restoration of all things." If Joseph Smith were indeed the prophet of the restoration, then the "Law of Worthiness," as it pertains to the House of the Lord, would be the same. Therefore, the Mormons do have a rule that requires the need for a temple recommend. To obtain this temple recommend requires a biannual worthiness interview with their local bishop and a member of the stake presidency to ensure one's purity in heart. Once a temple recommend is received, the member may enter into and participate in the learning of God's ways and in the ordinances performed.

Why Enter the House of the Lord?

Question: Having discussed the "Law of Worthiness," who is it that is allowed to enter into the House of the Lord?

From the Psalm of David, we learn that the people who are allowed to go into the House of the Lord are the people God chooses, or the "Elect of God."

> Psalms 65:4 – **Blessed is the man whom thou choosest, and causest to approach unto thee, that he may dwell in thy courts:** we shall be satisfied with the goodness of thy house, even of thy holy temple.

Question: Are you one of the chosen?

Question: Having established the House of the Lord, why is it that people go to the temples?

Although the reasons to go to the temple are many, we will only discuss the biblical reasons of why a person would go to the temple. What must be established is the type grouping of people who enter into the House of the Lord. The groups of people who enter into to the House of the Lord are the prophets, who spread the word of God and the "Elect of God," or the members of the church. Members of the church include the Jewish people throughout the Old and New Testaments, and the Christian converts during and after Christ's ministry. The Christian converts include both Jew and gentile.

The Prophet's Purpose in the Temples. The House of the Lord exists for the purpose of God Himself to come down and meet with the prophets. The House of the Lord is a very sacred, holy place where God periodically dwells. The first example is Moses. The Lord both instructed Moses that He would meet with him there and actually did speak to him in the "tabernacle."

> Exodus 29:42-46 – 42. This shall be a continual burnt offering throughout your generations at the door of the tabernacle of the congregation before the Lord: **where I will meet you, to speak there unto thee.**

> Leviticus 1:1 – **And the Lord called unto Moses, and spake unto him out of the tabernacle** of the congregation, saying,

A second example of God meeting His prophets in the temple is Solomon. God actually appeared unto Solomon.

> 2 Chronicles 1:6,7 – 6. And Solomon went up thither to the brazen altar before the Lord, which was at the tabernacle of the congregation, and offered a thousand burnt offerings upon it. 7. **In that night did God appear unto Solomon,** and said unto him, Ask what I shall give thee.

> 2 Chronicles 7:11,12 – Thus Solomon finished the house of the Lord, and the king's house: and all that came into Solomon's heart to make in the house of the Lord, and in his own house, he prosperously effected. 12. **And the Lord appeared to Solomon by night, and said unto him, I have heard thy prayer, and have chosen this place to myself for an house of sacrifice.**

A third example of God meeting His prophets is Ezekiel. The Lord's spirit actually filled the House of the Lord for Ezekiel.

> Ezekiel 43:4,5 – 4. **And the glory of the Lord came into the house** by the way of the gate whose prospect is toward the east. 5. So the spirit took me up, and brought me into the inner court; **and, behold, the glory of the Lord filled the house.**

The fourth example is David. David was able to hide from his enemies and was actually lifted up so that he could see his enemies around him.

> *Psalms 27:5,6 – 5. **For in the time of trouble he shall hide me in his pavilion: in the secret of his tabernacle shall he hide me;** he shall set me up upon a rock. 6. **And now shall mine head be lifted up above mine enemies round about me:** therefore will I offer in his tabernacle sacrifices of joy; I will sing, yea, I will sing praises unto the Lord.*

Then, David used the House of the Lord to seek the face of the Lord.

> *Psalms 27:8 – When thou saidst, "Seek ye my face; my heart said unto thee, **Thy face, Lord, will I seek.***

The Member's Purpose in the Temples. The second purpose of the temple is for the general membership of the church, both Jew and gentile. There are least six reasons why the general membership enter into the temples.

To Meet and Dwell With Them. The first reason is so the Lord could meet with them and dwell among them.

> *Exodus 29: 43-46 – 43. **And there I will meet with the children of Israel, and the tabernacle shall be sanctified by my glory.** 44. And I will sanctify the tabernacle of the congregation, and the altar: I will sanctify also both Aaron and his sons, to minister to me in the priest's office. 45. **And I will dwell among the children of Israel, and will be their God.** 46. And they shall know that I am the Lord their God, that brought them forth out of the land of Egypt, **that I may dwell among them:** I am the Lord their God.*

To Seek His Face. Not only are the prophets instructed or able to seek the face of the Lord, the general membership or *"Elect of God"* also has that same opportunity. They also enter into the temple to seek the face of God!

> *Psalms 24:6,7 – 6. **This is the generation of them that seek him, that seek thy face,** O Jacob, Selah. 7. Lift up your heads, O ye gates; and be ye lift up, ye everlasting doors; **and the King of glory shall come in***

> *Psalms 27:4 – One thing have I desired of the Lord, that will I seek after; that I may dwell in the house of the Lord all the days of my life, **to behold the beauty of the Lord, and to enquire in his temple.***

To Partake of the Lord's Spirit. A third reason to enter into the House of the Lord is for the members to partake of the Lord's spirit which has already been shown to be abundantly present.

> *Psalms 84:1-2 – **How amiable are thy tabernacles,** O Lord of hosts! 2. **My soul longeth, yea, even fainteth for the courts of the Lord:** my heart and my flesh crieth out for the living God.*

> *Psalms 84:4 – **Blessed are they that dwell in thy house:** they will be still praising thee. Selah.*

> *Psalms 84:10 – **For a day in thy courts is better than a thousand,** I had rather be a doorkeeper in the house of my God, than to dwell in the tents of wickedness.*

To See Visions. A fourth reason for the general membership of the church to enter into the temples is to be able to see visions, as did Zacharias in the New Testament.

> *Luke 1:21,22 – 21. And the people waited for Zacharias, and marveled that he tarried so long in the temple. 22. And when he came out, he could not speak unto*

*them: **and they perceived that he had seen a vision in the temple:** for he beckoned unto them, and remained speechless:*

To Make Sacred Covenants. A fifth reason is to make sacred covenants with the Lord.

> *2 Kings 11:4 – And the seventh year Jehoiada sent and fetched the rulers over hundreds, with the captains and the guard, **and brought them to him into the house of the Lord, and made a covenant with them, and took an oath of them in the house of the Lord,** and shewed them the king's son.*

> *Ezekiel 37:26,27 – 26. Moreover **I will make a covenant of peace with them; it shall be an everlasting covenant with them:** and I will place them, and multiply them, **and will set my sanctuary in the midst of them for evermore. 27. My tabernacle also shall be with them:** yea, I will be their God, and they shall be my people.*

More details of the covenants made are found in the next chapter *"The Covenant People."*

To Obtain a New Name. The sixth reason for the members to enter into the temple is a sacred reason. It is to obtain a new name. The Mormons have been receiving a "new name" in the temples for many, many years now. This "new name" is significant for the true Christians. It is part of the teachings of the Bible. The "new name" is also for the righteous members of His church.

> *Isaiah 62:1-3 – 1. For Zion's sake will I not hold my peace, and for Jerusalem's sake I will not rest, until the righteousness thereof go forth as brightness, and the salvation thereof as a lamp that burneth. 2. And the Gentiles shall see thy righteousness, and all kings thy glory: **and thou shalt be called by a new name, which the mouth of the Lord shall name.** 3. Thou shalt also be a crown of glory in the hand of the Lord, and a royal diadem in the hand of thy God.*

Again, Isaiah mentions the Lord's servants receiving a new name.

> *Isaiah 65:15 – And ye shall leave your name for a curse unto my chosen: for the Lord God shall slay thee, **and call his servants by another name:***

The apostle John writes in Revelations about the righteous members in the last days who "overcome" and receive a "new name."

> *Revelations 2:17 – He that hath an ear, let him hear what the Spirit saith unto the churches; To him that overcometh will I give to eat of the hidden manna, and will give him a white stone, **and in the stone a new name written, which no man knoweth saving he that receiveth it.***

Not only did the apostle John speak of this "new name" once, he also referred to it again.

> *Revelations 19:12 – His eyes were as a flame of fire, and on his head were many crowns; **and he had a name written, that no man knew, but he himself.***

In this section we have nineteen Biblical passages that explains why the prophets and general membership would go into the House of the Lord. The general Christian answer for temples is that "the temples are no longer needed."

Question: If God and Christ were to *"restore all things,"* would it be logical that the temples would be included amongst the many precious things of the Lord that would be restored?

Question: If God were to *"restore all things,"* wouldn't He again build temples so that He could appear to His prophets and children?

Question: If God were to *"restore all things,"* wouldn't He again instruct His prophets to build the holy Houses of the Lord, so that He could pour an abundance of His spirit upon His children?

Response to Position 5: The Mormons who go through the Temple are "crazy" because they wear special garments.

The Garments. According to Joseph Smith, the Lord again introduced special garments that are to be worn by the members of the church who entered into the temple and received the sacred ordinances. The Christians do not believe in the special temple garments and some actually mock the Mormons for wearing such "ridiculous" clothing.

The Old Testament and the Garments. In actuality, the Bible has many teaching about the sacred temple garments. This is what Moses writes.

> *Exodus 28:1,2, 40-42 – 1. And take thou unto thee Aaron thy brother, and his sons with him, from among the children of Israel, that he may minister unto me in the priest's office, even Aaron, Nadab and Abihu, Eleazar and Ithamar, Aaron's sons. 2.* ***And thou shalt make holy garments for Aaron thy brother for glory and for beauty.***

> *40. And for Aaron's sons thou shalt make coats, and thou shalt make for them girdles, and bonnets shalt thou make for them, for glory and for beauty. 41. And thou shalt put them upon Aaron thy brother, and his sons with him;* ***and shalt anoint them, and consecrate them, and sanctify them,*** *that they may minister unto me in the priest's office. 42.* ***And thou shalt make them linen breeches to cover their nakedness; from the loins even unto the thighs they shall reach:***

> *Exodus 39:1,28 – And of the blue, and purple, and scarlet, they made cloths of service in the holy place, and made the holy garments for Aaron;* ***as the Lord commanded Moses.*** *28. And a mitre of fine linen, and goodly bonnets of fine linen,* ***and linen breeches of fine twined linen,***

> *Leviticus 6:10 – And the priest shall put on his linen garment,* ***and his linen breeches shall he put upon his flesh,*** *and take up the ashes which the fire hath consumed with the burnt offering on the altar, and he shall put them beside the altar.*

Although these passages were written by Moses, all the instructions about the garments were actual revelations from the Lord that instructed Moses to prepare the *"fine twined linen breeches"* to be worn.

Isaiah received two visions about the last days that included the Lord directing the use of *"beautiful"* garments again that are referred to as *"the garments of salvation."*

> *Isaiah 52:1 – Awake, awake; put on thy strength, O Zion;* ***put on the beautiful garments,*** *O Jerusalem, the holy city: for henceforth there shall no more come into thee the uncircumcised and the unclean.*

> *Isaiah 61:10 – I will greatly rejoice in the Lord, my soul shall be joyful in my God;* ***for he hath clothed me with the garments of salvation,*** *he hath covered me with the robe of righteousness, as a bridegroom decketh himself with ornaments, and as a bride adorneth herself with her jewels.*

Question: If you have been known to mock these *"beautiful garments"* in the past, knowing now what the Lord thinks about these garments, will you mock them in the future?

Question: If these temple garments are actually *"the garments of salvation,"* can a

person receive true salvation if he or she does not have them to wear?

Ezekiel is another prophet who referred to the wearing of temple related garments.

> Ezekiel 42:14 – When the priests enter therein, then shall they not go out of the holy place into the utter court, **but there they shall lay their garments wherein they minister; for they are holy; and shall put on the other garments,** and shall approach to those things which are for the people.

The New Testament and the Garments. To demonstrate that the members are to continue to wear these garments that are made of fine linen, the apostle John even saw several visions of the last days.

One of these visions was the "armies of heaven," riding white horses, following Christ down from heaven. These armies were *"clothed in fine linen, white and clean."*

> Rev 19:13, 14 – And he was clothed with vesture dipped in blood: and his name is called The Word of God. 14. And the armies which were in heaven followed him upon white horses, **clothed in fine linen, white and clean.**

It is apparent that those people in heaven with Christ, will be "clothed in fine linen, white and clean."

Question: Are these pieces of *"fine linen,"* similar or the same as what was given to the prophet Joseph Smith, for the LDS members on this earth who go into the House of the Lord?

John's other vision mentions specific members in Sardis *"which have not defiled their garments,"* (which means they have not fallen into iniquity). These particular members go on to *"be clothed in white raiment."*

> Revelation 3:4,5 – 4. Thou hast a few names even in Sardis which have not **defiled their garments; and they shall walk with me in white:** for they are worthy. 5. **He that overcometh, the same shall be clothed in white raiment;** and I will not blot out his name out of the book of life, but I will confess his name before my Father, and before his angels.

Question: For a follower of Christ that will be "clothed in white raiment" and will not have his/her name "blotted out of the book of life," is it necessary to be wearing the "garments?"

Question: What happens to those followers of Christ who are not wearing the "garments" which are, according to Isaiah, the "garments of salvation?"

John's reference to the "garments" also comes with a warning to the churches.

> Revelation 3:6 – He that hath an ear, let him hear what the Spirit saith unto the churches.

John does not stop there. He receives another revelation from the Lord which states:

> Revelation 16:15 – Behold, I come as a thief. **Blessed is he that watcheth, and keepeth his garments,** lest he walk naked, and they see his shame.

The Lord has mentioned several times about his coming as a *"thief."* One was in the Book of Revelation. This was a warning right before He spoke of those who do not *"defile their garments, will not be blotted out of the book of life."*

> Revelation 3:3 – Remember therefore how thou hast received and heard, and hold fast, and repent. If therefore thou shalt not watch, **I will come on thee as a thief, and thou shalt not know what hour I will come upon thee.**

A second time that the Lord mentions coming at a time that will be unexpected is in Luke.

> *Luke 21:35 – 34. And take heed to yourselves, lest at any time your hearts be over-charged with surfeiting, and drunkenness, and cares of this life, and so that day come upon you unawares. 35.* **For as a snare shall it come on all them that dwell on the face of the whole earth.**

A third time that the Lord mentions that He will come suddenly, with no notice is in "the parable of the ten virgins."

> *Matthew 25:1-13 – 1. Then shall the kingdom of heaven be likened unto ten virgins, which took their lamps, and went forth to meet the bridegroom. 2. And five of them were wise, and five were foolish. 3. They that were foolish took their lamps, and took no oil with them: 4. But the wise took oil in their vessels with their lamps. 5. While the bridegroom tarried, they all slumbered and slept. 6. And at midnight there was a cry made, Behold, the bridegroom cometh; go ye out to meet him. 7. Then all those virgins arose, and trimmed their lamps. 8. And the foolish said unto the wise, Give us of your oil; for our lamps are gone out. 9. But the wise answered, saying, Not so; lest there be not enough for us and you: but go ye rather to them that sell, and buy for yourselves. 10. And while they went to buy, the bridegroom came; and they that were ready went in with him to the marriage: and the door was shut. 11. Afterward came also the other virgins, saying,* **Lord, Lord,** *open to us. 12. But he answered and said, Verily I say unto you, I know you not. 13.* **Watch therefore, for ye know neither the day nor the hour wherein the Son of man cometh.**

As John spoke in the quoted passages from Revelation, the wearing or having the special *"garments of salvation"* are directly related to the Lord's coming as a *"thief."* One should pay close attention to *"the parable of the ten virgins"* and ask your self a few questions.

Question: If, in the parable of the ten virgins, the oil in the lamp were replaced with the wearing of the "garments of salvation" which of the five virgins would you be grouped with, the five virgins who were wearing their "garments of salvation" or the five virgins who were not wearing their *"garments of salvation?"*

Christ's Statement About the Garments. Another admonition from Christ that is stated the same as in the parable of the ten virgins (Matthew 25:11).

> *Matthew 7:21 – Not every one that saith unto me,* **Lord, Lord, shall enter into the kingdom of heaven;** *but he that doeth the will of my Father which is in heaven.*

It is obvious from these passages that there will be many, possibly 50% or more, of the followers of Christ that will be denied entrance into the kingdom of God. In the parable of the marriage of the king's son, Jesus Christ gives another warning!

> *Matthew 22:11-14 – 11. And when the king came in to see the guests, he saw there a man which had not on a wedding garment: 12.* **And he saith unto him, Friend, how camest thou in hither not having a wedding garment? And he was speechless. 13.** *Then said the king to the servants,* **Bind him hand and foot, and take him away, and cast him into outer darkness; there shall be weeping and gnashing of teeth. 14. For many are called, but few are chosen.**

Again, the Lord is talking about Christians who believe in Him, but do not receive the proper guidance that comes from a prophet, which in this case is the requirement for "wedding garments." Members of the Mormon Church do receive special *"garments"* which are *"wedding garments"* in the temples. As Christ indicated, these *"wedding garments"* are critical to one's own salvation!

Question: Could the wearing of the *"garments of salvation"* be one of the deciding factors as to who is allowed into the kingdom of heaven?

Question: Does it matter whether or not you are wearing the *"wedding garments?"*

Question: Does your church offer the opportunity to wear the *"garments of salvation"* or do they mock the wearing of such clothing?

Question: What do you have to do to prepare yourself?

The Biblical Support Chart. The Christian position is that there is no need for temples in these days. After having gone through the Bible and studying each one of the Christian positions in relation to Joseph Smith's teachings about the need for temples, we again find 100% support from the Bible in all aspects of the temple.

THE BIBLICAL SUPPORT CHART

Is the following topic supported in the Bible?	Yes or No
Does the Bible support Joseph Smith's on the sacredness of the latter day temples where God may dwell? (Acts 7:48,49; 17:24; Exo 25:8,9; Exo 29:42-46; Lev 1:1; Deut 31:15; 2 Chron 1:6,7)	Yes
Does the Bible support the teachings of Joseph Smith that he a prophet was directed by God to build a temple? (2 Sam 7:5-7,13; 1 Kings 5:3-5; Hab 2:20; Zech 1:16; Zech 6:12,13)	Yes
Does the Bible support the teachings of Joseph Smith's that there will be temples in the last days? (Isa 2:2-3; Matt 17:11; Acts 3:19-21; Micah 4:1,2; Amos 9:11,12; Acts 15:16,17; Rev 7:15; Rev 11:1; Isa 4:6; Mal 3:1; Zech 14:16-21)	Yes
Does the Bible support Joseph Smith's teachings that there should be ordinances performed for the dead (i.e., baptism for the dead)? (1 Kings 7:23-25; 2 Chron 4:2-4; Jer 52:17,20)	Yes
Does the Bible support Joseph Smith's "law of worthiness" or temple recommend requirement for a person to enter into the temple? (1 Chron 22:6-11; Ezek 44:7-9; Psm 15:1-3; Psm 24:3-5; Isa56:6,7; Jer 7:1-7; Ezek 43:10-12; Num 1:51; Acts 21:26-31; Matt 21:12,13; Mark 11:15-18; Luke 19:45-46; John 2:14-16)	Yes
Does the Bible support Joseph Smith's teachings that a prophet and a person who enters the temples will be highly blessed and may even see or talk with God? (Psm 65:4; Exo 29:42-46; Lev 1:1; 2 Chron 1:6,7; 2 Chron 7:11,12; Ezek 43:4,5; Psalm 27:5,6; Psalm 27:8; Exo 29:43-46; Psm 24:6,7; Psm 27:4; Psm 84:1-2; Psm 84:4; Psm 84:10)	Yes
Does the Bible support Joseph Smith giving of "new names" in the temples? (Luke 1:21,22; Isa 65:15; Rev 2:17; Rev 19:12)	Yes
Does the Bible support Joseph Smith's implementation of wearing special temple/wedding garments? (Exo 28:1,2,40-42; Exo 39:1,28; Lev 6:10; Isa 52:1; Isa 61:10; Ezek 42:14; Rev 19:13,14; Rev 3:4,5; Rev 3:6; Rev 16:15; Rev 3:3; Matt 25:1-13; Matt 7:21; Matt 22:11-14)	Yes
Does the Bible support the fact that Joseph Smith has the saints wear as much white clothing as possible? (Rev 3:4,5; Rev 19:13,14)	Yes
Does the Bible support Joseph Smith's teachings that we should keep a genealogy of our ancestors and perform the temple ordinances for them? (Ezra 2:62; Mal 3:16-18; Matt 16:19; 18:18; Heb 11:32,33; 11:36-40; John 3:5,6; 1 Pet 3:18,19; John 5:25,28,29; 1 Pet 4:6; 1 Cor 15:29; Rom 14:9; 1 Cor 15:19; Pro 17:6)	Yes

Author's Note. After studying in the Bible the need for temples in the last days, it was not Joseph Smith who thought up the idea to build a temple. It is claimed by the Mormons and documented in the LDS scripture The Doctrine and Covenants that it was the Lord, through revelation, who instructed Joseph Smith to build a temple, gave the purpose for the temple, and the rules surrounding who may enter the temple. On December 27, 1832, in the city of Kirtland, Ohio, the Lord gave Joseph Smith the following first set of instructions:

> D&C 88:119 – *Organize yourselves; prepare every needful thing;* **and establish a house, even a house of prayer, a house of fasting, a house of faith, a house of learning, a house of glory, a house of order, a house of God;**

Then on August 2, 1833 in Kirtland, Ohio, the Lord gave the following second set of instructions:

> D&C 97:10-17 – 10. **Verily I say unto you, that it is my will that a house should be built unto me in the land of Zion,** *like unto the pattern which I have given you. 11. Yea, let it be built speedily, by the tithing of my people. 12. Behold, this is the tithing and the sacrifice which I, the Lord, require at their hands,* **that there may be a house built unto me for the salvation of Zion—**

The purpose for building this House of the Lord was included:

> 13. **For a place of thanksgiving for all saints, and for a place of instruction for all those who are called to work of the ministry in all their several callings and offices; 14. That they may be perfected in the understanding of their ministry, in theory, in principle, and in doctrine, in all things pertaining to the kingdom of God on the earth, the keys of which kingdom have been conferred upon you.**

Notice the parallel between these past two verses of instructions and the prophecy that Isaiah (Isaiah 2:2,3) and Micah (Micah 4:1,2) gave about the *"mountain of the house of the Lord shall be established"* where *"he will teach us of his ways."*

The next three verses are the instructions from the Lord of who may go into the house, or the *"law of worthiness."* It is from these instructions that the *"temple recommend"* system of the Mormon Church was set up.

> 15. **And inasmuch as my people build a house unto me in the name of the Lord, and do not suffer any unclean thing to come into it, that it be not defiled, my glory shall rest upon it; 16. Yea, and my presence shall be there, for I will come into it, and all the pure in heart that shall come into it shall see God. 17. But if it be defiled I will not come into it, and my glory shall not be there; for I will not come into unholy temples.**

After the completion of the Kirtland Temple, on April 3, 1836, the official dedication of the temple was made. At the dedication the Lord appeared to Joseph Smith and Oliver Cowdery and said:

> D&C 110:6-8 – 6. *Let the hearts of your brethren rejoice, and let the hearts of all my people rejoice, who have, with their might, built this house to my name. 7.* **For behold, I have accepted this house, and my name shall be here; and I will manifest myself to my people in mercy in this house. 8. Yea, I will appear unto my servants, and speak unto them with mine own voice, if my people will keep my commandments, and do not pollute this holy house.**

Following the traditions of the Bible that have been detailed in this chapter, the Lord established the same "House of the Lord" in the last days. As of this writing, there are over 129 sacred temples either built or in the design and construction phase. These temples are located all over the world so that the members may go in and "learn the ways of God," receive the special *"wedding garments,"* and make special covenants with the Lord—above and beyond the covenant of baptism. In these temples, many ordinances are made for the members beloved ancestors who will now be able to *"live according to God in the spirit."*

> *1 Peter 4:6 – For for this cause was the gospel preached also to them that are dead, that they might be judged according to men in the flesh, **but live according to God in the Spirit.***

To the Mormon's, the temples are very sacred places. As one can read from the biblical passages, all of the teachings of Joseph Smith concerning the temples are supported in the Bible. For the non-Mormons and anti-Mormons, you should ask yourself the following questions.

Question: Which church has more scriptural support for their particular position on temples?

Question: In regards to the "House of the Lord," which church has a more defined knowledge and practice with the Bible's true intent?

Question: Is it important for you and your eternal salvation to have the opportunity to wear the special "wedding garments?"

Question: Is it important for your ancestors and their eternal salvation to be able to *"live according to God in the Spirit?"*

Question: Which faith is more likely to be lead by *"crafty men, lying in wait to deceive?"*

NOTES

CHAPTER 15

THE COVENANT PEOPLE

From the earliest days of the church that Joseph Smith set up, the Lord spoke of establishing His everlasting covenant again with His people. It was on November 1, 1831 when the Lord revealed to Joseph Smith one of the purposes of restoring the church:

> D&C 1:22 – *That mine everlasting covenant might be established;*

Another example of the Lord establishing His covenant with Joseph Smith and His people is on February 16, 1832 when the Lord was explaining the different glories of heaven and what happens to the most just men on earth.

> D&C 76:69 – *These are they who are just men made perfect through Jesus **the mediator of the new covenant,** who wrought out this perfect atonement through the shedding of his own blood.*

According to the Mormon Church history, over the next thirteen years the Lord restored His fullness of the gospel to earth and one of the many precious truths that was established was the *"covenants"* that were so prevalent throughout the ages of the Bible.

When the Lord spoke of the last days, *"restoring all things"* and the *"times of restitution"*:

> Matthew 17:11 – *And Jesus answered and said unto them, **Elias truly shall first come, and restore all things.***

> Acts 3:21 – *Whom the heaven must receive **until the times of restitution of all things,** which God hath spoken by the mouth of all his holy prophets since the world began.*

The Lord meant that "all things" would be restored. When the Lord spoke about not "one jot or tittle will in no wise pass from the law:"

> Matthew 5:18 – *For verily I say unto you, Till heaven and earth pass, **one jot or one tittle shall in no wise pass from the law, till all be fulfilled.***

The Old Testament Oaths and Covenants. The Lord was speaking also about His covenants with His people that would be reestablished. A short history of the covenants made with His people starts in the Old Testament with Noah.

> Genesis 6:18 – ***But with thee will I establish my covenant;** and thou shalt come into the ark, thou, and thy sons, and thy wife, and thy sons wives with thee.*

> Genesis 9:16 – *And the bow shall be in the cloud; and I will look upon it, **that I may remember the everlasting covenant** between God and every living creature of all flesh that is upon the earth.*

The Lord also established His covenants with Abraham.

> Genesis 17:2-7 – 2. ***And I will make my covenant between me and thee,** and will multiply thee exceedingly. 3. And Abram fell on his face: and God talked with him, saying, 4. As for me, behold, **my covenant is with thee,** and thou shalt be a father of many nations. 5. Neither shall thy name any more be called Abram, but thy name shall be Abraham; for a father of many nations have I made thee, 6. And I will make thee exceeding fruitful, and I will make nations of thee, and kings shall come out of thee. 7. And I will establish my covenant between me and thee and thy seed after thee in their generations **for an everlasting covenant,** to be a god unto*

thee, and to thy seed after thee.

> *Genesis 26:3-5 – 3. Sojourn in this land, and I will be with thee, and will bless thee; for unto thee, and unto thy seed, I will give all these countries, **and I will perform the oath** which I sware unto Abraham thy father; 4. And I will make thy seed to multiply as the stars of heaven, and will give unto thy seed all these countries; and in thy seed shall all the nations of the earth be blessed; 5. Because that Abraham obeyed my voice, and kept my charge, my commandments, my statutes, and my laws.*

After Abraham, the Lord established His covenants with Moses.

> *Exodus 6:4 – **And I have also established my covenant with them,** to give them the land of Canaan, the land of their pilgrimage, wherein they were strangers.*

> *Exodus 19:5 – Now therefore, if ye will obey my voice indeed, **and keep my covenant,** then ye shall be a peculiar treasure unto me above all people; for all the earth is mine.*

> *Exodus 22:10,11 – 11. If a man deliver unto his neighbour an ass, or an ox, or a sheep, or any beast, to keep; and it die, or be hurt, or driven away, no man seeing it: 11. **Then shall an oath of the Lord be between them both,** that he hath not put his hand unto his neighbour's goods; and the owner of it shall accept thereof, and he shall not make it good.*

The first covenant the Lord made was the covenant to keep the commandments. It was with Moses that *"the words of the covenant"* were directly related to the Ten Commandments:

> *Exodus 34:28 – And he was there with the Lord forty days and forty nights; he did neither eat bread, nor drink water. And he wrote upon the tables **the words of the covenant, the ten commandments.***

> *Deuteronomy 4:13 – And **he declared unto you his covenant,** which he commanded you to perform, even ten commandments; and he wrote them upon two tables of stone.*

The Lord brought in other covenants.

> *Deuteronomy 29:1 – **These are the words of the covenant,** which the Lord commanded Moses to make with the children of Israel in the land of Moab, **beside the covenant which he made with them in Horeb.***

Another one of the covenants that the Lord made had to do with the "everlasting priesthood".

> *Numbers 25:10-13 – 10. And the Lord spake unto Moses, saying, 11. Phinehas, the son of Eleazar, the son of Aaron the priest, hath turned my wrath away from the children of Israel, while he was zealous for my sake among them, that I consumed not the children of Israel in my jealousy. 12. Wherefore say, Behold, **I give unto him my covenant of peace;** 13. And he shall have it, and his seed after him, **even the covenant of an everlasting priesthood;** because he was zealous for his God, and made an atonement for the children of Israel.*

Along with the Lord's covenants, there were also oaths that His people would swear to the Lord.

> *Numbers 30:2 – If a man vow a vow unto the Lord, **or swear an oath to bind his soul with a bond;** he shall not break his word, he shall do according to all that proceedeth out of his mouth.*

> *Deuteronomy 7:8 – But because the Lord loved you, and because **he would keep***

the oath which he had sworn unto your fathers, hath the Lord brought you out with a mighty hand, and redeemed you out of the house of bondmen, from the hand of Pharaoh king of Egypt.

*Deuteronomy 29:12,13 – 12. That **thou shouldest enter into covenant with the Lord thy God, and into his oath,** which the Lord thy God maketh with thee this day: 13. **That he may establish thee today for a people unto himself, and that he may be unto thee a God,** as he hath said unto thee, and as he hath sworn unto thy fathers, to Abraham, to Isaac, and to Jacob.*

The Lord established His covenant with Joseph.

*Genesis 50:25 – **And Joseph took an oath of the children of Israel,** saying, God will surely visit you, and ye shall carry up my bones from hence.*

The Lord established His covenant with Jacob, Isaac, and Abraham.

*Leviticus 26:42 – **Then will I remember my covenant with Jacob, and also my covenant with Isaac, and also my covenant with Abraham will I remember;** and I will remember the land.*

*1 Chronicles 16:14-17 – 14. He is the Lord our God; his judgments are in all the earth. 15. **Be ye mindful always of his covenant;** the word which he commanded to a thousand generations; 16. **Even of the covenant** which he made with Abraham, **and of his oath unto Isaac;** 17. And hath confirmed the same to Jacob for a law, **and to Israel for an everlasting covenant.***

*Psalm 105:8-10 – 8. **He hath remembered his covenant for ever,** the word which he commanded to a thousand generations. 9. **Which covenant he made with Abraham, and his oath unto Isaac;** 10. And confirmed the same unto Jacob for a law, and **to Israel for an everlasting covenant:***

To remain true to His way of doing things, the Lord established His oath and covenant with Solomon.

*1 Kings 2:43 – **Why then hast thou not kept the oath of the Lord,** and the commandment that I have charged thee with?*

*1 Kings 11:11 – Wherefore the Lord said unto Solomon, Forasmuch as this is done of thee, and **thou hast not kept my covenant and my statutes,** which I have commanded thee, I will surely rend the kingdom from thee, and will give it to thy servant.*

The Lord established His covenant with Jehoiada and his soldiers. He did this in the temple!

*2 Kings 11:4 – And the seventh year Jehoiada sent and fetched the rulers over hundreds, with the captains and the guard, **and brought them to him into the house of the Lord, and made a covenant with them, and took an oath of them in the house of the Lord,** and shewed them the king's son.*

The Lord established His covenant with Josiah in the temple.

*2 Kings 23:2,3 – 2. And the king went up into the house of the Lord, and all the men of Judah and all the inhabitants of Jerusalem with him, and the priests, and the prophets, and all the people, both small and great: and he read in their ears all **the words of the book of the covenant** which was found in the house of the Lord. 3. And the king stood by a pillar, and made a covenant before the Lord, to walk after the Lord, and to keep his commandments and his testimonies and his statutes with all their heart and all their soul, **to perform the words of this covenant*** *that were written in this book. And all the people stood to the covenant.*

The Lord established His covenant with Hilkiah and his king.

> *2 Chronicles 34:29-31 – 29. Then the king sent and gathered together all the elders of Judah and Jerusalem. 30. **And the king went up into the house of the Lord,** and all the men of Judah, and the inhabitants of Jerusalem, and the priests, and the Levites, and all the people, great and small: and he read in their ears all **the words of the book of the covenant** that was found in the house of the lord. 31. And the king stood in his place, and **made a covenant before the Lord,** to walk after the Lord, and to keep his commandments, and his testimonies, and his statutes, with all his heart, and with all his soul, **to perform the words of the covenant which are written in this book.***

Most of the past examples have been where the Lord established His oaths and covenants with the prophet and leaders of the faith. Not only did the Lord establish these oaths and covenants with the prophets, He also established His covenant with the general membership or with all the saints.

> *Psalm 50:5 – Gather my saints together unto me; **those that have made a covenant with me by sacrifice.***

> *Psalm 89:3 – **I have made a covenant with my chosen,** I have sworn unto David my servant.*

> *Nehemiah 9:38 – **And because of all this we make a sure covenant, and write it; and our princes, Levites, and priests, seal unto it.***

> *Nehemiah 10:29 – They clave to their brethren, their nobles, **and entered into a curse, and into an oath, to walk in God's law,** which was given by Moses the servant of God, and to observe and do all the commandments of the Lord our Lord, and his judgments and his statutes.*

The New Testament Oaths and Covenants. Many believe that with Christ's birth, ministry and atonement, there was no more need for the oaths and covenants of the Old Testament. The following teachings by some of the apostles, reconfirms that the oaths and covenants of the Old Testament prophets were still in effect.

Luke spoke of the covenant that Christ was to perform and that they should remember His holy covenant.

> *Luke 1:72,73 – 72. To perform the mercy promised to our fathers, **and to remember his holy covenant; 73. The oath which he sware to our father Abraham.***

Paul taught the following about the covenants that Christ made and the other members of saints made after they were in the church.

> *Romans 11:27 – **For this is my covenant unto them,** when I shall take away their sins.*

Paul taught the Galatian membership that if they are in Christ, then they still are under the covenant and "heirs according to the promise."

> *Galatians 3:17,29 – 17. And this I say, **that the covenant,** that was confirmed before of God in Christ, the law, which was four hundred and thirty years after, cannot disannul, that it should make the promise of none effect....29. And if ye be Christ's, then are ye Abraham's seed, and **heirs according to the promise.***

Paul taught the Ephesians that before they were members they were strangers to the covenants, now that they were members, they were no longer strangers to the covenant.

> *Ephesians 2:12 – That at that time ye were without Christ, being aliens from the commonwealth of Israel, and strangers from* **the covenants of promise,** *having no hope, and without God in the world:*

To the Hebrew saints Paul taught that to inherit the promises made to Abraham, they were to swear an oath themselves. In verse 19, Paul explained that this covenant was entered into "within the veil", which was in the temple. Everyone understands that the veil was in the temple, it is this same temple veil that was rent upon Christ's death.

> *Hebrews 6:12-19 – 12. That ye be not slothful, but followers of them who through faith and patience* **inherit the promises.** *13. For when God made promise to Abraham, because he could swear by no greater, he sware by himself, 14. Saying, Surely blessing I will bless thee, and multiplying I will multiply thee. 15. And so, after he had patiently endured, he obtained the promise. 16.* **For men verily swear by the greater: and an oath for confirmation is to them an end of all strife. 17. Wherein God, willing more abundantly to shew unto the heirs of promise the immutability of his counsel, confirmed it by an oath:** *18. That by two immutable things, in which it was impossible for God to lie, we might have a strong consolation, who have fled for refuge to lay hold upon the hope set before us: 19.* **Which hope we have as an anchor of the soul, both sure and steadfast, and which entereth into that within the veil;**

Paul taught that there was an oath to be made upon receiving the office of a priest in the Melchizedek priesthood.

> *Hebrews 7:20,21 – 20. And inasmuch* **as not without an oath he was made priest:** *21. (For those priests were made without an oath;* **but his with an oath** *by him that said unto him, The Lord sware and will not repent,* **Thou art a priest for ever after the order of Melchizedek:)**

If there is any doubt that the covenants made in the verses mentioned above were still the Old Testament covenants, Paul clears this up by teaching that Christ is now the "mediator of a better covenant" that had with it "better promises."

> *Hebrews 8:6 – But now hath he obtained a more excellent ministry, by how much also* **he is the mediator of a better covenant,** *which was established upon* **better promises.**

Paul continues to explain that there is a new covenant.

> *Hebrews 8:13 – In that he saith,* **A new covenant,** *he hath made the first old. Now that which decayeth and waxeth old is ready to vanish away.*

> *Hebrews 12:24 – And to Jesus* **the mediator of the new covenant,** *and to the blood of sprinkling, that speaketh better things than that of Abel.*

Christ's command to us to "be perfect, even as our Father which is in Heaven is perfect."

> *Matthew 5:48 –* **Be ye therefore perfect, even as your Father which is in heaven is perfect.**

Paul taught that the way for us to become perfect like our Father in Heaven is through "*the everlasting covenant.*"

> *Hebrews 13:20,21 – 20. Now the God of peace, that brought again from the dead our Lord Jesus, that great shepherd of the sheep, through the blood of* **the everlasting**

*covenant, 21. **Make you perfect in every good work to do his will,** working in you that which is wellpleasing in his sight, through Jesus Christ; to whom be glory for ever and ever. Amen.*

As noted above by Paul, this covenant is made within the veil of the temple.

Question: Does your church offer you the opportunity to make oaths and covenants in a sacred temple, so that you may reach the perfection of our Heavenly Father?

Covenants With the Latter Day House of Judah. In being specific, the Old Testament prophets taught that the Lord would, in the last days, reestablish His covenant with the House of Judah.

*Isaiah 55:3 – Incline your ear, and come unto me: hear, and your soul shall live; and **I will make an everlasting covenant with you,** even the sure mercies of David.*

*Jeremiah 32:40 – And I will **make an everlasting covenant with them,** that I will not turn away from them, to do them good; but I will put my fear in their hearts, that they shall not depart from me.*

*Ezekiel 16:60-62 – 60. Nevertheless **I will remember my covenant with thee** in the days of thy youth, **and I will establish unto thee an everlasting covenant.** 61. Then thou shalt remember thy ways, and be ashamed, when thou shalt receive thy sisters, thine elder and thy younger: and I will give them unto thee for daughters, but not by thy covenant. 62. **And I will establish my covenant with thee;** and thou shalt know that I am the Lord:*

*Jeremiah 50:4,5 – 4. In those days, and in that time, saith the Lord, the children of Israel shall come, they and the children of Judah together, going and weeping: they shall go, and seek the Lord their God. 5. They shall ask the way to Zion with their faces thitherward, saying, Come, and **let us join ourselves to the Lord in a perpetual covenant that shall not be forgotten.***

Covenants With the Latter Day Gentiles. Many church ministers still believe there is no need for the oaths, covenants, and temples in these latter days. They teach that the Lord will make these covenants with the House of Judah when He appears at His second coming. The prophets of old that prophesied of the last days actually saw the establishment of the ever-lasting covenant with the gentiles and the Jews before the second coming.

Isaiah saw that the Lord would *"make an everlasting covenant"* with the people in the last days.

*Isaiah 61:8 – For I the Lord love judgment, I hate robbery for burnt offering; and I will direct their work in truth, **and I will make an everlasting covenant with them.***

Jeremiah saw that the Lord would make a covenant with both the house of Israel and with the house of Judah.

*Jeremiah 31:31,33 – 31. Behold, the days come, saith the Lord, that **I will make a new covenant with the house of Israel, and with the house of Judah:** 32. Not according to the covenant that I made with their fathers in the day that I took them by the hand to bring them out of the land of Egypt; which my covenant they brake, although I was an husband unto them, saith the Lord: 33. **But this shall be the covenant that I will make with the house of Israel;** After those days, saith the Lord, **I will put my law in their inward parts, and write it in their hearts; and will be their God, and they shall be my people.***

Not only did Ezekiel see the establishment of the covenant with the people in the last days, he saw that the Lord would *"set my sanctuary,"* or *"tabernacle,"* or temple in the midst of them for evermore. Ezekiel saw that the covenant and the sanctuary would be established with the *"heathen,"* which are the "non-house of Judah" or gentiles.

> *Ezekiel 37:26-28 – 26. Moreover* **I will make a covenant of peace with them; it shall be an everlasting covenant** *with them: and I will place them, and multiply them,* **and will set my sanctuary in the midst of them for evermore. 27. My tabernacle** *also shall be with them: yea, I will be their God, and they shall be my people. 28.* **And the heathen shall know** *that I the Lord do sanctify Israel, when my sanctuary shall be in the midst of them for evermore.*

This is exactly what Joseph Smith taught—that the Lord restored His covenant and temples back to the earth.

The Apostasy and the Breaking of the Covenant. It was prophesied in the Old Testament that the covenant would be broken. Moses wrote about it.

> *Deuteronomy 29:25,26 – 25. Then men shall say,* **Because they have forsaken the covenant of the Lord God of their fathers, which he made with them when he brought them forth out of the land of Egypt:** *26. For they went and served other gods, and worshipped them, gods whom they knew not, and whom he had not given unto the:*

Isaiah also saw that the *"everlasting covenant"* would be broken. This is in direct relation to the apostasy from the church that Christ established.

> *Isaiah 24:5 – The earth also is defiled under the inhabitants thereof; because they have transgressed the laws, changed the ordinance,* **broken the everlasting covenant.**

The Lord confirmed the breaking of the *"everlasting covenant"* by the early church membership was a part of the apostasy.

> *D&C 1:14,15 – 14. And the arm of the Lord shall be revealed; and the day cometh that they who will not hear the voice of the Lord, neither the voice of his servants, neither give heed to the words of the prophets and apostles, shall be cut off from among the people; 15.* **For they have strayed from mine ordinances, and have broken mine everlasting covenant;**

Question: Does your church or faith teach that you have the opportunity to make further oaths and covenants with Heavenly Father and Jesus Christ?

Question: Would it be important to you to have the opportunity to make these oaths and covenants, to include the "new and everlasting covenant" with Heavenly Father and our Lord Jesus Christ?

The Biblical Support Chart. The Christian position on the Lord's oaths, covenants, and the new and everlasting covenant is one that is conflicting. Some say there is no need for the covenants of the Old Testament and some say nothing. Many Christians just do not know about these oaths and covenants.

Claiming to be the prophet of *"the restoration of all things"* Joseph Smith taught that these oaths and covenants are necessary for ones exaltation in the kingdom of God. The Biblical Support Chart lists the Bible passages that support these teachings of Joseph Smith.

THE BIBLICAL SUPPORT CHART

Is the following topic supported in the Bible?	Yes or No
Does the Bible support Joseph Smith's that special oaths and covenants should be made with the Lord? (Gen 6:18; Gen 26:3-5; Exo 6:4; Exo 19:5; Exo 22:10,11; Exo 34:28; Deut 4:13; Deu 29:1; Num 30:2; Deu 7:8; Deu 29:12,13; Gen 26:42; 1 Kings 2:43; 1Kings 11:11; 2 Kings 11:4; 2 Kings 23:2,3; 2 Chron 34:29-31; Psalm 50:5; Psalm 89:3; Neh 9:38; Neh 10:29; Luke 1:72,73; Rom 11:27; Gal 3:17,29; Eph 2:12; Heb 6:12-19; Heb 7:20,21; Heb 8:6,13; Heb 12:24)	Yes
Does the Bible support Joseph Smith's teachings obout an "everlasting covenant?" (Gen 9:16; Gen 17:2-7; Num 25:10-13; 1 Chron 16:14-17; Psalm 105:8-10; Heb 13:20,21)	Yes
Does the Bible support Joseph Smith's teachings that the Lord will establish His new covenant and the everlasting covenant with His people? (Isa 55:3; Jer 32:40; Ezek 16:60-62; Jer 50:4,5; Isa 61:8; Jer 31:31,33; Ezek 37:26-28)	Yes

Author's Note: Having a Mormon daughter who married my son-in-law, who is of the "saved Christian" faith and is quite anti-Mormon, has told me of comments and questions made to her about the Mormons from the members of these other churches that they attend. One of the questions posed to my daughter was:

Question: "Why are Mormons so committed?

One can read this book and find the answer to that question. It is God's commandment to "be perfect." All of the knowledge of the restoration of the fullness of the gospel of Jesus Christ, the *Book of Mormon*, the Priesthood, the temples, and etc. goes into making the Mormons a committed people who are seeking that *"perfection."* The path to *"perfection"* is making the additional oaths, covenants, anointing, endowment, and sealings that are made in the temples with the Lord.

It has been stated in both the latter days to Joseph Smith and in the New Testament days of Jesus Christ that *"unto whom much is given much is required."*

> D&C 82:2-4 – 2. *Nevertheless, there are those among you who have sinned exceedingly; yea, even all of you have sinned; but verily I say unto you, beware from henceforth, and refrain from sin, lest sore judgments fall upon your heads. 3.* **For of him unto whom much is given much is required; and he who sins against the greater light shall receive the greater condemnation.** *4. Ye call upon my name for revelations, and I give them unto you; and inasmuch as ye keep not my sayings, which I give unto you, ye become transgressors; and justice and judgment are the penalty which is affixed unto my law.*

> Luke 12:48 – *But he that knew not, and did commit things worthy of stripes, shall be beaten with few stripes.* **For unto whomsoever much is given, of him shall be much required:** *and to whom men have committed much, of him they will ask the more.*

When the Lord said *"unto whom much is given"* He was talking about the rewards of glory that He will give to each person who lived on the earth. Christ is talking about the three degrees of glory spoken of in **Chapter 12 – The Plan of Salvation – Post Mortal Life.** These three degrees of glory are the Celestial Kingdom, where Heavenly Father and Jesus Christ dwells, the Terrestrial Glory, where Jesus Christ's presence will also be, and the Telestial Glory, where both Heavenly Father and Jesus Christ will not even visit.

In order to receive the highest glory, the Celestial Glory, where both Heavenly Father and Jesus Christ will dwell, one must make these oaths and covenants, to include *"the new and everlasting covenant"* in one of the "Houses of the LORD" that have been built around the world by the Mormons.

NOTES

NOTES

CHAPTER 16

THE "GOD-MAKERS"

Author's Note: There has been much thought and prayer go into writing this chapter, which to the followers of Joseph Smith, is very special and sacred. As I contemplated whether I should include this chapter in the book or not, I fell back on to two different principles, one is Jesus Christ's own words of great warning when He said *"neither cast ye your pearls before swine."*

> *Matthew 7:6 – Give not that which is holy unto the dogs, **neither cast ye your pearls before swine,** lest they trample them under their feet, and turn again and rend you.*

> *D&C 41:6 – For it is not meet that the things which belong to the children of the kingdom should be given to them that are not worthy, or to dogs, **or the pearls to be cast before swine.***

I do not want to be guilty of *"casting this pearl before swine."*

After much contemplation as to whether to include this *"pearl"* in the book, I came to the conclusion that, after the many words and books written against Joseph Smith and his "God-maker" theory, that the *"pearl"* has already been cast. It is the purpose of this chapter to try, in the eyes of many, to retrieve the *"pearl"* and polish it up.

The second principle is the one of "personal inspiration." While writing this book much prayer, fasting, and scripture study was involved. It was through the inspiration of the Holy Ghost, and through the great support of my wife, CeLeste, that many of these Biblical scriptures were found that are included in this chapter. With the abundance of spiritual support in studying this topic in the Bible, I want to include this chapter in the book.

The Mysteries of the Kingdom of God. The Lord has held many secrets throughout the Bible, in both the Old Testament and the New Testament. He has periodically commented on them.

> *Deuteronomy 29:29 – **The secret things belong unto the Lord our God:** but those things which are revealed belong unto us and to our children forever, that we may do all the words of this law.*

> *Psalms 25:14 – **The secret of the Lord is with them that fear him; and he will shew them his covenant.***

God was very clear about His secrets when He spoke through the prophet Amos.

> *Amos 3:7 – **Surely the Lord God will do nothing, but he revealeth his secret unto his servants the prophets.***

In the New Testament, the Lord became very specific about his secrets and the "mysteries of the kingdom of heaven" and who will know them. His apostles Matthew, Mark, and Luke asked why He always spoke in parables. Jesus Christ answered them with this response:

> *Matthew 13:11,12 – 11. He answered and said unto them, **Because it is given unto you to know the mysteries of the kingdom of heaven,** but to them it is not given. 12. **For whosoever hath, to him shall be given, and he shall have more abundance:** but whosoever hath not, from him shall be taken away even that he hath.*

> *Mark 4:11,12 – 11. And he said unto them, **Unto you it is given to know the mystery of the kingdom of God:** but unto them that are without, all these things*

are done in parables: 12. That seeing they may see, and not perceive; and hearing they may hear, and not understand; lest at any time they should be converted, and their sins should be forgiven them.

Luke 8:10 – And he said, **Unto you it is given to know the mysteries of the kingdom of God:** *but to others in parables; that seeing they might not see, and hearing they might not understand.*

Having these three apostles write about "the mysteries of the kingdom of God" does give some weight of importance to these mysteries. Paul, in a letter to the Corinthians also spoke of these mysteries. Paul referred to themselves, the apostles, as *"the stewards of the mysteries of God."*

1 Corinthians 4:1 – Let a man so account of us, as of the ministers of Christ, **and stewards of the mysteries of God.**

Then Paul singles out one of the most important mysteries of God and that is the "mystery of godliness."

1 Timothy 3:16 – **And without controversy great is the mystery of godliness:** *God was manifest in the flesh, justified in the Spirit, seen of angels, preached unto the Gentiles, believed on in the world, received up into glory.*

In this passage Paul writes about how *"great is the mystery of godliness."* Paul then tells about how *"God was manifest in the flesh justified in the Spirit, seen of angels, preached unto the Gentiles, believed on in the world, received up into glory."* Many religious leaders would say that Jesus Christ and His mission is the *"great mystery of godliness."*

Question: If the majority of the Christian world already understands Jesus Christ and His mission, then how can that be the "great mystery of godliness?

In Paul's writings to the Colossians, he mentions this mystery again.

Colossians 1:26-28 – 26. **Even the mystery which hath been hid from ages and from generations, but now is made manifest to his saints:** *27. To whom* **God would make known what is the riches of the glory of this mystery among the Gentiles;** *which is Christ in you,* **the hope of glory:** *28. Whom we preach, warning every man, and teaching every man in all wisdom;* **that we may present every man perfect in Christ Jesus:** *29 Whereunto I also labour, striving according to his working, which worketh in me mightily.*

Paul mentions here that his work and labour—all he strives for and works mightily for—is that he *"may present every man perfect in Christ Jesus."* The *"mystery"* here is part of what Paul talked about in 1 Timothy 3:16 when he said *"and without controversy great is the mystery of godliness."* Paul states here that the mystery is *"how every man may be perfect in Christ!"*

NOTE: The concept that man may become perfect was explained in Chapter 5 and more will be explained on this later in this chapter.

Following the same pattern as in the Old and New Testaments, the Lord treated Joseph Smith the same way as the prophets and apostles of old. The Lord told Joseph Smith the following:

D&C 6:11,12 – 11. **And if thou wilt inquire, thou shalt know mysteries which are great and marvelous; therefore thou shalt exercise thy gift, that thou mayest find out mysteries, that thou mayest bring many to the knowledge of the truth, yea, convince them of the error of their ways.** *12. Make not thy gift known unto any save it be those who are of thy faith. Trifle not with sacred things.*

The Mysteries of Godliness. These are the teaching of Joseph Smith concerning the *"great mystery of godliness."*

> *Revelations 1:7 – He that hath an ear, let him hear what the Spirit saith unto the churches;*

One of the major Christian complaints about Joseph Smith is his doctrine on exaltation. Joseph Smith taught that if man can receive all the proper ordinances, overcome the world's temptations and trials, and endure to the end, man will be exalted with Christ. This is in a way, a chance for man to become like God the Father and Jesus Christ, or become a God.

This teaching, according to the Christians is blasphemy and is one of the main reasons why they believe the Mormons are a cult. It is also a reason why they believe the Mormons worship Satan. They have even coined the phrase that the Mormons are "the God-makers" (i.e., the title for this chapter).

The scriptures used for their support are many of the same in the section of the Personality of God. In several places in the Bible, it states that God is the first and the last, and beside me, there is no God.

> *Isaiah 43:10-11 – 10. Ye are my witnesses, saith the Lord, and my servant whom I have chosen; that ye may know and believe me, and understand that I am he:* **before me there was not God formed, neither shall there be after me. 11. I, even I, am the Lord; and beside me there is no saviour.**

> *Isaiah 44:6 – Thus saith the Lord the King of Israel, and his redeemer the Lord of hosts;* **I am the first, and I am the last; and beside me there is no God.**

> *Isaiah 45:21-23 – 21. Tell ye, and bring them near; yea, let them take counsel together: who hath declared this from ancient time? Who hath told it from that time? Have not I the Lord?* **And there is no God else beside me; a just God and a Saviour; there is none beside me.** *22. Look unto me, and be ye saved, all the ends of the earth:* **for I am God, and there is none else.** *23. I have sworn by myself, the word is gone out of my mouth in righteousness, and shall not return, that unto me every knee shall bow, every tongue shall swear.*

The Christians have several problems with Joseph Smith's teaching that mortal man may someday become a God like Christ. These are:

1. That Joseph Smith's "God-maker" theory is contradictory to the teachings of the Bible.
2. That Joseph Smith's teachings on exaltation is not supported in the Bible.
3. Since the Mormons believe in the exaltation theory, then the Mormons believe in a different God than the God of the Bible.

The Glory of Jesus Christ.

> *Revelations 2:11 –* **He that hath an ear, let him hear what the Spirit saith unto the churches;**

In order to understand what Heavenly Father's promise of "eternal life in His kingdom," one must understand what exactly is "the Glory of Jesus Christ." From the teachings of John and Paul, we learn that Jesus Christ was in the beginning with God, and was a God. Jesus Christ actually made all things to include the heavens and the earth.

> *John 1:1-3,14 – 1. In the beginning was the Word, and* **the Word was with God, and the Word was God. 2. The same was in the beginning with God. 3. All things were made by him; and without him was not any thing made that**

was made. 14. *And the Word was made flesh, and dwelt among us, (and we beheld his glory, the glory as of the only begotten of the Father,) full of grace and truth.*

Hebrews 1:1-3 – 1. *God, who at sundry times and in divers manners spake in time past unto the fathers by the prophets.* 2. *Hath in these last days spoken unto us by his Son,* **whom he hath appointed heir of all things, by whom also he made the worlds;** 3. *Who being the brightness of his glory, and the express image of his person, and upholding all things by the word of his power, when he had by himself purged our sins, sat down on the right hand of the Majesty on high;* 4. **Being made so much better than the angels, as he hath by inheritance obtained a more excellent name than they.**

Colossians 1:16 – **For by him were all things created,** *that are in heaven, and that are in the earth, visible and invisible, whether they be thrones, or dominions, or principalities, or powers:* **all things were created by him, and for him:**

Knowing now that Jesus Christ made all things, we learn in Timothy that Jesus was made flesh. Once Jesus Christ was born on this earth, He established the gospel of Jesus Christ, and taught it to all people. After teaching his gospel, He gave his life to atone for our sins. Jesus Christ was then resurrected.

1 Timothy 3:16 – And without controversy **great is the mystery of godliness:** *God was manifest in the flesh, justified in the Spirit, seen of angels, preached unto the Gentiles, believed on in the world,* **received up into glory.**

After successfully completing Christ's mission here on earth, Jesus was **"received up into glory"** or **"exalted"** in the kingdom of God. This exaltation included sitting on the right of God, and receiving power and authority to rule over the earth, angels, and nations.

Colossians 3:1 – If ye then be risen with Christ, seek those things which are above, **where Christ sitteth on the right hand of God.**

Philippians 2:9-11 – 9. **Wherefore God also hath highly exalted him,** *and given him a name which is above every name:* 10. *That at the name of Jesus every knee should bow, of things in heaven, and things in earth, and things under the earth;* 11. *And that every tongue should confess that Jesus Christ is Lord, to the glory of God the Father,*

Acts 2:33 – Therefore **being by the right hand of God exalted,** *and having received of the Father the promise of the Holy Ghost, he hath shed forth this, which ye now see and hear.*

1 Peter 3:22 – **Who is gone into heaven, and is on the right hand of God; angels and authorities and powers being made subject to him.**

In addition to the power and authority over all the people on the earth, Christ was also given the power to judge all mankind that lived on the earth.

John 5:22 – For the Father judgeth no man, but **hath committed all judgment unto the Son:**

It is the central belief of most Christian churches that Jesus Christ was and is **"exalted"** in the kingdom of God. Even though there is no dispute about the current position of Jesus Christ, the preceding scriptures were included in this chapter in order to provide a reminder of the magnitude of what Jesus was given by our Father in Heaven. Jesus Christ is a God.

It is important to understand that the *"inheritance of the kingdom of God"* that Jesus Christ received was the result of His fulfilling, in an outstanding manner, His mission here on earth. A question that could be asked at this point is:

Question: What does this knowledge, Jesus Christ's exaltation, have to do with us, as children of God?

The Elect of God.

> *Revelations 2:17 – He that hath an ear, let him hear what the Spirit saith unto the churches;*

From the very beginning of Jesus Christ's ministry, Jesus clearly taught that there were people who were "favored" in the eyes of God. These "favored" were taught differently than those who were not "favored." The first examples were Christ's teachings to the apostles. In the following passages, Jesus just finished teaching the parable of the sower and the apostles were asking Jesus, why he taught in parables. The answer was clear! There are those people that *"are given"* to know the mysteries of the kingdom of God and there are those people who will hear Christ but will not understand and will see, but will not perceive. Those people who *"are given"* to know the mysteries, will have more abundance.

> *Matthew 13:9-14 – 9. Who hath ears to hear, let him hear. 10. And the disciples came, and said unto him, Why speakest thou unto them in parables? 11. he answered and said unto them, **Because it is given unto you to know the mysteries of the kingdom of heaven, but to them it is not given. 12. For whosoever hath, to him shall be given, and he shall have more abundance:** but whosoever hath not, from him shall be taken away even that he hath. 13. Therefore speak I to them in parables: because they seeing see not; and hearing they hear not, neither do they understand. 14. And in them is fulfilled the prophecy of Esaias, which saith, By hearing ye shall hear, and shall not understand; and seeing ye shall see, and shall not perceive:*

> *Luke 8:8-10 – 8. And other fell on good ground, and sprang up, and bare fruit an hundredfold. And when he had said these things, he cried, He that hath ears to hear, let him hear. 9. And his disciples asked him, saying, What might this parable be? 10. And he said, **Unto you it is given to know the mysteries of the kingdom of God:** but to others in parables; that seeing they might not see and hearing they might not understand.*

Question: What is it that these children of God who *"hear and understand,"* and *"see and perceive"* will have in more abundance?

Before answering this question, more on the "favored people" or the *"elect"* of God should be revealed.

> *1 Thessalonians 1:4,5 – 4. Knowing, brethren beloved, **your election of God.** 5. For our gospel came not unto you in word only, but also in power, and in the Holy Ghost, and in much assurance; as ye know what manner of men we were among you for your sake.*

Paul is teaching the followers of Christ in Thessalonians that *"their election of God"* as having been called into the gospel, came not only in word, but power, and in the Holy Ghost. This election came not only here on earth, but *"from the beginning,"* the elect of God was chosen to have salvation to the *"obtaining the glory of our Lord Jesus Christ."*

> *2 Thessalonians 2:13,14 – 13. But we are bound to give thanks always to God for you, brethren beloved of the Lord, because **God hath from the beginning chosen you to salvation** through sanctification of the Spirit and belief of the truth: 14. Whereunto **he called you by our gospel, to the obtaining of the glory of our***

Lord Jesus Christ.

Paul taught both the Thessalonians and the Ephesians, that the favored were chosen from *"before the foundation of the world"* and that they were "predestinated to be adopted to Jesus Christ" or receive the gospel and be *"saved"* in this life.

> *Ephesians 1:4,5 – 4. According as **he hath chosen us in him before the foundation of the world, that we should be holy and without blame before him in love: 5. Having predestinated us unto the adoption of children by Jesus Christ to himself, according to the good pleasure of his will,***

> *Romans 9:10,11 – 10. And not only this; but when Rebecca also had conceived by one, even by our father Isaac; 11. (**For the children being not yet born,** neither having done any good or evil, **that the purpose of God according to election** might stand, not of works but of him that calleth;)*

Peter also taught the elect were chosen by *"the foreknowledge of God the Father."*

> *1 Peter 1:2 – **Elect according to the foreknowledge of God the Father,** through sanctification of the Spirit, unto obedience and sprinkling of the blood of Jesus Christ: Grace unto you, and peace, be multiplied.*

Now, after being taught that the *"favored people"* were *"chosen"* by God the Father, before this earth life, there are several other scriptures that refer to the *"elect of God."*

> *Colossians 3:12 – Put on therefore, **as the elect of God,** holy and beloved, bowels of mercies, kindness, humbleness of mind, meekness, longsuffering;*

> *2 Timothy 2:10 – Therefore **I endure all things for the elect's sakes, that they may also obtain the salvation which is in Christ Jesus with eternal glory.***

> *Titus 1:1 – Paul, a servant of God, and an apostle of Jesus Christ, **according to the faith of God's elect, and the acknowledging of the truth which is after godliness.***

> *1 Peter 2:9 – **But ye are a chosen generation,** a royal priesthood, an holy nation, a peculiar people; that ye should shew forth the praises of him who hath called you out of darkness into his marvelous light:*

> *2 John 1:1 – The elder **unto the elect lady and her children,** whom I love in the truth; and not I only, but also all they that have known the truth;*

The Lord speaking about Saul (Paul):

> *Acts 9:15,16 – But the Lord said unto him, Go thy way: **for he is chosen vessel unto me,** to bear my name before the Gentiles, and kings, and the children of Israel. 16. For I will shew him how great things he must suffer for my name's sake.*

Having heard what many of the apostles have taught about the *"elect of God"* Christ was very explicit in His prayer to Heavenly Father about the chosen that were given Him on this earth

> *John 17:1-12 – 1. These words spake Jesus, and lifted up his eyes to heaven, and said Father, the hour is come; **glorify thy Son, that thy Son also may glorify thee; 2. As thou hast given him power over all flesh, that he should give eternal life to as many as thou hast given him.** 3. And this is life eternal, **that they might know thee the only true God, and Jesus Christ, whom thou has sent.** 4. I have glorified thee on the earth: I have finished the work which thou gavest me to do. 5. And now, O Father, **glorify thou me with thine own self with the glory which I had with thee before the world was.** 6. I have manifested thy*

*name unto the men which thou gavest me out of the world; thine they were, and thou gavest them me; and they have kept thy word. 7. Now they have known that all things whatsoever thou hast given me are of thee. 8. For I have given unto them the words which thou gavest me; and they have received them, and have known surely that I came out from thee, and they have believed that thou didst send me. 9. I pray for them: I pray not for the world, but **for them which thou hast given me; for they are thine.** 10. **And all mine are thine, and thine are mine;** and I am glorified in them. 11. And now I am no more in the world, but these are in the world and I come to thee. Holy Father, keep through thine own name those whom thou hast given me, **that they may be one, as we are.** 12. While I was with them in the world, I kept them in thy name: those that thou gavest me I have kept, and none of them is lost, but the son of perdition; that the scripture might be fulfilled.*

Notice that in Christ's most critical prayer, that Christ prayed only for the "elect" and not everybody else! John understood this concept when he taught that those followers were "called and chosen."

*Revelation 17:14 – These shall make war with the Lamb, and the Lamb shall overcome then: for he is Lord of lords, and King of kings: and **they that are with him are called, and chosen, and faithful.***

Be Ye Therefore Perfect!

Revelations 2:17 – He that hath an ear, let him hear what the Spirit saith unto the churches;

Another principle that most Christians agree upon is the fact that Jesus Christ was the only perfect man on earth. The definition on this type of perfection is that Jesus Christ was without sin. Now, where Mormon's and other Christian religions differ in reference to the perfection of man is where Joseph Smith taught that man may become perfect. Jesus Christ own words support these teachings when he commanded all men to be perfect like Heavenly Father! These are Jesus Christ's own words:

*Matthew 5:48 – **Be ye therefore perfect, even as your Father which is in heaven is perfect.***

This was a commandment given to us. All commandments are—in the eyes of God—meant to be followed. Mormons believe that Heavenly Father or Jesus Christ will not give a commandment unless there is a way to accomplish it. There are some Mormons that believe this commandment to be perfect is attainable. The teachings of several of the New Testament apostles also supported this belief that we can become perfect in several gospel principals. Peter taught that after suffering for Christ, we could become perfect.

*1 Peter 5:10 – But the God of all grace who hath called us unto his eternal glory by Christ Jesus, after that ye have suffered a while, **make you perfect,** stablish, strengthen, settle you.*

Paul taught that a person who has charity, "*is the bond of perfectness.*"

*Colossians 3:14 – And above all these things put on charity, **which is the bond of perfectness.***

The apostles James and Timothy taught that through works, faith can be made perfect.

*James 2:22 – Seest thou how faith wrought with his works, **and by works was faith made perfect?***

*2 Timothy 3:17 – That the **man of God may be perfect,** thoroughly furnished*

> *unto all good works.*

This supports John's teaching that eternal life is for those who "know the only true God."

> *John 17:3 – And **this is life eternal, that they might know thee the only true God; and Jesus Christ,** whom that hast sent.*

Take care to what this passage does not say! It does not say *"and this is life eternal, that they might have faith in the only true God and Jesus Christ."*

It is the teaching of Joseph Smith that faith can be *"made perfect"* in small steps through living the commandments of God, making sacred covenants in the temple, being sealed to your spouse and children, wearing special temple garments, receiving a special "new name," receiving the "Holy Spirit of Promise," and your "calling and election made sure." As we perfect our living each commandment, we come closer to the perfection that Christ has commanded us to have. Examples of these principals are the commandments of "tithing," "keeping the Sabbath day holy" and "thou shalt not steal."

If a person keeps the law of tithing, and pays 10% of his/her earnings or increases, then that person is perfect in the law of tithing. If a person goes to church every Sunday, studies the scriptures, visits the sick, imprisoned, and needy, and does not partake in the purchase of goods and services on the Sabbath, then that person is perfect in keeping the Sabbath Day holy. Again, with the commandment that states that we shall not steal, a person who never steals anything is perfect in that commandment. The same principle applies for the other Ten Commandments.

Where perfection is hard to attain is in the two major commandments defined by Jesus Christ himself—love your Father in Heaven with all your heart mind and soul, and love your neighbor as you would want to be loved!

> *John 17:22-24 – 22. **And the glory which thou gavest me I have given them; that they may be one, even as we are one: 23. I in them, and thou in me, that they may be perfect in one;** and that the world may know that thou hast sent me, and hast loved them, as thou hast loved me. 24. Father, I will that they also, whom thou hast given me, be with me where I am; **that they may behold my glory,** which hast given me: for thou lovedst me before the foundation of the world.*

The apostle Paul commented on his personal state of perfection in a letter to the Philippians. Paul stated that he had not yet attained perfection in this life until he reaches the resurrection of the dead and receives a body "fashioned like unto" Christ's glorious body.

> *Philippians 3:11,12,20,21 – 11. If by any means I might attain unto the resurrection of the dead. 12. Not as though I had already attained, **either were already perfect:** but I follow after, if that I may apprehend that for which also I am apprehended of Christ Jesus.*
>
> *20. For our conversation is in heaven; from whence also we look for the Saviour, the Lord Jesus Christ: 21. **Who shall change our vile body, that it may be fashioned like unto his glorious body,** according to the working whereby he is able even to subdue all things unto himself.*

In the same manner, Jesus Christ did not consider himself completely *"perfect"* when he commanded us all to be perfect as stated in Matthew 5:48. *The Book of Mormon* account of Jesus Christ in the Americas, after Christ's resurrection, he commanded his sheep to *"be perfect, as both he and Heavenly Father is perfect."*

> *3 Nephi 12:49 – **Therefore I would that ye should be perfect even as I, or your Father who is in heaven is perfect.***

From this passage we learn that perfection is not just *"free from all sin,"* perfection also includes going through the death process and being resurrected with a glorious immortal body.

"Faith made perfect" is the actual *"getting to know God and Jesus Christ in this life"*—it is your *"calling and election made sure"* where you are guaranteed by Jesus Christ himself a place in the kingdom of our Heavenly Father.

> *2 Peter 1:10,11 – 10.* **Wherefore the rather, brethren, give diligence to make your calling and election sure: for if ye do these things, ye shall never fall: 11. For so an entrance shall be ministered unto you abundantly into the everlasting kingdom of our Lord and Saviour Jesus Christ.**

The reward for becoming perfect is great! This reward is part of the mystery that was spoken of:

> *Colossians 1:26-28 – 26.* **Even the mystery which hath been hid from ages and from generations, but now is made manifest to his saints: 27.** *To whom God* **would make known what is the riches of the glory of this mystery among the Gentiles;** *which is Christ in you,* **the hope of glory:** *28. Whom we preach, warning every man, and teaching every man in all wisdom;* **that we may present every man perfect in Christ Jesus:**

All who become "perfect in Christ" will become as Christ!

> *Luke 6:40 – The disciple is not above his master;* **but every one that is perfect shall be as his master.**

Exaltation vs Salvation.

> *Revelations 3:6 – He that hath an ear, let him hear what the Spirit saith unto the churches;*

> *Revelations 2:13 – He that hath an ear, let him hear what the Spirit saith unto the churches;*

> *Revelations 3:22 – He that hath an ear, let him hear what the Spirit saith unto the churches;*

From what we have learned about the *"elect of God"* is that *"they listen …and they hear, they see…and they perceive."* This *"elect of God"* also will receive the same *"glory"* that Jesus Christ received.

> *Ephesians 3:21 –* **Unto him be glory in the church by Christ Jesus throughout all ages, world without end.** *Amen.*

> *1 Peter 5:1 – The elders which are among you I exhort, who am also an elder, and a witness of the sufferings of Christ, and* **also a partaker of the glory that shall be revealed:**

> *1 Peter 5:4 – And when the chief Shephard shall appear,* **ye shall receive a crown of glory that fadeth not away**

> *1 Peter 5:6 – Humble yourselves therefore under the mighty hand of God,* **that he may exalt you in due time:**

> *1 Peter 5:10 – But the God of all grace,* **who hath called us unto his eternal glory by Christ Jesus,** *after that ye have suffered a while, make you perfect, stablish, strengthen, settle you.*

Paul also taught that we were predestined to obtain an inheritance.

> *Ephesians 1:9-11 – 9.* ***Having made known unto us the mystery of his will,*** *according to his good pleasure which he hath purposed in himself: 10. That in the dispensation of the fullness of times he might gather together in one all things in Christ, both which are in heaven, and which are on earth; even in him: 11.* ***In whom also we have obtained an inheritance, being predestinated according to the purpose of him who worketh all things after the counsel of his own will:***

Now, understanding that there is an *"elect of God,"* that this *"elect of God"* can become perfect, and this *"elect of God"* will receive the *"glory"* that Jesus Christ received. One must listen intently to what John's true message is in his writings in Revelations.

Most religions, in interpreting Revelations, try to figure out what is meant by the beasts, the angels, and the seals. The true meaning lies in the simple passages that are most often ignored. John writes the following warning time after time! This is the same warning that Jesus Christ gave when the apostles asked Jesus Christ why he spoke in parables. At this time, Jesus Christ was speaking about the two main groups of the Jewish faith, the Sadducees and Pharisees. John, having seen the future and knew of the many different Christian sects that would abound in the last days, was writing for the last day, and is speaking specifically to the many different modern day Christian "churches" i.e., the ministers, pastors, priests, and all heads of congregations and churches.

John gives the following warning seven times in the first three chapters of his writings.

> *Revelations 1:7 – He that hath an ear, let him hear what the Spirit saith unto the churches;*

> *Revelations 2:11 – He that hath an ear, let him hear what the Spirit saith unto the churches,*

> *Revelations 2:13 – He that hath an ear, let him hear what the Spirit saith unto the churches;*

> *Revelations 2:17 – He that hath an ear, let him hear what the Spirit saith unto the churches,*

> *Revelations 2:29 – He that hath an ear, let him hear what the Spirit saith unto the churches,*

> *Revelations 3:6 – He that hath an ear, let him hear what the Spirit saith unto the churches;*

> *Revelations 3:22 – He that hath an ear, let him hear what the Spirit saith unto the churches,*

Question: Are you and your church leaders listening?

In the last seven passages, John was speaking to the churches. The next passages from John are more to the individual and the leader. John speaks to the person or persons who *"overcomes,"* that is to each individual who has been born on this earth. The following passages lead to an end for those who *"overcome."*

In Revelation 2:17 John tells about those who overcome will eat of the hidden manna, will receive a white stone, and will receive a new name.

> *Revelation 2:17 – He that hath an ear, let him hear what the Spirit saith unto the churches;* ***To him that overcometh will I give to eat of the hidden manna, and will give him a white stone, and in the stone a new name written,*** *which no man knoweth saving he that receiveth it.*

The Mormons believe the white stone spoken of here is revelation. The *"new name"* is what is received when a person goes through the temple for the first time. This *"new name"* is a practice established by Joseph Smith, over 150 years ago and is discussed in detail in Chapter 14 – The Temples: "The House of the Lord."

The next time John speaks of *"those who overcome"* he tells them that they shall receive power over the nations and rule over them with a rod of iron.

> *Revelation 2:26-29 – 26.* **And he that overcometh, and keepeth my works unto the end, to him will I give power over the nations: 27. And he shall rule them with a rod of iron;** *as the vessels of a potter shall they be broken to shivers: even as I received of my Father. 28. And I will give him the morning star. 29. He that hath an ear let him hear what the Spirit saith unto the churches.*

Christ himself taught the apostles that the "faithful and wise steward" will be made ruler over His household or all that He has.

> *Luke 12:42-44 – And the Lord said,* **Who then is that faithful and wise steward, whom his lord shall make ruler over his household to give them their portion of meat in due season?** *43. Blessed is that servant, whom his lord when he cometh shall find so doing. 44.* **Of a truth I say unto you, that he will make him ruler over all that he hath.**

Question: Who are these nations that "those who overcome" will rule over?

The next passage is one of the most important of these passages. Christ tells us through John, that "those who overcome," will sit down with Christ on our Heavenly Father's throne!

> *Revelation 3:21,22 – 21.* **To him that overcometh will I grant to sit with me in my throne, even as I also overcame, and am set down with my Father in his throne. 22. He that hath an ear, let him hear what the Spirit saith unto the churches.**

Joseph Smith was personally taught by God the Father, Jesus Christ, Peter, James, and John, and many more angels and ancient prophets. Joseph Smith taught that for those *"who overcome"* will receive a form of Godhood. He taught that Heavenly Father will give all that he has to us...and that we will be joint heirs with Christ, which means we also may become a God. This was the same godhood doctrine that was referred to by John, Paul, Luke, and Matthew.

John taught:

> *Revelation 21:7 –* **He that overcometh shall inherit all things; and I will be his God, and he shall be my son.**

Paul taught:

> *Romans 8:16-18 – 16. the Spirit itself beareth witness with our spirit, that we are the children of God: 17.* **And if children, then heirs; heirs of God, and joint heirs with Christ; if so be that we suffer with him, that we may be also glorified together.** *18. For I reckon that the sufferings of this present time are not worthy to be compared* **with the glory which shall be revealed in us.**

Matthew taught:

> *Matthew 25:23 – His lord said unto him,* **Well done, thou good and faithful servant: thou hast been faithful over a few things, I will make thee ruler over many things: enter thou into the joy of the lord.**

Luke taught:

> *Luke 6:40 – The disciple is not above his master;* **but every one that is perfect shall be as his master.**

Several questions that must be asked to the churches, the many different Christian churches who profess that man may not achieve any type of exaltation or godhood are the following:

Question: How much truth do you have if you do not teach the doctrine of exaltation?

Question: To the leaders and teachers of Christian religions, if you do not teach your followers that they are potential heirs for exaltation and the way to achieve exaltation, are you deceiving your followers and keeping them from attaining exaltation?

Question: If you are not teaching the fullness of the restored gospel, are you at the straight and narrow gate that leads to eternal life and the kingdom of God, or are you at the broad gate and wide path that leads to destruction?

> *Matthew 7:13-14 – 13. **Enter ye in at the strait gate: for wide is the gate, and broad is the way, that leadeth to destruction, and many there be which go in thereat: 14. Because strait is the gate, and narrow is the way, which leadeth unto life, and few there be that find it.***

Now one can better understand what Timothy was talking about when he mentioned, *"great is the mystery of godliness:"*

> *1 Timothy 3:16 – And without controversy **great is the mystery of godliness:** God was manifest in the flesh, justified in the Spirit, seen of angels, preached unto the Gentiles, believed on in the world, **received up into glory.***

Question: Would there be a mystery of godliness if it were as simple as most Christians define God—That there is only one God!

> *Isaiah 44:6 – Thus saith the Lord the King of Israel, and his redeemer the Lord of hosts; **I am the first, and I am the last; and beside me there is no God.***

Several more questions for the leaders and followers of the different Christian churches:

Question: Are you listening?

Question: Are you one of Heavenly Father's chosen?

Question: Do you want to be a joint heir with Christ and sit on Heavenly Father's throne?

Ye Are Gods. While contemplating these questions about the exaltation of man, review the following passages in the Bible:

> *John 10:34-35 – 34. Jesus answered them, Is it not written in your law, I said, **Ye are gods?** 35. If he called them gods, unto whom the word of God came, and the scripture cannot be broken;*

> *Deuteronomy 10:17 – For the Lord your God is **God of gods,** and Lord of lords, a great God, a mighty, and a terrible, which regardeth not persons, nor taketh reward:*

> *Psalm 82:1 – **God standeth in the congregation of the mighty; he judgeth among the gods.***

> *Psalm 82:6 – I have said, **Ye are gods;** and all of you are children of the most High.*

> *Psalm 82:8 – **Arise, O God, judge the earth: for thou shalt inherit all nations.***

> *Revelations 3:21 – **To him that overcometh will I grant to sit with me in my throne, even as I also overcame, and am set down with my Father in his throne.***

The interpretation of some Christians of these verses calling people gods is the *"gods"* were military leaders that performed as judges. Never have the Christian leaders proclaiming this interpretation have given a verifiable reference for them being "gods" or temple guards.

After reading the scriptures pertaining to the *"elect of God"* achieving *"perfection,"* Christ sharing his *"glory"* and *"exaltation"* with those few who overcome, the passages calling the followers *"gods"* do become clear. They actually mean what the passage is saying—they (or you) are being called *"gods."*

Question: Are you a part of the fullness of Christ's teachings where, as Timothy taught, you are within grasp of reigning with Christ?

> *2 Timothy 2:12 – If we suffer, we shall also reign with him: if we deny him, he also will deny us:*

Question: Once you understand the meaning of *"the mystery of godliness,"* the *"elect of God,"* and our responsibility to become perfect—do these words of Christ have a new meaning?

> *John 14:12 – Verily, verily, I say unto you, **He that believeth on me, the works that I do shall he do also; and greater works than these shall he do;** because I go unto my Father.*

An example of the works that He performs is providing each of us the opportunity to be born, live, die and then be resurrected and live eternally.

Question: Could an example of the *"greater works than these shall he do"* be to create worlds?

> *Hebrews 1:2 – Hath in these last days spoken unto us by his Son, whom he hath appointed heir of all things, **by whom also he made the worlds;***

Question: Did Joseph Smith make up this *"Godmakers"* doctrine, or as Peter taught, is it part of the true teachings of Jesus Christ, where he will "exalt" us if we overcome?

> *1 Peter 5:6 – Humble yourselves therefore under the mighty hand of God, **that he may exalt you in due time:***

Question: Reading about the exaltation opportunity offered to you, does the following statement of Jesus Christ have more of a meaning?

> *Luke 12:48 – ...**For unto whomsoever much is given, of him shall much be required.***

If our Heavenly Father is going to offer us the opportunity to be *"exalted"* like Christ, it would go along with whoever receives *"exaltation,"* that they should be close to being *"perfect."* The idea of Christians being able to be "saved by grace by only believing in Jesus Christ breeds mediocrity. Mediocrity in ones efforts to follow the teaching of God will not be acceptable to our Heavenly Father. That is why Christ stated:

> *Matthew 7:21 – **Not every one that saith unto me, Lord, Lord, shall enter into the kingdom of heaven;** but he that doeth the will of my Father which is in heaven.*

The Terrestrial Glory is created for the mediocre.

The Biblical Support Chart. Probably the most controversial and significant teaching of the Prophet Joseph Smith is what the Christians have coined "The God-Maker." Here it is in all the "wisdom of man," the Bible overwhelmingly supports each aspect of the "The God-

Maker" teaching of Joseph Smith. Carefully study each topic and each scripture, it will mean your *"glory"* for you in all eternity!

THE BIBLICAL SUPPORT CHART	
Is the following topic supported in the Bible?	**Yes or No**
Does the Bible support Joseph Smith's teaching that the rewards after this life comes in glories? (John 1:1-3,14; Heb 1:1-3; Col 1:16; 1 Tim 3:16; Col 3:1; Phil 2:9; Acts 2:33; 1 Pet 3:22; John 5:22)	Yes
Does the Bible support Joseph Smith's teaching that certain people on this earth are God's elect? (1 Thes 1:4,5; 2 Thes 2:13,14; Eph 1:4,5; Rom 9:10,11; 1 Pet 1:2; Cjol 3:12; 2 Tim 2:10; Titus 1:1; 1 Pet 2:9; 2 John 1:1; Acts 9:15,16; John 17:1-12; Rev 17:14)	Yes
Does the Bible support Joseph Smith's teaching that the members of the church should strive to be perfect? (Matt5:48; 1 Pet 5:10; Col 3:14; James 2:22; 2 Tim 3:17; John 17:3; John 17:22-24; Phil 3:11,12,20,21; Luke 6:40)	Yes
Does the Bible support Joseph Smith's teaching that man may become ruler over nations with Jesus Christ? (Rev 2:26-29; Luke 12:42-44; Matt 25:23)	Yes
Does the Bible support Joseph Smith's teaching that the members may receive exaltation with Jesus Christ? (Eph 3:21; 1 Pet 5:4,10; Eph 1:9-11; 1 Pet 5:6)	Yes
Does the Bible support Joseph Smith's teaching that the people who overcome will receive what Christ receives? (Rev 3:21,22; Rev 21:7; Rom 8:16-18; Luke 6:40; 2 Tim 2:12)	Yes
Does the Bible support Joseph Smith's teaching that man may become a god? (John 10:34-35; Deut 10:17; Psalm 82:1,6; Rev 3:21)	Yes
Does the Bible support Joseph Smith's teaching about one's "calling and election made sure?" (2 Peter 1:10,11; John 14:16; John 14:21-23)	Yes

Author's Note:

> *Moses 1:39 – **For behold, this is my work and my glory—to bring to pass the immortality and eternal life of man.***

It is beautiful to know that God's whole purpose is to give other spirits—us—the opportunity to live eternally with a glorified body of flesh and bone, with our families. Now, with this knowledge combined with the knowledge of the *"mystery of godliness,"* I am totally awed at the tremendous love our Heavenly Father has for us! Our Heavenly Father loves us so much that all that He has will be ours!

> *Revelations 2:11 – **He that hath an ear, let him hear what the Spirit saith unto the churches;***

It is sad to think of the millions of people on the earth who refuse to listen and will be losing out on the great *"mystery of the godliness"* that Joseph Smith was truly given by Jesus Christ Himself.

> *Matthew 13:11 – **He answered and said unto them,** Because it is given unto you to know the mysteries of the kingdom of heaven, **but to them it is not given.***

It is my testimony that Joseph Smith and every prophet and apostle since Joseph Smith have been *"**the stewards of the mysteries of God."***

> *1 Corinthians 4:1 – **Let a man so account of us, as of the ministers of Christ, and stewards of the mysteries of God.***

To the non-Mormon and anti-Mormons. If you receive the Spirit of Truth and study the Bible, the *Book of Mormon,* The Doctrine and Covenants, and the Teachings of Joseph Smith, you will be able to unlock all of the mysteries of God and the universe from the beginning to the never arriving end, from the start to the never achieving finish.

It is there for the taking!

NOTES

CHAPTER 17

POLYGAMY

The official policy of the Church of Jesus Christ of Latter Day Saints is that no members will follow or participate in any kind of polygamy or plural marriage. This has been the policy for over 116 years, since September 24th, 1890. Any member of the Church who practices polygamy or plural marriage is excommunicated from the Church. The official policy and circumstances surrounding this policy can be read the Church publication called the Doctrine and Covenants.[24]

Not wanting to apologize or offer any side steps around the early years of the Church where Joseph Smith practiced polygamy I would like to quickly elaborate on the history. Although the Lord restored the law of polygamy to the early saints, this law was revoked on October 6, 1890 when President Wilford Woodruff declared the "manifesto." President Wilford Woodruff received a vision from the Lord of what would happen to the Church leadership, the temples, many members of the Church and their property if the Church did not renounce the practice of polygamy. In short, the leaders and many members of the church would be jailed, the temples would be taken away, and the work for our dead ancestors would be stopped. This all would happen by the United States government after it was determined that polygamy was against the law of the United States of America.

So in keeping with Joseph Smith's twelfth Article of Faith where we believe in living the law of the land…

> Twelfth Article of Faith – *We believe in being subject to kings, presidents, rulers, and magistrates, in obeying, honoring, and sustaining the law.*

…the Church officially ended the law of multiple wives.

The important principle to understand is that the Lord would *"restore all things"* which He did. The Lord did not say that everything would necessarily have to stay on earth until He came again for His Second Coming.

With these claims of the Prophet Joseph Smith and the ending of polygamy with the Prophet Wilford Woodruff, some 47 years later, if this principle was from the Lord, there would be some kind of support in the Bible for the practice of multiple wives being from or condoned by God. Here is what the Bible has to say about having multiple wives.

In following the theme of this book of *"every jot and tittle"* and the fact that the Lord will *"restore all things,"* if indeed the practice of polygamy was of God, then polygamy would have to be restored on the earth along with the fullness of the gospel.

A search of church history reveals that Joseph Smith, personally, did not want to institute the practice of having multiple wives. But Joseph Smith was commanded by Jesus Christ to institute the law of multiple wives. It was on July 12, 1843 that the first official commandment was written on multiple wives. It is recorded in the Doctrine and Covenants. This commandment of plural wives was given at the same time as the *"new and everlasting covenant"* covering *"the eternity of the marriage covenant"* was given. It reads:

> D&C 132:51-56 – 51. Verily, I say unto you: A commandment I give unto mine handmaid, Emma Smith, your wife, whom I have given unto you, that she stay herself and partake not of that which I commanded you to offer unto her; **for I did it, saith the Lord, to prove you all, as I did Abraham,** and that I might require an offering at your hand, by covenant and sacrifice.
>
> 52. **And let mine handmaid, Emma Smith, receive all those that have been**

given unto my servant Joseph, and who are virtuous and pure before me; and those who are not pure, and have said they were pure, shall be destroyed, saith the Lord God. 53. For I am the Lord thy God, and ye shall obey my voice; and I give unto my servant Joseph that he shall be made ruler over many things; for he hath been faithful over a few things, and from henceforth I will strengthen him.

54. And I command mine handmaid, Emma Smith, to abide and cleave unto my servant Joseph, and to none else. **But if she will not abide this commandment she shall be destroyed, saith the Lord; for I am the Lord thy God, and will destroy her if she abide not in my law.** *55.But if she will not abide this commandment, then shall my servant Joseph do all things for her, even as he hath said; and* **I will bless him and multiply him and give unto him an hundredfold in this world, of fathers and mothers, brothers and sisters, houses and lands, wives and children, and crowns of eternal lives in the eternal worlds.**

56. And again, verily I say, let mine handmaid forgive my servant Joseph his trespasses; and then shall she be forgiven her trespasses, wherein she has trespassed against me; and I, the Lord thy God, will bless her, and multiply her, and make her heart to rejoice.

Admitting that there is no firm writing in the Bible that indicates that polygamy was a commandment from God or Jesus Christ there is a lot that the Bible does say about the practice of polygamy and the people who practiced polygamy. I will go over what the circumstances were concerning the families who participated in polygamy and the relationships that these people had with God and Jesus Christ. The first person who we will study is Abraham.

Abraham Had Several Wives.

Genesis 16:1 – 1. **Now Sarai Abram's wife bare him no children:** *and she had an handmaid, an Egyptian, whose name was Hagar. 2. And Sarai said unto Abram, Behold now, the Lord hath restrained me from bearing: I pray thee,* **go in unto my maid; it may be that I may obtain children by her.** *And Abram hearkened to the voice of Sarai. 3.* **And Sarai Abram's wife took Hagar her maid the Egyptian, after Abram had dwelt ten years in the land of Canaan, and give her to her husband Abram to be his wife.**

Genesis 25:5,6 – 5. And Abraham gave all that he had unto Isaac. 6. **But unto the sons of the concubines, which Abraham had,** *Abraham gave gifts, and sent them away from Isaac his son, while he yet lived, eastward, unto the east country.*

Abraham's brother, Nahor, had a concubine.

Genesis 22:23,24 – 23. And Bethuel begat Rebekah: these eight Milcah did bear to Nahor, Abraham's brother. 24. **And his concubine, whose name was Reumah, she bare also Tebah, and Gaham, and Thahash, and Maachah.**

Genesis 26:34,35 – 34. **And Esau was forty years old when he took to wife Judith the daughter of Beeri the Hittite, and Bashemath the daughter of Elon the Hittite:** *35. Which were a grief of mind unto Isaac and to Rebekah.*

This plural marriage of Esau was a "grief of mind" to Isaac and Rebekah. The "grief of mind" could be because of two things. The first, Esau was not commanded by the Lord to enter into plural marriage thus being an "abomination" in the eyes of the Lord, or it could be that the two women were Hittites, and Esau was marrying out of the "faith."

Abraham's Fate With God.

Question: Was Abraham punished for having more than one wife?

The answer is no! In fact, Abraham became the father of what is currently around three billion people. The Christians, the Moslems, and the Jews all trace their spiritual lineage back to Father Abraham! Not only did Abraham become the father of all these religions God appeared to Abraham and talked with him on several occasions and God established His everlasting covenant with Abraham and his seed.

> *Genesis 17:2-4 – 2. And I will make my covenant between me and thee, **and will multiply thee exceedingly.** 3. And Abram fell on his face: **and God talked with him, saying,** 4. As for me, behold, my covenant is with thee, **and thou shalt be a father of many nations.***

> *Genesis 12:7 – **And the Lord appeared unto Abram,** and said, Unto thy seed will I give this land: and there builded he an altar unto the Lord, **who appeared unto him.***

> *Genesis 17:7 – And **I will establish my covenant between me and thee and thy seed after thee in their generations for an everlasting covenant,** to be a God unto thee, and to thy seed after thee.*

Jacob Had Several Wives. Jacob was given the blessing of being *"fruitful"* and being a *"multitude of people."*

> *Genesis 28:2,3 – 2. Arise, go to Padan-aram, to the house of Bethuel thy mother's father; and take thee a wife from thence of the daughters of Laban thy mother's brother. 3. **And God Almighty bless thee, and make thee fruitful, and multiply thee, that thou mayest be a multitude of people;***

Jacob did as he was commanded and ended up marrying two daughters of Jacob.

> *Genesis 29:15-23 – 15. And Laban said unto Jacob, Because thou art my brother, shouldest thou therefore serve me for nought: tell me, what shall thy wages be? 16. And Laban had two daughters: the name of the elder was Leah, and the name of the younger was Rachel. 17. Leah was tender eyed; but Rachel was beautiful and well favoured. 18. And Jacob loved Rachel; and said, I will serve thee seven years for Rachel thy younger daughter. 19. And Laban said, It is better that I give her to thee, than that I should give her to another man: abide with me. 20. And Jacob served seven years for Rachel; and they seemed unto him but a few days, for the love he had to her. 21. And Jacob said unto Laban, Give me my wife, for my days are fulfilled, that I may go in unto her. 22. And Laban gathered together all the men of the place, and made a feast. 23. And it came to pass in the evening, that he took Leah his daughter, and brought her to him; and he went in unto her.*

> *Genesis 29:25 – And it came to pass, that in the morning, behold, it was Leah: and he said to Laban, What is this thou hast done unto me? Did not I serve with thee for Rachel? Wherefore then hast thou beguiled me? 26. And Laban said, It must not be so done in our country, to give the younger before the firstborn. 27. Fulfill her week, and we will give thee this also for the service which thou shalt serve with me yet seven other years.*

> *Genesis 29:28 – And Jacob did so, and fulfilled her week: and he gave him Rachel his daughter to wife also.*

> *Genesis 29:30 – And he went in also unto Rachel, and he loved also Rachel more than Leah, and served with him yet seven other years.*

After the marriages to Leah and Rachel, there became a competition for Jacob's attention.

This competition was in the form of who could bare Jacob some sons. It is evident that the Lord had His hand in this "multiple wife" relationship when He opened up Leah's womb.

*Genesis 29:31-35 – 31. **And when the Lord saw that Leah was hated, he opened her womb: but Rachel was barren.***

Leah went on to have her first four sons, Reuben, Simeon, Levi, Judah.

*32. **And Leah conceived, and bare a son, and she called his name Reuben:** for she said, Surely the Lord hath looked upon my affliction; now therefore my husband will love me. 33. **And she conceived again, and bare a son;** and said, Because the Lord hath heard that I was hated, he hath therefore given me this son also: **and she called his name Simeon. 34. And she conceived again, and bare a son;** and said, Now this time will my husband be joined unto me, because I have born him three sons: **therefore was his name called Levi. 35. And she conceived again, and bare a son:** and she said, Now will I praise the Lord: **therefore she called his name Judah;** and left bearing.*

With Leah having four sons with Jacob, Rachel became very jealous.

*Genesis 30:1,2 – 1. And when Rachel saw that she bare Jacob no children, **Rachel envied her sister;** and said unto Jacob, Give me children, or else I die. 2. And Jacob's anger was kindled against Rachel: and he said, Am I in God's stead, who hath withheld from thee the fruit of the womb?*

Believing that Rachel was unable to have any children, she gave Jacob her maid, Bilhah, to wife so the children from Bilhah could be those of Rachel. Bilhah went on to have two sons Dan and Naphtali.

*Genesis 30:3-8 – 3. And she said, **Behold my maid Bilhah, go in unto her; and she shall bear upon my knees, that I may also have children by her. 4. And she gave him Bilhah her handmaid to wife: and Jacob went in unto her. 5.** And **Bilhah conceived, and bare Jacob a son.** 6. And Rachel said, God hath judged me, and hath also heard my voice, and hath given me a son; **therefore called she his name Dan. 7. And Bilhah Rachel's maid conceived again, and bare Jacob a second son.** 8. And Rachel said, With great wrestlings have I wrestled with my sister, and I have prevailed: **and she called his name Naphtali.***

Believing that she was unable to have more children, Leah, not wanting to be outdone by Rachel, gave Jacob her maid Zilpah. Jacob married Zilpah and had two more sons, Gad and Asher.

*Genesis 30:9-13 – 9. When Leah saw that she had left bearing, **she took Zilpah her maid, and gave her Jacob to wife. 10. And Zilpah Leah's maid bare Jacob a son. 11.** And Leah said, A troop cometh: and **she called his name Gad. 12. And Zilpah Leah's maid bare Jacob a second son.** 13. And Leah said, Happy am I for the daughters will call me blessed: **and she called his name Asher.***

Later on, God answered Leah's prayers to have more children, and Leah was able to bare her fifth and sixth sons, who were called Issachar and Zebulum.

*Genesis 30:16-20 – 16. And Jacob came out of the field in the evening, and Leah went out to meet him, and said, Thou must come in unto me; for surely I have hired thee with my son's mandrakes. And he lay with her that night. 17. **And God hearkened unto Leah, and she conceived, and bare Jacob the fifth son.** 18. And Leah said, **God hath given me my hire, because I have given my maiden to my husband:** and she called his mane Issachar. 19. **And Leah conceived*** *again, and bare Jacob the sixth son.* 20. *And Leah said, God hath endued me with a good dowry; now will my husband dwell with me, because I have born him six sons: and she called his name Zebulun.*

What is most interesting with Leah's last two son's that she had for Jacob, was that she gave thanks to God for these two sons, and that she thought she was blessed from God because she gave her maid to Jacob to wife.

*Genesis 30:18 – And Leah said, **God hath given me my hire, because I have given my maiden to my husband:***

Not only was Leah blessed by God, but Rachel was also blessed. God answered Rachel's prayers also by opening her womb where she had another son called Joseph.

*Genesis 30:22-24 – 22. **And God remembered Rachel, and God hearkened to her, and opened her womb.** 23. **And she conceived, and bare a son; and said, God hath taken away my reproach:** 24. **And she called his name Joseph; and said, The Lord shall add to me another son.***

Rachel did have another son who was called Benjamin.

*Genesis 35:17,18 – 17. And it came to pass, when she was in hard labour, that the midwife said unto her, **Fear not; thou shalt have this son also.** 18. And it came to pass, as her soul was in departing, (for she died) that she called his name Ben-oni: but **his father called him Benjamin.***

Jacob's Fate With God.

Question: What was God's response to Jacob taking sisters to wife, and taking these sister's maids to wife?

The answer is that God blessed Jacob abundantly with the following:

1. God changed Jacob's name to Israel.

   *Genesis 32:28 – And he said, **Thy name shall be called no more Jacob, but Israel:** for as a prince hast thou power with God and with men, and hast prevailed.*

   *Genesis 35:10 – And God said unto him, Thy name is Jacob: **thy name shall not be called any more Jacob, but Israel shall be thy name:** and he called his name Israel.*

2. The sons of these four wives Leah (6), Leah's maid Zilpah (2), Rachel (2), and Rachel's maid Bilhah (2) became the twelve tribes of Israel.

   *Genesis 35:11 – **And God said unto him, I am God Almighty: be fruitful and multiply; a nation and a company of nations shall be of thee, and kings shall come out of thy loins;***

   *Genesis 35:23-26 – 23. **The sons of Leah;** Reuben, Jacob's firstborn, and Simeon, and Levi, and Judah, and Issachar, and Zebulun: 24. **The sons of Rachel;** Joseph, and Benjamin: 25. **And the sons of Bilhah, Rachel's handmaid;** Dan, and Naphtali: 26. **And the sons of Zilpah, Leah's handmaid;** Gad, and Asher: these are the sons of Jacob, which were born to him in Padan-aram.*

3. God appeared to Jacob.

   *Genesis 32:30 – And Jacob called the name of the place Peniel: **for I have seen God face to face, and my life is preserved.***

   *Genesis 35:9 – **And God appeared unto Jacob again,** when he came out of*

Padanaram, and blessed him.

Moses Had more than one wife. Moses was first married after he fled Egypt. He married Zipporah, the daughter of Reuel. Zipporah had a son called Gershom.

> *Exodus 2:21,22 – 21. And Moses was content to dwell with the man: and he gave Moses Zipporah his daughter. 22. And she bare him a son, and he called his name Gershom: for he said I have been a stranger in a strange land.*

There is a second marriage recorded where Moses married an Ethiopian woman.

> *Numbers 12:1 – And Miriam and Aaron spake against Moses because of the Ethiopian woman whom he had married: for he had married an Ethiopian woman.*

What happened to Miriam for speaking against Moses?

> *Numbers 12:2-16 – 2. And they said, Hath the Lord indeed spoken only by Moses? Hath he not spoken also by us? And the Lord heard it. 3. (**Now the man Moses was very meek, above all the men which were upon the face of the earth.**) 4. And the Lord spake suddenly unto Moses, and unto Aaron, and unto Miriam, Come out ye three unto the tabernacle of the congregation. And they three came out. 5. And the Lord came down in the pillar of the cloud, and stood in the door of the tabernacle, and called Aaron and Miriam: and they both came forth. 6. And he said, Hear now my words: **If there be a prophet among you, I the Lord will make myself known unto him in a vision, and will speak unto him in a dream. 7. My servant Moses is not so, who is faithful in all mine house. 8. With him will I speak mouth to mouth,** even apparently, and not in dark speeches; and the similitude of the Lord shall he behold: wherefore then were ye not afraid to speak against my servant Moses? 9. And the anger of the Lord was kindled against them; and he departed. 10. And the cloud departed from off the tabernacle; and, behold, **Miriam became leprous, white as snow:** and Aaron looked upon Miriam, and, behold, she was leprous. 11. And Aaron said unto Moses, Alas, my lord, I beseech thee, lay not the sin upon us, wherein we have done foolishly, and wherein we have sinned. 12. Let her not be as one dead, of whom the flesh is half consumed when he cometh out of his mother's womb. 13. **And Moses cried unto the Lord, saying, Heal her now, O God, I beseech thee.** 14. And the Lord said unto Moses, If her father had but spit in her face, should she not be ashamed seven days? **Let her be shut out from the camp seven days, and after that let her be received in again. 15. And Miriam was shut out from the camp seven days: and the people journeyed not till Miriam was brought in again.***

Moses' Fate With God.

Question: What was God's response to Moses taking Zipporah and the Ethiopian woman to wife?

The answer to how God reacted to Moses taking two wives is that Moses became one of the greatest prophets Israel has ever known, and Moses was able to know God face to face.

> *Deut 34:10-12 – 10. **And there arose not a prophet since in Israel like unto Moses, whom the Lord knew face to face,** 11. In all the signs and the wonders, which the Lord sent him to do in the land of Egypt to Pharaoh, and to all his servants, and to all his land, 12. And in all that mighty hand, and in all the great terror which Moses shewed in the sight of all Israel.*

David Had Plural Wives. David, the great king of Israel, married the daughter of Saul, the first king of Israel.

> *1 Samuel 18:20,21 – 20. And Michal Saul's daughter loved David: and thy told Saul, and the thing pleased him. 21. And Saul said, I will give him her, that she may be a snare to him and that the hand of the Philistines may be against him, Wherefore Saul said to David,* **Thou shalt this day be my son in law in the one of twain.**

David then took Abigail and Ahinoam of Jezreel to wife.

> *1 Samuel 25: 42,43 – 42.* **And Abigail hasted,** *and arose, and rode upon an ass, with five damsels of hers that went after her; and she went after the messengers of David,* **and became his wife. 43.** **David also took Ahinoam of Jesreel; and they were also both of them his wives.**

Saul then gave David's first wife, Michal, to Phalti, the son of Laish.

> *1 Samuel 25:44 – But Saul had given Michal his daughter, David's wife, to Phalti the son of Laish, which was of Gallim.*

Immediately after David had become king over Israel, which was appointed by the Lord, David took more wives and concubines.

> *2 Samuel 5:12,13 – 12. And* **David perceived that the Lord had established him king over Israel,** *and that he had exalted his kingdom for his people Israel's sake. 13.* **And David took him more concubines and wives out of Jerusalem,** *after he was come form Hebron:* **and there were yet sons and daughters born to David.**

David's downfall was his lusting after Bathsheba, conceiving a child with her, and David's arrangement for Bathsheba's husband to be killed in battle.

> *2 Samuel 11:2-5 – 2. And it came to pass in an eveningtide, that David arose from off his bed, and walked upon the roof of the king's house: and from the roof he saw a woman washing herself; and the woman was very beautiful to look upon. 3. And David sent and enquired after the woman. And ones said, Is not this Bathsheba, the daughter of Eliam, the wife of Uriah the Hittite? 4. And David sent messengers, and took her; and she came in unto him, and he lay with her; for she was purified from her uncleanness: and she returned unto her house. 5. And the woman conceived, and sent and told David, and said, I am with child.*

After learning that Bathsheba was with David's child, David called in Uriah from the war front. David wanted Uriah to lie with Bathsheba, but Uriah, being a great leader did not feel he could indulge in the luxuries of being with his wife, while his soldiers were in the field without their wives.

David, who could not entice Uriah to go sleep with his wife, devised another plan. The following passages detail David's new plan for Uriah.

> *2 Samuel 11:14-17 – 14. And it came to pass in the morning, that David wrote a letter to Joab, and sent it by the hand of Uriah. 15. And he wrote in the letter, saying,* **Set ye Uriah in the forefront of the hottest battle, and retire ye from him, that he may be smitten, and die.** *16. And it came to pass, when Joab observed the city, that he assigned Uriah unto a place where he knew that valiant men were. 17. And the men of the city went out, and fought with Joab: and there fell some of the people of the servants of David;* **and Uriah the Hittite died also.**

After the death of Uriah, Bathsheba mourned for Uriah, and then was made David's wife.

> *2 Samuel 11:26,27 – 26. And when the wife of Uriah heard that Uriah her*

*husband was dead, she mourned for her husband. 27. **And when the mourning was past, David sent and fetched her to his house, and she became his wife, and bare him a son. But the thing that David had done displeased the Lord.***

The Lord was very displeased with David for having Uriah killed in battle. The Lord sent Nathan to David with a parable that incited David's anger against a rich man. Then Nathan told David that the rich man in the parable was David himself. This is what Nathan told David:

> *2 Samuel 12:7-12 – 7. And Nathan said to David, Thou art the man. Thus saith the Lord God of Israel, I anointed thee king over Israel, and I delivered thee out of the hand of Saul; 8. And I gave thee thy master's house, and thy master's wives into thy bosom, and give thee the house of Israel and of Judah; and if that had been too little, I would moreover have given unto thee such and such things. 9. Wherefore hast thou despised the commandment of the Lord, to do evil in his sight:* **thou hast killed Uriah the Hittite with the sword, and hast taken his wife to be thy wife, and hast slain him with the sword of the children of Ammon.** *10. Now therefore the sword shall never depart from thine house; because thou hast despised me, and hast taken the wife of Uriah the Hittite to be thy wife. 11. Thus saith the Lord, Behold, I will raise up evil against thee out of thine own house, and I will take thy wives before thine eyes, and give them unto thy neighbour, and he shall lie with thy wives in the sight of this sun. 12. For thou didst it secretly: but I will do this thing before all Israel, and before the sun.*

David's Fate With God. From the previous words of Nathan, it was clear to David that he had sinned by having Uriah killed in battle and then taking Bathsheba to wife. David realized his sin and admitted the sin was against the Lord. David was punished for this, in the very way Nathan explained. Nathan told David that he would not die from this but the son born from this relationship would die.

> *2 Samuel 12:13-15,18 – 13. And David said unto Nathan, I have sinned against the Lord. And Nathan said unto David,* **The Lord also hath put away thy sin; thou shalt not die. 14. Howbeit, because by this deed thou hast given great occasion to the enemies of the Lord to blaspheme, the child also that is born unto thee shall surely die. 15. And Nathan departed unto his house. And the Lord struck the child that Uriah's wife bare unto David, and it was very sick.***
>
> *18. **And it came to pass on the seventh day, that the child died.***

Reviewing the words that the Lord spoke to David, through Nathan, were the words of David's punishment for what he did to Uriah. These words were:

> *2 Samuel 12:11 – **Thus saith the Lord, Behold, I will raise up evil against thee out of thine own house, and I will take thy wives before thine eyes, and give them unto thy neighbour, and he shall lie with thy wives in the sight of this sun. 12. For thou didst it secretly: but I will do this thing before all Israel, and before the sun.***

The second part of David's punishment was carried out when an "evil" entered. It took over David's kingdom and slept with David's concubines. This evil that was raised against David turned out to be from his own house. The person who took over the kingdom and slept with David's concubines—was David's own son Absalom.

Absalom attacked David's kingdom, and David had to flee.

> *2 Samuel 15:13,14 – 13. And there came a messenger to David, saying, **The***

hearts of the men of Israel are after Absalom. 14. And David said unto all his servants that were with him at Jerusalem, Arise, and let us flee; for we shall not else escape from Absalom: make speed to depart, lest he overtake us suddenly, and bring evil upon us, and smite the city with the edge of the sword.

After taking over the city, Absalom went and slept with David's concubines.

2 Samuel 16:20-22 – 20. Then said Absalom to Ahithophel, Give counsel among you what we shall do. 21. And Ahithophel said unto Absalom, Go in unto thy father's concubines, which he hath left to keep the house; and all Israel shall hear that thou art abhorred of thy father: then shall the hands of all that are with thee be strong. 22. So they spread Absalom a tent upon the top of the house; and Absalom went unto his father's concubines in the sight of all Israel.

David's Repentance. There are signs that David was very remorseful and repented of his sins.

2 Samuel 15:30 – And David went up by the ascent of mount Olivet, and wept as he went up, and had his head covered, and he went barefoot: and all the people that was with him covered, every man his head, and they went up, weeping as they went up.

David regained his kingdom.

2 Samuel 22:1-4 – 1. And David spake unto the Lord the words of this song in the day that the Lord had delivered him out of the hand of all his enemies, and out of the hand of Saul. 2. And he said, The Lord is my rock, and my fortress, and my deliverer; 3. The God of my rock; in him will I trust: he is my shield, and the horn of my salvation, my high tower, and my refuge, my saviour; thou savest me from violence. 4. I will call on the Lord, who is worthy to be praised: so shall I be saved from mine enemies.

An early sign that David was forgiven was after Bathsheba's son died, David went back into Bathsheba to lie with her, and she had another son who was named Solomon. This son "was loved by the Lord."

2 Samuel 12:24 – And David comforted Bathsheba his wife, and went in unto her, and lay with her: and she bare a son, and he called his name Solomon: and the Lord loved him.

After this experience, David gave good advice, by the Spirit of the Lord.

2 Samuel 23:1-3 – 1. Now these be the last words of David. David the son of Jesse said, and the man who was raised up on high, the anointed of the God of Jacob, and the sweet psalmist of Israel, said, 2. The Spirit of the Lord spake by me, and his word was in my tongue. 3. The God of Israel said, the Rock of Israel spake to me, He that ruleth over men must be just, ruling in the fear of God.

In the last days of David, he said this:

1 Kings 1:29 – And the king sware, and said, As the Lord liveth, that hath redeemed my soul out of all distress,

Solomon had plural wives. In David's last days, he made his son, Solomon, the son of Bathsheba who the "Lord loved," king of Israel.

1 Kings 1:30 – Even as I sware unto thee by the Lord God of Israel, saying, Assuredly Solomon thy son shall reign after me, and he shall sit upon my throne in my stead; even so will I certainly do this day.

David charges to Solomon to keep the commandments of the Lord.

> *1 Kings 2:1-4 – 1. Now the days of David drew nigh that he should die; and he charged Solomon his son, saying, 2. I go the way of all the earth: be thou strong therefore, and shew thy self a man; 3.* **And keep the charge of the Lord thy God, to walk in his ways, to keep his statutes, and his commandments, and his judgements, and his testimonies, as it is written in the law of Moses, that thou mayest prosper in all that thou doest, and whithersoever thou turnest thyself:** *4. That the Lord may continue his word which he spake concerning me, saying, If thy children take heed to their way, to walk before me in truth with all their heart and with all their soul, there shall not fail thee (said he) a man on the throne of Israel.*

Solomon's first wife was the daughter of the Pharaoh, king of Egypt.

> *1 King 3:1 – And Solomon made affinity with Pharoah king of Egypt,* **and took Pharaoh's daughter, and brought her into the city of David, until he had made an end of building his own house,** *and the house of the Lord, and the wall of Jerusalem round about.*

In the end, Solomon ended up having seven hundred wives and three hundred concubines.

> *1 Kings 11:1-6 – 1.* **But king Solomon loved many strange women,** *together with the daughter of Pharaoh, women of the Moabites, Ammonites, Edomites, Zidonians, and Hittites; 2. Of the nations concerning which the Lord said unto the children of Israel, Ye* **shall not go in to them, neither shall they come in unto you: for surely they will turn away your heart after their gods:** *Solomon clave unto these in love. 3.* **And he had seven hundred wives, princesses, and three hundred concubines: and his wives turned away his heart.**

Solomon's Fate with God. Solomon did not fair so well with God after having taken seven hundred wives and three hundred concubines. The sin that Solomon committed was not having plural wives, it was Solomon turning his heart away from God and worshiping the idols and false gods of the strange wives and concubines.

> *1 Kings 11:4-6 – 4. For it came to pass,* **when Solomon was old, that his wives turned away his heart after other gods: and his heart was not perfect with the Lord his God, as was the heart of David his father.** *5. For Solomon went after Ashtoreth the goddess of the Zidonians, and after Milcom the abomination of the Ammonites. 6.* **And Solomon did evil in the sight of the Lord, and went not fully after the Lord, as did David his father.**

> *1 Kings 11:9-10 – 9.* **And the Lord was angry with Solomon, because his heart was turned from the Lord God of Israel, which had appeared unto him twice, 10. And had commanded him concerning this thing, that he should not go after other gods: but he kept not that which the Lord commanded.**

The punishment for not repenting and not stopping the worship of false gods was that Solomon was to lose the kingdom. **Note that Solomon was not in trouble for having seven hundred wives and three hundred concubines.**

> *11. Wherefore the Lord said unto Solomon, Forasmuch as this is done of thee, and* **thou hast not kept my covenant and my statutes, which I have commanded thee,** *I will surely rend the kingdom from thee, and will give it to thy servant.*

A Plural Wife Review. From the King James version of the Bible, we have most of the great prophets and kings of the Old Testament having plural wives. These include the following:

1. Abraham (2 wives and concubines)
2. Jacob (4 wives)
3. Moses (2 wives)
4. David (many wives and concubines)
5. Solomon (700 wives and 300 concubines)

Question. What were the accomplishments of these prophets and leaders?

1. Abraham – Father of the "Covenant Race" or "House of Israel."
2. Jacob (Israel) – Continued the "covenant" from Abraham, father of the 12 tribes of Israel.
3. Moses – Great prophet who freed Israel from slavery, set up the "Law of Moses," received the keys of the priesthood and the keys for the gathering of Israel.
4. David – Great king over Israel.
5. Solomon – Great king over Israel and built the House of the Lord, which is known as the Solomon Temple.

Question: How close were these leaders to the Lord?

1. Abraham – The Lord appeared to Abraham and talked with him several times.

   *Genesis 17:2-4 – 2. And I will make my covenant between me and thee, **and will multiply thee exceedingly.** 3. And Abram fell on his face: **and God talked with him, saying,** 4. As for me, behold, my covenant is with thee, **and thou shalt be a father of many nations.***

   *Genesis 12:7 – **And the Lord appeared unto Abram,** and said, Unto thy seed will I give this land: and there builded he an altar unto the Lord, **who appeared unto him.***

2. Jacob – Knew God *"face to face."*

   *Genesis 32:30 – And Jacob called the name of the place Peniel: **for I have seen God face to face, and my life is preserved.***

3. Moses – Knew God *"face to face."*

   *Exodus 33:11 – **And the Lord spake unto Moses face to face, as a man speaketh unto his friend...***

   *Deut 34:10 – **And there arose not a prophet since in Israel like unto Moses, whom the Lord knew face to face,***

4. David – Was a prophet and conversed many times with the Lord.

   *1 Samuel 23:2 – Therefore David enquired of the Lord, saying, Shall I go and smite these Philistines? **And the Lord said unto David,** Go, and smite the Philistines, and save Keilah.*

   *1 Samuel 23:4 – Then David enquired of the Lord yet again. **And the Lord answered him and said,** Arise, go down to Keilah; for I will deliver the Philistines into thine hand.*

In the next verse the Lord speaks to David while he had more than one wife.

   2 Samuel 2:1,2 – 1. And it came to pass after this, that David enquired of the Lord, saying, Shall I go up into any of the cities of Judah? And the Lord said unto him, Go *up. And David said, Whither shall I go up? And he said, Unto Hebron. 2. So David went up thither, **and his two wives also,** Ahinoam the Jezreelitess, and Abigail Nabal's wife the Carmelite.*

The next passage has the Lord making David king over Israel, and David immediately takes more concubines and wives.

*2 Samuel 5:12,13,19 – 12. **And David perceived that the Lord had established him king over Israel, and that he had exalted his kingdom for his people Israel's sake.** 13. **And David took him more concubines and wives out of Jerusalem,** after he was come from Hebron: and there were yet sons and daughters born to David.*

After taking more concubines and wives, the Lord talks with David—not about having multiple wives and concubines—but about going up to war with the Philistines.

*19.And David enquired of the Lord, saying, Shall I go up to the Philistines? Wilt thou deliver them into mine hand? **And the Lord said unto David, Go up: for I will doubtless deliver the Philistines into thine hand.***

5. Solomon – had two accounts where the Lord appeared unto him and talked with him. Each of these appearances are recorded twice in the Bible. The first appearance was for God to give Solomon whatever he wanted.

*1 Kings 3:5-15 – 5. **In Gibeon the Lord appeared to Solomon in a dream by night:** and God said, Ask what I shall give thee.*

*2 Chronicles 1:7 – **In that night did God appear unto Solomon,** and said unto him, Ask what I shall give thee.*

The second appearance was when Solomon finished the "House of the Lord." The Lord appeared unto Solomon because the Lord was pleased with the temple.

*1 Kings 9:1,2 – 1. And it came to pass, when Solomon had finished the building of the house of the Lord, and the king's house, and all Solomon's desire which he was pleased to do, 2. **That the Lord appeared to Solomon the second time, as he had appeared unto him at Gibeon.***

*2 Chr 7:11,12 – 11. Thus Solomon finished the house of the Lord, and the king's house: and all that came into Solomon's heart to make in the house of the Lord, and in his own house, he prosperously effected. 12. **And the Lord appeared to Solomon by night, and said unto him, I have heard thy prayer, and have chosen this place to myself for an house of sacrifice.***

The Biblical Support Chart. After learning about some of the greatest prophets and leaders of the Old Testament, these having multiple wives, we see that each of these prophets were never reprimanded for having multiple wives. The only exception is if the lifestyle took them astray from the true commandments of God as was in David and Solomon's cases. Each of these Old Testament prophets, after having multiple wives had visits from the Lord and were able to converse with the Lord. Each of them, when walking uprightly before the Lord, was favored by the Lord even when they had multiple wives.

From these experiences in the Old Testament, it can be supported that Joseph Smith, also a great prophet, who saw both Heavenly Father and the Lord Jesus Christ, was given the law of polygamy by Jesus Christ Himself.

THE BIBLICAL SUPPORT CHART

Is the following topic supported in the Bible?	Yes or No
Does the Bible support Joseph Smith's teaching that polygamy, or the taking of more than one wife, could be from God? (Gen 16:1; 25:5,6; 22:23,24; 26:34,35; 28:2,3; 29:15-35; 30:3-20; 35:11,17,18; Exo 2:21,22; Num 12:1-16; Deu 34:10-12; 1 Sam 18:20,21; 25:42-44; 2 Sam 5:12,13: 11:2-5, 14-17,26,27; 12:7-18; 16: 20-22; 1 Kings 1:30; 2:1-4; 3:1; 11:1-6)	Yes

Author's Note: We have here four great prophets of the Old Testament who actually saw God *"face to face."* Each conversed with God on a regular basis, they all had multiple wives, and they all were still in good standing with God.

In comparing these great Old Testament prophets with the prophet Joseph Smith we have several similarities. These similarities are:

1. Like the Old Testament prophets, Joseph Smith saw God "face to face."

> **Joseph Smith—History 17. ...** *When the light rested upon me I saw two Personages, whose brightness and glory defy all description, standing above me in the air. One of them spake unto me, calling me by name and said, pointing to the other—This is My Beloved Son. Hear Him!*

2. Like the Old Testament prophets, Joseph Smith was able to talk to God on a regular basis. The Doctrine and Covenants are full of examples where Jesus Christ appeared to and would talk with Joseph Smith to give him instructions on how to organize and direct the Church.

Returning to the biblical passage about false prophets:

> *Matthew 7:15,16 – 15. Beware of false prophets, which come to you in sheep's clothing, but inwardly they are ravening wolves. 16.* **Ye shall know them by their fruits.** *Do men gather grapes of thorns, or figs of thistles?*

One must ask him/herself a very important question:

Question: Is Joseph Smith a false prophet and did he try to deceive his followers with the doctrine of plural wives?

If you have always been taught that having multiple wives was wrong and not of God, and you now answer that question with "well, maybe polygamy could be from God," then you should ask yourself the next question:

Question: If my church leaders have always taught me that polygamy was wrong and not of God, then who is the "deceiver"—Joseph Smith or my leaders?

Question: In the spirit of the "every jot and tittle" and the Lord "restoring all things" passages—if four of the greatest Old Testament prophets participated in plural marriages, was the Lord bound to restoring the practice of plural marriage in these last days?

NOTES

CHAPTER 18

THE BLACKS AND THE PRIESTHOOD

The second most controversial teaching of Joseph Smith was the policy of not allowing the blacks to receive the priesthood and temple ordinances. This church policy withstood from Joseph Smith's time through the turbulent 1960's when the United States were finally offering the black American's the rights afforded them by the constitution. During the early 1970's, this policy withstood the United States government's pressure to abolish this policy.

Question: In spite of all this government and social pressure, why did the church refuse to extend the "priesthood and temple blessings" to the blacks?

The answer is quite simple…it is because the Lord Jesus Christ is the head of the church, not the president or the apostles. The Lord Jesus Christ knows what is best for His church and His saints. It was not until June 8, 1978 that through a revelation from the Lord to the then President, prophet, seer, and revelator of the Church, Spencer W. Kimball, that *"all of the privileges and blessings which the gospel affords"* be extended to every worthy member of the Church *"without regard for race or color."*

This solution is great for the people who have testimonies of the divinity of the prophet Joseph Smith. It is for the people who do not yet believe in the sacred calling of Joseph Smith that must be shown some kind of biblical support for this policy. The problem that must be addressed here is, as the "anti-Mormons" claim, the policy of Joseph Smith is very prejudicial and as some have claimed is bigotry. These two terms are defined as:

> prejudice – 2c. an irrational attitude of hostility directed against an individual, a group, a race, or their supposed characteristics.[25]

> bigot – one obstinately or intolerantly devoted to his own opinions and prejudices.[26]

As these "anti-Mormons" use these terms to over-emphasize the Joseph Smith policy on the blacks and the priesthood, one can see that their claims are exaggerated. At no time in the history of the Mormon Church has there been an *"irrational attitude of hostility"* directed towards the blacks. In fact, it is historically recognized that there were members of the church who were of the black race since the days of Joseph Smith. Black members of the church have always been extended the fellowship and baptism into the Church.

As we learned in **Chapter 4: The Priesthood,** it is a requirement for a person to receive the ordinance of baptism by the proper authority in order to enter into the kingdom of God.

> *John 3:5-7 – 3. Jesus answered, Verily, verily, I say unto thee,* **Except a man be born of water and of the Spirit, he cannot enter into the kingdom of God.**

Never in the history of the Church has the Church denied the ordinance of baptism to a qualified (fully repentant) person of the black race or any other color or culture. Therefore, the blacks have never been denied the opportunity to enter into the highest degree of "glory"—the Celestial Kingdom. The only opportunity the blacks were denied was the opportunity to receive the "priesthood and temple blessings."

Additionally, those who have known the church, also know that there have been the dark colored or black skins of the Pacific Islanders who have always received the priesthood and temple blessings of the Church.

Biblical Support. In following the theme of this book—if Joseph Smith was a true prophet, there would be some kind of Biblical support for all of Joseph Smith's teachings—or he would not be a true prophet. It is now my, the author's responsibility to show that there has been similar policy, i.e., keeping the "priesthood and temple blessings" from certain groups or races of people, in both the Old and New Testaments of the Bible. I will not address policies of prejudice and bigotry, as there were no such policies in the Mormon Church.

This policy and practice of the Lord not extending the "priesthood and temple blessings" to certain groups of people will be easier to identify and prove than any other topic in this book. It is clear in the Bible and almost all Christian religions agree with most of the following policies that were in practice in the Bible:

1. In the Old Testament, the Jews were the only ones allowed the higher priesthood. (See **Chapter 4: The Priesthood**)

2. In the Old Testament, the Jews with the priesthood were the only ones allowed into the temples. (See **Chapter 14: The Temples**)

3. In the Old Testament, the Levites were the only ones who received the Aaronic Priesthood. When they could not prove their genealogy as being from the levites, they were "put from the priesthood."

   *Ezra 2:62 – These sought their register among those that were reckoned by genealogy, but they were not found: **therefore were they, as polluted, put from the priesthood.***

4. In the New Testament, the Lord Jesus Christ did not preach His new gospel to anybody but the Jews.

5. It was after His resurrection that Christ extended the "priesthood and temple blessings" to the gentiles in the Mediterranean area. These "priesthood and temple blessings" were not preached to the African nations or the Asian nations.

   *Romans 2:10 – But glory, honour, and peace, to every man that worketh good, **to the Jew first, and also to the Gentile:***

   *Ephesians 3:5,6 – 5. **Which in other ages was not made known unto the sons of men, as it is now revealed unto his holy apostles and prophets by the Spirit; 6. That the Gentiles should be fellow heirs,** and of the same body, and partakers of his promise in Christ by the gospel:*

6. It is clear in all the mainstream Christian religions of today, with the exception of the Catholic Church, the priesthood is not a blessing that is afforded to them. The Catholic Church still claims to hold the priesthood, which was handed down from Pope to Pope since the apostle Peter. All other Christian religions are breakaway apostate groups from the Catholic Church or a non-denominational start up that does not even claim the priesthood is necessary. (See **Chapter 1: The Apostasy and Chapter 4: The Priesthood**)

7. It is clear that in all the Christian religions, the blessings of the temple are not extended to their membership. (Each Christian Church who declare, "there is no need for temples" unfortunately excludes themselves and their membership. See **Chapter 14: The Mormon Temples**)

It is interesting to note that in the beginning of the Old Testament, this policy of not extending the "priesthood and temple blessings" to all people was from the Lord, Himself!

Question: Would you call the Lord prejudiced and a bigot?

Of course not! The "all knowing" Lord first set up His Kingdom on earth through the Jewish people. He was also known to withdraw the "priesthood and temple blessings" from the Jewish people when they lost their ability to keep His commandments and remain pure. After Jesus

Christ was crucified, He extended the "priesthood and temple blessings" to the gentiles in the Mediterranean area. This was the second group of people who received these blessings.

When there is a first and a second, there must also be a first and a last! In the case of the "priesthood and temple blessings," a portion of the descendants of Abraham, the tribe of Judah, was the first to receive these blessings. The last to receive the "priesthood and temple blessings" were the blacks, on June 8, 1978.

Question: Why were the blacks the last to receive the "priesthood and temple blessings?"

As explained in **Chapter 13, The Plan of Salvation: The Mortal Earth Life,** we are here on earth to prove our faith in God. Maybe this policy of the "priesthood and temple blessings" being withheld from the blacks was to test one or all of the following groups of people:

1. The blacks.
2. The members of the LDS Church who were around when the change came to allow the blacks into the priesthood and temples.
3. The anti-Mormons who seem to degrade this policy of Joseph Smith, when in fact it was and always has been the policy of the Lord to keep the "priesthood and temple blessings" from some groups of people.
4. All of the current modern day Christian religions who do not have the "priesthood and temple blessings" afforded to them while in their church.

Author's Note: It is my observation that the negative movement against Joseph Smith and the particular policy of not offering the "priesthood and temple blessings" to the blacks was and is a ruse used by the "anti-Mormons" in order to persecute Joseph Smith and the members of The Church of Jesus Christ of Latter Day Saints. This persecution is in fact *"an irrational attitude of hostility directed against an individual, a group, a race, or their supposed characteristics,"* in this case, against Joseph Smith and the members of The Church of Jesus Christ of Latter Day Saints.

This persecution has been directed, in the most part, from other Christian religions that do not have the "priesthood and temple blessings" in their own churches.

Reviewing again the following scriptures:

> *Matthew 7:13,14 – 13.* **Enter ye in at the strait gate:** *for wide is the gate, and broad is the way, that leadeth to destruction, and many there be which go in thereat:* *14.* **Because strait is the gate, and narrow is the way, which leadeth unto life, and few there be that find it.**

> *Matthew 7:21-23 – 21.* **Not every one that saith unto me, Lord, Lord, shall enter into the kingdom of heaven;** *but he that doeth the will of my Father which is in heaven. 22. Many will say to me in that day, Lord, Lord, have we not prophesied in thy name? And in thy name have cast out devils? And in thy name done many wonderful works? 23.* **And then will I profess unto them, I never knew you: depart from me, ye that work iniquity.**

It is clear that many Christian religions that accept the Lord and think to do His will, will not *"enter into the kingdom of heaven."*

Reviewing again the parable of the "10 virgins" (Matthew 25:1-13), there will be half of the virgins that are not prepared with enough oil in their lamps, and will be shut out of the "marriage supper of the Lamb" (Revelation 19:7-10).

Question: What do you think the Lord will do about a person who condemns the

policy of Joseph Smith of not offering the "priesthood and temple blessings" to the blacks, when in fact, this has been the policy of the Lord since the beginning of the Old Testament?

The answer:

> *Matthew 10:41 – **He that receiveth a prophet in the name of a prophet shall receive a prophet's reward; and he that receiveth a righteous man in the name of a righteous man shall receive a righteous man's reward.***

It was prophesied in Isaiah that at some point all people will be afforded the right to the "priesthood and temple blessings" or the covenants offered by the Lord. At one point, in the following example, *"the eunuchs"* and *"the sons of strangers"* were apparently not offered the *"priesthood and temple blessings."* But in the end— *"all people"* will have the temple blessings, which include the opportunity to make the sacred covenants with the Lord in the *"**Holy Mountain**"* (temple) where they can be *"**joyful in my house of prayer!**"*

> *Isaiah 56:3-7 – 3. **Neither let the son of the stranger, that hath joined himself to the Lord, speak, saying, the Lord hath utterly separated me from his people:** neither let the eunuch say, Behold, I am a dry tree. 4. For thus saith the Lord unto the eunuchs that keep my sabbaths, and choose the things that please me, and take hold of my covenant; 5. Even unto them will I give in mine house and within my walls a place and **a name better than of sons and of daughters: I will give them an everlasting name, that shall not be cut off.** 6. **Also the sons of the stranger, that join themselves to the Lord,** to serve him, and to love the name of the Lord, to be his servants, every one that keepeth the sabbath from polluting it, and taketh hold of my covenant; 7. **Even them will I bring to my holy mountain, and make them joyful in my house of prayer:** their burnt offerings and their sacrifices shall be accepted upon mine altar; **for mine house shall be called an house of prayer for all people.***

Question: How could have Joseph Smith truly been a prophet, if he had allowed everybody to have the "priesthood and temple blessings" from the beginning of the restoration?

Question: It is possible that this prophesy of Isaiah's could not have been fulfilled if the "priesthood and temple blessings" were not withheld from somebody?

Recalling the following prophecy:

> *Matthew 5:17, 18 – 17. Think not that I am come to destroy the law, or the prophets: I am not come to destroy, but to fulfill. 18. For verily I say unto you, Till heaven and earth pass, **one jot or one tittle shall in no wise pass from the law, till all be fulfilled.***

The Biblical Support Chart. Joseph Smith clearly taught that the "priesthood and temple blessings" should be withheld from the blacks. This policy lasted until June 8, 1978, when the then president of the Church, Spencer W. Kimball, received a revelation from the Lord permitting everybody without regard to race or color would be given the opportunity to receive the "priesthood and temple blessings." This policy is clearly supported by the Bible in both the Old and New Testaments where the Lord only allowed the Jewish people into the priesthood and the temples. It was not until after Christ's resurrection that He sent the twelve apostles to the gentiles living in the Mediterranean area with the gospel and the "priesthood and temple blessings." It was not until after the restoration of the gospel that the "priesthood and temple blessings" were extended to all people, without regard to race or color.

Isaiah 56:7 – ...for mine house shall be called a house of prayer for all people.

THE BIBLICAL SUPPORT CHART	
Is the following topic supported in the Bible?	**Yes or No**
Does the Bible support Joseph Smith's policy of excluding the "priesthood and temple blessings" from the blacks? (Ezra 2:62; Rom 2:10; Eph 3:5,6; Isa 56:3-7)	Yes

NOTES

NOTES

CONCLUSION

BEWARE THE SERPENT

Now, having finished comparing most of Joseph Smith's teachings with the King James Version of the Bible, I want to thank those who have completed this book with me. Hopefully, you have learned something new and have grown closer to our Heavenly Father, Jesus Christ, the Bible and the teachings of Joseph Smith.

If you have kept a count of the Biblical Support Chart, you should notice that 83 of the teachings and policies of Joseph Smith have 100% support from the Bible, even the most wild and crazy ones! This is where Christ's warning is critical to understand.

> *Matthew 7:15 – 15.* **Beware of false prophets,** *which come to you in sheep's clothing, but inwardly they are ravening wolves. 16.* **Ye shall know them by their fruits.** *Do men gather grapes of thorns, or figs of thistles?*

"Beware of false prophets" is such a great warning because of the different religious leaders over the last two hundred years who have declared to be prophets, specifically and including Joseph Smith. Jesus Christ, knowing that there would be true prophets gave us a way to know which prophets are actually called of God and which ones are **"ravening wolves"** waiting to deceive us—the serpents!

The way Christ gave a sincere Christian to know the difference between a true prophet and a false prophet is **"by their fruits ye shall know them."** This book was written specifically to challenge **"the fruits"** of Joseph Smith, i.e., his teachings and the organization that he set up on this earth—The Church of Jesus Christ of Latter Day Saints.

> *Matthew 7:20 –* **Wherefore by their fruits ye shall know them.**

In the Biblical Support Chart at Appendix 1, there are 90 of **"the fruits"** of Joseph Smith with the scriptural support cited. As stated earlier, 100% of those teachings and policies have some kind of backing from the Bible. As commanded by Jesus Christ, Joseph Smith was perfect in his teachings.

> *Matthew 5:48 –* **Be ye therefore perfect, even as your Father which is in heaven is perfect.**

From the Biblical Support Charts from each chapter, I have compiled a Biblical Support Challenge to all non-members and wavering members of the Church of Jesus Christ of Latter Day Saints. This challenge is found in Appendix 1. I invite all Christians to take that challenge and compare their teachings with those of their religious leaders and churches. This will help them find out how close to perfection they are in their teachings.

I would like to offer a few last words to the different groups of readers that could read this book.

To the LDS Church Member. I want to thank you for your support in reading this book. I hope it has strengthened your testimony as it has mine. I am thoroughly amazed at the amount of scriptural support the Bible gives to Joseph Smith's teachings and the organization of Christ's Church here on earth. This study has given me a deeper insight to the wonderful works of Joseph Smith and his position as Prophet of the restoration.

To the Wavering LDS Church Member and Friends of the Church Who are Investigating. It is to you, the LDS Church members who are being drawn away by various types of anti-Mormon information, and to the friends of the LDS Church who are studying, investigating, and maybe even testing the truthfulness of the teachings of the Prophet Joseph Smith that this book was primarily written for.

I hope that you studied the different teachings in this book as they compare to the Bible. I sincerely hope that you will apply the Biblical Support Challenge to the Church that you are currently considering or affiliated with. Knowing that most Christian churches do not have or acknowledge a prophet at the head of their church, you can still apply this challenge to your religious leader's teachings and church organization. Then, with the results of your challenge, it will be easy to compare Joseph Smith's result of 100% support with your church's resulting percentage.

Having completed the Biblical Support Challenge, only you can answer what is best for yourself… While you contemplate what is best for you, remember what the Bible has to say about prophets:

> *Amos 3:7 – **Surely the Lord God will do nothing, but he revealeth his secret unto his servants the prophets.***

> *Matthew 10:41 – **He that receiveth a prophet in the name of a prophet shall receive a prophet's reward; and he that receiveth a righteous man in the name of a righteous man shall receive a righteous man's reward.***

Among the many fruits from Joseph Smith are the temple promises from God that your family will be *"sealed"* together and become *"heirs together of the grace of life."*

> *2 Corinthians 1:22 – **Who hath also sealed us,** and given the earnest of the Spirit in our hearts.*

> *1 Peter 3:7 – Likewise, ye husbands, dwell with them according to knowledge, giving honour unto the wife, as unto the weaker vessel, **and as being heirs together of the grace of life;** that your prayers be not hindered.*

Again, it is only up to you which "rewards" you will go after—those of a righteous man, or those of a prophet. It is your choice whether you want to spend eternity with your family or not!

To the Anti-Mormon. If you are still with me I congratulate you and hope that you will sincerely take the Biblical Support Challenge in Appendix 1. In the Foreword, I made it clear that one or even both of us could possibly fall into the category of deceivers—the serpents. Christ clearly warned of this when He said:

> *Ephesians 4:11-14 – 11. **And he gave some, apostles; and some, prophets; and some, evangelists; and some, pastors and teachers; 12. For the perfecting of the saints, for the work of the ministry, for the edifying of the body of Christ: 13. Till we all come in the unity of the faith, and of the knowledge of the Son of God, unto a perfect man,** unto the measure of the stature of the fullness of Christ: 14. **That we henceforth be no more children, tossed to and fro, and carried about with every wind of doctrine, by the sleight of men, and cunning craftiness, whereby they lie in wait to deceive;***

> ### Beware the Serpent!

Having 100% biblical support for all the teachings and policies of Joseph Smith clearly puts the Mormons at an advantage at not being the deceiver or the serpent! The Bible clearly states that many Christians who believe they will be saved will not be allowed into the kingdom of God.

> *Matthew 7:13,14 – 13. **Enter ye in at the strait gate:** for wide is the gate, and broad is the way, that leadeth to destruction, and many there be which go in thereat:*

14. Because strait is the gate, and narrow is the way, which leadeth unto life, and few there be that find it.

*Matthew 7:21-23 – 21. **Not every one that saith unto me, Lord, Lord, shall enter into the kingdom of heaven;** but he that doeth the will of my Father which is in heaven. 22. Many will say to me in that day, Lord, Lord, have we not prophesied in thy name? And in thy name have cast out devils? And in thy name done many wonderful works? 23. **And then will I profess unto them, I never knew you: depart from me, ye that work iniquity.***

Knowing that many Christians will not be allowed into the kingdom of God, it is important for you to identify whether or not you are a part of the deceivers. In referring back to the parable of the ten virgins where five of them did not have a sufficient amount of oil.

Question: Are you going to be the one who leads a part of those approximate 50% of the Christians away from entering into the kingdom of God?

*Matthew 25:11-13 – 11. **Afterward came also the other virgins, saying, Lord, Lord, open to us. 12. But he answered and said, Verily I say unto you, I know you not. 13. Watch therefore, for ye know neither the day nor the hour wherein the Son of man cometh.***

This parable of the 10 virgins is very important because it let's everybody know that not having the *"oil"* for the lamp will keep one from entering into the kingdom of God.

Question: Could it be that one of the following five elements that you are not teaching may be the missing "oil" for one of the sincere Christians that you lead away?

1. The proper baptism by one with the proper authority is a very important factor for one to enter into the kingdom of God.

   *John 3:5 – Jesus answered, Verily, verily, I say unto thee, **Except a man be born of water and of the Spirit, he cannot enter into the kingdom of God.***

   *Ephesians 4:5 – **One Lord, one faith, one baptism.***

Question: Have you been baptized by somebody who has the Aaronic or Melchizedek Priesthood?

2. Having a sacred "House of the Lord" or temple will be important during the last days because Jesus Christ will be "suddenly" coming to it!

   *Malachi 3:1 – Behold, I will send my messenger, and he shall prepare the way before me: **and the Lord, whom ye seek, shall suddenly come to his temple,** even the messenger of the covenant, whom ye delight in: behold, he shall come, saith the Lord of hosts.*

Question: Does your church have a sacred temple that the Lord can suddenly come to in the last days?

Question: If not, are you prepared to miss out on the information that will be given by the Lord during that meeting?

3. Not wearing the special *"wedding garments"* is definitely an element that will keep a person from entering into the kingdom of God. It is clearly stated that a person *"not having on a wedding garment"* is definitely cast out. That person is part of the *"many who are called,"* but not one of the few who are *"chosen."*

   *Matthew 22:11-14 – 11. And when the king came in to see the guests, he saw there a man which had not on a wedding garment: 12. **And he saith unto him, Friend, how camest thou in hither not having a wedding garment? And he*** *was speechless. 13. Then said the king to the servants, **Bind him hand and foot, and take him away, and cast him into outer darkness; there shall be weeping and gnashing of teeth. 14. For many are called, but few are chosen.***

Question: Are you or any of your followers wearing the special *"wedding garments?"*

Statement: If not, then you are missing some "oil!"

4. Having the temple work completed for your ancestors is also an important element of one entering into the kingdom of God.

> *Hebrews 11:40 – **God having provided some better thing for us, that they without us should not be made perfect.***

Question: Have you completed the temple work for your dead ancestors?

Warning: Doing the work for your ancestors is a very time consuming process that could be the *"oil"* that is not in your lamp when the bridegroom comes. Believe me...by the time you get this done, the door will be shut!

5. Following a prophet that will be raised up in the last days.

> *Acts 3:22,23 – 22. For Moses truly said unto the fathers, **A prophet shall the Lord your God raise up unto you of your brethren, like unto me; him shall ye hear in all things whatsoever he shall say unto you. 23. And it shall come to pass, that every soul, which will not hear that prophet, shall be destroyed from among the people.***

From a blessing given from *The Book of Mormon* prophet Lehi to his son Joseph.

> *2 Nephi 3:11 – **But a seer will I raise up out of the fruit of thy loins;** and unto him will I give power to bring forth my word unto the seed of thy loins—and not to the bringing forth my word only, saith the Lord, but **to the convincing them of my word, which shall have already gone forth among them.***

Joseph then prophesied about this latter day prophet that would be named after him.

> *2 Nephi 3:15 – **And his name shall be called after me; and it shall be after the name of his father.** And he shall be like unto me; for the thing, which the Lord shall bring forth by his hand, **by the power of the Lord shall bring my people unto salvation.***

Statement: If you decide not to follow a true prophet of God, then when you are awarded a Terrestrial Glory, you cannot complain. After all, you made the decision!

> *Matthew 10:41 – **He that receiveth a prophet in the name of a prophet shall receive a prophet's reward; and he that receiveth a righteous man in the name of a righteous man shall receive a righteous man's reward.***

These elements just mentioned may seem small and insignificant to you, but they do fall under the following scripture:

> *Matthew 5:18 – For verily I say unto you, Till heaven and earth pass, **one jot or one tittle shall in no wise pass from the law, till all be fulfilled.***

All the small details of what the prophets of old have stated will *"be fulfilled,"* whether you believe in the *"jot or tittle"* element or not. The dilemma is whether you are going to continue to *"deceive"* yourself and your followers or repent and set things right. The quickest way to find out what you should do is go to the promise made in the *Book of Mormon.*

> *Moroni 10:3-5 – 3. Behold, I would exhort you that when ye shall read these things,*

if it be wisdom in God that ye should read them, that ye would remember how merciful the Lord hath been unto the children of men, from the creation of Adam even down until the time that ye shall receive these things, and ponder it in your hearts. 4. **And when ye shall receive these things, I would exhort you that ye would ask God, the Eternal Father, in the name of Christ, if these things are not true; and if ye shall ask with a sincere heart, with real intent, having faith in Christ, he will manifest the truth of it unto your, by the power of the Holy Ghost. 5. And by the power of the Holy Ghost ye may know the truth of all things.**

You may know the truth of all things! Through the prophet Joseph Smith, the Lord has said something special to those who actually follow Moroni's promise and receive testimonies and the truth:

D&C 20:14 – **And those who receive it in faith, and work righteousness, shall receive a crown of eternal life.**

Following the Lord's admonition in the above passage, He also added this:

D&C 20:15 – **But those who harden their hearts in unbelief, and reject it, it shall turn to their own condemnation—**

If you, the "anti-Mormon," have read even a portion of this book and sincerely studied the biblical passages quoted, you will never be able to say that you have not been warned.

Referring back to the commandment from the Lord to become perfect, we all have the duty to strive for this perfection. To show the importance of *"becoming perfect"* it is written in Psalms of the Second Coming of Christ. It is quite clear who will be preserved when the *"fire comes to devour!"*

Psalms 50:1-5 – 1. **The mighty God, even the Lord, hath spoken, and called the earth from the rising of the sun unto the going down thereof. 2. Out of Zion, the perfection of beauty, God hath shined. 3. Our God shall come, and shall not keep silence:** *a fire shall devour before him, and it shall be very tempestuous round about him.* **4. He shall call to the heavens from above, and to the earth, that he may judge his people. 5. Gather my saints together unto me; those that have made a covenant with me by sacrifice.**

There are four important points to this passage:

1. **"The perfection of beauty, God hath shined"** are the members of the Church that Christ has restored on the earth that are striving to become perfect.

2. There will be a fire that **"comes to devour."**

3. The Lord will **"gather His saints"** to be protected. These **"saints"** are the members of Christ's church.

4. These **"saints"** are those who have **"made a covenant with the Lord by sacrifice."**

The meaning of this message is that the people who are striving to become perfect, are *"saints"* (or members of the Church of Jesus Christ), who have *"made a covenant with the Lord"* which are the covenants made in the House of the Lord or temple. These saints will be gathered and protected from the great *"fire"* of the last days.

Not all is lost here for the non-saints! It was mentioned in the chapter on the post-mortal life about the different glories that will be our reward that Christ will give to all of us.

Matthew 16:27 – For the Son of man shall come in the glory of his Father with his angels; ***and then he shall reward every man according to his works.***

When one thinks about every man receiving a reward from Christ—there is something very beautiful. Each Christian, the Mormons and the anti-Mormon, will actually get what he or she is expecting. To the Christians who believe in only one heaven, that they will live eternally in the presence of Jesus Christ, who does not believe in marriage in the resurrection will receive exactly what they believe in—an eternal life in the Terrestrial Glory with the presence of Jesus Christ and without their families.

For those Mormons who believe in obtaining exaltation, being joint heirs with Christ, being sealed for eternity with their families, and actually work for these blessings will receive exactly that—an eternal life in the Celestial Glory in the presence of our Heavenly Father, Jesus Christ, and our families. (There is definitely sound evidence for the exaltation teaching of Joseph Smith!)

This is the beauty of a loving Heavenly Father with a plan of salvation that will reward almost all of mankind with something better than this life! My testimony to you is that God the Father and His Son Jesus Christ, as two separate beings with glorified bodies of flesh and bone, appeared to the Prophet Joseph Smith and restored the fullness of Christ's gospel through him. I know that all the teachings of Joseph Smith and the organization that he restored are all true, are all perfect, and are from the only true God. It is our responsibility to get to know God and His son.

> *John 17:3 – **And this is life eternal, that they might know thee the only true God, and Jesus Christ, whom thou hast sent.***

It is my prayer that all who have read this book will be inspired to continue their investigation into who are the real God the Father and Jesus Christ.

APPENDIX

THE BIBLICAL SUPPORT CHALLENGE

To the non-LDS Church member: Hopefully, having read this book you have a better feel for Joseph Smith, his teachings, policies, and church organization. Knowing now that all of Joseph Smith's teachings do have some kind of support from the Bible, I now want to make a challenge to you.

Understanding that the interpretations of the Biblical passages used in this book may differ, there are many of these teachings that are plain and simple. It is my challenge to you to review the following chart and compare your churches or your religious leader's teachings and organization to those listed. Write a "yes" or a "no" in the last column under "Your Church." At the end, count the number of "yes" answers and divide it by the total number of items listed. This will give you a percentage of how your church's or religious leader's teachings compare with the teachings of the Bible.

THE BIBLICAL SUPPORT CHALLENGE			
Chap-Topic	Are the following topics supported in the LDS Church and Your Church?	LDS Church	Your Church
1-1	Does the Bible support the teaching of an Apostasy? Does your church teach the apostasy? (Isaiah 24:5; 29:13, Amos 3:7; Isa 60:2; Amos 8:11; 2 Thes 2:2,3,7; Acts 20:29-31; 1 Cor 11:18,19; Titus 1:15,16; Gal 1:6,7; 2 Tim 3:1-7; 4:3,4; 2 Tim 1:15; 1 Tim 4:1; 2 Tim 2:16-18; Matt 24:5,24)	Yes	—
2-2	Does the Bible support the teaching of the Restoration of the gospel of Jesus Christ in the last days? Does your church believe there will be a restoration? Isaiah 11:11,12; 24:5; 29:13-16; 60:2; Jer 31:31; Dan 2:44; Amos 8:11; Mal 4:5,6; Joel 2:28; Acts 3:19-21;Matt 17:12,13; Eph 1:10; Rom 11:25; Rev 14:6; Acts 3:22,23; Amos 3:7; Matt 17:1-8.	Yes	—
3-3	Does the Bible support naming the general membership of the Christ church, saints? Does your church call it's members saints? (Deut 33:2,3; Psalms 50:5, 89:7;97:10; Rom 1:7; 1 Cor 1:2; 2 Cor 1:1; Eph 1:1; Phil 1:1; Col 1:2)	Yes	—
3-4	Does the Bible support the organization of the church with prophets and apostles? Does your church have a living prophet at the head? (Amos 3:7; Eph 2:19-22; 1 Cor 12:27,28; Eph 4:11-14; Acts 3:22,23)	Yes	—
3-5	Does the Bible support the continued need for having 12 apostles? Does your church have 12 living apostles? (Acts 1:21-26)	Yes	—

THE BIBLICAL SUPPORT CHALLENGE			
Chap-Topic	Are the following topics supported in the LDS Church and Your Church?	LDS Church	Your Church
3-6	Does the Bible support that the fullness of the Church of Jesus Christ should be based on revelation? Does your church claim to have current revelation from God and Jesus Christ? (Matt 16:13-18; Gal 1:6-12; 2:2; 1 Cor 13:2; Prov 29:18)	Yes	—
4-7	Does the Bible support the existence of the Aaronic Priesthood? Does your church have the Aaronic Priesthood? (Num 3:3,8-10; 18:1,7,8; Joshua 18:7)	Yes	—
4-8	Does the Bible support the existence of the Melchisedek Priesthood? Does your church have the Melchisedek Priesthood? (Gen 14:18; Psalms 110:4; Heb 5:6; 5:10)	Yes	—
4-9	Does the Bible support the division of the two priesthoods as one being a lesser priesthood than the other? Does your church believe there are two priesthoods, one greater than the other? (2 Kings 23:4; Heb 7:1,2,4; 7:11,12; 5:5,6; 5:8-10)	Yes	—
4-10	Does the Bible support Joseph Smith's claim that one needs to have the "power" given to him to be a church leader? Does your church believe they need "power" to be a leader? If yes, who gave them this power? (John 3:5-7; Acts 19:1-6; Matt 28:18; 1 Cor 4:20; Matt 10:1; Luke 10:19; Acts 6:8; Heb 5:1,4; Exo 28:1; 40:12-15)	Yes	—
4-11	Does the Bible support Joseph Smith's teaching that one must be baptized by the proper authority in order to enter into the kingdom of God? Does your church believe that it is necessary for a person to be baptized by the proper authority to enter into the kingdom of God? (John 3:5-7)	Yes	—
5-12	Does the Bible support Joseph Smith's teaching that one must be spiritually reborn—or baptized by fire? Does your church believe in being spiritually reborn—or baptized by fire? (Matt 3:11; John 1:33; Acts 1:5; 1 Peter 1:22,23; Acts 2:4)	Yes	—
5-13	Does the Bible support Joseph Smith's teaching that receiving the Holy Ghost is a gift, after baptism? Does your church give the gift of the Holy Ghost after baptism? (John 7:39; John 20:22; Acts 2:38; Acts 10:45)	Yes	—

THE BIBLICAL SUPPORT CHALLENGE			
Chap-Topic	Are the following topics supported in the LDS Church and Your Church?	LDS Church	Your Church
5-14	Does the Bible support Joseph Smith's teaching that the gift of the Holy Ghost is given by the "laying on of hands"? Does your church give the gift of the Holy Ghost by the "laying on of hands". (1 Tim 4:14; 2 Tim 1:6; Hebrews 6:2)	Yes	—
5-15	Does the Bible support Joseph Smith's teaching that the gift of the Holy Ghost overcomes all common sense and earthly wisdom? Does your church profess receiving spiritual inspiration over the common sense and wisdom of man? (1 Cor 2:4,5; 2 Cor 1:12; 1 Cor 2:10-16)	Yes	—
5-16	Does the Bible support Joseph Smith's teaching that the members receive testimony through the Holy Ghost? Does your church encourage its members to receive testimonies of all things spiritual? (John 15:26; 1 John 5:6; John 5:34; John 8:32; John 21:24; 1 Cor 1:6; 2 Tim 1:8)	Yes	—
5-17	Does the Bible support Joseph Smith's teaching that one may become perfect? Does your church encourage its members to become perfect? (Matt 5:48; Col 4:12; Gen 6:9; Job 1:8; Luke 6:40; John 17:23; Eph 4:11,12; Col 1:28; 2 Tim 3:17; Heb 12:23)	Yes	—
5-18	Does the Bible support Joseph Smith's teaching about the Holy Spirit of Promise? Does your church teach about the Holy Spirit of Promise? (Eph 1:13,14; Eph 4:30; Eph 2:12, 19-22)	Yes	—
5-19	Does the Bible support Joseph Smith's teaching about one's "calling and election made sure?" Does your church teach that you can receive your "calling and election made sure?" (2 Peter 1:10,11; John 14:16; John 14:21-23; D&C 130:3; 67:10)	Yes	—
6-20	Does the Bible support the Joseph Smith's teaching of the church being one organization? Is your church organized where there is one church and they are all the same in organization and function? (1 Cor 14:33; Eph 4:3,4; 1 Cor 1:10,11; 1 Cor 12:13,25; Phil 2:2; 3:16-19; 1 Tim 1:3,7-10; Heb 13:9)	Yes	—
6-21	Does the Bible support the strictness of Joseph Smith's teaching of the church having one doctrine? Does your church have one doctrine throughout all congregations? (Heb 13:9; Eph 4:11-14; Matt 7:13,14; 21-23; 25:1-13)	Yes	—

THE BIBLICAL SUPPORT CHALLENGE			
Chap-Topic	Are the following topics supported in the LDS Church and Your Church?	LDS Church	Your Church
7-22	Do the six biblical contradictions listed in this chapter support Joseph Smith's teaching that there are contradictions in the Bible? Does your church believe that there are contradictions in the Bible? (Acts 9:7 & Acts 22:9; 1 Cor 5:9; Matt 27:5 & Acts 1:18; Eph 2:5-9 & Gal 6:7-20; John 10:30 & Gen 1:26,27, Gen 32:30, Acts 7:55,56; John 1:18 & Gen 12:7, Gen 32:30, Ex 24:9-11)	Yes	—
7-23	Does the Bible support Joseph Smith's teaching that there are missing scriptures from the Bible? Does your church believe that there are missing scriptures from the Bible? (Exo 24:4,7; Num 21:14; Josh 10:13; 2 Sam 1:18; Ezek 37:15-17; Luke 4:17-20)	Yes	—
8-24	Does the Bible support Joseph Smith's claim that the Book of Mormon came out of the ground? Does your church have a book that would fulfill these scriptural passages? (under "every *jot and tittle*")(Isa 29:1-4; Psalms 85:11)	Yes	—
8-25	Does the Bible support Joseph Smith's claim that the Book of Mormon could have been sealed? Does your church have a book that would fulfill these scriptural passages? (under "*every jot and tittle*") (Isa 29:11,12)	Yes	—
8-26	Does the Bible support Joseph Smith's claim that the Book of Mormon could be another scripture? Does your church have a book that would fulfill these scriptural passages? (under "*every jot and tittle*") (2 Tim 3:15-17)	Yes	—
8-27	Does the Bible support the claim that a book will be written that contains the history of the tribe of Judah, one of the twelve tribes of Israel? Does your church have a book that would fulfill these scriptural passages? (under "*every jot and tittle*") (Ezk 37:15-18)	Yes	—
8-28	Does the Bible support Joseph Smith's claim that the Book of Mormon is the history of tribe of Ephraim, one of the twelve tribes of Israel? Does your church have a book that would fulfill these scriptural passages? (under "*every jot and tittle*") (Ezk 37:15-18)	Yes	—

THE BIBLICAL SUPPORT CHALLENGE			
Chap-Topic	Are the following topics supported in the LDS Church and Your Church?	LDS Church	Your Church
8-29	Does the Bible support the claim of the Book of Mormon that it contains the history of a family from Jerusalem that went across the ocean to another land? Does your church have a book that would fulfill these scriptural passages? (under "*every jot and tittle*") (Gen 11:8; Gen 48:15-19; Gen 49:22-26; Deut 33:13-16; Isa 16:8)	Yes	—
8-30	Does the Bible support the Book of Mormon's account of Jesus Christ visiting the people in the Americas? Does your church have a book that would fulfill these scriptural passages? (under "*every jot and tittle*") (Matt 15:24; John 10:16)	Yes	—
9-31	Does the Bible support the teaching that man was created in the image of God? Does your church teach that man was created in the image of God? (Gen 1:26,27; 5:1,3; 9:6; 6:3; James 3:9)	Yes	—
9-32	Does the Bible support the teaching that God the Father and His son Jesus Christ each have a body of flesh and bone? Does your church teach that God the Father and Jesus Christ both have a separate body of flesh and bone? (Gen 5:1,3; Gen 9:6; Gen 6:3; James 3:9; Gen 32:30; Exo 24:10; Exo 33:11; Exo 31:18; Exo 33:21-23; Num 12:7,8; Deu 9:10; Mark 16:19; Act 7:55-56; Matt 3:16,17; Matt 4:4; Matt 17:5; Heb 1:3; Heb 1:3; Rev 22:4; Luke 24:36-40; Phil 3:20,21; 1 John 3:2; 2 Cor 4:4; Phil 2:6; Col 1:14,15)	Yes	—
9-33	Does the Bible support the teaching that God the Father and His son Jesus Christ are two different personages? Does your church teach that God the Father and His son Jesus Christ are two different personages? (John 17:11,20-22, 1 Cor 6:17; John 10:30; Matt 3:16,17; Acts 7:55,56; Heb 1:1,2,5; Psalm 136:2; Deu 10:17; Psalm 82:1,6; 1 Cor 8:5)	Yes	—
9-34	Does the Bible support the teaching of Joseph Smith that man can see God? Does your church teach that man can see God? (Gen 12:7; 32:30; Exo 24:9-11; 33:11; 1 King 3:5; 9:2; Isa 6:1-5; Job 42:5; Amos 9:1; Acts 7:2; 7:55,56; Rev 22:3-5; John 20:18; Matt 28:9; Luke 24:15,16,34; 1 Cor 15:6,7, Acts 26:13-16; John 20:24-29; Luke 24:36-40; John 6:46)	Yes	—

THE BIBLICAL SUPPORT CHALLENGE			
Chap-Topic	Are the following topics supported in the LDS Church and Your Church?	LDS Church	Your Church
9-35	Does the Bible support Joseph Smith's teaching that Christ created the world? Does your church teach that Christ created the world? (John 1:1-3,14; Heb 1:1-3; Col 1:16; Heb 11:3; Eph 3:21)	Yes	—
9-36	Does the Bible support Joseph Smith's teaching that Jesus Christ is the God of the Old Testament? Does your church teach that Jesus Christ is the God of the Old Testament? (Isa 43:11; 45:21; Acts 4:10-12; 13:23; Phil 3:20; Titus 2:13; 1 Tim 4:10;)	Yes	—
9-37	Does the Bible support Joseph Smith's claim that Jesus Christ will be the judge? Does your church teach that Jesus Christ will be our final judge? (John 5:21,22; John 5:27)	Yes	—
10-38	Does the Bible support Joseph Smith's teaching that "saved by grace" is defined as – "salvation from sin is given to all men and women who are born on earth"? Does your church teach that all men and women who are born on earth are saved? (1 Cor 15:22,23; Luke 3:6; John 3:17; 5:25,28,29; 1 Peter 3:18-20; 1 Peter 4:6; Isa 45:23; Rom 14:11; Phil 2:10,11)	Yes	—
10-39	Does the Bible support Joseph Smith teaching that "eternal salvation" is where only certain men and women may live in the presence of God the Father and Jesus Christ, in the actual kingdom of God? Does your church teach that only certain men and women may live in the presence of god the Father and Jesus Christ, in the actual kingdom of God? (John 17:3; Heb 5:9; John 3:5; Mark 16:15,16; Matt 7:13; 7:21; 16:27; 7:24-27; 25:14-30; 13:3-9; Gal 6:7,8)	Yes	—
10-40	Does the Bible support Joseph Smith's teaching that one's religious "works" here on earth is critical to entering into the kingdom of God? Does your church teach that one's religious "works" are critical to entering into the kingdom of God? (James 1:22; 2:14-25; Gal 6:7,8; Rev 20:12,13; Matt 16:27)	Yes	—
11-41	Does the Bible support Joseph Smith's teaching that Jesus Christ existed before this life? Does your church teach that Jesus Christ existed before this life? (John 8:58; Col 1:17; 1 Cor 15:46; John 1:1-3,14; 6:38; 6:51,62; 8:58; 16:28-33; 17:4,5; 1 Pet 1:18-20)	Yes	—

THE BIBLICAL SUPPORT CHALLENGE			
Chap-Topic	**Are the following topics supported in the LDS Church and Your Church?**	**LDS Church**	**Your Church**
11-42	Does the Bible support Joseph Smith's teaching that Jesus Christ is the literal son of God? Does your church teach that Jesus Christ is the literal son of God? (Matt 3:17; 17:5; Mark 9:7; Luke 9:35; 2 Pet 1:17)	Yes	—
11-43	Does the Bible support Joseph Smith's teaching that Jesus Christ is literally God's first born? Does your church teach that Jesus Christ is literally God's first born son? (Psm 89:27; Rom 8:29; Col 1:15; Heb 1:6)	Yes	—
11-44	Does the Bible support Joseph Smith's teaching that we are all sons of God? Does your church teach that we are all sons of God? (Psm 82:6; Hos 1:10; Mal 2:10; Matt 5:48; Acts 17:28,29; Rom 8:16; Eph 4:6; Heb 12:9; Job 32:8)	Yes	—
11-45	Does the Bible support Joseph Smith's teaching that our spirits were first in heaven with God before this life? Does your church teach that you existed as a spirit in heaven with God before your were born in this life? (1 Cor 15:45,46; Job 38:4-7; Eccl 12:7; John 3:13; Jer 1:4,5; Job 1:6)	Yes	—
11-46	Does the Bible support Joseph Smith's teaching that there was a war in heaven that included Lucifer and all men who are born on earth? Does your church teach that there was a war in heaven that included Lucifer and all men who are born on earth? (Job 1:6; Rev 12:7-9; 8:10-12; Isa 14:12-16; Luke 10:18)	Yes	—
12-47	Does the Bible support Joseph Smith's teaching that all men born on this earth will resurrect? Does your church teach that all men born on this earth will resurrect?	Yes	—
12-48	Does the Bible support Joseph Smith's teaching on the judgement day? Does your church teach that there will be a judgement day? (Rev 20:12,13; 22:12; 1 Pet 1:17; Rom 14:10; Matt 16:27)	Yes	—
12-49	Does the Bible support Joseph Smith's teaching on the existence of multiple heavens? Does your church teach that there are multiple heavens? (Psm 33:6; 102:25; Heb 1:10; Psm 104:2; Isa 40:22; 55:9; Joel 2:30; 2 Cor 12:2)	Yes	—
12-50	Does the Bible support Joseph Smith's teaching on Paradise? Does your church teach that there is a place called Paradise (in heaven)? (Luke 23:42,43)	Yes	—

THE BIBLICAL SUPPORT CHALLENGE			
Chap-Topic	Are the following topics supported in the LDS Church and Your Church?	LDS Church	Your Church
12-51	Does the Bible support Joseph Smith's teaching that we will receive a "glory" depending on our works here in this life? Does your church teach that you will receive a "glory" depending on your works here in this life? (Psm 62:7; 84:11; Prov 4:9; Jer 2:11; 1 Cor 15:40,41; Phil 3:20,21)	Yes	—
12-52	Does the Bible support Joseph Smith's teaching of the existence of a Celestial glory being the highest glory man can receive? Does your church teach that there is a Celestial glory which will be the highest glory that you can receive? (2 Pet 1:17; 2 Cor 3:7-11; 2 Cor 4:17; Col 1:26-28; 1 Pet 5:1; 5:4; 5:10; Jer 2:11)	Yes	—
13-53	Does the Bible support Joseph Smith's teaching on the importance of man being born with a body of flesh and bone? Does your church teach the importance of you being born with a body of flesh and bone? (Gen 1:26,27; Phil 3:20,21; 1 Cor 15:40,41; Matt27:52,53; Rom 8:23; Act 24:15; 1 Cor 15:21,22)	Yes	—
13-54	Does the Bible support Joseph Smith's teaching on importance of demonstrating faith in God & Jesus Christ? Does your church teach on the importance of demonstrating faith in God & Jesus Christ? (Mark 11:22; Habab 2:4; Rom 1:17; Gal 3:11; Heb 10:38; 2 Cor 5:6,7; Heb 11:1; John 20:29)	Yes	—
13-55	Does the Bible support Joseph Smith's teaching on the requirement of repenting for our sins? Does your church teach on the requirement of our repenting of our sins? (Matt 3:2; Mark 1:15; Mark 6:12; Acts 17:30; 2 Pet 3:9; Acts 3:19; Eph 5:5; Luke 13:3)	Yes	—
13-56	Does the Bible support Joseph Smith's teaching that we should follow strict adherence to God's commandments? Does your church teach that there should be strict adherence to God's commandments? (John 14:15; 14:21-23; Exo 20:3-17; 34:28; Deut 4:13; Matt 22:36-40)	Yes	—
13-57	Does the Bible support Joseph Smith's teaching that all Christians should pay a full tithing to the Lord? Does your church teach that you should pay a full tithing (10% of your income) to the Lord? (Gen 14:20; Heb 7:1,2; Gen 28:22; Lev 27:30; Num 18:26; Deut 12:6; 14:22; 2 Chron 31:5; Mal 3:8-10; Matt 17:11; Matt 5:17,18)	Yes	—

THE BIBLICAL SUPPORT CHALLENGE			
Chap-Topic	Are the following topics supported in the LDS Church and Your Church?	LDS Church	Your Church
13-58	Does the Bible support Joseph Smith's teaching that there is a health commandment known as the Word of Wisdom? Does your church have formal teaching of a health commandment that all members should follow? (Lev 10:9-11; Num 6:2,3; Eccl 10:17; Isa 5:22; Deu 14:2-21; Eph 5:17,18; Col 2:16; 1 Tim 3:1-3; 1 Cor 6:10; Dan 1:8; 1 Cor 3:16,17)	Yes	—
13-59	Does the Bible support Joseph Smith's teaching that homosexuality should not be an accepted practice? Does your church teach that homosexuality should not be an accepted practice? (Lev 18:22; 20:13; Rom 1:18,26,27; 1 Tim 1:9,10; Jude 1:7; 1 Cor 6:9,10)	Yes	—
13-60	Does the Bible support Joseph Smith's temple ordinances of the endowment and anointing? Does your church provide you with the opportunity to receive a temple ordinance of the endowment and anointing? (Luke 24:49; Exo 28:41; 30:25; 30:29-31; Lev 8:10; 2 Sam 1:14; 2 Cor 1:21; 1 John 2:20; 2:27)	Yes	—
13-61	Does the Bible support Joseph Smith's teaching that we can receive the ordinance of eternal marriage? Does your church provide you with an ordinance that will bind you with your spouse for eternity? (Luke 20:27-33; Matt 22:23-30; Mark 12:23-25; Luke 20:35; Matt 16:19; John 3:5,6; Matt 18:18; 1 Cor 11:11; Eph 5:31,32; John 17:11; 1 Peter 3:7; 2 Cor 1:22; Neh 9:38; 10:1-27, 29; Isa 49:8; Gen 2:18; 2:24; Eccl 3:14; Matt 10:41)	Yes	—
13-62	Does the Bible support Joseph Smith's teaching that all Christians are required to endure to the end in living God's laws? Does your church teach you that you are required to endure to the end in living God's laws? (Matt 10:22; 24:13; Mark 13:13; 4:11-17; 4:24,25; 2 Tim 4:3,4; Heb 6:15; James 5:11; 1 Cor 13:7)	Yes	—
13-63	Does the Bible support Joseph Smith's teachings that we should keep a genealogy of our ancestors and perform the temple ordinances for them? You're your church teach you to keep a genealogy of your ancestors perform the temple ordinances for them? (Ezra 2:62; Mal 3:16-18; Matt 16:19; 18:18; Heb 11:32,33; 11:36-40; John 3:5,6; 1 Pet 3:18,19; John 5:25,28,29; 1 Pet 4:6; 1 Cor 15:29; Rom 14:9; 1 Cor 15:19; Pro 17:6)	Yes	—

THE BIBLICAL SUPPORT CHALLENGE

Chap-Topic	Are the following topics supported in the LDS Church and Your Church?	LDS Church	Your Church
14-64	Does the Bible support Joseph Smith's teaching on the sacredness of the latter day temples where God may dwell? Does your church teach on the sacredness of the latter day temple where God may dwell? (Acts 7:48,49; 17:24; Exo 25:8,9; Exo 29:42-46; Lev 1:1; Deut 31:15; 2 Chron 1:6,7)	Yes	—
14-65	Does the Bible support the teachings of Joseph Smith that he, a prophet was directed by God to build a temple? Does your church teach that your leaders are directed by God to build a temple? (2 Sam 7:5-7,13; 1 Kings 5:3-5; Hab 2:20; Zech 1:16; Zech 6:12,13)	Yes	—
14-66	Does the Bible support the teachings of Joseph Smith's that there will be temples in the last days? Does your church teach that there will be temples in the last days? (Isa 2:2-3; Matt 17:11; Acts 3:19-21; Micah 4:1,2; Amos 9:11,12; Acts 15:16,17; Rev 7:15; Rev 11:1; Isa 4:6; Mal 3:1; Zech 14:16-21)	Yes	—
14-67	Does the Bible support Joseph Smith's teachings that there should be ordinances performed for the dead (i.e., baptism for the dead)? Does your church teach that there should be ordinances performed for the dead? (1 Kings 7:23-25; 2 Chron 4:2-4; Jer 52:17,20)	Yes	—
14-68	Does the Bible support Joseph Smith's "law of worthiness" or temple recommend requirement for a person to enter into the temple? Does your church teach that there should be a "law of worthiness" or temple recommend required before a person can enter into a temple? (1 Chron 22:6-11; Ezek 44:7-9; Psm 15:1-3; Psm 24:3-5; Isa56:6,7; Jer 7:1-7; Ezek 43:10-12; Num 1:51; Acts 21:26-31; Matt 21:12,13; Mark 11:15-18; Luke 19:45-46; John 2:14-16)	Yes	—
14-69	Does the Bible support Joseph Smith's teachings that a prophet and a person who enters the temples will be highly blessed and may even see or talk with God? Does your church teach that you, while in a temple of God, may see or talk with God? (Psm 65:4; Exo 29:42-46; Lev 1:1; 2 Chron 1:6,7; 2 Chron 7:11,12; Ezek 43:4,5; Psalm 27:5,6; Psalm 27:8; Exo 29:43-46; Psm 24:6,7; Psm 27:4; Psm 84:1-2; Psm 84:4; Psm 84:10)	Yes	—

THE BIBLICAL SUPPORT CHALLENGE

Chap-Topic	Are the following topics supported in the LDS Church and Your Church?	LDS Church	Your Church
14-70	Does the Bible support Joseph Smith giving of "new names" in the temples? Does your church give you "a new name?" (Luke 1:21,22; Isa 65:15; Rev 2:17; Rev 19:12)	Yes	—
14-71	Does the Bible support Joseph Smith's implementation of wearing special temple/wedding garments? Does your church provide you with special temple/wedding garments? (Exo 28:1,2,40-42; Exo 39:1,28; Lev 6:10; Isa 52:1; Isa 61:10; Ezek 42:14; Rev 19:13,14; Rev 3:4,5; Rev 3:6; Rev 16:15; Rev 3:3; Matt 25:1-13; Matt 7:21; Matt 22:11-14)	Yes	—
14-72	Does the Bible support the fact that Joseph Smith has the saints wear as much white clothing as possible? Does your church encourage you to wear as much white clothing as possible? (Rev 3:4,5; Rev 19:13,14)	Yes	—
15-73	Does the Bible support Joseph Smith's teaching that special oaths and covenants should be made with the Lord? Does your church give you're the opportunity to make special oaths and covenants with Lord? (besides baptism) (Gen 6:18; Gen 26:3-5; Exo 6:4; Exo 19:5; Exo 22:10,11; Exo 34:28; Deut 4:13; Deu 29:1; Num 30:2; Deu 7:8; Deu 29:12,13; Gen 26:42; 1 Kings 2:43; 1Kings 11:11; 2 Kings 11:4; 2 Kings 23:2,3; 2 Chron 34:29-31; Psalm 50:5; Psalm 89:3; Neh 9:38; Neh 10:29; Luke 1:72,73; Rom 11:27; Gal 3:17,29; Eph 2:12; Heb 6:12-19; Heb 7:20,21; Heb 8:6,13; Heb 12:24)	Yes	—
15-74	Does the Bible support Joseph Smith's teaching about an "everlasting covenant" with the Lord? Does your church offer you the opportunity to make an "everlasting covenant" with the Lord? (Gen 9:16; Gen 17:2-7; Num 25:10-13; 1 Chron 16:14-17; Psalm 105:8-10; Heb 13:20,21)	Yes	—
15-75	Does the Bible support Joseph Smith's teachings that the Lord will establish His new covenant and the everlasting covenant with His people? Does your church teach that the Lord has established His new covenant and the everlasting covenant with your church members? (Isa 55:3; Jer 32:40; Ezek 16:60-62; Jer 50:4,5; Isa 61:8; Jer 31:31,33; Ezek 37:26-28)	Yes	

THE BIBLICAL SUPPORT CHALLENGE

Chap-Topic	Are the following topics supported in the LDS Church and Your Church?	LDS Church	Your Church
16-76	Does the Bible support Joseph Smith's teaching about being the steward of the mysteries of the kingdom of God? Does your church claim to be stewards of the mysteries of the kindom of God? (Deut 29:29; Psalm 25:14; Amost 3:7; Matt 13:11,12; Mark 4:11,12; Luke 8:10; 1 Cor 4:1; 1Tim 3:16; D&C 6:11,12)	Yes	—
16-77	Does the Bible support Joseph Smith's teaching that certain people on this earth are God's elect? Does your church teach that its church members are God's elect? (1 Thes 1:4,5; 2 Thes 2:13,14; Eph 1:4,5; Rom 9:10,11; 1 Pet 1:2; Col 3:12; 2 Tim 2:10; Titus 1:1; 1 Pet 2:9; 2 John 1:1; Acts 9:15,16; John 17:1-12; Rev 17:14)	Yes	—
16-78	Does the Bible support Joseph Smith's teaching that man may become ruler over nations with Jesus Christ? Does your church teach that you may become a ruler over nations with Jesus Christ? (Rev 2:26-29; Luke 12:42-44; Matt 25:23)	Yes	—
16-79	Does the Bible support Joseph Smith's teaching that the members may receive exaltation with Jesus Christ? Does your church teach that you may receive exaltation with Jesus Christ? (Eph 3:21; 1 Pet 5:4,10; Eph 1:9-11; 1 Pet 5:6)	Yes	—
16-80	Does the Bible support Joseph Smith's teaching that the people who overcome will receive what Christ receives? Does your church teach that if you overcome, then you will receive what Christ receives? (Rev 3:21,22; Rev 21:7; Rom 8:16-18; Luke 6:40; 2 Tim 2:12)	Yes	—
16-81	Does the Bible support Joseph Smith's teaching that man may become a god? Does your church teach that you may become a god? (John 10:34-35; Deut 10:17; Psalm 82:1,6; Rev 3:21)	Yes	—
17-82	Does the Bible support Joseph Smith's teaching that polygamy or the taking of more than one wife is of God? Does your church teach that polygamy or the the taking of more than one wife is of God? (Gen 16:1; 25:5,6; 22:23,24; 26:34,35; 28:2,3; 29:15-35; 30:3-20; 35:11,17,18;Exo 2:21,22; Num 12:1-16; Deu 34:10-12; 1 Sam 18:20,21; 25:42-44; 2 Sam 5:12,13: 11:2-5, 14-17,26,27; 12:7-18; 16: 20-22; 1 Kings 1:30; 2:1-4; 3:1; 11:1-6)	Yes	—

	THE BIBLICAL SUPPORT CHALLENGE		
Chap-Topic	Are the following topics supported in the LDS Church and Your Church?	LDS Church	Your Church
18-83	Does the Bible support Joseph Smith's policy of excluding the "priesthood and temple blessings" from the blacks? Does your church believe that it was okay for the church to withhold the "priesthood and temple blessings" from certain people at certain times in the history of the world? (Ezra 2:62; Rom 2:10; Eph 3:5,6; Isa 56:3-7)	Yes	—
	Count the Number of "Yes" answers, write them here.	83	83
	Divide the number of "Yes" answers by 86.	83	—
	This is your Church's percentage of support from the 98 biblical topics, policies, beliefs, truths and etc that were discussed in this book.	**100%**	—

Question: What is your Biblical Support Challenge percentage?

Question: How well does the Bible support your Church leader's teachings and church organization?

In the Forward I mentioned that I have over the years been told by other church members and other church leaders that the teachings of God and church, whoever church it may be, must make sense and appeal to the wisdom of the learned religious leaders. As in **Chapter 5 – The Holy Ghost,** the scriptures explain that the things of God are spiritual and must be understood by the spirit, not under the earthly wisdom of man. Again, in defiance of the teachings of the apostle Paul, I made this Biblical Support Challenge to appeal to the common sense and the earthly wisdom of man. If your Biblical Support Challenge percentage did not at least reach the 75% mark, I would be very concerned for my own potential for entering into the kingdom of God!

With the comparison of the common sense results of Joseph Smith's 100% accuracy and the results of your churches percentage, I would think it would be very wise for you to read the following passages and meditate upon them.

> *1 Corinthians 2:13 – Which things also we speak, not in the words which man's wisdom teacheth, but which the Holy Ghost teacheth; comparing spiritual things with spiritual.*

> *1 Cor 2:4, 5 – And my speech and my preaching was not with enticing words of man's wisdom, but in demonstration of the Spirit and of power: 5. That your faith should not stand in the wisdom of men, but in the power of God.*

> *2 Cor 1:12 – For our rejoicing is this, the testimony of our conscience, that in simplicity and godly sincerity, not with fleshly wisdom, but by the grace of God, we have had our conversation in the world, and more abundantly to you-ward.*

> *1 Cor 2:10-16 – But God hath revealed them unto us by his Spirit: for the Spirit searcheth all things, yea, the deep things of God. 11. For what man knoweth the*

> *things of a man, save the spirit of man which is in him? Even so the things of God knoweth no man, but the Spirit of God. 12. Now we have received, not the spirit of the world, but the spirit which is of God; that we might know the things that are freely given to us of God. 13. Which things also we speak, not in the words which man's wisdom teacheth, but which the Holy Ghost teacheth; comparing spiritual things with spiritual. 14. But the natural man receiveth not the things of the Spirit of God: for they are foolishness unto him: neither can he know them, because they are spiritually discerned. 15. But he that is spiritual judgeth all things, yet he himself is judged of no man. 16. For who hath known the mind of the Lord, that he may instruct him? But we have the mind of Christ.*

After meditating about the past passages, I sincerely ask, in the spirit of God and the Holy Ghost, that you pick up the *Book of Mormon* and again read the promise of the angel Moroni.

> *Moroni 10:3-5 – 3. Behold, I would exhort you that when ye shall read these tings, if it be wisdom in God that ye should read them, that ye would remember how merciful the Lord hath been unto the children of men, from the creation of Adam even down until the time that ye shall receive these things, and ponder it in your hearts.*
>
> *4. And when ye shall receive these things, I would exhort you that ye would ask God, the Eternal Father, in the name of Christ, if these things are not true; and if ye shall ask with a sincere heart, with real intent, having faith in Christ, he will manifest the truth of it unto you, by the power of the Holy Ghost. 5. And by the power of the Holy Ghost ye may know the truth of all things.*

If you read the *Book of Mormon* and follow this promise, I know that you will find great joy in the spiritual world and things of God and Jesus Christ. I testify that this promise from the angel Moroni is true because Moroni is truly the angel spoken of by John in the Book of Revelations.

> *Revelations 14:6 – And I saw another angel fly in the midst of heaven, having the everlasting gospel to preach unto them that dwell on the earth, and to every nation, and kindred, and tongue, and people.*

It is this angel Moroni that has given the Church of Jesus Christ of Latter Day Saints the many pearls that were discussed in this book! It is this angel Moroni that is represented on the spirals of many of the LDS temples all over the world!

NOTES

INDEX

REFERENCES

1 "Christian Religions – A Comparative Chart Vol. II", Rex Bennettt, Copyright 1985, 3080-148th Avenue S.E., Suite 112, Bellevue, Washington 98007.

2 The Great Apostasy, by James E. Talmage, Deseret Book Company, Salt Lake City, Utah, 1909, pages 161-163.

3 John Wesley's Works, Vol. VII, 89:26-27.

4 How to Escape Religion Guilt Free, Scott R. Stahlecker, Universe, Inc., New York, 2004.

5 Joseph Smith—History, Doctrine & Covenants, excerpts from verses 3-26.

6 Webster's Ninth New Collegiate Dictionary, Merriam-Webster Inc., Publishers, Springfield, Mass, USA, 1990, page 158.

7 San Antonio Express News, Saturday, October 2, 2004, Life Section, Dr. Billy Graham's Column.

8 The Articles of Faith of the Church of Jesus Christ of Latter-Day Saints, Joseph Smith, 8th Article.

9 Joseph Smith—History. Chapter 1, verses 16 and 17. From the Extracts from the History of Joseph Smith, The Prophet, History of the Church, Vol. 1, Chapters 1-5.

10 Ibid. Random House, page 1226.

11 Joseph Smith—History. Chapter 1, verses 16 and 17. From the Extracts from the History of Joseph Smith, The Prophet, History of the Church, Vol. 1, Chapters 1-5.

12 Joseph Smith—History. Chapter 1, verses 16 and 17. From the Extracts from the History of Joseph Smith, The Prophet, History of the Church, Vol. 1, Chapters 1-5.

13 R. Philip Roberts, Mormonism Unmasked, 1998, Broadman & Holman Publishers, Nashville, Tennessee, page 133.

14 Ibid., page 181.

15 The Random House College Dictionary, the Unabridged Edition, 1980, Random House, Inc., New York.

16 Documentary History of the Church, Volume VI, pages 365-366.

17 Webster's New World Compact School and Office Dictionary, Cleveland & New York, 1988, page 184.

18 Webster's Ninth New Collegiate Dictionary, Merriam-Webster Inc., Springfield, Massachusetts,1990, page 446.

19 D.H.C., Vol, IV, page 599.

20 D.H.C., Vol. IV, page 569.

21 D.H.C., Vol. IV, pages 425-426.

22 D.H.C., Vol, IV, page 599.

23 D.H.C., Vol VI, pages 365-366.

24 Doctrine And Covenants of the Church of Jesus Christ, 1981, Official Declaration-1, pages 291-293.

25 Webster's Ninth New Collegiate Dictionary, Merriam-Webster Inc., Springfield, Massachusetts, 1990, page 928.

26 Ibid., page 149.

ABOUT THE AUTHOR
KENDALL L. MANN

In 1972 at the age of 18, Kendall L. Mann was baptized into the Church of Jesus Christ of Latter Day Saints. The very next year he served a two-year LDS mission to Argentina. He received a degree in Judicial Administration at Brigham Young University. He received a Masters Degree in International Relations from St. Mary's University, San Antonio, Texas. He is currently a high school Spanish teacher. Throughout his life he has met many people who charge the Mormons with being a cult. During the many discussions that followed he found that one of the major accusations of the anti-Mormons was that Joseph Smith did not believe in the Bible or the God of the Bible.

It was the lack of LDS information on how to use the Bible to answer the many anti-Mormon questions that Kendall decided to write Beware the Serpent. Using only the Bible to test the teachings of the Prophet Joseph Smith Kendall has filled a void that many LDS members and friends of the Church will use for many years to come.